Dickson's
WORD TREASURY

Books by Paul Dickson

Think Tanks

The Great American Ice Cream Book

The Future of the Workplace

The Electronic Battlefield

*The Mature Person's Guide to Kites, Yo-Yos, Frisbees,
and Other Childlike Diversions*

Out of This World

The Future File

Chow: A Cook's Tour of Military Food

The Official Rules

The Official Explanations

Toasts

Words

There Are Alligators in the Sewers & Other American Credos
(with Joseph C. Goulden)

*Dickson's Joke Treasury: An Anthology
of Gags, Bits, Puns, and Jests
and How to Tell Them*

Names

On Our Own: A Declaration of Independence for the Self-Employed

The Library in America

Family Words

The Dickson Baseball Dictionary

The New Official Rules

What Do You Call a Person From . . . ?

Slang!

Timelines

Baseball's Greatest Quotations

On This Spot: Pinpointing the Past in Washington, D.C.
(with Douglas E. Evelyn)

Dickson's
WORD TREASURY

*A Connoisseur's Collection of
Old and New,
Weird and Wonderful,
Useful and Outlandish
Words*

Paul Dickson

John Wiley & Sons, Inc.
New York ■ Chichester ■ Brisbane ■ Toronto ■ Singapore

*To my mother, Isabelle C. Dickson,
who first taught me there was no
such thing as "mere words" or, as a writer named
C. J. Ducase once put it, to speak of "mere words" is
much like speaking of "mere dynamite."*

In recognition of the importance of preserving what has been written, it is a policy of John Wiley & Sons, Inc., to have books of enduring value published in the United States printed on acid-free paper, and we exert our best efforts to that end.

This is a revised and expanded edition of *WORDS* (New York: Delacorte Press, 1982). Copyright © 1982 by Paul Dickson. Some writing has appeared in slightly different form in *Word Ways, Creative Living, Newsday,* and *Smithsonian* magazine.

Grateful acknowledgment is made for permission to reprint excerpts from the following publications:
CALL MY BLUFF by Frank Muir and Patrick Campbell. Reprinted by permission of the publisher, Methuen London Ltd. and Frank Muir.
OUNCE DICE TRICE by Alastair Reid, drawings by Ben Shahn. © 1958 by Alastair and Ben Shahn. By permission of Little, Brown and Company in association with the Atlantic Monthly Press.
The poem by David Stern appears with his personal blessing.

Library of Congress Cataloging-in-Publication Data

Dickson, Paul.
    Dickson's word treasury : a connoisseur's collection of old and new, weird and wonderful, useful and outlandish words / Paul Dickson.
        p.   cm.
    Rev. and expanded ed. of Words. 1982.
    Includes bibliographical references and index.
    ISBN 0-471-55168-6
    1. Vocabulary.   2. English language—Glossaries, vocabularies, etc.   I. Dickson, Paul. Words.   II. Title.
    PE1449.D52   1992   91-25819
    428.1—dc20

Printed in the United States of America

10 9 8 7 6 5 4 3 2 1

Printed and bound by Courier Companies, Inc.

Contents

INTRODUCTION

I first became fascinated with words when I was a kid playing word games with my family at the dinner table. We would try to come up with a word that was obscure or long or hard to pronounce so that we could dazzle my parents. Because of these games, I know that there is a brook in Connecticut called the *Naramyacknowwhosankatankashonk* and that *mappula* is the name for the handkerchief used to signal the start of the action in Roman games.

This led me to word collecting, my adult hobby, and word collecting led me to a perhaps obvious conclusion, but one that escaped me for a long long time. It is that language is a great source of fun. The experts call this "recreational linguistics," but that's too stuffy for the pure, unadulterated fun I'm talking about.

I know, of course, that the primary function of language is communication, and there is nothing funny or amusing about a statement like,"Help, fire!" or "I think I'm about to be very, very sick." Nor is there much joy in most of what passes by our eyes during the workday, especially when it is labeled "memo," or "report," or has the word "official," or "federal," or "policy" in its title.

I'm talking about the part of language that would appeal more to a den of Cub Scouts—jokes, puns, riddles, whacky accents, and word games—than to the folks who write the books people in the computer industry insist on calling "documentation."

I'm also talking about many other things including crossword puzzles, the game of Hangman, Scrabble, dictionary browsing, and, of course, word collecting. I'm also sincerely fascinated with the fact that *typewriter* is one of the longest words that can be written using only the top letter bar of the typewriter and that recent words, like *raunchy* and *humungous,* drive the scholars crazy because they can't figure out where they came from.

I approach my word collecting with a zeal that borders on the compulsive. I confess that in the name of collecting I have labored through the driest scholarly publications to find the odd gem like *nutation,* which is the wobble in the earth's axis caused by the pull of the moon.

I candidly admit spending time that could have been used increasing the gross national product compiling totally useless, but altogether satisfying, collections including 315 phobias and 74 gums (from *alk gum* through *zapota gum*). I have just started a nut list because so many of the names for nuts are just that: *guru nut, vomit nut, hiccup nut,* and *canary nut,* for starters.

I must report that in my hunt for words I have dug deeply into the trash barrels at the post office looking for odd catalogs thrown away by people picking up their mail. Had I been too proud to dig in the trash, I never would have found the tool catalogs that showed me there is really no such thing as a plain pair of pliers, but rather scores of differently named pliers, including nine that begin with the letter *L* (*lineman's side pliers, lock ring pliers, long-handled diagonal cutting pliers, long-nose pliers, long-nose side cutting pliers, long-nose tip cutting pliers, long-reach needle nose pliers, long-reach short-nose duckbill pliers,* and *looping pliers*).

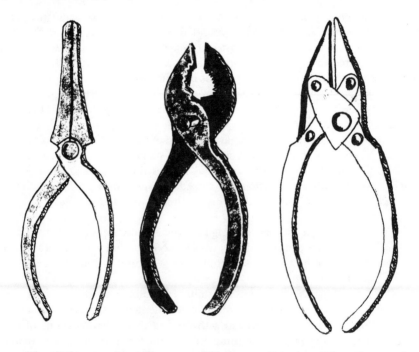

The slightest nudge will set me off in a new direction. When I saw a sign in the window of a costume and novelty shop that proclaimed, "Yes, We Have Warts!" (presumably the kind you glue on), it got me to respond, "Yes, but what kind of warts?" With the help of my *Dictionary of Dermatological Words, Terms and Phrases,* I learned that one can grow an *acuminate wart, anatomic wart, common wart, digitate wart, fig wart, filiform wart, flat wart, mosaic wart, necrogenic wart, paraungual wart, periungual wart, plane wart, plantar wart, prosector's wart, senile wart, subungual wart, venereal wart,* or a *vulgar wart.*

Speaking of highly specialized dictionaries, I am obsessed with them. My hoard now includes such works as *The Dictionary of Paper, The Dictionary of Gambling, The Glossary of Meteorology,* and *The Dictionary of Magic.* I have three dictionaries of citizen band radio slang, and I am on the track of a second logger's dictionary.

Besides accumulating odd dictionaries and words, I have collected verbal and written oddities of every description—talk show euphemisms for death ("She was just coming into her own when she left us"), punny names for places that cut and dress hair (Hair Today, Lunatic Fringe, Rape of the Lock, Delilah), and newspaper headlines of parochial school football victories (Sacred Heart Slams Our Lady of Mercy, 38–6). I even have a small but prized collection of dictionary entries that lead you nowhere (one not very old dictionary explains that *halicore* is a noun meaning *the dugong*).

I also admit to using up other people's time in my endless quest for collector's items. I have imposed myself on army colonels, bartenders, and antique dealers in the hope of coming up with a great military acronym, drinking term, or name for an obscure piece of furniture. I always talk with people who sit next to me on airplanes, in the shameless hope that I might be able to exploit them for a few professional terms. This is how I found that computer workers use the interchangeable terms *abend* (abortive termination) and *abterm* (abnormal termination), and I have actually wangled several interviews with Frederick C. Mish, the editorial director of the G. & C. Merriam Company, to nail down the answer to such important questions as whether or not *angry* and *hungry* are the only English words that end in -*gry*. (The answer is on page 206.) My visits to the Merriam Company in Springfield, Massachusetts, also enabled me to see—and drool on—its files, which contain 13 million citations on the use of individual English words. Quite simply, it is the greatest English word collection in the world. There is a report on this fascinating American institution in the chapter entitled *Wordland.*

Finally, I confess that I am not only a word collector, but also a word exhibitionist who has spent much time displaying parts of his collection. This book is based on an earlier collection, *Words,* and includes many additions and new exhibits.

What follow are 58 separate museum-style displays containing elements of the overall ever-growing collection. I hope not only that you enjoy them, but that you get hooked on words in the process.

Acronyms

An Assembly of Antic Abbreviations

Americans, as a rule, employ abbreviations to an extent unknown in Europe. Life, they say is short and the pace is quick; brevity, therefore, is not only the soul of wit, but the essence of business capacity as well. This trait of the American character is discernable in every department of the national life and thought. . .

> *John S. Farmer*, Americanisms—Old and New
> *(London: 1889)*

Although acronyms existed before World War II, they have proliferated in the period from 1940 to the present. Even their name is modern, having been coined under federal auspices during the war. The term *acronym* (from *akros*, meaning tip, plus *onym*, name) was first introduced to scholars in a 1943 issue of *American Notes and Queries*, which traced it to Bell Telephone Laboratories, which had created the word as a title for a pamphlet written to keep workers abreast of the latest initialized titles for weapons systems and agencies.

Acronyms are best described as pronounceable formations made by combining the initial letters or syllables of a string of words. Two classic examples are SCUBA (Self-Contained Underwater Breathing Apparatus) and RADAR (RAdio Detection And Ranging). These two have reached the highest status an acronym can reach: becoming so widely accepted that they are treated as regular words. Both scuba and radar are now written virtually exclusively in lower case.

Beyond the pure acronym, there are two significant variations. The first is the initialism, which is a straight forward combination of letters rattled off as letters (ACLU, NFL, COD, etc.). The second is the portmanteau or telescope word, which is a blend of two or more words in which the roots are generally recognized. The U.S. Navy loves portmanteaus: NAVFORKOR (NAVal FORces, KORea) and BUPERS (BUreau of PERSonnel) are two of many.

For the word collector, acronyms offer a fertile and fascinating area. For one thing, new ones are created daily. The Gale Research Co. of Detroit, which publishes the *Acronyms, Initialisms, and Abbreviations Dictionary* (AIAD), put out its first edition in 1960 with 12,000 entries. The seventh edition contains 211,000 entries; the eighth edition which came out in late 1982, easily broke the quarter-million mark; and the 1987 edition had more than 400,000 terms and weighed about 16 pounds.

I have collected acronyms for more than 20 years. These are my favorites:

ABBA. Swedish pop group whose name is an acronym made from the first names of the members of the group: Agnetha, Benny, Bjorn, and Anni-frid.

ABRACADABRA. The name of a pioneering listing of 400 "space-age" abbreviations first published by the Raytheon Company in the early 1960s, when a collection of 400 was sizable. ABRACADABRA stood for ABbreviations and Related ACronyms Associated with Defense, Astronautics, Business, and RAdio-electronics.

ABSCAM. The famed code name for the FBI foray into the murky realm of congressional ethics. Early stories said the name stood for AraB SCAM, which disturbed some Arab-Americans. The FBI claimed it stood for Abdul Enterprises, which was the name of the front group for the operation.

ACNE. Action Committee for Narcotics Education.

ACORN. ACronym-ORiented Nut.

ACRONYM. Allied Citizens Representing Other New York Minorities, and the fictional Acronyms Can Really Obsess Neurotic Young Man.

ADCOMSUBORDCOMPHIBSPAC. For a long time the longest acronym in captivity. It was, for instance, the longest of 45,000 entries in the 1965 edition of the *Acronyms, Initialisms, and Abbreviations Dictionary*. It is from the U.S. Navy and officially stands for Administrative Command, Amphibious Forces, Pacific Fleet Subordinate Command, although it is derived from ADministrative COMmand, SUBordinate COMmand, amPHIBiouS forces, PACific fleet. It still has not been bettered in English, although if it ever is, the new champion probably will come from the Navy, which seems to have a special penchant for long acronyms. Another Navy creation: COMSERFORSO-PACSUBCOM for COMmander, SERvice FORce, SOuth PACific SUBordinate COMmand.

According to the *1989 Guinness Book of World Records,* the longest acronym is a 56-letter monster from the Soviet Union describing a scientific laboratory.

ALOHA. Aboriginal Lands Of Hawaiian Ancestry, the name of an effort to compensate aboriginal residents for lands taken from them in the nineteenth century.

ALTAIR. A third-generation acronym from the Pentagon that contains two earlier acronyms: ARPA (for Advanced Research Projects Agency) Long-range Tracking And Instrumentation RADAR (RAdio Detection And Ranging). Such acronyms embedded within other acronyms have been termed *tour de force acronyms* by Kenneth H. Bacon in an article on the subject in *The Wall Street Journal.* Bacon used the Army's SCAMPERS as an example: Standard Corps Army MACOM (for Major Army COMmand) PERsonnel System.

APPALLING. The creation of the late Theodore M. Bernstein, *New York Times* editor and expert on English usage, for Acronym Production, Particularly At Lavish Level, Is No Good.

APPLE. Advanced Propulsion Payload Effects. NASA.

ARISTOTLE. Annual Review and Information Symposium on the Technology Of Training and LEarning, an Air Force formulation. ARISTOTLE is but one of a number of classic acronyms. Among others, PLATO (Programmed Logic for Automated Training Operation), ADONIS (Automatic Digital ONline Instrument System), SOCRATES (System for Organizing Content to Review And Teach Educational Subjects), and CASSANDRA (Chromatogram Automatic Soaking, Scanning ANd Digital Recording Apparatus).

AWOL. Absent WithOut Leave. Armed Forces. The author has encountered several applications of AWOL including American Way of Life and, from an ad for a furniture company, Almost Wholesale Or Less.

BEDOC. BEDs OCcupied. Army.

BESS. The official acronym for no less than three NASA satellites: Biological Experiment Scientific Satellite; Biomedical Experiment Scientific Satellite; and Biomedical Experiment Support Satellite. The confusion this must generate may be incalculable.

BICYEA. Top-of-the-line ice cream from Bresler's. The name is an acronym for Best Ice Cream You Ever Ate. It is pronounced *bye-che-ya.*

BIRD. One of many examples of what happens to the names of prestigious international organizations when their names are (1) translated and (2) acronymized. BIRD stands for *Banque Internationale pour la Reconstruction et le Development,* or the International Bank for Reconstruction and Development.

BIRDDOG. Basic Investigation of Remotely Detectable Deposits of Oil and Gas. U.S. Geological Survey experimental satellite project.

BOGSAAT. Acronym cynically applied to the preferred technique of high-level decision making in America. It stands for a Bunch Of Guys Sitting Around A Table.

BOLTOP. Better On Lips Than On Paper. It is one thing to write SWAK on the back of a sealed envelope, but if you really mean business, write SWAK-BOLTOP!

BOMFOG. Brotherhood Of Man, Fatherhood Of God. Term that journalists have attached to the pious, homily-ridden blather of politicians. It is often referred to as *bomfoggery*. Garry Wills traced the origin of the term in a column in the *Washington Star*. He said it dates back to when Nelson Rockefeller was on the campaign trail: "When Nelson was winding up a campaign speech, he liked to orchestrate the coda around 'the Brotherhood of Man Under the Fatherhood of God' and that phrase was a signal to accompanying journalists to sidle back toward the campaign bus."

BURP. BackUp Rate of Pitch, a NASA term for a type of spacecraft motion. It also stands for Brewers United for Real Potables, an association of home brewers of beer.

BUSWREC. Ban Unsafe Schoolbuses Which Regularly Endanger Children.

BX. According to NASA Reference Publication 1059, "Space Transportation System and Associated Payloads: Glossary, Acronyms and Abbreviations," published in January 1981, BX stands for box. What's more, FLG stands for flag and FLP for flap. One is hard-pressed to think of a situation in which an abbreviation that saves only one letter actually saves time and causes less confusion. The Army uses BX to refer to Base eXchange—an updated version of the PX, which stood for Post eXchange.

Cabal. There is a legend that this word is an acronym for the names Clifford-Ashley-Buckingham-Arlington-Lauderdale, who were conspiratorially inclined cabinet members in the court of Charles II. It actually derives from the Hebrew *cabala* ("full of hidden mystery"), but makes a nice story anyhow.

CAUTION. Citizens Against Unnecessary Tax Increases and Other Nonsense, a group formed in St. Louis in the early 1970s to oppose a large bond issue.

CHAMPION. Compatible Hardware And Milestone Program for Integrating Organizational Needs. Air Force.

CHASE. Cut Holes And Sink 'Em, a Navy Ammunition Disposal System.

CHRIST. Christians Heeding Righteousness Instead of Satanic Tyranny, a conservative religious organization.

CIA. Not only the Central Intelligence Agency, but the Culinary Institute of America, Califorina Institute of the Arts, Computer Industry Association, and Cotton Importers Association.

CINCUS. Short-lived U.S. Navy acronym for Command-IN-Chief U.S. Fleet, which was dropped in 1942 because it was pronounced *sink us*.

CLAIM. Chemical Low-Altitude Missile. Air Force.

COBOL. COmmon Business Oriented Language. A disproportionate number of names for computer programs, like COBOL, are acronyms or portmanteaus. For instance, FORTRAN is a compression of FORmula TRANslation, and JOVIAL stands for Joules Own Version International Algebraic Language. SNO-BOL stands for StriNg Oriented symBOlic Language, a language used in manipulating strings of symbols.

COED. Computer Operated Electronic Display.

COLA. Cost Of Living Adjustment, but also Maine's Congress of Lakes Associations.

COO. Chief Operating Officer, as in a January 30, 1990, *USA Today* headline: "Spindler named COO at Apple."

COYOTE. Call Off Your Old Tired Ethics.

CREEP. Committee for the RE-Election of the President. This acronym is infamous in politics as it stood for the group working for President Nixon during Watergate.

CROC. The Committee for the Recognition of Obnoxious Commercials, an ad hoc group that provides toilet bowl-shaped awards to reluctant Madison Avenue winners.

CRUD. Chalk River Unidentified Deposit. From the U.S. Nuclear Regulatory Commission's *Handbook of Acronyms and Initialisms.*

DACOR. An IBM product DAta CORrection system that had to be renamed when the acronym for its first name was figured out. It was originally called the Forward Error-Control Electronics System. Then there is the certainly apocryphal story that Tiffany's once refused to inscribe the silver collection plates of the First Unitarian Church of Kenebunkport with initials.

DASTARD. Destroyer Anti-Submarine Transportable ARray Detector.

DIED. Department of Industrial and Economic Development (of Ohio). Now defunct.

DIMPLE. Deuterlum Moderate Pile Low Energy reactor, a British nuclear reactor.

DISCO. Defense Industrial Security Clearance Office.

DONG. Danish Oil and Natural Gas, according to *Platt's Oilgram News.*

DUA. Acronym that shows how acronyms have created confusion even on the other side of the moon. During the Apollo 12 mission while astronauts were making their seventh lunar revolution, there was some minor trouble with an emergency light in the spacecraft. Controllers in Houston diagnosed the problem and said,

"We think we've figured it out, your DUA was off."
After a few seconds of silence, the response from Apollo 12 was,
"What is a DUA?"
"Digital Uplink Assembly," replied Houston.

DUMB. Deep Underground Mountain Basing. Department of Defense missile acronym.

EGADS. Created for the signal used to destroy a missile in flight: Electronic Ground Automatic Destruct System.

EIS. Environmental Impact Statement. This is the kind of acronym that bureaucrats and members of Congress use every day and expect the rest of us to understand. A few years ago a Massachusetts congressman proclaimed in a headline in a newsletter to constituents, "Air Force to do EIS on PAVE PAWS." PAVE PAWS is an Air Force radar system that stands for Precision Acquisition of Vehicle Entry-Phased Array Warning System. EIS is pronounced *ice*, which makes it even more confusing.

FADD. Fight Against Dictating Designers, one of several groups that sprang up to protest changes in fashion in the early 1970s. Another group whose sole purpose was to fight the turn from mini to midi was GAMS, for Girls/ Guys Against More Skirt.

FAGTRANS. First Available Government TRANSportation, term used in military transportation orders.

FASGROLIA. The FASt GROwing Language of Initialisms and Acronyms, term created by *Time* in 1966 to describe the phenomenon.

FIDO. Freaks, Irregulars, Defects, Oddities a coin collector's term for a minting error.

FROG. Free-Rocket Over Ground, a U.S. designation for a Soviet missile system. (Author's note: When I first heard this acronym, I was a reporter covering military appropriations hearings in the late 1960s. Until I was told what FROG stood for, I was stunned by what seemed to be undue congressional and military alarm over small Russian amphibious animals.)

FUBAR. One of a series of military acronyms for things that are less than 100 percent perfect. FUBAR, which stands for Fouled-Up Beyond All Recognition (in the cleaner of two explanations), dates back to World War II. See also FUBB, FUMTU, JANFU, NABU, SAPFU, SUSFU, TARFU, and TUIFU. Snafu is the granddaddy of them all.

FUBB. Fouled-Up Beyond Belief.

FUMTU. Fouled-Up More Than Usual.

GASSAR. General Atomic Standard Safety Analysis Report. Nuclear Regulatory Commission.

GLCM/SLCM. Respectively, these stand for Ground-Launched Cruise Missile and Sea-Launched Cruise Missile and often have been discussed in Congress in recent years. They are pronounced *CLICK-em* and *SLICK-em*.

GODORT. GOvernment DOcuments Round Table, a librarians' organization. It underscores the fact that even librarians can create awkward acronyms that resemble sounds made by someone with severe indigestion. It is hardly an aberration, as the "Acronyms Appendix" to the American Library Association's publication list also features such units as MAGERT (Map And GEography Round Table) and LIRT (Library Instruction Round Table).

GOO. Get Oil Out, the name of the citizens' group formed in California after an oil slick appeared off Santa Barbara in 1969. GOO was such an appropriate and memorable acronym that it may have helped the group gain prominence.

GOOBS. Going Out Of Business Sale. This acronym is used by Washington, D.C. area consumer groups that act as watchdogs over stores that are regularly going out of business.

GWIBIT. Guild of Washington Incompetent Bureaucratic Idea Throatcutters. The term was coined in 1943 by Representative Karl E. Mundt, who explained at the time, "A gwibitzer is not to be confused with a kibitzer; the latter merely stands on the sidelines and watches while the former sits in the path of progress and trips those who traverse it."

HADES. Hypersonic Air Data Entry System.

HAIR. High Accuracy Instrumentation Radar.

HAL. A crypto-acronym from the film *2001: A Space Odyssey.* The film's demonic computer, HAL, reveals his true identity when each letter of the acronym is advanced one letter to IBM.

HAWK. Homing All-the-Way Killer, an aptly named missile. HIP in the context of this weapon stands for HAWK Improvement Program.

HINT. Puckish TV news talk for Happy Idiot News Talk. HINT takes place, for instance, when the weatherperson is thanked for providing a nice weekend. "I'll see what I can dish out for the next few days," is the common humble reply.

HO. Habitual Offender in police acro-jargon.

HOLLAND. Home Our Love Lasts And Never Dies or Have On Little Lace and No Drawers. An envelope acronym and an alternative to SWAK for Sealed With A Kiss. A naughty cousin to HOLLAND is NORWICH (Knickers Off Ready When I Come Home). Such envelope notations were popular during World War II.

HUT. Television business term for Households Using Television. This sets up situations in which neighborhoods are described in terms of their "HUT percentages."

Iacocca. Writer Ed Lucaire reports: "Many workers in Detroit . . . contend that Iacocca really does stand for I Am Chairman Of the Chrysler Corporation of America.

IGOR. Intercept Ground Optical Recorder. NASA.

INFANT. Iroquois Night Fighter And Night Tracker system. A Vietnam-era weapons system produced for the Army by the Hughes Aircraft Co. Martial acronyms like INFANT and BAMBI (Ballistic Anti-Missile Boos Intercept) are among many innocuous or innocent-sounding names for fearsome realities. These fly in the face of Winston Churchill's admonition that military things should have military names and that he would never send British troops off to fight in something called Operation Begonia or the like.

IRAN. Inspection and Repair As Necessary. NASA.

JANFU. Joint Army-Navy Foul-Up. World War II. Not to be confused with

JAAFU (Joint Anglo-American Foul-Up) or JACFU (Joint American-Chinese Foul-Up).

Jeep. Name derived from GP for General Purpose, which was the vehicle's original designation. Jeeps—now being phased out by the Army—are being replaced with High Mobility Multipurpose Wheeled Vehicles (words that do not lend themselves to an easy nickname).

JOOM. Junior Observers Of Meteorology. During World War II, JOOMs were trained to replace Weather Bureau staff who had gone to war. The JOOMs were one of a number of wartime four-letter personnel including British FANYs (First Aid Nursing Yeomanry), WAVES (Women Accepted for Voluntary Emergency Services), and WASPs (Women's Auxiliary Service Platoon, an American unit in the Panama Canal Zone).

JUMPS. Joint Uniform Military Pay System.

KISS. Keep It Simple Stupid. An acronym used when things are getting too complex.

LANTIRN. Low Altitude Navigation Targeting InfraRed system for Night. Air Force.

LEGO. Building-block toy that got its name from the Danish *leg godt* for "play good."

LEM. NASA's Lunar Excursion Module. This was the original name for the moon landing craft that was abruptly changed to LM for Lunar Module. *Time* reported in its February 14, 1969, issue, "On the theory that Lunar Excursion Module (LEM) was too frivolous a name for the moon landing craft, NASA gravely renamed it Lunar Module, thus reducing the friendly LEM to the now unpronounceable LM."

LOX. Liquid OXygen. Gaseous OXygen, on the other hand, is GOX.

MA. One of the 50 two-letter state abbreviations that the Postal Service has been pushing since 1963, when it began putting them on postmarks. MA is one of eight of these designations that begin with M—MA, MD, ME, MI, MN, MO, MS, and MT. MA stands for MAssachusetts but is easy to confuse with Maine and Maryland. No less confusing are AK, which stands for Alaska but could just as easily represent Arkansas, and CO, which is Colorado's code, not Connecticut's. Few people have mastered the two-letter system, which was, after all, designed for "machine readability." A growing underground is quietly subverting the system by writing out names like Ohio and Iowa and using old-fashioned abbreviations like Mass. and Penn. for what have officially become MA and PA.

A game can be played with these state abbreviations by coming up with words using only the code. National Public Radio's "Weekend Edition" conducted a Memorial Day (as in ME-MO-RI-AL) 1991 contest to come up with a good dictionary example of such a construction. The winner was Ganymede (GA-NY-ME-DE), the cup-bearer of the gods.

MAD. Mutual Assured Destruction, a concept of nuclear planning.

MADDAM. Multiplexed Analog to Digital, Digital to Analog Multiplexed, a Coast Guard computer system term.

MAP. Modified American Plan. One of a number of acronyms and abbreviations commonly used in the travel industry. Others include FIT (Foreign Independent Travel), APEX (Advanced Purchase EXcursion), and B&B (Bed and Breakfast).

MECCA. Master Electrical Common Connector Assembly. NASA.

MOBIDIC. MOBIle DIgital Computer, a computer scheme at the National Bureau of Standards.

MUDPAC. Melbourne University Dual-Package Analog Computer.

MUDPIE. Museum and University Data Processing Information Exchange.

NABU. Non-Adjusting Ball-Up, a contemporary addition to military screw-up acronyms of the FUBAR school.

NASA. The National Aeronautics and Space Administration. It is an example of a successful acronym in that when the word NASA is spoken or written, people generally know what is being referred to—that is, if they are not members of either the North American Swiss Alliance (NASA), the National Association of Synagogue Administrators (NASA), North Atlantic Seafood Association (NASA), or The North American Saxophone Alliance (NASA).

NATO. The North American Treaty Organization to most, but not to the National Association of Theatre Owners.

NECCO. New England Confectionery COmpany, producers of the famous NECCO wafers.

NIMBY. Not In My BackYard. This is the name for the urge to oppose hospitals, nuclear power plants, halfway houses, liquor stores, and just about anything else that can be opposed. Those who oppose, usually in the name of protecting real estate values, are known as NIMBYs. Clearly implied in this is having the benefit of the installation as long as it is in another neighborhood.

NMI. As far back as World War I, the U.S. Army has used this designation, which stands for No Middle Initial, to complete the names of military personnel. NMI, in effect, became the middle name of great numbers of Americans.

NOIP. The National Orchestral Institute Philharmonic. This is a decidedly uncharacteristic acronym for a group that thrives on harmony.

NOSE. National Odd Shoe Exchange.

NW-NW. No Work-No Woo. This was the slogan adopted by women workers at the Albina shipyards in Portland, Oregon, during World War II. According to the *Reader's Digest* of January 1944, "They agreed not to date men who were absent from work."

OAO. One And Only. An acronym used at the U.S. Naval Academy for one's sweetheart.

OTE. OverTaken by Events. An abbreviation that has begun cropping up with regularity in Washington in recent years and applied to such things as reports and budget requests: "If we don't get that report done, we may be OTE."

ONO. Or Nearest Offer. ONO is often used in British classified ads.

PAUSE. People Against Unconstitutional Sex Education. PAUSE is part of a galaxy of morally upright groups that also includes MOMS (Mothers for Moral Stability) and POPS (People Opposed to Pornography in Schools).

PAW. People for the American Way, a now-established group that was created to offset the influence of the religious right wing. A good acronym for punny headlines: "TV Ads Give the Moral Majority PAWS," for instance, from the *Washington Post*. PAW was also the name of an advertising campaign—Pets Are Wonderful—launched by the pet food industry to offset negative cat and dog stereotyping.

PAWOB. Passenger Arriving WithOut Baggage. This is airlinese for a person whose bags have been mislaid or misdirected en route.

PAWS. Phased Array Warning System. Air Force.

PITS. Payload Integration Test Set. NASA.

POETS. Piss Off Early, Tomorrow's Saturday. This is British office equivalent of TGIF (Thank God It's Friday).

POGO. Polar Orbit Geophysical Observatory, a NASA satellite.

POLF. Parents Of Large Families. POLF was used during the period of the national "War on Poverty."

POME or POM. Prisoner Of Mother England. According to the seventh edition of the *Acronyms, Initialisms, and Abbreviations Dictionary*, this term was originally used in the nineteenth century to describe a convict in an Australian penal colony and then developed into "pom" or "pommie" as a nickname for any Englishman found Down Under—as opposed to a native Aussie. "A second theory," says the AIAD, "maintains that the nickname is short for 'pomegranate,' a red fruit, and refers to the sunburn that fair-skinned Englishmen quickly acquire upon arrival in Australia." *Pomieland* is an Australian nickname for England.

Posh. Ultra-smart, luxurious. Several British authors claim it is an acronym for "Port Out, Starboard Home." Norman Moss explains in his book *What's the Difference? A British/American Dictionary:* "On the ships taking Britain's imperial officials and their families to the Far East, the most sought after and most expensive cabins were on the port side of the ship on the way out and the starboard side on the way home, because these were the ones most shielded from the strong sun." Even more specific is the explanation from William Manchester's *The Last Lion-Winston Spencer Churchill 1874–1932*. "The Peninsula and Oriental Steam Navigation Company's four-week voyage between the mother country and Calcutta . . . had become a legend. The worst part of the passage was crossing the Red Sea. Those who could afford relative comfort bought . . . port-side cabins going out to India and starboard cabins for the trip home; in time, 'Port Out, Starboard Home' became the acronym POSH."

In all Merriam-Webster dictionaries the word *posh* is listed with the notation "origin unknown." This has occasioned a steady stream of letters and calls from people who have solved the posh mystery. Almost always, the story goes along the lines of the Moss explanation—that the acronym POSH was first used by the Peninsular and Oriental Steam Navigation Company in the nineteenth century. A good story, but one that has no basis in fact. For one thing, the word *posh* does not show up in print until 1918 and, more to the point, no ticket or any other reference to P.O.S.H. has been found. Merriam-Webster encloses this information in a cordial letter to those who have reported the "Port Out, Starboard Home" discovery.

Such fascinating but totally unsupported word histories are known as "folk etymologies." David Justice, whose specialty at Merriam-Webster is etymology, reports that many of these are like posh in that their explanation involves initials. Others, with no obvious support, include: *cop*, which many people think is short for City's Official Police; *tip*, which allegedly came from a box marked "To Insure Promptness" into which one would drop a coin; and *gorp*, the backpackers' snack that some swear came from "good old raisins and peanuts."

Justice adds that people tend to be amused and taken in by these explanations, even such wild ones as Ford being short for Found On Road Dead, or BVD standing for Bottom Very Dry.

Meanwhile, Justice himself works on establishing the true history of a word. When asked which one word that now carries the notation "origin unknown" he would like to crack, he mentions *kludge*, which is defined as "a system and esp. a computer system made up of poorly matched components."

POT. Portable Outdoor Toilet. Army.

POTUS. President Of The United States. According to *The Wall Street Journal,* this acronym was a favorite of Lyndon Johnson's but displeased Richard Nixon, who preferred to be called "the President" and did away with PO-TUS. It was also used during the Kennedy Administration.

Research conducted by Louis Milliner of New Orleans says that the term actually dates back to 1879 and the administration of Rutherford B. Hayes. It was part of a code copyrighted by Walter P. Phillips, which was described as "A throroughly tested method of shorthand arranged for telegraphic purposes and contemplating the rapid transmission of press reports; also intended to be used as an easily acquired method for general and court reporting." POTUS was composed of two Phillips Code abbreviations: POT for President Of and US for United States. Phillips also used SCOTUS for Supreme Court Of The United States. As Milliner notes: "This was more properly an acronym inasmuch as pure Phillips would have been SCTOTUS.

The code also provided YA for yesterday, YAM for yesterday morning, and YAP for yesterday afternoon. Correspondent Milliner adds, "It was through YAP that I first heard about the code. I read about a newspaper telegrapher who, unfamiliar with that cable base, copied a story and handed his editor an item about the Island of Yesterday Afternoon.

POWER. A federal writing course. Producing Organized Writing and Effective Reviewing.

PRAM. Productivity, Reliability, Availability and Maintainability office. Air Force.

QANTAS. For Queensland And Northern Territory Aerial Services (since 1920). This proves that one of the few ways to get around the u-follows-q rule is through an acronym.

RALPH. Reduction and Acquisition of Lunar Pulse Heights. NASA. Also, The Royal Association for the Longevity and Preservation of the Honeymooners, a TV series that featured Jackie Gleason as Ralph Kramden.

REPULSE. An FBI acronym-code name for an effort to counter attempts by Soviet KGB agents to link the name of J. Edgar Hoover with that of a Johnson administration aide arrested on a morals charge in 1964. REPULSE stood for Russian Efforts to Publish Unsavory Love Secrets of Edgar.

ROSE. Rising Observational Sounding Equipment (which by any other name . . . ?).

ROY G BIV. Acronymic aide-memoire for the colors of the rainbow: red, orange, yellow, green, blue, indigo, violet.

RUNCIBLE. Originally a nonsense word created by Edward Lear, but now a no-nonsense acronym in computerdom standing for Revised Unified New Computer with Its Basic Language Extended.

SAHAND. Society Against "Have A Nice Day."

SANTA. Souvenir And Novelty Trade Association.

SAP. Society for Applied Spectroscopy.

SAPFU. Surpassing All Previous Foul-Ups.

SAPT. Special Assistant to the President for Telecommunications, during the Johnson administration.

SATIRE. Semi-Automatic Technical Information REtrieval.

SCOOP. A New York anti-dog litter-group: Stop Crapping On Our Premises.

SCOPE. One of many examples of identical acronyms that read out differently depending on whether you are talking about a computer system or a program to rehabilitate former prisoners. Some of the SCOPEs: System for the Co-ordination Of Peripheral Equipment; Service Center Of Private Enterprise; Senior Citizens' Opportunities for Personal Enrichment; Supportive Council On Preventive Effort; Summer Community Organization and Political Education program; State Commission On Public Education; Scripps Cooperative Oceanic Productivity Experiment; and Select Council On Post-high-school Education.

SCROD. A Maine group, The Special Committee to Restore the Ogunquit Dunes. What is so interesting is that an old and dubious etymology for scrod, the generic name for young fish, is that derived from an old fish market sign for the catch of the day, which read Special Catch Recieved on Dock (SCROD).

SEE. Stop Everything Environmentalists. This a derisive term with no official standing.

SHAZAM. The word that Billy Batson uttered in the comic books to become Captain Marvel. It stood for the wisdom of Solomon, the strength of Hercules, the stamina of Atlas, the power of Zeus, the courage of Achilles, and the speed of Mercury.

For Mary Batson, who changed into Mary Marvel, SHAZAM stood for the grace of Selena, the strength of Hippolyta, the skill of Ariadne, the fleetness of Zephyrus, the beauty of Aurora, and the wisdom of Minerva.

SINS. Situational Inertial Navigation System. Navy.

SLOP. Satellite Low Orbit Bombardment.

SMEAR. Span/Mission Evaluation Action Request. NASA.

SMOOSA. Save Maine's Only Official State Animal, a Main group attempting to end the annual moose season.

Smynorca. Acronyms spelled backwards, a creation of San Francisco columnist Herb Caen to describe "a set of catchy initials for which words must then be found."

Snafu. Situation normal: all fouled-up. This Army acronym, which goes back at least to World War II, has long ago achieved lowercase status. It now is listed as an adjective, a verb, and a noun in *The Random House Dictionary of the English Language.*

SNOOTLOCK. Philip Chaplin of Toronto reports, "Senior Naval Officer On The Lakes Of Canada, the post was held by Commodore Sir James Yeo in the War of 1812. If it was not treated as an acronym, it should have been."The excess K was presumably added to give heft to the term.

SNORT. Supersonic Naval Ordnance Research Track. Nothing to sniff at, this administrative project was running along at a cost of $1 million a year in the 1980s.

SOW. Statement Of Work. Common military usage.

SSSH! The Michigan-based Society for Silent Snowmobiles Here!

SOS. Many have claimed that this distress call is an acronym for Save Our Ship. Not so. It is simply three easily remembered and transmitted letters in Morse code.

SOYBEAN. Society Of Yonkers-Bred Emigrees, Although Nostalgic or Sons Of Yonkers, But Escaped As Necessary. This is a group formed by Rick Winston of Adamant, Vermont, upon hearing that the author of this book, a Maryland resident, also hailed from Yonkers, New York.

ST. WAPNIACL. Prior to 1947, schoolchildren had only to recall the name of this saint and they would know not only the names of the government departments but the order in which they were created:

State 1789	Navy 1789
Treasury 1789	Interior 1849
War 1789	Agriculture 1862
Attorney General 1789	Commerce 1903
Post Office 1789	Labor 1913

This came to an end when War and Navy were consolidated in 1947.

SUNFED. Special United Nations Fund for Economic Development.

SUSFU. Situation Unchanged; Still Fouled-Up.

SWAG. Scientific Wild-Assed Guess. SWAG is good for bluffing, as in "I used the SWAG methodology."

SWAMI. Standing-Wave Area Motion Indicator.

TARFU. Things Are Really Fouled-Up.

3-H. The late Hubert H. Humphrey, as abbreviated by certain tabloids. "3-H Mourns RFK" was one headline using the abbreviation.

TUIFU. The Ultimate In Foul-Ups.

UNIVAC. UNIVersal Automatic Computer. The name of the world's first commercial computer, delivered to the Bureau of the Census in 1951.

UTTAS. Utility Tactical Transport Aircraft System, a helicopter that is pronounced *yew-tahs.*

VAMP. One of the earliest recorded acronyms, if not the earliest. VAMP, re-discovered by William and Mary Morris, dates back to the mid-nineteenth century, when it was used in firefighting circles for Voluntary Association of Master Pumpers. Prior to the Morrises' revelation, it had been broadly concluded that the earliest English acronym was ANZAC, a World War I designation for the Australian and New Zealand Army Corps. In any event, ANZAC had at least one other military antecedent in FANY for First Aid Nursing Yeomanry.

WAFFLE. Wide Angle Fixed Field Locating Equipment.

WAMPUM. Wage And Manpower Process Utilizing Machines. This is one of many acronyms used in recent years at the Bureau of Indian Affairs.

WANAP. WAshington National AirPort, as stated on military travel orders.

WASP. Wyoming Atomic Simulation Project, among others.

WATSUP. The Wessex Association for The Study of Unexplained Phenomena, a group of British UFO spotters.

WBFP. Recent addition to the classified real estate advertising vocabulary. It stands for Wood Burning Fire Place.

WHAM. Cynical acronym used by U.S. troops during the war in Vietnam for "Winning the Hearts And Minds of the people."

WONG. Weight On Nose Gear. NASA.

WUMP. White, Urban, Middle-class, Protestant.

YAWYE. You Are What You Eat.

ZEBRA. Zero Energy Breeder Reactor Assembly. British nuclear project.

ZIP. The Zip in Zip Code stands for Zone Improvement Plan.

2

Alimentary Words

*A Hearty Ration of Terminology from
Either Side of the Kitchen Door*

Acetarious. Applied to plants used in salads.

Albedo. The white, pithy inner peel of citrus fruits.

Alliaceous. Having the definite aroma of garlic.

Analeptic. Word for a diet that is restorative or promotes good health.

Bain marie. Double boiler; two pots.

Bard. To cover meat with strips of bacon.

Basin. The dimple at the bottom of an apple.

Batrachivorous. Frog-eating. Along with *arachnivorous* (spider-eating) and *xy-livorous* (wood-eating), one of the more obscure *vorous* words in the language.

Beestings. The first milk taken from a cow after giving birth to a calf. It is especially rich.

Bench tolerance. Baker's term for the property of dough that allows it to ferment at a rate slow enough to prevent overfermentation while it is being made up into bread, buns, or whatever, on the bench.

Benedict. To prepare an egg for eggs benedict. One of an increasing number of food nouns becoming verbs, it was first spotted in a Nieman-Marcus catalog in an offering for a home windmill capable of generating "more than enough wattage to brew her morning coffee, benedict an egg . . ."

Biggin. In a coffeepot, the perforated basket that contains the grounds.

Bletting. The spotted appearance of very ripe fruit when decomposition has begun.

Bobeche. A circular wax-catcher that fits over a candle. It is pronounced *bow-besh.*

Brackle. To break bread or cake or crumble them into pieces.

Broccoflower. Cross between cauliflower and broccoli.

Bromatology. A treatise or essay on food, a study of food.

Bullition. Act or state of boiling.

Burette. An oil and vinegar cruet.

Butterboat. A small gravy boat used for melted butter.

Cafetorium. A large room common to industrial and military installations that combines the functions of a cafeteria and an auditorium.

Carapace. The upper shell of lobsters, crabs, crayfish, and turtles.

Catsup. Rare spelling of ketchup after the end of 1988 when Del Monte dropped catsup from its bottles and followed Heinz and Hunt's to the K-word.

Celtuce. Celery-lettuce. A lettuce with an edible stalk that tastes like a lettuce and celery combination.

Cepivorous. Onion-eating.

Chela. The large claw of a lobster or crab.

Chex. Imperfect but usable eggs sold at a reduced price. Chex are commonly eggs that are cracked but have membranes that are intact.

Clementine. The hybrid produced from an orange and a tangerine.

Cockle. Valentine candy in the shape of a heart with a small message on it like "Love Ya" or "Snookums." It has been pointed out that the shape of a cockle-shell rather resembles a heart.

Coil. Stew produced from odds and ends, originally a hobo term that may be linked to the traditional Irish stew, *colcannon.*

Coral. Lobster ovaries, which turn a bright coral when cooked.

Crumber. Miniature carpet-sweeper for removing crumbs from a table.

Cutlet bat. A bat or mallet used to pound cutlets or other meat before cooking them.

Daffle. An oven mop.

Deaconing. The practice of putting the best-looking food on top, such as putting the most attractive fruit on the top of a basket.

Dragées. Marginally edible silver balls used to decorate baked goods. Pronounced *drazhees*.

Dredge. To coat or sprinkle a piece of food with a dry ingredient such as flour, sugar, or crumbs. Not to be confused with dusting, which is coating pans or work surfaces with flour, starch, or some other dry substance.

Dredger. Device used by bakers to dredge sugar on your doughnuts.

Elutriate. To purify by washing or straining.

Erythorbate. Full name sodium erythorbate. It is a chemical food additive used to give a pink color to hot dogs, bologna, and other cured meat. As it can be heard as "earth bait,"—suggestive of earthworms, it may be the basis for periodic rumors that certain lunch meats contain worms.

Eggfoam. Lightly beaten egg used to coat food before it is fried.

Épergne. A series of bowls attached to an ornamental metal stem. Pronounced *ip-urn*.

Eupeptic. Having good digestion. The opposite of dyspeptic.

Farctate. Full; stuffed. A farctated diner is one who could not eat another morsel.

Farinaceous. Mealy.

Fletcherize. To chew thoroughly and specifically—30 chews to the mouthful. From American nutritionist Horace Fletcher, who advocated the practice.

Flipper. One of three specific terms for a deviant can of food. The three are *flipper, springer,* and *sweller*. The U.S. Navy, which uses a lot of canned goods, gives these three official definitions:

> **Flipper—** A can of food that bulges at one end, indicating food spoilage. If pressed, the bulge may "flip" to the opposite end. Can and contents should be discarded.
>
> **Springer—** A marked bulging of a food can at one or both ends. Improper exhausting of air from the can before sealing, or bacterial or chemical growth may cause swelling and spoilage.
>
> **Sweller—** A can of food having both ends bulging as a result of spoilage. Swellers should be discarded, except molasses, in which this condition is normal in a warm climate.

Floret. A small flower or one of a cluster of flowers, such as those of broccoli or cauliflower.

Franconia. Browned, as whole potatoes are browned with a roast.

Frill. Paper decoration on the bone end of a chop.

Frizzle. The process of cooking in fat until crisp and curled at the edges.

Frutarian. Consumer who believes that most food, even many vegetables, are harmful and must rely on fruit as the major source of nutrition.

Full-tilt boogie. Term used by humorist Jean Shepherd, which he insists is known to all aficionados, for pizza with everything: "anchovies, sausage, green peppers, double cheese, onions, and the greasy thumbprints of Vinnie himself."

Funistrada. A "nonsense" food name created by the U.S. armed forces for use in preference surveys along with 375 real foods. The idea was to use funistrada and two other nonsense names as a control to see if those taking the poll were paying attention. In a 1974 survey, funistrada ranked relatively high: above such things as eggplant, instant coffee, apricot pie, harvard beets, canned lima beans, grilled bologna, and cranberry juice. The other two nonsense names used in these surveys are buttered ermal and braised trake, neither of which rank as high as funistrada.

Gastrology. The science of keeping oneself well and happily fed.

Gemel. A fused set of cruets for oil and vinegar with divergent spouts.

Grazing. Term for sampling food that came into its own in the 1980s. This list of food terms, which were additions to the *Merriam-Webster 9th New Collegiate Dictionary,* includes the date each made its American debut. This list becomes a capsule history of gustatory change:

Al dente—1947	Food processor—1974
Beef Wellington—1965	Frittata—1931
Bialy—1965	Granola—1971
Bok choy—1938	Gyro—1971
Burrito—1957	Havarti—1957
Carbonara—1963	Health food—1882
Charbroil—1968	Jimmies—1947
Clams casino—1952	Junk food—1971
Crudites—1966	Kiwifruit—1966
Dashi—1961	Lekvar—1958
Falafel—1951	Marinara—1949
Fettuccine Alfredo—1961	Nacho—1969

Nouvelle cuisine—1977
Osso buco—1935
Pastina—1945
Paupiette—1889
Peking duck—1955
Phyllo—1950
Pig out—1978
Pita—1951
Refried beans—1957
Reuben sandwich—1966
Salad bar—1973
Scotch egg—1809
Shell steak—1971

Sloppy joe—1968
Snow cone—1964
Souvlakia—1950
Steak tartare—1955
Subgum—1938
Sushi—1898
Tabbouleh—1965
Tetrazzini—1951
Veggie—1966
Yakitori—1964
Ziti—1929
Zuppa inglese—1941

Experts at Merriam-Webster point out that a number of new food terms have come into the language since their massive *Third International Dictionary* was published in 1961. One could, in fact, feast well at a post-1961 alphabetical buffet that would feature: aioli, bananas foster, caldo verde, chimichanga, dim sum, dagwoods, designer pizza, empanadas, frijoles refritos, green goddess dressing, italian sandwiches, lane cake, moussaka, quiche lorraine, steak diane, vegeburgers, western omelets, and yakitori. Besides the food itself, you find such essential food-related items as the doggy bag, salad bar, and wok.

Green chop. What cole slaw is called in some places such as church suppers in parts of rural Maryland.

Hachoir. A crescent-shaped chopping knife with two handles used with a circular bowl into which hit fits. It is also called a *mezzaluna,* which is Italian for half-moon.

Hand-cut. Culinary term of the nineties to enhance the menu value of pasta and vegetables, as in: "Hand-cut Tagliatelle with Lemon Zest, Julienned Parma Ham and Dried Peperoncino in a Sweet Cream Reduction." Menu talk of the nineties may not be able to rival that of the eighties when a $1.95 side salad became, quoting from a very real menu, ". . . a blend of fresh greens tossed tenderly with Saint Germain's + herb dressing from the secret files of the Master Alchemist topped with an array of freshly shredded vegetables for your palatal delight."

Kissingcrust. Crust formed where one loaf touches another in the oven.

Limequat. Lime/kumquat hybrid.

Limivorous. Mud-eating. Here is an old word that has not been used very often; however, with the advent of mud-wrestling as a bar sport it may be ready to come into its own.

Mandoline. Vegetable slicer with an adjustable blade. The vegetable is rubbed up and down the mandoline.

Moggy. A Yorkshire treacle cookie.

Mother. A slime of yeast and bacteria that forms on fermenting liquids and is used to turn cider into vinegar. Sediment in vinegar is also called mother.

Nidorous. Resembling the smell or taste of roasted fat.

Nubbin. A small or imperfect ear of corn.

O'Brien. A style of preparing sautéed vegetables with pimentos and diced green peppers.

Oligophagous. Eating only a limited number of specific foods.

Papillote. Frilly paper hat used to decorate the end of a cutlet or other bone. Pronounced *pappy-lote.*

Piggin. A wooden tub with a handle shaped by continuing one of the staves above the rim. Today small piggins are often found in restaurants as butter holders.

Pipkin. A tiny pan for melting butter.

Plumcot. Plum/apricot hybrid.

Pobbies. Small pieces of bread that have been squashed together with milk and fed to birds and baby animals.

Poltophagy. The prolonged chewing of food, in which the food is reduced to a semiliquid state.

Prosage. Vegetarian sausage made of pure vegetable protein.

Ramekin. A small individual casserole.

Rasher. One thin slice of bacon.

Rimmer. Implement for ornamenting the edge of a piecrust.

Roasting jack. Device for turning a roasting spit.

Roux. A mixture of flour and fat used in cooking as a thickening agent. Rhymes with blue.

Runcible spoon. A three-pronged fork, curved like a spoon, that is usually used for serving. Runcible is a nonsense word coined by Edward Lear. Originally Lear variously applied the word to spoons, hats, cats, and geese.

Runnels. Runways that appear on platters to catch juices.

Rutmus. Mixture of mashed potatoes and turnip with hot butter sauce.

Scotch hands. Two wooden handles used for shaping balls of butter.

Semese. Half-eaten.

Skirt. The technical term in the ice cream business for the little globule of ice cream that appears at the base of a scoop of ice cream on a cone. Certain ice cream scoopers have been advertised for their ability to avoid "over-serving and wasteful skirt."

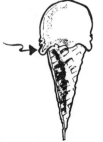

Sneeze guard. The clear plastic or glass shield that hovers over salad bars, cafeteria lines, and the like.

Sugar spots. The name for the brown flecks that appear on banana skins.

Tiffin. Midmorning snack or luncheon.

Tomalley. The "green stuff" of cooked lobster. It is the liver of the creature, and to many it is a great delicacy. "[It] is the quintessence of the creature and the nearest we mortals can come to the ambrosia of the Greek gods" is what writer Robert P. Tristram Coffin wrote in a typical tomalley testimonial.

Tomato shark. Implement used in peeling and removing stems from tomatoes.

Trencher. Shallow bowl-shaped slab of bread that holds a meaty stew and absorbs its juices. In early medieval England, before dinner plates were used, people commonly ate from trenchers and then ate the trencher.

Turophile. Cheese fancier. A coinage of Clifton Fadiman's.

Veganism. Extreme vegetarianism. A vegan excludes dairy products as well as meat.

Wham. Meatless ham made of textured soy.

Whye. Cross of wheat and rye.

Witloof chicory. Better known as Belgian endive.

Yingling. Candy made of peanuts, butterscotch chips, and Chinese noodles. The mix is boiled and formed into a small haystack.

Zarf. Holder for a handleless coffee cup. Contemporary zarfs are made of plastic.

Zester. A small rake-like tool used to shave the top layer of skin from an orange or lemon. These shavings are used to flavor such things as sauces and icings.

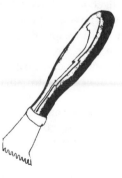

3

Animal Talk I

Words from the Other Species

Aculeate. Equipped with a sting (adj.) or an insect with a sting (noun).

Anoestrum. Period between the "heats" of animals.

Baculum. Small bone in the penis of certain mammals.

Barbel. A slender tusk-like appendage that appears on the lips of certain fish.

Barrow. A neutered pig.

Byssus. The "beard" that mollusks use to attach themselves to rocks and other objects. Rhymes with vices.

Calks. The projections at the ends of horseshoes that help horses keep their footing.

Carapace. The upper body-shell of tortoises, lobsters, crabs, and other crustaceans.

Caruncles. The fleshy appendages on the upper part of the necks of turkeys. See *snood* this chapter.

Corvine. Crow-like; pertaining to a crow.

Croches. The small knobs on the antlers of deer and other similarly antlered animals.

Cygnet. A young swan.

Dewclaw. The little claw behind a dog's foot; the false hoof of a deer.

Dewlap. The loose skin that hangs from the neck of an ox or cow.

Dowcet. A testicle of a deer or rabbit.

Eft. The name for a newt during the period of its life when it lives on land.

Ephemeromorph. Biologist's term for forms of life that are so low they cannot be classified as either animal or vegetable.

Epizootic. Describing a disease that is widespread in animals, as opposed to epidemics, which are human.

Flews. The large upper lips of certain dogs, such as bloodhounds, which hang down pendulously.

Fornix. The upper shell of an oyster.

Furcula. The clavicular bone of a bird; the wishbone.

Gablocks. Spurs used by fighting cocks.

Gallayak. The noted writer L. Sprague de Camp informed the compiler of this in a letter: "... when I was in Alaska in 1924, at the Government Agricultural Station I saw a calf said to be a cross between a yak and a Galloway. They called it a gallayak."

Geep. The offspring of a sheep and a goat, also called a *shoat.*

Grilse. Young salmon.

Gruntle. The snout of a pig.

Hinnable. Able to neigh or whinny.

Hinny. The offspring of a horse and a she-ass.

Implumous. Without feathers.

Joey. A baby kangaroo.

Jumar. The offspring of a cow and horse, which is biologically impossible. A *jumart* is the supposed offspring of a bull and a mare.

Koomkie. Trained female elephant used to decoy wild males.

Labtebricole. Living in holes.

Lutrine. Otter-like.

Mordacity. Likely to bite, a biting quality.

Nasicornous. Having the horn on the nose.

Necropsy. An animal autopsy.

Nide. A single hatching of pheasants.

Nuddle. To rub or push with the nose; to press close to the ground with the nose, as an animal does.

Pannage. Pig food. This term is more commonly used in Britain than America.

Petulcous. Butting like a ram. Overly aggressive.

Ranarium. A frog farm.

Scut. A very short tail, such as that of a hare.

Snood. The vermiform appendage dangling from the upper beaks of male turkeys. It is tumescent and can be extended and retracted.

Suint. Oily sebum of sheep from which lanolin can be extracted, sometimes glibly referred to as the dried perspiration of sheep. Rhymes with truant.

Talpoid. Mole-like; having talpoid characteristics.

Tantony. The smallest pig in a litter.

Trocar. Tool inserted into a bull or cow to relieve intense gas pressure that sometimes results from eating too much clover. In a recently revealed letter that Harry Truman sent an old friend in 1951, the former president said he wished he could apply a trocar to the "stuffed shirts" in government. "You know what happens when you stick one of them into an old bull that's clovered. The report is loud and the wind whistles—but the bull usually comes down to size and recovers."

Ungual. Pertaining to or having a nail, hoof, or claw.

Wattle. The fleshy growth on the neck or face of the turkey and other fowl. Chickens have a pair of them suspended from the lower mandible, where the chin should have been.

Weanel. A newly weaned animal.

Wether. A castrated male sheep.

Yakalo. An animal that is half yak and half buffalo.

Zebrula. The product of a union of a horse and zebra.

Zobo. Reported cross between a zebra and a yak.

Zum. A cross between a yak and a cow, also called a *dzo*.

4

Animal Talk II

"In a Pig's Eye," You Say

Our language is loaded with "animalisms"—words and phrases that use animal images and metaphors. There is a zoo full of them that we are hardly aware of saying, or, to use an animalism, they roll off the tongue *like water off a duck's back*. A baseball announcer tells us that a *southpaw* is warming up in the *bullpen*; we are told that our destination is only ten miles away *as the crow flies*; and, if we are *dog-tired*, we think about taking a *catnap*. We can be *mad as a wet hen*, *happy as a clam*, or clumsy as a *bull in a china shop*. In matters of war and peace, we are variously described as *hawks* or *doves*, and if we pay no attention to such matters, we are thought to be *ostrich-like*. If we make too much of something, we are said to be *making a mountain out of a molehill*.

By using these terms and phrases every day, we reveal something about ourselves. For one, they constantly remind us that human ways and animal ways may not be all that far removed from one another. This could be why they are so easily said and understood. In human terms, there is, for instance, no question what we mean when we speak of a *snail's pace*, say someone is *eagle-eyed* or *henpecked*, or refer to pranks as *monkeyshines*. Sometimes we use animalisms to express contempt. To refer to a crowd of humans as *cattle* or a *herd of sheep* is to suggest rude stupidity or doltish docility.

Animalisms also tell us something about human nature itself. When we talk of the *fox guarding the hen house* or say that someone is as *sly as a fox*, we

31

are commenting on human, not animal, behavior. The linguistic fox is a stand-in for human deception (unless we are doing the *fox-trot*) and shows us throwing off our less desirable characteristics on an animal as if to make them sound more acceptable. Someone who *drinks like a fish* is someone who gives the fish a bad name. Oddly, the vocabulary of alcohol abuse is loaded with animalisms—*drunk as a coot, skunked, fish-eyed, boiled as an owl*, etc.—not one of which has any basis in reality.

One indication of the degree to which such terms and phrases have taken hold is to scan Darryl Lyman's book *The Animal Things We Say*. This book, published in 1983, contains hundreds of animalisms (along with their origins) as well as many animal-related words, some of which we seldom recognize as such. In a fascinating chapter on "Animals Hidden in Words," Lyman shows us, for instance, that *ukulele* is Hawaiian for "jumping flea," that the pasta *vermicelli* is Italian for "little worms," and that *muscle* comes from the Latin *musculus* for "little mice" (presumably because muscles rippling under the skin look like small rodents). He also points out that many everyday words and phrases come from the relationship of humans to one specific animal. Horses and horse racing, for example, give us such expressions as *also-ran*, to *bridle*, *by a nose, champ at the bit, neck and neck, spur*, and *well-groomed*.

After browsing through Lyman's book, one gets the feeling that it is all but impossible to utter more than a few sentences before running into at least one animal reference. Browsing, by the way, is an animal term according to Lyman who writes, "Tender young shoots, twigs and leaves on trees and shrubs are called browse. When casually nibbling on such material, an animal is said to *browse*. The idea of browsing has been figuratively applied to humans; to inspect something is a leisurely way *to browse*. *To browse* at a library means to 'nibble' at the books."

Then there are scores of comparisions in which humans become *cross as a bear, busy as a beaver, poor as a church mouse, sick as a dog*, or *meek as a lamb*. One can list these similies *until the cows come home*.

Sound is another concept that we relate to animals. People and things *purr like a kitten, honk like a goose, cackle like a hen, quack like a duck, bark like a dog*, or *growl like a bear*. We also *snarl, snort, yelp, grunt, chatter*, and *bellow*—all from a longer list of terms Lyman says were created to describe animal noises and were then appropriated to describe human sounds.

We commonly use animal names for all sorts of human labeling and symbolism: fraternal lodges (Lions and Moose); teams (Tigers and Orioles); automobile models (Mavericks and Mustangs); and mascots. We even use the name of one animal to name another: *fox terrier, bullfrog, sea cow, deer fly*, and *horseshoe crab* to name a few.

Another way to see the extent to which animalisms permeate the language is to take one animal and look at the phrases to which it is tied. An aggressive male is a *wolf* who may or may not *wolf* down his food. Poor people work to *keep the wolf away from the door*, and if they are evicted we say *they have been thrown to the wolves.* We are told not to *cry wolf* and to beware of a *wolf in sheep's clothing.*

It is easy to determine why the wolf's linguistic image is not a nice one. Human folklore is populated with wolves (and werewolves) who are rapacious, cruel, and dangerous. From childhood we are horrified by the big bad wolf in stories like "Little Red Riding Hood" and "The Three Little Pigs."

Speaking of pigs, we have *pig Latin* (fake Latin: Latin as pigs might speak it) and call people *pigheaded,* to say nothing of *hog wild, road hog, hogwash, whole hog,* and *living high on the hog* (where the best cuts of meat are). We have also been told that *you can't make a silk purse out of a sow's ear.* Our porcine-human comparisons are hardly flattering: *fat as a pig, greedy as a hog, dirty as a pig,* and we liken a messy human habitation to a *pigsty* or *pigpen.*

These human visions are often off the mark. We have turned the owl into a universal symbol of wisdom, yet no scientific evidence suggests that this is a particularly smart bird, just as nothing suggests that the loon is loonly. The wise image we have given to the owl probably comes from its wise and solemn looks, and it has been suggested that the loon's crazy image does not come from the bird at all but from the fact that *loon* sounds like *lunatic.*

Where do all these words and phrases come from?

Everywhere.

Some are self-explanatory or nearly so. There can be little question about the inspiration for expressions like *locking the barn doors after the horse has been let out* and *as jumpy as a cat on a hot tin roof. Cockoo* as applied to humans comes from the little mechanical bird that pops out of the face of clocks; *ugly duckling* comes from the Hans Christian Andersen story of the same name; and to *have an albatross around one's neck* is to recall the hapless Ancient Mariner from Samuel Taylor Coleridge's famous poem. Both *holy cow* and *sacred cow* come from the Hindu veneration of that animal. TV *rabbit ears* and *alligator clips* are aptly descriptive of the shape of the object in question, and terms like *crow's nest, dovetail, fleabag, cat burglar,* or *pack rat* leave little to the imagination.

Others, however, have stories behind them that are often rooted in antiquity. Aesop's fables, the Bible, and the works of Shakespeare account for a number. In his classic, *Phrase and Word Origins,* Alfred H. Holt was able to track *a little bird told me* (meaning "I don't want to reveal my source") to the Koran, the Bible (Ecclesiastes 10:20), Shakespeare, and Swift. Still others have defied generations of etymological sleuthing. It is still anyone's guess why we say it is *raining cats and dogs.* Others are mere linguistic infants having come into the language in the twentieth century (*can of worms* for a mess, *horse-and-buggy* as an adjective for old fashioned, and *bat out of hell,* which was a slang expression of World War I aviators).

Humans are still creating animalisms in such terms as *cold duck, cattle call,* and *pig out.* The current cliche for an elaborate presentation is a *dog and pony show,* and it is no longer enough to say that something is a mere *can of worms* but *a whole, new can of worms.* The word *foxy* means something quite different than it did a generation ago, and recently when a new term was sought to describe people whose attitudes towards arms were neither that of a *hawk* or *dove*, they became *owls.* Computer slang also has its share of animalisms including *moby* (from *Moby Dick*) for something immense and *bug* for a mistake or problem. The noted computer scientist Grace Hopper once traced the term *bug* to an early computer that malfunctioned because of a real bug that had gotten inside the machine.

A very small collection of animal words and phrases and their origins is offered here to show how varied their sources of inspiration are.

Bulls and bears. The Wall Street bull probably got his name from the fact that bulls toss their heads upwards (a human bull buys in anticipation of a rise in prices). The bear of the financial markets probably took his name from a once common expression "to sell the skin before you bag your bear." At one point, people who put their money on a falling market were known as "bear-skin jobbers."

Dog days. This term for the hottest days of the summer comes from Sirius, the dog star. According to the late John Ciardi who discussed the term in his *Browser's Dictionary*, the star rises with the sun during the period from the middle of July to the end of August. Romans looked at the bright star and explained their hot summers by saying that Sirius added to the heat of the sun.

Flog a dead horse. Logic would interpret this as an image of futility that came off the farm as a dull-witted plowman tried to get extra work from his dead horse. This is pure horsefeathers according to John Ciardi who pointed out in his *Second Browser's Dictionary* that it is, in fact, a nautical idiom. Ciardi's research lead to a period of time—called the "dead horse"—during which British merchant seamen were paid in advance after signing on for a voyage. A sailor could draw no additional pay until the "dead horse" payment was worked off or "flogged."

Fly in the ointment. One of many animalisms that come from the Bible. In his *Dictionary of Cliches*, James Rogers traces this phrase to Ecclesiastes 10:1: "Dead flies cause the ointment of the apothecary to send forth a stinking savor; so doth a little folly him that is in reputation for wisdom and honor."

Happy as a clam. According to John Gould in his book *Maine Lingo*, the northern New England expression comes from the longer original "happy as a clam at full tide." Gould's explanation: "When the tide is full, nobody is digging clams."

In a pig's eye. In *The Animal Things We Say*, Darryl Lyman says there is evidence that this term for balderdash comes from a nineteenth-century shipboard game in which a person was blindfolded, turned around three times, and told to locate the eye of a pig outlined on the deck. "The odds against marking the correct place were great. Therefore, uttering something impossible is analogous to putting a mark *in a pig's eye.*"

Let the cat out of the bag. This way of saying that a secret has been revealed was discussed in E. C. Brewer's *Dictionary of Phrase and Fable* published in the nineteeth century: "It was formerly a trick among country folk to substitute a cat for a suckling pig, and bring it in a bag to market. If any greenhorn chose 'to buy a pig in a polk,' without examination, all very well; but if he opened the sack, 'he let the cat out of the bag' and the trick was disclosed."

Lion's share. From Aesop's lion who came up with a formula for dividing the pack's kill as follows: he got one quarter because it was his prerogative, another quarter was his because of his courage; and the third quarter was for his dam and cubs. As for the last quarter, he said, "let who will dispute it with me." Presumably, someone else got the fourth portion as the phrase means the largest share rather than all. The phrase *to cry wolf* also comes from Aesop's fables.

Monkey wrench. Some have written that this came from the appearence of the tool, but the documentation lies on the side of a man named Monk who invented it while working for the Springfield, Massachusetts, firm of Bemis and Call in 1856. First called Monk's wrench, it was turned into monkey wrench. It became part of an idiom for sabatoge (to throw a monkey wrench into the machinery).

There are more linguistic ties between humans and animals than the images and metaphors that have come into speech. Linguists have long been fascinated that English provides a separate vocabulary for animals in groups; hence, *a bevy of quail, a cloud of gnats, a kindle of kittens, a shrewness of apes, a pride of lions, a gam of whales,* and *a rag of colts,* to name a few. James Lipton, whose *Exaltation of Larks* was devoted to these collective terms, says that they were codified in the fifteenth century at a time when English was expanding. He goes on to argue that the fanciful *exaltation* is as legitimate a term for larks as *school* is for fish. Just for the record, men come in *bands* and angels in *hosts.* We have also come up with an elaborate and specific set of terms for where animals live (including *nests, roosts, warrens, hives, kennels, burrows,* and *dens*) and a host of animal adjectives (ranging from the familiar *canine* and *feline* to the rarer examples like *ranine* and *otarine,* which relate, respectively, to frogs and seals). The crow even has its own adjective: *corvine.*

Another rich area is the animal names that appear on the map. Of these, many come from the shape of a geographic feature that resembles the animal (Moosehead Lake) or a form of life that dominated the place (Mosquito Island). Conversely, place names have been widely applied to animals. Dog breeds serve as a prime example of this with the *Boston* (Massachusetts) *Terrier, Afghan* (from Afghanistan) *Hound, Skye* (in the Hebrides) *Terrier, Dalmatian* (the region in Yugoslavia), *Airedale* (from the Aire River Valley in Yorkshire, England), *Chihuahua* (from the North Mexican state), and *Spaniel* (named for its native Spain).

Finally, there is the most fertile area of them all, the names that we give to animals. For starters we are content with a simple generic name like *pigeon*, but then we must come up with dozens of breed and species names. Pigeon breeds include such splendid names as *Birmingham Roller, Chinese Owl, Giant Runt, Ice,* and *English Pouter.* Chicken names include *Buff Orphington* and the *Penciled Wyandotte.* This trend even continues in the insect realm. The price list from Al's Tarantula Ranch, a Kenmore, Washington, establishment catering to the "tarantula hobby," contains a fascinating array of popular names including the *Velvet Red Rump, Costa Rican Zebra, Pink Toe Tree Tarantula, Flame Knee,* and *Yellow Banded Tree Tarantula.* At $185 dollars, the most expensive spider on the list was an adult female *Goliath Bird Spider.*

The proud owner of a Goliath Bird Spider would not only have a pet with a popular name but also a Latin taxonomic name (*Theraphosa leblondi*). The owner might also want to give that particular spider a pet name and for this might want to consult Jean E. Taggart's book *Pet Names,* which suggests 30 appropriate names for pet spiders on the order of *Trapper* (after the way they bag their prey) and *Silas Marner* (a weaver in the George Eliot book of the same title). The Taggart book even lists names for pet rats including *Whiskers* and *Ta Ka,* a Native American name for rat. Beyond spiders and rats, there are the individual names we give to other pets, zoo animals, and race horses.

Naming the family pet is a personal event and often connected with a story or event. Friends of the author's lost a cat named *Carnation.* When a carbon-copy kitten was found they felt the only natural name for her was *Reincarnation.* Author Christopher Morley named his cats *Shall* and *Will* because "no one can tell them apart." *New York Times* columnist William Safire has written, "I used to have a German shepherd named Henry, after Henry A. Kissinger, because at one time I was irritated with my Nixon Administration colleague and wanted to be able to say 'Down Henry!' after a hard day at the West Wing."

Some give pets generic names—*Tabby, Spot,* and *Fido* (from the Latin for "faithful")—while others tend to human names like *Peter, Elizabeth,* and David Letterman's oft-mentioned dog, *Bob.* A Chicago veternarian has written that people who give their pets human names tend to be more closely attached to their animals, while another vet has concluded that a pet name reveals something about the owner, for instance, a family of lowly economic or social status may name a pet *Princess* or *King.*

Recent surveys have shown that *Rover* is still the most popular dog name in America, and that there are more cats named *Sam* than any other. Other top dog names include *Spot, Max, Lady, Pepper,* and *Muffy,* while *Kitty, Tiger, Boots,* and *Princess* are popular cat names.

If a horse is a thoroughbred and is to be registered with the Jockey Club in New York for listing in the *American Stud Book,* the name must not be any longer than 18 letters, not duplicate another active horse's name (15 years must elapse before it can be used again), not be a trade name, and must lie within the bounds of good taste. This set of rules all but insures a steady stream of odd horse names.

Famed trainer Woody Stephens was recently asked what was the worst horse name he had ever heard, and he quickly replied, "I've heard some terrible names but probably Bug Juice was the worst." Ranking right up there would have to be *Bates Motel* (a famous colt of the early 1980s named for the place where Norman Bates ran amok in the movie *Psycho*), *Disco Inferno, Cold Shower,* and *You Name It.* The latter was a horse that raced in the late 1960s and was so named after the Jockey Club had turned down a number of names and the exasperated owner finally scrawled "you name it!" across the application.

Zoo animals get their names for a host of reasons. Some are given names appropriate to the country they came from, such as *Ling-Ling* and *Hsing-Hsing* who were gifts of the People's Republic of China, while others are given playful crowd-pleasing names like *Starlet O'Hara* at the—where else?—Atlanta Zoo. Then there is the hard-to-resist urge to give Zoo llamas names like *Llulu* and gnus names like *Gnancy*.

Finally, some zoo animal names are commonly selected because they "fit" the image of the animal in question. Powerful gorilla names with African overtones are a case in point. *Ramar, Sampson, Tanga, Shamba, Colo, Maximo, Massa, Tomoka, Kumba, Big Man, Togo, Binga, Baltimore Jack, Tomoka, Kanda, Bushman,* and *Bamboo* are the names of American zoo gorillas past and present.

The most famous name for a real gorilla (as opposed to the likes of King Kong and Mighty Joe Young) was that bestowed on a large animal obtained by the Ringling Brothers-Barnum & Bailey Circus in 1937. He was originally called Buddy, but the circus staff hunted for a name that would convey his large size. They found a giant named *Gargantua* who was the hero of a satire by Rabelais. The ape became *Gargantua the Great* and the adjective *Gargantuan* has been popular ever since. Example: "People seem to have a gargantuan repertoire of animalisms."

5

Antonyms

An Aggregation of Rare Counter Terms

Often one form of an English word is much more popular than its opposite. Here are some of the more unusual antonyms.

Adiabolist. To the devil what an atheist is to God.

Amitular. Auntly actions or qualities. Created by Bergen Evans to rectify a "reprehensible omission" of the English language, which has never had a counterpart for *avuncular*, which refers to uncle-ish behavior.

Antapology. The reply to an apology; saying "That's all right" after someone has apologized for stepping on your foot.

Ante-jentacular. Before breakfast, as opposed to the more commonly heard *post-prandial* (after dinner).

Autonym. A writer's own name; the opposite of *pseudonym*.

Cacophemism. Using a harsh or cruel expression where a milder one would be proper; the opposite of *euphemism*. Some would argue that a *dysphemism* is another opposite—albeit in the other direction—of euphemism. Using a disparaging or belittling term to describe something that deserves more is a dysphemism. It is, for instance, dysphemistic to speak of a mansion as a shack or a BMW as a jalopy.

Ciplinarian. One who teaches disorder. The opposite of *disciplinarian*.

Clairaudient. Able to hear things not actually present in the same manner that a *clairvoyant* is able to see things not actually present. A *clairsentient* is able to perceive sensations not actually present.

Clement. Describing pleasant, mild weather; not inclement.

Cuckquean. A female cuckold.

Dystopia. The opposite of a utopia, such as the state imagined in George Orwell's *1984* or the film *Rollerball. Anti-utopia* is another term used to describe this state.

Gruntle. To put in a good humor. It is the positive opposite of *disgruntle* and is seldom used for the simple reason that it sounds like a bad-humored word. A marvelous collection of "Words Rarely Used in Their Positive Form," from *advertent* (giving attention—the flip of *inadvertent*) to *wieldy* (strong; manageable—not *unwieldy*), appears in *The Book of Lists #2* by the Wallace family.

Illth. The opposite of *wealth.*

Marcidity. The state of great leanness. *Obesity*'s opposite extreme.

Merman. The male counterpart of the *mermaid.*

Misandry. Female hatred of males. A rare word for the female equivalent of *misogyny.*

Monoglot. Unlike the *polyglot* or the person who is bilingual, the monoglot speaks only one language.

Nescience. Ignorance—a far cry from *prescience.*

Nullibicity. The ubiquitousness of ubiquitousness as a word leads to the question of its opposite. Nullibicity is the state of being nowhere. *Nullibiety* means the same thing.

Onymous Not anonymous.

Paravail. The opposite of *paramount.*

Pedipulate. *Manipulation* by foot.

Pessimal. *Optimal*'s opposite.

Philogynist. A lover of women; the *misogynist*'s opposite number.

Sannup. *Squaw*'s husband; married male Indian.

Sedentes. Those who remain in one place; the opposite of *migrants*. Pronounced *said-en-tays*. Writer L. Sprague de Camp notes, "About "sedentes,' there ought to be a word 'sessor' for sedentary organisms, on the analogy of 'cursor'; but my Webster's 2nd International does not list it."

Spintry. Male *whore*.

Tarassis. Male equivalent of *hysteria*, which borrows from the Greek for uterus (the same borrowing used in hysterectomy).

Ubiety. Thereness; being in a place; the opposite of *absence*.

Urning. A word for a male homosexual. An extremely rare word, which was reintroduced in Theodore M. Bernstein's *Dos, Don'ts & Maybes of English Usage.* He hunted the term down in reaction to the common belief that there was no English word for exclusively male homosexuality. The word is pronounced *oorning* and the practice is *urningism*.

Another possibility is *comasculation*, which appears in Josefa Heifetz Byrne's collection of words, *Mrs. Byrne's Dictionary,* and is defined as "homosexuality between men."

6

Bluff Words

A Swarm of Stumpers

"Call My Bluff" is the name of the long-popular British television game show that pits two teams of three against each other. A word is given to team A along with its true definition. Team A then presents the true definition along with two outlandish fabrications to team B, whose job is to sort out the right definition. Team B is then given a word, and the team with the most successful record at the end of the show wins. The only rule is that one of the three definitions given must be true.

To give an example of how it works, here is how the word *bonze* was handled by the mainstays of the show, Frank Muir and Patrick Campbell, which is quoted from their book, *Call My Bluff.*

1. "Bonze" is a rather secret trade-word still used in the world of bootmaking, especially among the high-class gentlemen's bootmakers in St. James. A bonze is the tracing made of the outline of a customer's foot from which, of course, the "last" is cut. At one particular bootmaker's they still have the bonzes of Lord Nelson and Disraeli, and of at least one duke of whom it is said in the trade that he had "a bonze like a boat."

2. "Bonze" is derived from the Portuguese word *"Bonze,"* and is an impolite but not necessarily offensive name for a Japanese clergyman.

41

You might wonder why the Portuguese, who live a very very long way away from the possibility of seeing even a Japanese layman, would feel the need for an impolite word for a Japanese cleric, but they do, and it's "bonze." It's also impossible to understand why some English dogs are called Bonzo, but they are.

3. "Bonze" was a game resembling ninepins which was prohibited-by-statue, during the fifteenth and sixteenth centuries, on the grounds that it was knocking over too many public figures. It wasn't played in a pub or bowling alley, but out-of-doors, where there was more room for power-play bonzing: i.e., bashing hell out of ninepins painted to look like the government of the day.

The correct answer is *2*.

The following is a collection of real words and their real definitions that are ideally suited to *Call My Bluff* and other recreational wordplay.

Acinaceous. Consisting of or full of kernels.

Anomphalous. Without a navel. Medieval paintings of Adam and Eve often showed the couple anomphalously.

Apricate. To bask in the sun; to sunbathe.

Asitia. Lack of appetite; dislike of food.

Aspergillum. Rod or brush used for sprinkling holy water.

Bagasse. Sugarcane refuse.

Bandoline. A hairdressing made from quinces.

Banghy. Porter's shoulder yoke in India. Also, *bangy*.

Bastinado. That form of torture in which the soles of the feet are beaten with a stick or rod.

Bottomry. A loan to equip or repair a ship.

Burke. To kill by suffocating with the hand or a wet plaster. Named after a William Burke who with an accomplice killed 15 people in this manner and sold their bodies to medical students for dissection. The method was employed because it left no telltale marks of violence. (Burke was hanged in 1829 in Edinburgh.) The word is also used figuratively in the sense of stifling or smothering an investigation or other proceeding.

Capoletti. Triangular-shaped ravioli.

Cenotaph. A tombstone in memory of someone buried somewhere else at some other time.

Circumforaneous. Wandering from house to house.

Chiliomb. The sacrifice of 1,000 animals.

Chryselephantine. Made of gold and ivory.

Coruscate. To give off glitter or sparkles of light; to be brilliantly witty.

Cratch. A crib for corn and other grain, which is raised off the ground to protect its contents from water, rodents, and other hazards.

Cromlech. Prehistoric table-like monument made by placing a flat rock on top of two vertical rocks or a circle of rocks. Pronounced *chrome-leck*.

Danegeld. Public blackmail. A danegeld was occasionally levied to pay off the Danes who invaded England in the days before William the Conqueror.

Eellogofusciouhipoppokunurious. Very good; very fine.

Eriff. A two-year-old canary.

Errhine. Made to be snuffed into the nose.

Exigent. Urgent; needing immediate attention. A good word to use on packages and letters, since everybody else writes *rush* or *urgent*.

Fenks. Whale blubber refuse; rotten blubber. At one time used as manure in farming.

Fescue. A small stick used by teachers to point to specific letters or numbers.

Flabellum. A large fan carried by attendants to the Pope; or a fan used to keep flies away from the Communion wine.

Futtocks. The upright curved ribs of a ship coming up from the keel.

Gadroon. A small-scale, ruffle-like ornamentation used on furniture and silver as a decorative edging.

Ganch. To execute by impaling on hooks.

Gelogenic. Tending to produce laughter.

Helminthous. Infested with worms.

Hippocaust. The burning of a horse in sacrifice.

Ichor. In mythology, the fluid that ran instead of blood in the veins of the gods.

Ignivomous. Vomiting fire.

Impavid. Without fear.

Izzard. Ancient term for the letter z.

Jargoon. A second-rate zircon.

Keckle. To preserve from chafing by covering with canvas, tape, or whatever. A cable is sometimes keckled with rope. Primarily a nautical term.

Kex. Dried hemlock; the dry, usually hollow stem of various herbacious plants, especially of large umbelliferous plants, such as cow parsnips, wild chervil, etc. It is an antiquated word that has come back into its own with the advent of Scrabble.

Kheda. An enclosure for capturing wild elephants.

Mansuetude. Tameness; sweetness of temper.

Meniscus. The curved upper surface of liquid in a tube.

Mesothesis. That which is put in the middle to serve as a balance, or compromise, to opposing principles.

Mulm. The organic sediment that gathers at the bottom of an aquarium.

Musnud. The cushioned throne of an Indian prince.

Mycocide. An agent that kills mold.

Nigroglobulate. To blackball.

Noria. An apparatus for raising water, made up of buckets attached to a wheel.

Nummamorous. Money loving.

Ogygian. Incomparably ancient, antediluvian. Pronounced *oh-gigi-ann*.

Ormolu. Bronze or brass that has been gilded.

Podsnappery. Self-satisfied philistinism. From the character Podsnap in Dickens's *Our Mutual Friend.*

Ptarmic. That which causes sneezing.

Pushkin. A strainer hung on a barrel faucet to catch and strain cider, vinegar, or whatever.

Quisquillous. Made of rubbish.

Rammish. Strongly scented.

Roorback. A false report circulated to damage the reputation of a political candidate. The term dates back to 1844 when two New York State newspapers published extracts from a book, *Roorback's Tour Through the Western and Southern States* by Baron von Roorback, which contained libelous material about presidential candidate James K. Polk. Among other things, he was accused of being involved in the slave trade. The book and its author were both nonexistent.

Rundle. Another word for a ladder rung. A completely superfluous word since rung rings so true.

Sanguisugent. Bloodsucking.

Saponify. To convert to soap.

Scissel. The strip of metal from which the blanks for coins have been cut. Rhymes with missile.

Scree. A pile of debris at the base of a cliff.

Sectile. Capable of being cut easily with a knife.

Silurian. Terribly old. The Silurian is part of the Paleozoic era. Mark Twain used the word to indicate doddering old age.

Sjambok. Whip made from rhinoceros or hippopotamus leather.

Spraints. The droppings of an otter.

Stummel. The shank and bowl of a wooden pipe—that is, all save the stem.

Ucalegon. A neighbor whose house is on fire.

Urbacity. Excessive or foolish pride in one's city.

Withy. Flexible and tough.

Yclept. Denoting called or named. It is the past participle of the archaic verb *clepe*. Pronounced *ee-klept*.

Ylem. The primordial stuff from which the various elements of matter were formed—neutrons, protons, etc. Pronounced *eye-lem*.

Body English

*Words for Things
You Can't Run Away From*

Aconal. Relating to the elbow. An archaic term with a host of possible modern applications ranging from mass transportation to pro basketball.

Acronyx. Ingrown nail.

Aspectabund. Of a pleasantly changing countenance.

Axilla. The armpit.

Blype. A piece of skin that peels off after a sunburn.

Buccula. Double chin.

Canthus. The point at either end of each eye where the upper and lower lids meet.

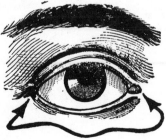

Carminative. Relating to farting; that which induces gas.

Cellulite. Fat, a name created to describe those dimpled formations on one's thighs and backsides. Some maintain that the term is just a fancy synonym for fat and was, in fact, created to "sell you lite" beer, "sell you lite" frozen dinners, etc.

Cerumen. Earwax.

Chaetophorous. Bristle-bearing; in need of a shave.

Cilia. An eyelash.

Circadian. Having to do with bodily cycles, such as those that are interrupted by jet air travel.

Columella. The fleshy part of the nose, just above the lip, that separates the nostrils.

Dolichopodous. Having long feet.

Dorsum. The back part of the tongue.

Embrasure. The space between the teeth.

Exungulation. Paring the nails.

Frenulum. The thin muscle under the tongue, also the thin muscle under the penis.

Furfuration. The falling of dandruff from the scalp, or other situations in which dead skin falls in small particles.

Gelasin. A dimple in the cheek that appears when one smiles.

Geromorphism. Looking older than one's real age.

Gnathion. The tip of the chin.

Gonion. Either end of the lower jaw, the part just under the ear.

Hallux. Big toe.

Hirci. Armpit hair.

Hircinous. With a goat-like odor.

Horripilation. Shuddering sensation, as one feels when one's "hair stands on end"; gooseflesh.

Laxcrimae crocodilorum. Crocodile tears.

Lanugo. The peach fuzz hair that covers the body of newborn humans—a term given new popularity by Dr. T. Barry Brazelton.

Lentiginous. Heavily freckled.

Lunula. The white crested-shaped part of the fingernail at the base of the nail.

Macrotous. Large-eared.

Melanotrichous. Having black hair.

Noop. The sharp point of the elbow. An old word, native to Scotland.

Olecranon. The "funny" bone, the projecting bone of the elbow.

Opisthenar. The back of the hand.

Oscitancy. The act of yawning.

Ozostomia. Evil-smelling breath.

Paedomorphism. The process of growing young; the retention into adult life of those human traits associated with childhood. *Gerontomorphism* is the opposite process of growing old.

Pandiculation. A stretching and yawning, as people are likely to do just before or after sleeping.

Papauliferous. Pimply.

Patrician. One of many named beards. The Patrician is a very long, very full, almost rectangular beard like the kind that adorns the Smith Brothers on the cough drop box. A beard-trimming chart, published by W. W. Bode of San Francisco around 1888, names no less than 15 distinct styles including the Dundreary, the Vidette, and the San Diego.

Paxwax. The neck tendon—properly, the nuchal ligament.

Pelosity. The degree of body hair.

Philtrum. The indentation in the middle of the upper lip just below the nose. This word's rarity was underscored by an editorial that appeared in the *Washington Star* in late 1969, which expressed distress that "there is still no satisfactory term in English to describe...the indentation in the center of the human upper lip." One of the paper's readers set the record straight.

Plook. Scottish word for a nasty boil or pimple.

Podobromhidrosis. Smelly feet.

Popliteal. Pertaining to the hollow area at the back of the knee.

Pronasale. The tip of the nose.

Pseudosmia. False smell-perception.

Purlicue. The space between the index finger and the extended thumb.

Pygia. A pain in the rump.

Racklettes. The little lines on the wrist.

Sclera. The white of the eye.

Sciapodous. Having very large feet.

Sexdigitism. The state of having six fingers or six toes on a hand or a foot.

Simity. The state of being pug-nosed.

Snoach. The breath through the nose.

Steatopygic. Having excessively fat buttocks; bottom-heavy.

Sternutation. Sneezing.

Tragus. The fleshy bump on the ear between the face and the ear cavity.

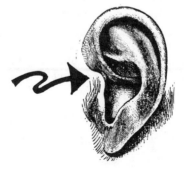

Ulotrichous. Having woolly hair.

Uvula. The thing that hangs down from the back of the mouth (which children invariably think is a tonsil).

Vellus. Short, downy hairs found on the face, not beard hairs, as well as the rest of the body.

Vomer. The slender bone separating the nostrils.

8

British Words

A Volley of Transatlantic Differences

This collection of lesser-known examples of British English was, in part, inspired by a series of quotations:

> Yet another foreign language—that of America.
> —*George Bernard Shaw*

> We and the Americans have much in common, but there is always the language barrier.
> —*Oscar Wilde*

> We are divided by a common language.
> —*Winston Churchill*

> The chief editor of the *Oxford English Dictionary,* Robert Burchfield, said recently that in 200 years or so Americans and Britons would be unintelligible to one another and not be able to converse without a translator.
> —The New York Times, *Editorial,*
> *July 31, 1981*

The first week I was in America I was in a luncheonette and I heard one of the countermen tell the other "to burn the English." All I could think was I hope they don't think I'm English.

—*Philip Young, Belfast, Maine, who came to the United States from Scotland*

Affiliation order. A paternity suit.

Anorak. A parka.

Anti-bounce clip. Shock absorber.

Anti-clockwise. Counterclockwise.

Arterial road. Main road.

Articulated lorry. Tractor-trailer truck.

Assurance. Insurance.

Aubergine. Eggplant.

Balaam. Fillers; items used to fill newspaper space.

Bank holiday. Legal holiday.

Banknote. Paper money.

Bed sitter. Studio apartment.

Beetroot. Beet.

Big dipper. Roller coaster.

Bobbin. A scientist or technologist.

Bombing. Actors in England say a play is bombing if it is doing very well.

Book. To reserve.

Boot. Trunk of a car.

Boot-to-bonnet. Bumper-to-bumper.

Boudoir biscuits. Ladyfingers.

Brackets. Parentheses.

Bradshaw. Timetable.

Brainstorm. Sudden madness.

Brake-van. Caboose. It is also called a *guard's van*. In England a caboose is the kitchen on the deck of a ship.

Brothel-creepers. Men's shoes with thick crepe soles.

Bumf. Paperwork. This commonly used term of the British bureaucracy comes from the World War II slang word for toilet paper, *bumfodder*.

Bump cap. Hard hat.

C-3. 4-F.

Cab rank. Taxi stand.

Capsicum. Green or bell pepper.

Casual ward. Flophouse.

Cause-list. A trial calendar.

Charabanc. An open bus with no aisle and a door for each seat, like an extended convertible and commonly used for sightseeing.

Coach. A closed single-decker bus.

Chicory. Endive.

Chucker-out. Bouncer.

Cleg. Horsefly.

Clever biscuit. Noel Coward's translation of "smart cookie" into English.

Codswallop. Nonsense.

Commercial traveler. Traveling salesperson.

Corf. A creel, a container for fish.

Corn. The grain commonly grown in the district; wheat in England, oats in Scotland.

Cornet. Ice cream cone.

Cos. Romaine.

Counterfoil. Check stub.

Courgettes. Zucchini squash.

Crisps. Potato chips. British *chips,* on the other hand, are French fries.

Cubby. Glove compartment.

Cuffuffle. Slang for a dither; agitated.

Cutting. A newspaper clipping.

Dear. Expensive.

Death duties. Estate taxes.

De-bag. To take someone's pants off as a joke.

Dixie. Iron pot.

Doggo. To be in hiding, to lay low.

Dogsbody. A person who will do the odd jobs that nobody else wants to do.

Drawing pins. Thumbtacks.

Dual carriageway. Divided highway.

Elevenses. Coffee at 11:00 A.M.

Endive. Chicory.

Engaged tone. Busy signal.

Erk. The lowest rank in the RAF.

Face flannel. Washcloth.

Fanlight. Transom.

Fanny. The female pudenda.

Fiddle. A flim-flam.

Fish slice. Spatula or pancake turner.

Fixings. Hardware.

Fleck. Lint. On the other hand, *lint* in England means surgical dressing.

Flex. Electric cord.

Flyover. Overpass.

Fruiterer. Store selling vegetables and fruit.

Full stop. Period in punctuation.

Fully found. All expenses paid.

Fubsy. Fat and squat.

Gash. Spare parts or leftover parts that can serve as spares.

Gaudy. A university or college reunion dinner.

Gazump. To raise the price of something after someone has agreed to buy it. According to Norman Moss in his *What's the Difference? A British/American Dictionary,* "It comes from an archaic colloquial term 'gazumph,' to swindle, which in turn comes from Yiddish."

Geyser. Water heater.

Go-down. A warehouse when used as a noun.

Gooseberry. The fifth wheel at a party or other gathering.

Grabbe. To grope for.

Grotty. Inferior, dirty, or shabby. Stems from *grotesque.*

Guggle. Gurgle.

Hairgrips. Bobby pins.

Hairslide. Barrette.

Hayter. A rotary mower. This began as a trade name but has since become the word for any such mower.

Hessian. Burlap.

Hoarding. A billboard.

Holiday. Vacation.

Humour. One of a number of words in which the British use *ou* where American's settle for *o. Smoulder, labour, mould, honour,* and *colour* are other examples. *Glamour* is the same on either side of the Atlantic.

Interval. Intermission.

Ironmongery. Hardware.

Jacket potato. Baked potato.

Jollop. Gobble.

Kerb. The stone forming the edge of the pavement.

Ladder. A run in a stocking.

Layabout. Hobo or bum.

Lay-by. Roadside rest area.

Li-lo. Air mattress. Originally a brand name, but increasingly being used for all air mattresses.

Lido. A public swimming pool. A municipal swimming pool is often called a *corporation swimming-bath.*

Locum. One doctor covering for another; a clergyman's temporary replacement.

Loose chippings. Gravel.

Mercer. A silk dealer; a shop dealing in expensive fabrics.

Motorway. Turnpike.

Multiple shops. Chain store.

Mutes. Professional pallbearers.

Nappy. A diaper.

Navvy. Construction worker.

Nissen hut. Quonset hut.

Nought. Zero.

Noughts and crosses. Ticktacktoe.

Old boy/Old girl. Alumnus or alumna of a secondary school.

Outgoings. Expenses (as in household expenses) and overhead (as in business overhead).

Pavement. Sidewalk.

Pedestal. Toilet bowl.

Pelmet. Curtain valance.

Pillar box. Mailbox in the form of a truncated pillar.

Pimp. Small bundles of kindling wood.

Pip, the. A state of depression, from the poultry disease. "He gives me the pip" means "I'm fed up with him."

Pip. To beat by a small margin.

Plait. Braid, as both a noun and the verb *to braid.*

Planning permission. Building permit.

Plimsolls. Sneakers.

Plough. The Big Dipper, a.k.a. the *Great Bear.*

Ponce. Pimp, both noun and verb.

Press stud. Snap fastener.

Punter. Speculator.

Putty. British nautical slang for muddy bottom.

Road diversion. Detour.

Roadworks. Road repair.

Roneo. To mimeograph or duplicate.

Rubber. Eraser.

Run-away. A drain.

Shave hook. Paint scraper.

Sick. Vomiting.

Skew-wiff. Cockeyed.

Skirt. Flank steak.

Slut's wool. A marvelous piece of British slang for dust balls or "dust bunnies."

Small ad. Want ad.

Speech day. End of the year awards ceremony at school.

Stumer. A bad check.

Surgery. A doctor's office or the collection of patients in the office. To say that a doctor has a large *surgery* is to say he has an office full of patients. Briton Jimmy Jump of Essex adds, "Members of Parliament and city/town councillers also hold regular *surgeries* when ordinary citizens can go along with their problems, suggestions and complaints. Usually they are held weekly."

Suspenders. Garters. (What Americans call suspenders are called braces in England.)

Terjubilee. Sesquicentenary; 150 years. A proper jubilee in 50 years.

Theatre. Operating room.

Tick (someone) off. To reprimand.
Tiddler. A minnow.
Turn-ups. Trouser cuffs.
Twee. Self-consciously, or overbearingly, cute.
Undercut. Tenderloin.
Underground. Subway.
Unit trust. Mutual fund.
Verge. The grassy strip at the edge of a highway.
Wellies. Galoshes.
Whitlow. Infected fingernail.
Winklepickers. Pointed shoes.
Winkle pin. A bayonet.
Works. Factory.
Zizz. A snooze or nap.

9

Burgessisms

*A Treasury of Rare Coinages
from an American Original*

> He loves machinery, and intricacies of technique. He adores the extravagant, the outrageous. But he used his gift always to demonstrate the absurdities of life. He creates his characters only to destroy them. He formulates complex theories . . . and blows them up with blasts of laughter. He is amused at everything, respects nothing.
>
> *—Gelett Burgess on Gelett Burgess*

Gelett Burgess (1866–1951) was an American humorist who loved tours-de-force. One of his favorites was minting words. He coined *bromide* (for a platitudinous bore) and *blurb* (a self-serving book announcement or testimonial), both of which have become part of the language. In 1914 he published *Burgess Unabridged: A New Dictionary of Words You Have Always Needed,* which contained scores of elaborately defined and illustrated words of his own manufacture. Today this brilliant work is largely forgotten and can only be found on the shelves of a few very large libraries despite the fact that the book was reissued by Archon Books in 1986 with a new introduction by yours truly. The book contains one major contribution to the language after another, as well as a blurb from Willard Espy:

Laugh until you drool salivous!
Back is Burgess, redivivus!
Burgess Unabridged will wow
Lovers of the Purple Cow!

In order to once again attempt to spark a Burgess revival, here are 40-odd annotated examples.

Agowilt. *n.* (1). Sickening terror, sudden unnecessary fear. (2). The passage of the heart past the epiglottis, going up.

(The fear that comes the minute after you have thrown a burnt match in a wastebasket, the terror that comes after an unexpected elevator jerk, and the startle that comes when your foot reaches for the extra step that isn't there in the darkness are all examples supplied by Burgess. Since this phenomenon was named, the automobile has brought with it countless new instances, ranging from the "Oh no! I've locked the keys in the car" agowilt to the sudden fear, which occurs when you have driven halfway to a vacation spot, that you have forgotten to turn the oven off.)

Allibosh. *n.* A glaringly obvious falsehood; something not meant to be actually believed; a picturesque overstatement. (From seed catalogs to circus posters, Burgess found allibosh all around him, including "verbal alliboshes" too numerous to mention: "No, I don't think you're a bit too fat, you are just nice and plump.)

Bimp. *n.* A disappointment, a futile rage. *v.* To cut, neglect, or forsake.

(Burgess elaborates: "Did you get that raise in your salary on New Year's Day, or did you get bimped? Were you forgotten on Christmas? Did you draw to a flush and fail to fill? You get bimped. Did you find you had no cash in your pocket when it came time to pay the waiter? Did that firm cancel its order? Bimps!")

Bleesh. *n.* (1). An unpleasant picture; vulgar or obscene art. (2). An offensive comic-supplement form of humor. *a.* Revolting, disgusting, coarse.

Cowcat. *n.* (1). A person whose main function is to occupy space. An insignificant or negligible personality. (2). A guest who contributes nothing to the success of an affair; one invited to fill up, or from a sense of duty. (3). An innocent bystander.

Diabob. *n.* (1). An object of amateur art; anything improbably decorated; handpainted. (2). Any decoration or article of furniture manufactured between 1870 and 1890.

(Burgess had his eye on the hammered brasswork, tortured wood, hand-decorated linen, and tooled leather of his time. The most diabobical of today's goods are those colorful paintings on black velvet that are sold by the side of the road and invariably feature the the Last Supper, the New York skyline, or Elvis in concert.)

Digmix. *n.* (1). An unpleasant, uncomfortable, or dirty occupation. (2). A disagreeable or unwelcome duty. *v.* To engage in a necessary but painful task.

(Burgess supplied many examples of the digmix, including dishwashing, fish cleaning, getting a divorce, and taking a child to the dentist).

Drillig. *n.* A tiresome lingerer; a button-holer.

("The Ancient Mariner was a drillig," according to Burgess, along with many golfers, door-to-door book salepeople, and banquet speakers who note the late hour, promise a few short words, and then drone on for more than an hour.)

Eegot. *v.* A fair-weather friend; one who is overfriendly with a winner. A success-worshiper.

Fidgeltick. *n.* (1). Food that is a bore to eat; anything requiring painstaking and ill-requited effort. (2). A taciturn person, one from whom it is hard to get information.

(Pistachios and artichokes are Burgess's prime examples of edible fidgelticks, while a human type would be a railroad official from whom you were trying to get information after an accident.)

Fud. *n.* (1) In a state of déshabille, or confusion. (2). A mess, or half-done job.

(Remarkably, Burgess created this word years before the invention of pastel-colored plastic hair curlers and the late-twentieth-century custom of proudly wearing them to shopping malls.)

Gefoojet. *n.* (1) An unnecessary thing; an article seldom used. (2) A tool; something one ought to throw away, and doesn't. (3) The god of unnecessary things.

Gixlet. *n.* (1) One who has more heart than brains. (2) An inveterate host; an irresistible entertainer.

(Among other things, a gixlet buys you a drink when you don't want one, pays your fare, and apologizes when he steps on your foot. "The Gixlet, in short," concludes Burgess, "is the joyous, friendly dog, that leaps with muddy paws upon your clean, white trousers.")

Gixlety. *adj.* Brutal kindness; misguided hospitality; an overdose of welcome.

Gloogo. *n.* 1. A devoted adherent of a person, place, or thing. (2) A married person in love with his or her spouse after the first year. (3) Anything that can be depended on. *adj.* Loyal, constant. Foolishly faithful without pay.

Goig. *n.* A suspected person; one whom we distrust instinctively; an unfounded bias; an inexplainable aversion.

Gowyop. *n.* (1) A state of perplexity, wherein familiar persons or things seem strange. (2) A person in an unfamiliar guise.

(Gowyops commonly occur when we run into someone who used to have a beard or has gained 128 pounds since we last saw them.)

Gubble. *n.* (1) A murmuring of many voices. (2) Society chatter. *v.* To indulge in meaningless conversation.

("It's like some huge, slimy reptile, with a hundred mouths," he adds, "all murmuring.")

Gubblego. *n.* A crowded reception, a talking contest.

Hygog. *n.* (1) An unsatisfied desire. (2) An anxious suspense.

("Did you ever wait for a sneeze that wouldn't come?" Burgess asks. "It is a hygog.")

Hygogical. *adj.* Unattainable; next to impossible.

Igmoil. *n.* (1) A quarrel over money matters; a sordid dispute. (2) The driving of a hard bargain; a petty lawsuit.

("To lose a friend through an igmoil is the most sordid tragedy of life.")

Impkin. *n.* A superhuman pet; a human offspring masquerading in the form of a beast; an animal that is given overabundant care.

(Burgess adds, "Impkins are canine and feline, but their parents are usually asinine.")

Jirriwig. *n.* (1) A superficial traveler. (2) The Philistine abroad. (3) A bromide in search of himself. *v.* To travel with one's eyes shut. To destroy opportunity.

Jujasm. *n.* (1) A much-needed relief; a long-desired satisfaction. (2) An expansion of sudden joy.

(The first warm day of spring, the moment a baby stops crying in the middle of the night, and a hot drink after a sleigh ride are all jujasmic commonplaces.)

Kripsle. *n.* A worrying physical sensation, an invisible annoyance absorbing one's attention.

(Kripsles abound, with two of the commonest examples being the emerging of a hole in one's sock and the real or imagined looseness of a tooth. Since this term was coined, millions have been made as Madison Avenue has exploited our fear of kripsles, especially those relating to odor. Burgess also gave us *kripsly*, an adverb that is magnificently displayed and understood in the sentence "Walking on spilt sugar is kripsly.")

Looblum. *n.* (1) A pleasant thing that is bad for one; rich, but dangerous, food. (2) A flatterer; flattery.

(Burgess's looblum list includes cigars, green apples, morning cocktails, cocaine, black coffee at night, and hot mince pie.)

Mooble. *n.* (1) A mildly amusing affair; a moderate success. (2) A person or thing over whom it is difficult to be enthusiastic.

(Burgess's further explanation: "The Samoans have a word which means, 'A-party-is-approaching-which-contains-neither-a-clever-man-nor-a-pretty-woman.' It's a mooble—a fairly good play, a dinner-party where the menu makes up for the dramatis personae—moobles!")

Nodge. *n.* (1). The only one of its kind or set. (2) A person who doesn't "fit in"; a Martian.

(Like so many of these words, this one has immediate application. Odd socks, single gloves, and the person who shows up at a natural-food potluck in a tuxedo carrying a bag of Moon Pies will never again lack for a generic name in my mind.)

Nulkin. *n.* (1) The core or inside history of any occurrence. A true but secret explanation. (2) Facts known, but not told.

("Why is a book popular? Publishers strive in vain to discover the literary nulkin.")

Oofle. *n.* (1) A person whose name you cannot remember. (2) A state of forgetfulness regarding a friend or thing. *v.* (1) To try to find out a person's name without asking. (2) To talk to an unknown person without introducing him to a nearby friend.

(This word is remarkable for two reasons. First, that it was not coined before 1914, and second, that once coined, such a useful word has been all but forgotten—*oofled.*)

Paloodle. *n.* (1) One who gives unnecessary or undesired information. (2) Uncalled-for advice. (3) A recital of obvious details. *v.* To give the above; to assume omniscience.

Pawdle. *n.* (1) One who is vicariously famous, rich, or influential. (2) A person of mediocre ability, raised to undeserved prominence. *v.* To wear another's clothes.

(Where was this word when we needed it? O Donald Nixon, O Billygate!)

Rowtch. *n.* One who has elaborate gastronomic technique. *v.* (1) To accomplish strange maneuvers over food by means of a knife and fork. (2) To eat audibly or with excessive unction.

(One could compile an encyclopedia of rowtching techniques, starting with some of the examples that Burgess identified—vegecide, for instance, which is the refined habit of cutting well-cooked vegetables with a knife and fork when a fork will do—and continuing to more recent developments. The modern salad bar alone provides a host of examples including the fabled "crouton drop," which is the ability to drop a full ladle of croutons on top of a salad plate that has already been loaded to the point where it would appear to be impossible to add anything more.)

Spillix. *n.* (1) Undeserved good luck; accidental success. (2) A luck stroke beyond one's normal ability.

(Spillix allows you to overhear a fascinating conversation, find money on the street, win a lottery, or score a hole in one.)

Tintiddle. *n.* (1) An imaginary conversation. (2) A witty retort, thought of too late, a mental postscript.

Udney. *n.* (1) A beloved bore; one who loves you but does not understand you; a fond but stupid relative. (2) An old friend whom you have outgrown.

(Burgess clearly understood and had compassion for udneys, having written of them, "You go to them in your troubles and you forget them in your pleasures. You hate to write to them, but manage to scrawl hasty and vapid notes.")

Voip. *n.* Food that gives no gastronomic pleasure; any provender that is filling, but tasteless. *v.* To eat hurriedly, without tasting.

("Every morning,"explained Burgess, "millions of Americans go forth sustained for work but cheated out of the pleasures of a real repast—they have merely fed on voip." To think that he identified voip decades before the introduction of synthetic eggs, engineered tomatoes, hamburger extenders, imitation potato chips, vending-machine pastry, and innumerable dry breakfast cereals.)

Wog. *n.* Food on the face; unconscious adornment of the person.

(A Burgess word that is pure genius. Once one has heard this word, it is practically impossible to see someone with spinach or whatever on his or her face and not think "wog." Unfortunately, for a number of years this word was used in Britain as ugly pejorative slang for a nonwhite male. [It has been said to be an acronym for "wily Oriental gentleman."] One hopes that the Burgessism dominates. An indication that it may is that the *New York Times* columnist Russell Baker devoted his whole column of August 30, 1981, to various wogs—egg wogs, oily lettuce wogs, fishwogs—and what to do about them.)

Wox. *n.* A state of placid enjoyment; sluggish satisfaction.

("After your long tramp in the rain, after your bath and hot dinner, you sit by the fire in a wox.")

Yamnoy. *n.* (1) A bulky, unmanageable object; an unwieldy or slippery parcel. (2) Something you don't know how to carry. *v.* (1) To inflict with much luggage. (2) To carry many parcels at once.

Yowf. *n.* (1) One whose importance exceeds his merit. A rich or influential fool. (2) Stupidness, combined with authority.

("You find the yowf sitting at the Captain's table on shipboard; and at the speaker's dais at banquets. He is top-heavy with importance, and soggy with self-esteem.")

Curses

A Pack of Proposed Profanities

Swearing is no longer worth a damn. Its effects have been subverted by forces ranging from the R-rated movie to the Nixon White House tapes. We need a fresh start with a whole new set of obscenities and nasty epithets to work with. Admittedly, the words in my collection—old ones, new ones, and new applications of existing words—are not yet that shocking, but should this book get banned from a small-town library, we are in business.

Amplexus. The rutting of frogs and toads. Because of both the sound of the word and its meaning, amplexus deserves better than to be hidden away in the pages of unabridged dictionaries. It is a fine expletive: AMPLEXUS!

Asterisk. Stephen Leacock once suggested that this was a fine word form swearing. "'Asterisk!' shouted the pirate," wrote Leacock. "'I'll make it two asterisks,' snarled the other, 'and throw in a dash.' "

The written asterisk symbol also has a certain power. Burgess Johnson, in the introduction to his *Lost Art of Profanity*, quotes from an opinion by Judge Hammond of the Supreme Judicial Court of Massachusetts:

The Watch and Ward Society of Boston years ago brought charges against a certain magazine for printing obscene matter, and my old friend the late Kendall Banning was forced to defend the publication. He felt sure that he could make a case, and during the train ride to Boston he had a sudden idea, and began jotting down such nursery rhymes as he could recall. Then he crossed out significant words and submitted asterisks. In court he asked permission to read these rhymes. They later appeared in a privately printed brochure which aroused delight or horror, according to the state of the reader's mind. A mere sampling will serve here:

A dillar, a dollar
A ten-o'clock scholar,
What makes you *** so soon?
You used to *** at ten o'clock,
But now you *** at noon.

Jack and Jill went up the hill to *******
Jack fell down and broke his ***
And Jill came tumbling after.

Johnson goes on to report that the courtroom broke out in laughter and that Banning made his point.

Auxospore. One of many all-purpose swear words created by Gelett Burgess, the master of word creation. Auxospore appears in a passage from Burgess's *Find the Woman*, which was published in 1911. In the passage a truck driver, who has gotten in the way of a parade organized by a society to ban profanity, is addressed by the angry Dr. Hopbottom, who is the head of the society:

The doctor shook his fist again and started in earnest. His voice began with calmness and deliberation, but soon rose high—it swept forth in a majestic declamation full of all sorts of forte, staccato and crescendo effects to the noble climax.

"See here, you slack-salted transubstantiated interdigital germarium, you rantipole sacrosciatic rock-barnacle you, if you give me any of your caprantipolene paragastrular megalopteric jacitation, I'll make a lamellibranchiate gymnomixine parabolic lepidopteroid out of you! What diacritical right has a binominal oxypendactile advoutrous holoblastic rhizopod like you got with your trinoctial ustilaginous Westphalian holocaust blocking up the teleostean way for, anyway! If you give me any more of your lunarian, snortomaniac hyperbolic pylorectomy, I'll skive you into a megalopteric diatomeriferous auxospore! You queasy Zoroastrian son of a helicopteric hypotrachelium, you, shut your logarithmic epicyclodial mouth! You let this monopolitan macrocosmic helciform procession go by and wait right there in the anagological street. And no more of your hedonistic primordial supervirescence, you rectangular quillet-eating, vice-presidential amoeboid, either!"

Bigsix. For years publishers and broadcasters have spoken of "the big six" to refer collectively to the words piss, fart, shit, fuck, cock, and cunt. Why not shout "Bigsix" as collective verbal shorthand for the full half dozen? Or call someone "a bigsixing s.o.b."

Bombschmutt. Writer Sherry Suib Cohen introduced this word in an article on four-letter words in *Westchester* magazine. It was created by a student in one of her creative-writing classes who said, "I don't think sex and elimination are obscene. What's obscene to me is war. I think 'bombschmutt!' would be a marvelous curse."

Bumbledicking. Word used to great effect in Preston Jones's play *The Oldest Living Graduate.*

Cacademoid. Insult word for academics created by Reinhold Aman, editor of *Maledicta, the International Journal of Verbal Aggression.* It is a blend of caca, the childish word for feces, and academic. According to *Time,* Aman created the word to describe those who did not appreciate the work he was doing.

Codszooks! A 17th-century oath.

Coprolite. A fossilized turd. John Ciardi, for one, believes that this word should be brought into general use because there are so many coprolites among us.

Culch. An old Maine expletive used in the sense of "Rubbish!" "Bull!" or "Bullshit!" It is Ripe for revival.

Curpin. An old term for chicken rump that could easily be applied metaphorically.

Dicknailing. Epithet used by Rufus Sanders, the pseudonym of Lloyd Barto, in his column for the *Montgomery Advertiser* that ran in the 1880s and 1890s. "Squire Rogers jumped on him with a ring-tail, dicknailing reply" is a line from one of his columns. He also pioneered the use of the word *flugens,* as in "It was cold as the flugens that day."

Eesle. In Boontling, the invented language of the early settlers of California's Anderson Valley, *eesle* was the word for asshole. It was used both in the pejorative and as a greeting ("You old eesle") in the same way that one would say, "How are you doing, you old bastard?"

Expletive deleted. This became a household term with the release of the transcript of Richard Nixon's White House tapes. Then as now, it is a useful stand-in for a true, blue streak of cussin'.

Feague. Defined in Francis Grose's 1785 *Classical Dictionary of the Vulgar Tongue* as ". . . to put ginger up a horse's fundament, to make him lively and carry his tail well; it is said, a forfeit is incurred by any horse dealer's servant who shall show a horse without first feagueing him. Used figuratively for encouraging or spiriting one up." *Magnificent word!*

Fico. From Samuel Johnson's dictionary, "An act of contempt done with the fingers, expressing a fig for you."

Foutra. A old word of deep contempt. Used, for instance, by Shakespeare: "A foutra for the world and wordlings base." (*Henry IV,* Part II) The Bard's term seems to be a borrowing of the French *foutre* whose primary meaning is "to thrust, poke, or beat" but which has acquired a secondary meaning of "to fuck."

Fud. According to the *Oxford English Dictionary,* this is the proper term for a rabbits anus. This gives added zest to the word *befuddle.*

Fugh. (Pronounced *foo.*) An old exclamation of disgust. It looks stronger when written than when said. Also written as *phew.*

Fumet. Deer dung. Pronounced *foo-mitt.*

Gardyloo. An archaic warning cry that was made when waste water was tossed out the window. *Gardyloo* was the English corruption of the French *"Gardez de l'eau,* for "Watch out for the water."

Golter-yeded gawpsheet. Old English insult recorded in Elizabeth Mary Wright's *Rustic Speech and Folklore.* Its original meaning has been lost, but it has a marvelous ring to it.

Hagbadek. One of five new swearwords created by Burges Johnson in his *Lost Art of Profanity,* which is based on the assertion that *b's, d's, g's, h's,* and *k's* have the greatest objurgatory value. The other four: "Bodkogh!" "Khigbod!" "Dakadigbeg!" and "Godbekho!"

$100 noun/$100 verb. After a 1991 ordnance went into effect in Quincy, Massachusetts, that made swearing in public a $100-fine offense, Stan Grossfeld wrote in the Boston *Globe*: "All too often, we tolerate obscene language from ($100 noun) who don't give a ($100 noun) about decent law-abiding citizens like you and me. That ($100 noun) has got to stop."

Immerd. To cover with dung.

Infandous. Too odious to be spoken or written.

Jobjam. An all-purpose curse word created by Booth Tarkington, who sometimes used it with "dobdab." In a novel one of his characters tells someone "to go to the jobjam dobdab bastinadoed Hellespont helm!"

Klaxoveedesteen. From Thomas L. Rose of Conroe, Texas, who heard it during a game of *Trivial Pursuit* when a team of cheaters invented it to keep from losing. "It is an impressive swearword."

Kodak. In *The Lost Art of Profanity,* Burges Johnson suggested that kodak was an excellent swearword that George Eastman wasted on a gadget. Other wasted swearwords on Johnson's list: "Kleenex!" "O Hemorrhoids!" "Gestalt!" and "Lydia Pinkham!"

Lewdster. A lecher; one given to illegal pleasures. A lewder than lewd word that goes back to Samuel Johnson's work.

Malaga. Alexandre Dumas introduced this swearword in his *Vicomte de Bragelonne.* The essayist Alfred George Gardiner later wrote of *Malaga*: "It is a good swearword. It has the advantage of meaning nothing and that is precisely what a swearword should mean. It should be sound and fury, signifying nothing. It should be incoherent, irrational, a little crazy like the passion which evokes it."

Maledicta balloon. Cartoonist's term for one of those lines of typographical swears appearing over a character's head: %$@#*+ "@!!.

Mundungus. This very old word was first used to describe dung or odorous garbage, but later came to be used most commonly to describe vile-smelling tobacco. It begs to be sworn with.

Odsplut. A very old British oath that is believed to be a minced version of "God's blood."

Pissabed. Dandelion. Samuel Johnson included this term in his dictionary as "A yellow flower growing in the grass." It comes from the French *le pissenlit* for "the piss in bed," which derives from its diuretic qualities. Correspondent Blaine C. McKusick has researched the term and found this from *Good's Study of Medicine* (1822) "It [the dandelion] posesses unquestionably diuretic properties, and hence, indeed, its vulgar name of piss-a-bed." It would also seem to be a good term of rage, more to the point than, say, calling someone a bastard.

Pornogenitone. Son of a harlot. From the Greek.

Pox and Piles. Common curse of the Middle Ages.

Pricklouse. An archaic term of contempt for a tailor that could be brought back for general contempt.

Riggafrutch. A new expletive that had its debut in Bill Sherk's *Brave New Words*. It was coined by Bob Krueger, a Toronto music teacher.

Slutch. A blend of slut and bitch.

Swyve. Chaucer's copulatory verb.

Taffy. Time was when people would say taffy when they encountered hot air, making it the Pollyannaish equivalent of B.S. It is innocuous in the extreme . . . so innocuous, in fact, that it has a certain shock value to it that makes it a good swearword. However, do not use it around anyone who is Welsh as it is considered a slur (from a nursery rhyme, "Taffy was a Welshman, Taffy was a thief.").

Tath. Cattle dung, or grass that grows near it. It begs to be used as an expletive of incredulity.

Ted. To spread manure.

Tunket. Old New England word for hell (as in "As sure as tunket . . ."). It comes from *Tophet*, an Old Testament name for the place where human sacrifice was made by fire.

Umslopogus. This is the name of a Zulu chief in an H. Rider Haggard novel, which Burges Johnson felt should have been used instead as a swearword.

Uzzard. A rare gem of a word unearthed by Ivor Brown, British word-hunter *extraordinaire*. An *uzzard* is a third-generation bastard; a bastard by a bastard out of a bastard.

Waxyquez. All-purpose swearword composed of the five letters—*q, w, x, y* and *z*—that have been banned from the Esperanto alphabet. Should fill a need, as Esperanto is short on swearwords, especially those made from taboo letters. Created by the author.

Worms in your marrow! A curse used by William Blake.

Decorative Words

An Array from Art and Architecture

Abbozzo. A preliminary sketch; rough.

Afterimage. Experiencing a sensation of color after the stimulus has been removed. Positive afterimage occurs when one can still see a bright image after the eyes have been closed. Negative afterimage occurs when one looks at a blank area after seeing intense color and sees the complementary color to the original.

Arris fillet. A triangular piece of wood or other material used to raise the covering of a roof against a chimney or wall so as to throw off the rain.

Ashlar. Term used to distinguish square-cut, carefully laid masonry from masonry that uses rough, odd-shaped stones. The latter is called *rubble* masonry.

Autotelic. A work that creates its own reason for being, as opposed to a work that is *didactic.*

Boast. To dress or shape a stone. The outward face of the stones used in churches are usually *boasted.*

Bocage. Supporting, ornamental background for a ceramic figure.

Breastsummer. A large horizontal beam supporting an exterior wall over an opening such as a large window.

Brunneous. Dark brown. Brunneous is one of a number of marvelous color words. Some other fine examples:

Caesious. Pale blue-green. Pronounced *see-zee-ous*.

Castaneous. Chestnut-colored.

Cesious. Blue-gray.

Eau-de-nil. Light green; literally, the water of the Nile. Pronounced *ode-a-nil*.

Ferruginous. Iron rust-colored.

Festucine. A straw-color between green and yellow.

Filemot. The color of a dead leaf.

Glaucous. Green with a bluish-gray tinge.

Modena. Deep purple.

Pavonine. Having the iridescence of a peacock's tail.

Phenicious. Red with a slight mixture of gray.

Puniceous. Bright or purplish red.

Subfusc. Dusky; dingy.

Taupe. Mole-colored. Rhymes with *rope*.

Chroma. The intensity, saturation, or brilliance of a color. Primary colors have high chroma while greyish colors (terra cotta, olive) have low chroma.

Contrapposto. The opposing twist between masses. Commonly used to describe the contrast between the directions of shoulders and hips in the human figure.

Corbiesteps. Steps forming the end of a gable in a masonry building. They are also known as *crowsteps* and *corbelsteps*.

Corbie is Scots for crow.

Craquelure. The web of hairline cracks common to old oil paintings. Pronounced *crack-lure*.

Crenelate. To notch a building, such as the squared notch in the battlement of a fort or castle.

Cribble. To decorate wood or metal by making small dots or punctures on the surface.

Dentils. In classical architecture, a decorative row resembling teeth.

Écorché. The name for the skinned or flayed anatomical figure used by artists to study muscles.

Empaquetage. Work of art consisting of a tightly wrapped object ranging up to and including buildings. A form of conceptual art.

Engobe. In pottery, a decoration made by applying liquid clay to the body of the object being made.

Fenestration. The pattern or scheme of a building's windows. *Defenestration,* on the other hand, is the act of throwing a person or an object out of a window.

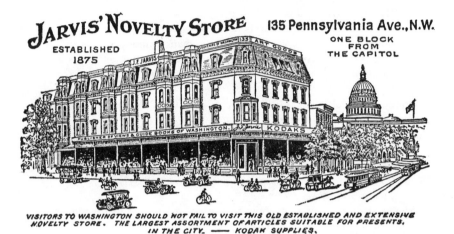

JARVIS' NOVELTY STORE 135 Pennsylvania Ave., N.W.

ESTABLISHED 1875

ONE BLOCK FROM THE CAPITOL

VISITORS TO WASHINGTON SHOULD NOT FAIL TO VISIT THIS OLD ESTABLISHED AND EXTENSIVE NOVELTY STORE. THE LARGEST ASSORTMENT OF ARTICLES SUITABLE FOR PRESENTS, IN THE CITY. —— KODAK SUPPLIES.

Fillister. The groove on the outer edge of a window frame into which the glass is fitted.

Grimthorpe. To do a rotten job of restoration. From Lord Grimthorpe, who at the end of the last century attempted the restoration of St. Albans' abbey in Hertfordshire, England.

Grotesque. A stone carving of a face on a building placed so that water drips off its nose. A gargoyle on the other hand is designed so the water spouts out of its mouth.

Halation. The quality of light that makes the light-colored area of a painting seem larger than a dark one even though they are the same size.

Hob. The projecting corner of a fireplace. *Hobnob* comes from the sociable habit of sitting around the hob while drinking.

Imbrication. The decorative effect of overlapped edges, such as found on roof tiles and fish scales.

Impasto. Layers of pigment in a painting; a thick and paste-like application of paint.

Inglenook. A chimney corner; a corner by the fire.

Interfenestral. Between windows.

Kibosh. Adding cement or plaster to a sculptured or wooden form. From this comes the old expression "to put the kibosh on," meaning to change in shape or form; to finish off.

Loggia. An arcade or passageway open on one side. Present in classical architecture as well as motels.

Mahlstick. A stick with a knob at one end that is held across the face of a painting as a rest for the artist's hand. It is often used in painting fine detail.

Maquette. A room in miniature.

Muntin. Narrow wood separations between panes of glass in windows, bookcase doors, etc. Also known as *muttins* and *mutts*. Some people also call them *mullions;* yet there are those who go on to claim that a *mullion* is a vertical separation while a *muntin* can go in any direction (vertical, horizontal, diagonal).

Nogging. Material (brick, cloth, cement, etc.) used to pack the wall crevices of a wooden or log house.

Noodle. To overwork a painting or other work of art by adding too much detail, redefining, and "correcting." It is a critical term commonly applied to a work that lacks vigor.

Nosing. The part of a stair step that projects over the riser.

Oda. A room in a harem.

Oubliette. Dungeon that can only be gotten in and out of through a ceiling trapdoor. Pronounced *ou-blee-et.*

Patinate. To produce an artificial appearance of age on wood or metal.

Perron. A landing and staircase outside of a building, leading from the first floor.

Plinth. The base of a column or pedestal, usually square.

Putto. It means small boy and is applied in art to the many cherubs that appear in Renaissance painting. The plural is *putti.* Pronounced *poo-toe* and *poo-tea.*

Pyrography. The art of woodburning.

Quadriga. A sculpture of a chariot drawn by four horses, often seen atop a monument.

Rived. Wood that has been split, not sawed. Old houses often have riven timbers or panels. Rhymes with tithed.

Sfumato. The blending of colors through indistinguishable gradations; very smooth transition.

Shake. Hand-split wood shingle.

Skintle. To build unevenly with bricks in order to produce a quaint or picturesque effect.

Slaister. To paint or color in an ill and vulgar manner. Even with the advent of punk and new wave, slaister has been relegated to the limbo of a crossword-puzzle word. Ivor Brown, a fan of the word, has written that it ". . . gives a rich and odious suggestion of bad, greasy makeup and of lips crudely incarnadined."

Spall. Construction term for the disintegration of concrete surfaces or corners.

Stipple. In painting, achieving a color tone by making many small dots.

Stomp. A cigar-sized roll of gray paper, pointed at either end, that is used by artists to blend or soften the effects of charcoal or pastels. Sometimes called a *stump*.

Toe-hole. An indented area of the base of a counter, such as that commonly found at the bottom of kitchen counters. Also known as a *kick space*.

Tortillon. A small stomp (see also) about the size of a small pencil and usually pointed at only one end.

Weepers. Holes built into masonry to allow for drainage.

Zoophoric column. A column that either bears or supports the figure of an animal.

Dicksonary

*Some 50 Words Created by the Author
in Response to Being Placed in the Last
Quarter of the Twentieth Century*

Ambiguletter. A letter of the alphabet that is so written that it could be one
of two letters, say, an *a* or an *o*. The author has been using these for years
to save hours looking things up.

Anthonize. To give the public what the public does not want. Named for the
Anthony dollar coin that looked and felt like two bits. The government is a
prominent anthonizer (the nine-digit zip, the new two-dollar bill, etc.), but
private industry also contributes (Billy Beer, nonmelting ice cream, Nehru
jackets, etc.).

Anchortease. Incessant blurbing of upcoming stories on 30-minute television
newscasts: "Coming right up, a candid look at incest."

Appal. To appall with bad spelling. For instance, a 1985 press release for
Jonathan Kozol's *Illiterate America* contained this line, "An eloquent plea
that Americans recognize the appaling frequency of illiteracy in this country." More? A headline in a newspaper called *New Haven Country Woman*:
"SAT Scores Apalling."

Barristrate. Willfully depicting the human condition in terms of lechery, greed,

72

and buffoonery. Derives from Chuck Barris, who has given us "The Gong Show," "The Newlywed Game," and "Three's a Crowd."

Baskinrobbinsitus. That sudden pain one gets in the sinuses when one eats ice cream too fast.

Baudinize. To promote a book, film, or other property with excessive zeal. Named for Robert Baudin, the disgruntled, publicity-seeking author who in 1979 flew over Manhattan threatening to fly his plane into the window of the company that published his autobiography.

Beepoop. To create a serious situation through a feeble attempt at humor. Term suggested by the flap that ensued when Governor Lee Dreyfus of Wisconsin told the 1980 State Honey Queen that he and his wife call honey "bee poop." This, of course, occasioned passionate protests from the Wisconsin Beekeepers Association, the Wisconsin Honey Producers Association, and others.

BeLee. To commit modest, harmless fraud against those willing to be exploited. Named for the many Bruce Lees who appeared after the actor's death: Bruce Lai, Bruce Li, Lee Bruce, etc. BeLee rhymes with melee.

Bibliorts. Things other than bookmarks used by people to mark a place in a book—ticket stubs, laundry lists, etc. From *biblio-*, the Greek prefix for book, and *orts,* an old, little-used term for scraps.

Boxecrate. To desecrate an area with your standard flat, square, determinedly dull glass and concrete office buildings and apartments.

Btubore. A person who never seems to stop talking about how energy-efficient they have become. Recent woodstove converts are often the worst btubores. The term comes from BTU, the British thermal unit and is pronounced *bit-too-bore.*

Bureaugance. A blend word of bureaucrat + arrogance formed to cover that particular level of determined arrogance that is common to Senate aides, postal authorities, IRS functionaries, and the pandas at the National Zoo.

Centicipation. Something that has fallen far below that which had been anticipated; a 99 percent failure. The metric prefix *centi-* (for one-hundredth) is used in commemoration of American metric conversion, thus far a perfect example of *centicipation.*

Comchoutword. Word or words that appear on printed tapes generated by new computerized check-out machines. The words are generally shortened, so that one occasionally finds unnerving or odd items on the tape. Writing in the *Washington Post*, Ellen Ficklin told of her surprise at finding that she had bought cannibalistic-sounding MANSOUPMIX (actually a package of Manischewitz soup makings). Comchoutwords are hidden within the bars of bar codes.

0   12345 67890

Cosellian. The highest level of smug self-certainty, as in "Cosellian cocksured-ness." Inspired by an evening some years ago of watching *Monday Night Football* with the sound turned on. Common Cosellian statements include: "As I have repeatedly stated and is being proven here tonight"; "The con-clusive proof of what you have been hearing from me all along"; and "As— —-confided to me before the game."

Elegate. To attempt to elevate something minor into a major scandal. To seize upon something as a Watergate-like incident when it is nothing of the sort— "Billygate," for instance.

Euphecide. The tendency to create such outlandish euphemisms to describe things that all euphemistic speech is suspect. The following are bogus ex-amples created for J. Baxter Newgate II and his syndicated *National Chal-lenge,* but they sound like they were lifted from a federal report: "simulated penmanship" (forgery), "time-honored award recipient" (prisoner), "highly coordinated, state-supported highway maintenance team" (chain gang), "art-ful asset appropriation" (embezzlement), "aptitude shortfall" (stupidity), "cash flow displacement" (bank robbery), "energy conservation" (sloth), and "adverse behavior quarters" (stockade).

Fabricist. A person who discriminates based on the fabric and/or the clothing of others. Liberals who feel that they harbor no prejudices will often toss off lines like: "It was horrible! Half the men in the room were wearing polyester leisure suits and one of them was wearing—are you ready for this?— white socks and a white belt."

Fidocanesis. Process by which owners come to look more and more like their pets.

Frugalflaunt. Conspicuous *non*consumption; to flaunt one's frugality. Putting your compost heap in the front yard is frugalflaunting, as is going to a sumptuous buffet and taking only bean sprouts and parsley. A frugalflaunt *(n.)* is a person who says he wants a Cuisinart but is holding off until they come out with a solar-powered model.

Glenhaven. A name that is so innocuous or trite that you find it difficult to recall. Cedar crest, plaza central, long ridge, and harbor view are all glen-havens.

Gnusman/Gnuswoman. The ruthless, compulsive punster. So called because one of these would take a small child to the zoo on the off chance that the child will ask, "What's a gnu?" and he or she would be able to reply, "Not much. What's a gnu with you?" Times and fashions change, but this type is a constant. A manual on the art of conversation published in London in 1867 contains this description, which sounds just like the gnusperson down the block: "You see by his manner that he does not take the least interest in what you are saying, but is on the watch for anything that suggests a pun or verbal quirk, with which he ruthlessly interrupts you, even although you may be at the most telling or interesting part of your story, and forthwith bursts into a roar of laughter as if he had really said something excessively clever.''

Hojonate. A one-word compression of a multiworded name for a company, product, or service. From Hojo, which is the hojonate of Howard Johnson. Citgo, Memco, Artco, and Nabisco are common hojonates. Also a verb, *to hojonate*, which is to compress for commercial purposes.

Hrusk. To advance the cause of mediocrity. From the name of Senator Roman Hruska of Nebraska who defended Nixon Supreme Court nominee Clement Haynesworth. Hruska answered those who argued that Haynesworth was mediocre with the point that there are many mediocre people in America deserving representation by a mediocre Supreme Court justice. Hrusking is now part of the American way of life.

Inflatuate. *n.* A blend word from *inflation* and *infatuate*, the inflatuate is a person with a seeming inability to talk of anything but prices and their rise. Although the times may be largely responsible for bringing this economic Hyde out of many a mild-mannered Jekyll, it does not make their behavior any less infuriating.

Internacast. To bring internal matters to the attention of outsiders. The staffs at certain hotels and restaurants are expert internacasters who tell you the manager's policy on overtime, how the busboys never clear station #6, and that the cashier has fallen arches because she has to stand all the time.

Konvenience. A convenience that can only be reached by car, hence much less a convenience. For reasons unclear, many konveniences often feature forced *k*'s in their signs: Kwik-stop, Kash 'n Karry, etc.

Loxocration. The process of saying something nasty to a person in such a way that the person is bewildered. For instance, using the rare word *rebarative* for repulsive or the obscure *foraminated* for bored. Loxocration is an effective means of venting one's spleen without getting punched in the nose.

Mangainanize. To imagine that everyone around you has more sex, makes more money, and so forth. Word derives from the Mangainans of Polynesia who are said to be the most highly sexed folks in the world.

McWord. An awkwardly pretentious mix of languages or traditions—Miss Piggy's use of *moi*, the name of Wayne Newton's mansion (Casa Shenandoah), and Scots-Irish-surnamed food (McMuffin, McChicken, etc.).

Miragones. Short-lived advertising and marketing miracles—fabrics with *celaperm*, razor blades with *diridium*, deodorant with *lumium*, and so forth. Miragones can be found only in the pages of old magazines.

Mxyzptlk. A person with a particularly difficult name to pronounce. Mxyzptlk is one of Superman's multitude of archenemies. An example of a Mxyzptlkian character was Joe Btfsplk, who used to appear in Al Capp's "Li'l Abner."

Neckar. To test or try something in such a way as to invite disaster: "He neckared the brakes on his new Ford by racing up close to a brick wall and then slamming down on the pedal at the last moment." The term comes from a river of the same name in Western Germany, where the prime example of modern neckaring took place in 1979. The U.S. Army helped German authorities test a new bridge spanning the river by driving 34 of its heaviest fully manned M60 tanks onto the structure. It sagged but did not collapse.

Nork. A product that looks especially appealing in its original context—an ad, a catalog, a hotel gift shop—but that loses all appeal very shortly after you get it. Norks are especially common at Christmas and include such items as automatic wine-bottle decorkers, cute hors d'oeuvres sticks, towels with clever inscriptions, and multipurpose electronic gizmos commonly advertised in airline inflight magazines. Most norks are mail-order items.

GIRLS Your father, brother, husband or sweetheart will appreciate this as a present.

THE ROTARY HAT IRON.

As necessary to the toilet as a hat brush. Heat in the gas jet. If not kept by your furnisher, will be sent by mail on receipt of $1.25.

CATALOGUE SENT FREE.

EDWIN B. STIMPSON & SON,
31 Spruce Street, New York.

Nusnobs. Unlike your old snobs with their fairly rigid and predictable set of things to look down on, nusnobs are relativists who look down on whatever they are not. If, for example, a nusnob lives in the city, he can't imagine the living hell of the suburbs, he can only speak of the urban nightmare. Nusnobs are only fun when paired off against one another.

Othodgeous. A sleazy, down-at-the-heels ambience; sleazy-cozy. Word derives from (and was coined at) the old O.T. Hodge Chili Parlor at 814 Pine Street, St. Louis. It is a quintessentially othodgeous place. It is pronounced *oath-odge-ous.*

Peiaster. *v.* To inadvertently create confusion; to bestir the bureaucracy without meaning to. Another eponym, this one for Earnest Peia of Morris Plains, New Jersey, who by following an old family tradition of naming sons after the father created great confusion at the Social Security Administration. By 1980, when the Associated Press reported on the 66-year-old man's dilemma, Peia had been issued three different Social Security numbers. Pronounced *pea-astor.*

Peru. Offending unintentionally; bothering B, who is innocent, in an attempt to get to A. A classic peru took place during the Iranian hostage period when the *Washington Post* went out to tweak Iran in an editorial entitled "Is Iran Welshing?" The editorial presumably rolled off the backs of the Iranians but infuriated people of Welsh descent in the Washington area.

Peru can be used as both a noun and verb (to peru someone or something, or a peru was committed). The name of the South American nation is used as it is entirely innocent in this matter.

Pibble. A name or a term written to look like what it says, such as:

The inspiration for this word came from a letter from Sara Gump of Savannah, who insisted that she was unable to come up with a proper name for such words, which are commonly used in advertising. I immediately decided to call them pibbles as I had been long concerned with the fact that there was no *pibble* in English.

Prflop. Public relations effort that falls on its face. In June 1981, a classic case took place when a New York public relations firm sent the *Wall Street Journal* three loaves of a new 100 percent natural whole wheat bread. Because they lacked preservatives, two arrived covered with mold. Great publicity for preservatives.

Productese. Designer conversation; talk in which product names are forced for reasons of status. Sample: "Don't spill your Perrier, you might get lime on your Top Siders!"

Punburn. The pain that comes with a pun that has not been expressed. For instance, a friend calls to say that he is in the hospital and has fallen in love with the woman who has been attending him there. You get off the phone and punburn ensues as you realize you should have said, "You mean to say, you took a turn for the nurse."

Punstore. The very specific kind of place—now in proliferation—that uses a cute or atrocious pun to announce itself. It is particularly common to new places that cut or dress hair (Rape of the Lock, Headmaster, Lunatic Fringe) and maternity shops (Heir Apparent, Great Expectations). Frank Mankiewicz has looked at the trend and asked, "Will banks succumb? . . . the Bread Box?"

Redfox. *v.* To regulate in an excessive and foolish manner; to use regulation in such a manner that the worst fears of the antiregulators are realized. It is named for Red Fox denims manufactured by Charles Henson of Georgia. After making these pants for close to 30 years, Henson was told by the Federal Trade Commission that he could no longer use the name because they were not made with the fur of red fox.

Smirkword. A word or phrase that you can never again think of in the same light after learning of an earlier or alternative meaning. Cleveland, for instance, is a name that has had an entirely new ring to it after I discovered that it was once common slang for the female pudendum. Another example is flux, a Victorian euphemism for diarrhea. The leading smirkword in contemporary speech is nitty-gritty. According to John Train in his *Remarkable Words,* this was, "originally, black slang for the inner end of a vagina."

SpaceBarBrokeThings. Generic name for trendy names with no breathing room discovered while writing a book with WordStar (not to be confused with WordPerfect) for HarperCollins with the first version printed with LaserJet. HolyCow!

Sullivan. *v.* To initiate a reform that results in a reinforcement of that which was being reformed. Named for New York State Assemblyman Peter M. Sullivan, who proposed and had enacted a law requiring that all consumer contracts be written in plain English. When the lawyers had finished with the language of his law, it came out, in Sullivan's words, ". . . long, complex and downright fuzzy."

Tabscanitize. To scan the headlines of supermarket tabloids and then find that you are stuck with those headlines for the rest of your life and that nothing you can do will purge them from your brain . . . EVANGILIST EXPLODES IN PULPIT . . . BIGFOOT'S GOT MY WIFE (AND, BOY IS SHE MAD!) . . .

STATUE OF ELVIS SPOTTED ON MARS ... PRETTY TEENTOASTED IN TANNING BED ... MEMPHIS WOMAN SEES IMAGE OF ELVIS IN OATMEAL ...

Tikitacky. South Seas kitsch; that particular Polynesian look featured in souvenir shops that relies heavily on gaudy plastic flowers, faces carved from coconut shells, and the heads of ancient gods cut from lava-textured plastic. Real world examples include the Tiki God Party Lights, Fu Manuchu Tumbler, Kahuna "Little Joe" Mug offered in the Archie McPhee ("Outfitters of Popular Culture") catalog.

Translute. Translate + convolute; more than a bad translation, but rather one with a complete change of meaning. A classic translution took place in 1977 when President Carter's statement to the Polish people, "I wish to learn your opinions and understand your desires for the future," was given as "I desire the Poles carnally."

Woeperson. Although we can all think of things that have changed for the worse over the years, the woeperson sees everything in terms of decline, decadence, and desperation. Even a 21-year-old woeperson feels that everything was better when he was younger. One of the cruelest things you can do to a woeperson—equivalent to telling a hypochondriac how well he is looking—is to tell one that your last conversation got you to thinking about all the things that have improved.

Word word. There are situations in which it is necessary to repeat a word in order to make sure someone knows what you are talking about. For instance, you might be asked, "Are you talking about an American Indian or an Indian Indian?" or "Oh, you're talking about grass grass. I thought you were talking about grass."

From what I have been able to determine, there is no word for this phenomenon, and "word word" seemed to be a logical name to give it.

Wurst Case Scenario. The compulsion of newspaper food section editors to punch up an otherwise dull story about leeks or sorrel with a ghastly headline pun. Here are a few of the best examples—hence worst—from the *Washington Post*: "Thai It, You'll Like It," "Breads of Kneadless Effort," and "One Bite and Your Spirits Will Sorrel."

Zisterous. Relating to reform that will be of greatest benefit to the reformer. Derives from the name Barry Zister, who, as Connecticut State Consumer Counsel, tried to persuade the phone company to print directories backward from Z to A every odd year to offset the competitive advantage of coming first—like AAAAAA Diaper Service.

Dress Words

Terms to Go from Head to Toe

Aglet. The covering at the end of a shoelace.

Aiguillette. An ornamental cord, usually pointed, worn over the left shoulder with some military uniforms. It is worn by military aides to U.S. Presidents and by high-ranking officers. In the British military tradition, it is worn on the left by staff officers and the right by honorary aides to the Queen or a Governor General.

Airplane-back. The portion of a cuff link that is poked through the cuff holes and then held in place as it is folded out like the wings of an airplane.

Beaver. The movable portion of a suit of armor that protects the mouth and chin.

Biretta. Square cap with projections on top worn by Catholic ecclesiastics. It has a pom-pom in the center.

Bottu. Indian forehead-marking used to indicate caste. Rhymes with tattoo.

Brassard. A badge worn on the arm; an armband such as the Military Police wear (with the initials MP on it).

Clock. Decoration on the side of stockings or socks, also known as a *quirk*.

Five-eighths length. In the trade, the name of a garment that reaches halfway between the hips and knees.

Forre. Handkerchief bordering.

Fourchettes. Strips running along the sides of glove fingers that serve to connect the front and back of the glove. Pronounced *four-shet*.

Furblow. Gathered ruffles and festoonery embellishing a woman's dress.

Fustanella. Short white skirt worn by men in Greece on certain ceremonial occasions.

Gibus. Collapsible opera hat that can be flattened when not in use. From the nineteenth-century Parisian hatter of the same name, who invented it. Pronounced *jiboo*.

Gigot. A leg-of-mutton sleeve that is extremely full at the shoulder and narrows at the elbow.

Gimme caps. The popular one-size-fits-all baseball-style caps bearing the embroidered logo of John Deere, International Harvester, or whatever. According to *Newsweek*, the terms originated when farmers would say to tractor salesmen, "Gimme one of them caps."

Godet. A triangular piece of fabric added to a garment to give it extra fullness.

Goose. Tailor's long-handled pressing iron.

Habille. The dress of a striptease artist at the beginning of the act.

Hand. Garment industry term for the feel of a fabric.

Hauberk. Medieval metal tunic.

Havelock. Cloth hanging down from the back of a soldier's hat as protection against the sun.

Hog washers. Alternative name for coveralls, bib overalls, overalls, etc.

Kaffiyeh. Arab headdress made from a folded piece of cloth of the type worn by Yasir Arafat. Pronounced *ka-fee-ya*.

Keeper. The loop located next to the buckle on a belt. It keeps the end of the belt in place.

Kiltie. The extended shoe tongue, usually fringed, that folds over and covers the laces. These are common on golf shoes and are sometimes called a *kiltie tongue*.

Klompen. Dutch wooden shoes. If they were carved in France or Canada, they would be called *sabots*. Sabotage was invented when French workers threw their *sabots* into working machinery.

Lifeline. On a necktie, this is the thread that holds the lining in place and runs from one end to the other. A good lifeline has a tied loop of extra thread at both ends to permit extra give.

Loft. Term used to describe the springiness of wool as it comes back to shape after being crumpled.

Loup. A half-mask.

Maddy. A madras middy.

Maillot. Fashion industry term for the one-piece bathing suit, from the French word for tights.

Mappula. Name for the handkerchief used to signal the start of the action in Roman games.

Monokini. Woman's swimsuit consisting of the bottom half only.

Muckender. An old, much franker, word for handkerchief.

Nerd pack. In some circles, the name for those shirt-pocket plastic pouches for holding pens and pencils.

Pannier. A woman's overskirt gathered bustle-like on each side of her body. The term comes from an earlier meaning: pairs of baskets hanging over the sides of mules or packhorses.

Petasus. Broad-brimmed hat of the ancient world; also the winged model worn by Mercury, messenger of the gods.

Phonytail. Artificial hair in the style of a ponytail, used by *Seventeen* in the 1950s and 1960s.

Pickelhaube. The classic Prussian spiked helmet.

Placket. The opening, containing a zipper or other fastening device, that enables one to get in and out of slacks or a skirt.

Presser foot. The flat, foot-like piece of metal at the business end of the sewing machine arm. It sits next to the needle and keeps the fabric flat and in place.

Psyche. Mirror in an adjustable frame that reflects a person at full length.

Retro. Fashion term for "retrogressive" and the opposite of futuristic.

Romal. A whip made from a horse's briddle reins when they are tied together. A Western term from the Spanish *ramal,* a branch road or ramification.

Rowel. The wheel of a spur. The vocabulary of the old West included a number of words and phrases for specific rowels, such as the sunset or sunburst rowel, which was one with many points.

Size lining. Retail talk for grouping merchandise by size, as opposed to *price lining,* which refers to grouping items by their price range.

Skigs. Shoe-business word for a slow-moving item.

Snood. A hairnet often attached to the back of a hat to hold hair in place. In her *Fashion Dictionary,* Mary Brooks Picken reports that a snood was originally a "Fillet formerly worn around the head by young women in Scotland and considered an emblem of chastity."

Soutache. The narrow braid trimming commonly used to border men's pajamas and bathrobes.

Sporran. A leather pouch covered with fur and ornamented, which hangs in front of a Scottish kilt. It was originally intended to serve as a pocket for the day's ration.

Swacket. Fashion industry term for a sweater that buttons like a jacket.

Talaria. The sandals with wings worn by Mercury.

Tapadero. Toe-fender for Western stirrups. Often shortened to taps. It derives from the Spanish verb *tapar,* to close or cover.

Tassets. Parts of a suit of armor that protect the genitals.

Thrion. The fig leaf garb favored by Adam and Eve.

Toe box. The area at the front of a shoe that should allow for plenty of toe room.

Toe cap. The material covering the toe of the shoe.

Togate. Wearing or dressed in a toga.

Turnback. The curved end of a clothes hanger.

Vamp. The upper part of a shoe.

Wamus. The frontiersman's fringed hunting shirt, usually made of buckskin.

Wase. The circular headcovering or pad used by porters when carrying loads on their heads. A straw pad.

Drinking Words

A Jeroboam of Terms for the Bibulous

Aerometer. Instrument used for measuring specific gravity, which is the difference between the weight of a beverage and a similar amount of water. In England the excise tax on beer is based on specific gravity.

Agrafes. The cage that holds a champagne cork in place. Believe it or not, there is actually a second word for this same thing, which is a *coiffe*. Both are French words. Agrafes is pronounced *a-graph*.

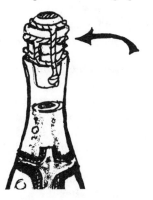

Alegar. Vinegar made from ale or beer; malt vinegar.

Balderdash. Adulterated wine.

Barm. The froth on beer. Sometimes called *fob*.

Beer comb. A special spatula used to scoop foam from the tops of beer glasses and mugs.

Beeswing. Filmy tartar scales that form in some wines after a long period of storage. So called because they look like the wings of bees.

BIB. Short for Bottled in Bond.

Billet. The thumbpiece on the lid of a stein or tankard.

Binned. Term for bottles stored in tiers.

Bottle stink. The term for an unpleasant smell from a wine bottle, which disappears after the bottle is allowed to stand uncorked for a short time. It is not to be confused with terms for permanent harm, such as *corky* (spoiled by a bad cork) or *pricked* (see also).

Bottle ticket. A small plaque hung around the neck of a bottle or decanter with the name of the beverage on it. Often made of silver.

Bouge. The "belly" of a cask; the point where the circumference is the greatest. It is also called the *bilge*.

Bright. *Racked* (see also) beer as opposed to that with the *lees* (see also) left in.

Brimmer. A glass so full that the liquid touches the brim. Although the liquid has climbed to the brim, there is a slight depression or hollow in the center of the surface. A *bumper,* on the other hand, is a brimmer too which extra drops have been added to fill the hollow to a bump. The difference between a brimmer and a bumper can be demonstrated by floating a cork fragment on the surface. In a brimmer, the cork will float to the edge, while it will sit in the middle of a bumper.

Bumper. See *Brimmer*.

Bung hole. The aperture through which beer enters a cask. The bung hole is filled with a *shive*.

Calibogus. A mix of rum and spruce beer.

Capsule. The metal foil or plastic cap that covers the top of a wine bottle, which must be removed before the cork can be removed. Capsules usually carry a logo or trademark.

Classically sculptured. Pretentious wine term for a well-balanced vintage.

Comet wine. Wine made during a year in which a major comet appears. Since the comet year of 1811, which was also a great vintage year, there have been those who insist that comet wines are great wines.

Denaturant. A substance added to alcohol to make it unfit for drinking, but without destroying its use for other commercial purposes—hairdressing, for instance.

Départ. The final taste of wine in the mouth. French.

Draff. The spent grains of malt left after the production of whiskey.

Dunder. The dregs left after the distillation of rum. In some rum-making processes, dunder from one run is added to the next for added flavor.

Elongated. When applied to wine, it means that water has been added. If this seems too euphemistic, consider the French term for elongated, *mouillage*.

Épluchage. The process of picking over the grapes to eliminate bad ones. French.

Feints. The last liquid from a still.

Ferruginous. When speaking of beer, this term refers to a taste like water with high iron content. Like wine tasting, beer tasting has its own set of terms, which include *austere, beery* (typical of beer), *Brackish, bright, clean, dank, flabby, skunky, swampy,* and *tinny.*

Fliers. White, fluffy particles that float in white wines. Fliers are most likely to appear when the wine is transported from a warm to a colder climate.

Flight. An assemblage of three wines served together in two ounce glasses for the purposes of comparing taste.

Fob. Brewer's term for beer froth. Sometimes called *barm.*

Foreshots. The first liquid to come out of a still.

Gantry. A four-footed wooden stand for barrels.

Gaugers. Revenue officers who measure contents.

Gyle. A quantity of beer brewed at one time; a brewing. Beer kegs carry a stenciled gyle number to indicate which brewing it came from.

Hemorrage. Beer and tomato juice—sometimes employed as a hangover remedy.

Hogen-mogen. Said of strong booze; an exclamation and a description.

Horse's neck. Old soda fountain term for ginger ale with vanilla ice cream.

Jirble. To pour out a drink unsteadily.

Katzenjammer. A cat's whining, literally, but most often applied to a hangover.

Lees. The dregs of wine or beer.

Legs. Streaks that run down the side of a glass after wine has been swirled in it. Wine with pronounced streaks is said to have "good legs."

Long list. The full listing of wines offered by a fine restaurant.

Mini-pétillance. Slight sparkle or crackle in a wine.

Mocktail. Drink with no alcohol.

Muddler. The technical name for a swizzle stick, sometimes called a *mosser.*

Muselage. Muzzling champagne corks by the addition of the traditional tin cap. French.

Must. The unfermented, freshly pressed grape juice used for wine making.

Nebuchadnezzar. The largest champagne bottle size, capable of holding 104 glasses. It is larger than the 83-glass *Balthazar,* 62-glass *Salmanazar,* 41-glass *Methuselah,* 31-glass *Rehoboam,* 21-glass *Jeroboam,* and 10-glass *Magnum.* Your standard *bottle* holds a mere five glasses. Putting all this into bottles, we have:

Magnum = 2 bottles	Salmanazar = 12 bottles
Jeroboam = 4 bottles	Balthazar = 16 bottles
Rehoboam = 6 bottles	Nebuchadnezzar = 20 bottles
Methuselah = 8 bottles	

Nip. One-sixth of a quartern (a 5-oz. measure).

Noggin. A quarter of a pint.

Oast. A kiln for drying hops.

Oenology. The art and science of wine making. Pronounced *e-nology*.

Peated. Scotch taster's term for the degree to which a particular Scotch has a smoky or peaty character. A Scotch may be "well pleated," "lightly peated," etc.

Perry. Pear cider made along the same lines as apple cider.

Plonk. Cheap, ordinary table wine. British slang.

Pomace. The substance remaining after the juice has been extracted from apples, grapes, or whatever. Pomace is often used as animal food.

Pony. Half a jigger, three-quarters of a shot, an ounce.

Potheen. Irish name for illegally distilled whiskey.

Pricked. Of wine that has turned to vinegar. The term may be an anglicization of the French *piqué*, which refers to a wine that has become or is becoming vinegary.

Punt. The concave area at the bottom of certain wine bottles. It allegedly gives strength to the bottle and is not there to give the false impression of extra quantity.

Racked. Wine or beer that has been separated from its *lees*.

Shebeen. Illegal Irish drinking den.

Shive. A circular wooden plug that is hammered into the hole in a cask after it has been filled.

Short dog. Small, cheap bottle of wine.

Shuked or Shooked. Said of wine casks that have been taken apart, with the staves bundled for ease of transport.

Sling. Used as a synonym for cocktail, as in Singapore Sling, but originally liquor mixed with flavored water.

Soda back. Current bar talk for soda on the side.

Spile. A small peg that fits into a hole in the *shive* (see also) of a cask.

Stillion. A stand for a beer keg or wine cask.

T&T. Tanqueray and tonic, a bar call.

Tastevin. The small silver saucer that is used for wine tasting. Tastevins are often hung around the neck of a wine steward by a chain as a symbol of authority.

Ullage. What is not in a cask or bottle; that which is left after evaporation, leakage, or use.

Ullaged. Said of a bottle or cask, part of whose contents have spilled, been consumed, or evaporated.

Vallinch. Long glass tube used for taking samples for casks.

V.S.O. Initialism associated with cognac for Very Special Old. *V.S.O.P.* stands for Very Special Old Pale, and *V.V.S.O.P.* stands for the same thing except that an extra Very is thrown in for good measure.

Weeper. A wine bottle that is leaking through its cork.

Well succeeded. Said of wines that have fulfilled the expectation of their vintage.

Wine cradle. Basket used to serve wine at a slant.

Working. Continuing fermentation. Overdevelopment.

Worm. The business end of a corkscrew.

Worn. Term for wine that has been too long in the bottle or spirits that have been too long in the cask.

XXX Originally, X stood for the number of times a liquor had been distilled, so that XXXX stood for the strongest and purist. Later it came to mean simply the strength of a liquor or beer. Today the system is in disuse.

Zymurgy. The branch of industrial chemistry that deals with fermentation, distillation, and wine making.

15

Ecretsay Onguestay

From Arague to the Vague Specific, the Art of Covert Talk

When I was a kid, my aunt and my mother were able to converse fluently in a secret language that, I was later to learn, is called *Turkey Irish*. I could not understand a word of it. This used to drive me crazy, especially around Christmas when they would openly but secretly jabber on about impending surprises. I am now in the process of becoming fluent in Turkey Irish so that my children will not be deprived of the confounding beauties of a secret tongue.

Arague. Language in which *arag* is introduced before vowels. Pararagimaragararagily faragound aragin aragenglaragand.

Back slang. This is primarily a British habit by which slang is created by spelling words backward. *Ecilop* is slang for police. Iona and Peter Opie, in their *Lore and Language of Schoolchildren,* report that it is common to boys in certain trades ". . . where it is spoken to ensure that the customer shall not understand what is being said ('*Evig reh emos delo garcs dene*'—'Give her some old scrag end')."

Boontling. A contraction of Boonville Lingo, Boontling is a language that was created by the early residents of upper Anderson Valley in Mendocino County, California. In his book, *Boontling: An American Lingo,* Charles C. Adams termed it ". . . a deliberately contrived jargon which was spoken ex-

90

tensively between 1880 and 1920." Writing about it in the *Christian Science Monitor*, Raymond A. Lajoie said, "When spoken, it sounds like English that is not quite understandable, like a kind of double-double talk. . . . When written, it looks like someone used a typewriter with his fingers crossed."

One of the reasons the language was created was to allow adults to gossip without fear of their children or outsiders understanding. As a result, Adams reports, approximately 15 percent of the language was made up of "nonch harpins"—objectionable talk. A few "nonch harpins":

Burlap: To have sexual intercourse, sometimes *burl*. Other words for the same act: *Bow* and *geech*.
Keeboarp: Premature male orgasm.
Dreef: Interrupted coitus.
Squirrel ribby: An erect penis.
Moldunes: Breasts.
Afe: A fart.

Carving verbs. In Elizabethan England there existed a special vocabulary for the table that included specific verbs for carving various game, fish, and poultry. In his dictionary, *Words, Facts and Phrases,* Eliezer Edwards writes, ". . . persons using the wrong term were looked upon with some pity and contempt." Here is a collection of those verbs, gathered from a variety of sources:

Allay a pheasant	Gobbet a trout	Tame a crab
Barb a lobster	Lift a swan	Thigh a pigeon
Break a hare	Mince a plover	Thigh a woodcock
Chine a salmon	Rear a goose	Trench a sturgeon
Culpon a trout	Sauce a capon	Transon an eel
Disfigure a peacock	Scull a tench	Tusk a barbel
Dismember a hen	Side a haddock	Umbrace a mallard
Display a quail	Splat a pike	Unjoint a bittern
Fin a chevin	Splay a bream	Unlace a coney
Fract a chicken	Spoil a hen	Unlatch a curlew
Frush a chub	String a lamprey	Wing a partridge

Cockney rhyming slang. Foreigners are mystified by this East End of London lingo in which *apples and pears* means stairs, *tit for tat* stands for hat, *tea-leaf* for thief, *Johnny Horner* for corner, and *raspberry tart* is fart. Because of the popularity of the television show "The East Enders," on which it is used, many more people have been exposed to it. Ross Reader, who grew up in London, offers this explanation and sample glossary: "The principle of rhyming slang is that instead of using the word you mean, you choose an expression that rhymes with it. For instance, instead of the word 'stairs' you say 'apples and pears'. To cause even more confusion, you can drop the second half of the expression. For instance 'hat' becomes 'tit for tat', which is abbreviated to 'titfer'. For years I used 'titfer' for 'hat' and 'butcher's' for 'look' (as in 'Let's have a butcher's' for 'Let's have a look') and I did not realise that I was using rhyming slang. Another well-known word is 'rabbit' for 'talk'. ('She is rabbiting on all day.') The rhyme here is rabbit-pork = Talk. This is obscure, I don't know what rabbit-pork is, presumably some kind of meat. To U.S. denizens, 'pork' and 'talk' don't rhyme, which does not help. It is thought that rhyming slang was invented so that outsiders would not understand but I think it is just for the joy of creating new words."

REAL WORD	RHYMING SLANG
wife	trouble-and-strife
trousers	round-the-houses (pronounced 'rahnd the 'ahses', because Cockneys do not pronouce their aithches)
pub(lic house)	rub-a-dub
look	butcher's hook
row (argument)	bull and cow
mouth	north and south
feet	plates of meat
pissed (i.e. drunk)	'Mozart and Liszt' or 'Brahms and Liszt'
eyes	mince pies
titties (bosoms)	Bristol Cities (named for football team)
balls (testicles)	cobbler's awls
boots	daisy roots

Double Dutch. A secret language in which vowels are pronounced normally but consonants become syllables:

b—bub	j—jug	p—pup	v—vuv
c—cash	k—kuk	q—quack	w—wash
d—dud	l—lul	r—rug	x—xux
f—fuf	m—mum	s—sus	y—yub
g—gug	n—nun	t—tut	z—zub
h—hutch			

It takes practice even to say hello and good-bye—hutchelullulo and gu-goodudbubyube. Billy in Double Dutch becomes Bubilullulyuh. The secret key to Double Dutch was revealed in an article by Dr. James F. Bender in the *New York Times Magazine* of December 31, 1944. Not only did he reveal the secrets of Double Dutch, Opish, Pig, and Turkey Irish (see below), but he asserted that no less than 50 million Americans spoke one or more synthetic tongues.

Eggy-peggy. A primarily British language in which *eg* or *egg* is inserted before each vowel. Nancy Mitford refers to it in her *Love in a Cold Climate:* "Lady Montdore...led me to the table and the starlings went on with their chatter about my mother in 'eggy-peggy,' a language I happened to know quite well. 'Egg-is shegg-ee reggealleggy, pegg-oor swegg-eet?' "

A related phenomenon is the old and still common practice of English public schoolboys chopping off the final syllable of a word and adding -ers. Examples provided by translator George Kirby: "Webster had spaghetti for breakfast" which becomes "Webbers had sapgers for breakers." Stark naked becomes "starkers" and marmalade becomes "marmers."

Framis. Double-talk for double-talk. Unfortunately, this form of talking does not enjoy the same popularity it did prior to and through World War II. Well done, it is a skillful blend of meaningful and meaningless words that when delivered leads the listener to think he is either hard of hearing or losing his mind. Or more to the point: a durnamic verbal juberance with clear mokus, flaysome, and rasorial overtones. In 1943, *Life* magazine carried an article on double-talk by George Frazier that contained some hints for those wishing to master it. The most important:

—Certain sounds work better than others. Some of them are: *oil, urf, erris, eufen, orsin, awn,* and *urma.* You can create a basic vocabulary prefixed by consonants or syllables.

—The best way to start is with short sentences or phrases. Frazier suggested asking a waiter for such unprocurable dishes as:

Steefils on toast
Kerbits and milk
Zilts with sauerkraut
Vimilforty cheese kribbles from Holland

—Never smile while talking.

—Use enough legitimate words to convince the listener that you are not talking framis.

A fine example of rhymed framis is the following which appeared in an ad for comedian Bert Leslie in the December 20, 1917, *Variety*:

To The Gecks
May the Fusssel Spras
Dil the mosley pass
And the Guncas
Gale your comepus
So praze your wimp
And fill your limp
And poo your luxing flogears
Prall your dit
Fose your lit
And brott to Happy New Years

Perhaps the single greatest practitioner of the art was the late Al Kelly. His work was captured by Bob Considine whose column was a repository for such things as this from a Kelly St. Patrick's Day banquet speech:

"Since time imarilad, the history of St. Patrick and its quobists hair been a great maln in my plybs. Each year thoumats of people grail the streets to verblym the marching multridits as they parade in glariv states . . . It's the rimz of the Irish and the slags of torpins which made this St. Patrick's of lamarod of successful stayvs. Thank you!"

Jerigonza. Spanish Pig Latin in which the letter *p* is inserted after each vowel, turning *buenos dias* into *bupepnos dipaps*. It was described by a B. Sacto-Hirano in the second edition of *A Pamphlet on the Four Basic Dialects of Pig Latin.* Another Spanish version has the syllable *ti* (pronounced tee) inserted before every syllable. *Viva Espana* would become *Tivitiva Tiestipatina.*

King Tut. This language is described in Alan Milberg's *Street Games.* Vowels stay the same. A *u* is added to every consonant and then the consonant is repeated. *T* becomes *tut* and *b* becomes *bub.* Double consonants are expressed with the word *square—gg* becomes *gug square.* All *y*'s become *yuk.* Nunotut tuthuhatut easusyuk tuto mumasustuterur!

Opish. Pronounced *ah-pish.* Vowels remain the same, but *op* is added after each consonant so that, for example, the first three days of the week become: Moponopdopayop, Topuesopdopayop. Wopedopnopesopdopayop. A variation uses *ob.*

Pig Latin. Easiest to use and the most popular of the secret languages, Pig Latin is based on two simple rules: (1) Take the first letter of the word that is to be said, put it at the end of the word, and then add *ay.* (2) Do not invert letters if the word begins with *a, e, i, o,* or *u,* but add *ay* to the end of the word. It'say eallray eryvay implesay. A variant form uses *kee* in place of *ay,* which is impleskee ootkee.

Platysyllabic Pig. The name given to a form of Pig Latin in Brig. Gen. Cyclops Stonebone's *Pamphlet on the Four Basic Dialects of Pig Latin.* It divides words into syllables and inserts *iv* (the *iv* of ivory) after the initial consonant. Box becomes bivox. It becomes more complicated with givigivantivic wivords.

(The author of the aforementioned pamphlet was actually William Murray Cheny, who published one of the few scholarly works on Pig Latin in 1953.)

Ruly English. A language invented by Simon M. Newman for the Patent Office in the 1950s in which every word has only one conceptual meaning and each concept has only one word to describe it. It was created to get away from regular "unruly" English in which, for instance, the word "through" has 13 distinct meanings. Ruly features many "between" words, such as *resilrig* to describe a state between resilience and rigidity. Somewhat rigid is *sli resilrig* and very flexible is *subresilrig.*

Rx. On a doctor's prescription, s.o.s. does not mean that the patient is in distress but that the drug ordered is to be taken "if necessary." Other notations commonly used in doctor/pharmacist communications:

aa	of each	p.r.n.	when required
ad lib	as desired	q.d.	every day
b.i.n.	twice a night	q.i.d.	4 times a day
c	with	q.s.	as much as required
caps	capsule	q.4 h.	every 4 hours
gm	gram	s	without
gtt	a drop	stat	immediately
o.d.	right eye	t.i.d.	3 times a day
o.m.	every morning	t.i.n.	3 times a night
p.c.	after meals		

Short-order code. Although not used as commonly as it once was, short-order cooks, waiters, waitresses, and soda jerks developed an elaborate set of code words and numbers. The words are not impossible to figure out (Adam and Eve on a raft = two poached eggs on toast), but numbers contain no clues to their meaning. Here are the most commonly used numbers:

2½—Small glass of milk.
5—Large glass of milk.
13—White bread; also, the boss is nearby.
14—A special order; stand by for something out of the ordinary.
19—Banana split.
21—Limeade. (This and other numbers ending in 1 call for a single, 22 is a call for 2 limeades, 23 for three and so forth.)
22—Customer's check has not been paid.
23—Scram; leave me alone, I'm working.

30—The end, the place is closing.

33 Red—Coca-Cola with cherry syrup.

36—Postum.

41—This can stand for either a lemonade or a small glass of milk.

48½—To be fired; someone who has been 48½ed has just been discharged.

51—Hot chocolate.

55—Root beer.

55½—Small root beer.

66—An empty bowl or glass; dirty dishes.

73—Best wishes.

81—Glass of water.

86—Sold out or unavailable, as in "86 the banana cream pie."

87½—Look at the beautiful girl out front.

88—Love and kisses.

95—There is a customer walking out without paying.

98—Look out, the assistant manager is near.

99—Beware, the manager is approaching.

Turkey Irish. A language in which *ab* is inserted before vowels. It is one of the rarest. Dr. James Bender wrote in his 1944 *New York Times Magazine* article that it showed up only in certain communities, such as Yonkers, New York, but would be unheard of a few miles away. Habavabe aba nabicabe dabay.

Tutahash. Like Double Dutch except that the letters *c, h, r, w, x, y,* and *z* are respectively rendered *cus, hash, rur, w, x, yum,* and *zuz.*

Vague specific. An important concept and term created by Richard B. Gehman in an article in *Collier's* in 1949. It refers to the habit of "referring vaguely to specific persons or things." Gehman gave many examples, including this conversation from under his own roof:

"Here," my wife said, "you can take these."

"Where do you want them?"

"Oh, put them out there somewhere."

"With the others?"

"No," said my wife decisively, "put them with those things behind the others."

Famways

The Legend and Lore of the Living Room

> Your family, like every other family, has a language of its own, consisting of unintelligible catch phrases, favourite but not generally known, quotations, obscure allusions, and well-tried, but not intrinsically humorous family jokes.
>
> —*A.A. Milne "Christmas Party," in* A Table Near the Band and Other Stories

If a great (or great, great) grandparent went down with the *Titanic* when it rammed into an iceberg, that would be a stunning fact for the family genealogist to record. It would constitute the most direct link possible between a family and that terrible 1912 shipping disaster, which is still regarded with awe and horror.

But what if there was a rakish great, great grandfather who had a berth paid for on the ship, but did not go down with it? What if, according to the family version of the tale, he missed the boat because he could not leave a poker table where he was in the process of amassing a bundle of money?

You have always had your doubts about this story's authenticity—"Did he actually let an expensive ticket go to waste? Maybe he just *thought* about going on the Titanic."—but it still gets told and retold at family gatherings. Over time, details get added to the story as somebody vaguely recalls once being told that Ty Cobb stopped by to watch a few hands of the poker game.

True or false, the story of the poker game is a legitimate part of a family's tradition known as family folklore. It is as surely folklore as the story of George Washington and the cherry tree or Paul Bunyan and his blue ox. A story or anecdote, however, is just one element of family folklore. The term is a collective name for all of the rituals, customs, stories, legends, and shared experiences that are commonly distilled, embellished, and reworked over time. Collectively, it is what makes your household different from all others.

Interest in family folklore is increasing. "It was boosted by the Bicentennial, "Roots," and the Smithsonian Folklife Program and just seems to keep on going," explains Steven J. Zeitlin, a folklorist currently serving as the director of the nonprofit organization City Lore: The New York Center for Urban Folk Culture. He has been involved in several family folklore projects at the Smithsonian (more on this shortly) and is keenly interested in the subject.

He is also an advocate who hopes that more families involve themselves in what he terms "their living cultural heritage." Zeitlin also sees family folklore as an important alternative to the notion of family that comes to us from Hollywood and Madison Avenue. "This is the real grass roots family rather than some prepackaged version offered to us in prime time."

Zeitlin believes that the new awareness of and fascination for family folklore, like conventional genealogy, is growing as people become increasingly aware of the importance of their own family history. Zeitlin says that family folklore is not separate from genealogy, but rather an important facet of it. If the traditional "family tree" research is historic genealogy, family folklore is cultural genealogy. The former is more likely to be recorded in black and white, the latter passed down in stories, expressions, and rituals. If history is reality; folklore is stylized reality.

"The recording of military records and the precise attention to birth dates is not everyone's cup of tea," say Zeitlin, "some people are much more interested in what the family was about—what made grandpa laugh and which traditions were brought over from another country. To many people the cultural heritage of their own family is much more accessible and fascinating than historic detail." He adds, "Some people are much more comfortable tape-recording stories from a grandparent than digging through court records."

But if family folklore is not courthouse records and immigration lists, then what is it exactly?

An exact answer is difficult because so many things can qualify—from a joke, to a grace or blessing, to a home video, to the exact way Uncle Fred recounts the moment he *almost* ran into Marilyn Monroe. In time, it can range from a story that is a hundred years old to all that stuff that, at this very moment, is festooned with magnets from your refrigerator door. (Several years ago, Sid Moody of the Associated Press made the point clearly in an article: "The icebox has become the keyhole through which to spy on the private lives of America. . . . That it also hold ice cream is besides the point.")

Lest there be any question, family folklore comes in wildly diverse packages: sad, mundane, noble, touching or, as often the case, silly or goofy. Customs can be tied to great events, such as the Depression or the Civil War, or totally familial ones. They can take physical form in a family recipe scribbled on a sheet of paper or a reel of home movies.

That said, here are a few common forms of family folklore.

Creatures of Custom

Outside of oft-told stories, perhaps the most common form is that of a simple custom or tradition. These can be as straightforward as planning a major prank for April Fool's Day to reserving a corner of the kitchen wall as a place to mark and date the growth of children.

Many have to do with the observance of a holiday. An old friend tells of his grandparents' first Thanksgiving in America after arriving from Italy. Not knowing about traditional stuffing, they loaded their turkey with ravioli. In that family the "traditional" stuffing is still ravioli. In another family there is a holiday tradition of giving and re-giving a hideous, green doll—Mr. Greenbean—to an unsuspecting member of the family. The trick is finding a way to package the doll (fitting it into a can, for example) so that it looks like a conventional gift.

Sometimes a holiday tradition becomes so extraordinary that it makes the news. A few days after Christmas in 1968, the Associated Press carried the story of a 109-year-old fruitcake. Under a Tecumseh, Michigan, dateline, the story began: "When Fridelia Ford died in 1878, she left behind an edible heirloom that has been kept in the family for more than a century." It seems that the woman died before the cake had aged properly, and it was decided to keep it uneaten in her honor. Periodically, the family appoints a new guardian whose job it is to make sure that nobody nibbles at it.

Verbal Heirlooms

Another grouping involves verbal traditions ranging from a pet joke to an unorthodox frame of reference for something otherwise mundane. A Milwaukee woman, Cate Pfeifer, confesses that she comes from a family of bad housekeepers and serious readers. As she puts it, "We discuss our homes in terms of allusions to the circles of hell in Dante's *Inferno*. My mother will ask about my apartment and I will tell her that it is at the circle reserved for virtuous pagans."

Names and nicknames are a fertile field for family folklorists. Mary M. Stolzenbach of Vienna, Virginia, reports on the extent to which her family has gone with names: "One of our family customs was re-christening the dog whenever we thought of another good name. He was at various times 'Uncle Grandma,' 'Fifi,' and 'Cadwallader P. Terwilliger.' His real name was 'Kitty.' "

Then there are words and phrases that have so infatuated this author that he recently published a collection of them in a book called *Family Words*. These are the verbal oddities that have been fashioned to fill in the blanks of everyday life. Many of these special words and phrases are of this generation, while others date back into another century.

Often these words and the reasoning behind them is known only to the family. For instance, it is called "Number 26," and in one family it describes that moment when something occurs in the mind of a cat that sends it, inexplicably, on a high-speed tear through the house, usually skidding on the kitchen floor in the process. It is over just as quickly as it started. The term and the concept came from the family of Dave Matheny of Minneapolis, a writer for the *Star Tribune*.

But why Number 26? "Well," says Matheny, "we came up with a theory about cats which is that they lay around the house generating random numbers while they sleep. They lay there slowly running through numbers—91, 256, 41, 111—when all of a sudden the number 26 comes up and that triggers the tear through the house. We figured that was the only explanation for it."

One finds that family words tend to be about homey and homely things: pets, kids, the kitchen, simple emotions, and the like. Here are some of the most recent additions to the collection as well as a few of the author's favorites from *Family Words*:

Ackazooma. The stem protruding from the core of the apple. From Frank Whitby of Littleton, Colorado, who says, "As I was sure that the akazooma *had* to be removed *before* eating, I was unprepared for a world full of ackazooma-intact apple eaters when I reached the age of seven years. Thus, the tradition of ackazooma removal before eating an apple has continued into my adulthood."

Antook. A Chicago woman proudly brought home an antique brick, which the dealer told her had been used to keep people warm in a sleigh after it had been warmed. Her family created the word "antook" to describe the brick and other dubious antiques.

Applaudience. An audience that has come to applaud; specifically, those composed of parents and grandparents who go to children's piano and dance recitals. Presumably the term was created to reassure a child nervous about "all those people" who would be at the recital.

Asyou. The bottom or top step of the stairs where things are put—from "As you go up/down take this with you." From Faith M. Thompson, Claremore, Oklahoma.

Bastarda. Female bastard, from Susan Fenwick Reed, Chapel Hill, North Carolina.

Bip. A North Carolina woman said her daughter created this word for the kind of person who buttons the top button of a sports shirt and wears black socks to a picnic.

Blesper. The cotton or wool stuffing that occasionally comes out of upholstered furniture. From Larry Broadmore of San Fernando, California, who says of it, "I have no idea where the name came from—but this substance was to me like 'the blood' of the furniture, and therefore very important and mysterious."

Blutz. According to Joanne Lee, who reported it, it "is a verb which describes putting one's open mouth on the partially submerged anatomy (any part that's big enough will do) in a swimming pool (or a bathtub if it's big enough) with lips held slackly and sort-of blowing to produce bubbles, or at least a lot of water activity and noise. The action can be accompanied by a humming sound if one is able to do it. It's pronounced in such a way as *not* to rhyme with clutz . . . but more like the 'u' in the color blue. A guy I was in love with when I was 13 or 14 used to do it to me all the time (whenever we were in the water together). I don't recall it was particularly erotic, but it sure felt nice."

Boogoeaster. Child's rendition of ego-booster.

Booning. Dipping bread or toast in the yolk of a sunny side-up egg. From Dan Rodricks, Baltimore writer and radio personality.

Budabuda. The inside of the lower lip, so called because it is used in conjunction with the forefinger to make the sound "budabuda."

Buffalo style. From Joan Gilbert of Portland, Maine, who reports it was "first used by my then six-year-old brother who misheard the word "buffet"; now a generic term for any casual, nonseated meal, as in 'It's too hot to fuss with dinner; let's just eat buffalo style.' "

Cheese and trees. Broccoli and cheese. From the Leslie Morgan family, Lewisville, Texas.

Chinese nose picker. Staple remover. From Jeanie Evans, Detroit.

Chipslunch. The crusty, greasy remains in a frying pan after you've cooked hamburgers for lunch or dinner. This word is often used in an abstract adjectival form as in, "What a chipslunchlike day."

Clara. Nobody in the family can recall why, but this is what is said when a man's trousers or woman's slacks are strategically stuck in the wrong place.

Cortsty. An endearment meaning cute, lovable. From Stephen V. Masse, Amherst, Massachusetts.

Cuddle-huddle. A group hug between two or more family members or close friends; used especially when there is great need for emotional support. From Cathleen R. Robertson of Bloomington, Minnesota.

C.Y.K. This stands for Consider Yourself Kissed and was given to me by a woman whose father was a germ-conscious doctor who would say "C.Y.K." to the kids when he put them to bed during cold season.

Didit. Raised highway lane markers that make the sound "didit, didit" when you ride over them.

DMZ. Dumped Magazine Zone. A corner of the living room for magazines and newspapers. From Shelly Waters of Dallas.

Eekser. The lever on an ice cube tray, so called because of the noise it makes when pulled.

Fardo. The embarassment you feel for somebody else.

Flipper catcher. Basket for household remote controls. From Shelly Waters of Dallas.

Fowlenzia. One of many names for the unspecified disease that attacks children when they either (a). don't wash their hands, (b). eat too much Halloween candy, or (c). let the dog lick their faces. Other diseases of the same severity include *scagamoga* and *fisterous*.

Frudenda. [sing. pl. *frudendum*.] Items handmade by grandmothers and other elderly ladies using drycleaner bags, nylon net, artificial flowers, etc. Purpose unknown. From Mary Ann Raimond, Boynton Beach, Florida, who says it was originally coined by her mother.

Futzamutza. This is what unlabled cheeses that remain in the refrigerator too long become in one family.

Gerbiling. Worrying, talking too much, running around, doing aimless little things. From Patricia Spaeth, Port Townsend, Washington.

Glect. To smother with attention and concern; the opposite of *neglect*. From a New York City man with a glectful aunt.

Goozlum. Mix of algae and cow saliva found on water cattle drink. From Dave Duron, Baltimore.

Grunter. That bathroom one uses when one needs maximum privacy. From Diantha Thorpe.

Hahas. Child's word for glasses. The term comes from the sound you make when you breath heavily on them to steam them up for cleaning. Hahas, which are spelled "h-a-h-a-s", should actually be pronounced with a loud breathy sound.

Hardway store. A do-it-yourself hardware store in the family of Sam Sherstad of Garland, Texas.

Hooptoot. Short for "hop to it" meaning to get moving; from David Kopaska-Merkel who got it from his wife.

Hup hups. Quick drawn-in breaths that are leftover from crying. This is from Norma C. Finnegan of St. Paul who has actually compiled a small dictionary of her own family's family words called *Finneganisms*. (Another Finniganism is *beewa* for the pleated paper separating cookies in cookie boxes. They are so named because they can be manipulated like an accordian.)

Iguanas. The little brown, burnt potato chips you inadvertently eat that come in every bag. From Nancy Mayerman, Williamsville, New York.

Macaroni-stay-home. Colander in one Italian-American family. From a first generation mother.

Melvin. The rubbery crust that forms on the top of pudding. A third-generation family word believed to go back to a neighborhood kid named Melvin who loved to scrape the "melvin" off pudding.

Metutials. Small, irksome chores that must be done before anything else can be done. "I'll do it after my metutials" gives nasty tasks a certain dignity according to the woman whose family uses it.

Moux. Elegant name for the ball in the toilet tank, from a Denver woman who points out that you can suggest to your spouse that "the upstairs moux is stuck" at a fancy dinner party without raising an eyebrow.

Nerky. A blend of nerd and jerky created in one household to describe one particularly misshapen, ill-fitting, and hence, nerky, baseball cap.

Niblings. Nieces and nephews collectively.

Ploop. Ploop, a friend tells me, is the roll of fat that commonly appears after the holidays and *ploops* down over the belt.

Plunk-plunk. The sound that the first glass of milk made when it came out of the *bottle*. From Mrs. M.L. Isenberg of St. Louis who points out ". . . cardboard cartons do not contain 'plunk-plunks.' "

P'Skinny. High-pitched feeble fart from Beth Ryan and Howard Wittels, Wayzata, Minnesota.

Routin. The whitish wrinkles that you develop on your fingers from being in the tub too long. From the H. Robert Frenzel family of Arlington, Texas.

Rubber husbands. One divorcee's term for those rubber pads used to turn pesky jar tops.

Runaround. A particularly vicious hangnail that will, if pulled hard, runaround the finger in an arc of bloody pain.

Shobun. The term invented on the spot by a teenager to describe the outfit of a Sumo wrestler seen on television.

Snestle. To settle down snugly, say, with a good book on a rainy night, or a house that is snestled into the landscape. From Marie E. Johnson, La Conner, Washington.

Sunday bag. This is a better class of paper bag saved for use on Sundays or holidays when bringing food or gifts to other people's houses. The Chicago lady whose family uses the term says that a supermarket bag is for everyday, but that one from Marshall Field and Co. is a Sunday bag.

Tinkletorium. Bathroom.

Toad cloth. Any dishrag that has gotten too wet and clammy to dry dishes. From Jane Tesh, Mt. Airy, North Carolina.

Up the wooden hill. Time to go to bed. From Elizabeth Watts, New York City.

Vamoosification Leavetaking, from David C. Kopaska-Merkel.

Washing machine music. Rock music with a heavy beat. Submitted to the collection by Ross Reader who got it from his father. He explains, "When you hear it from a certain distance, for instance when it is coming through the wall from a neighboring house, you cannot hear the tune but only the beat, and it sounds like the rhythmic reverberations of a washing machine."

Waybacker. A child adept at holding his or her head back for hair-washing. From Penny Veldman, Royal Oak, Michigan.

Wiggleyfon. The sheathed string on a hooded sweatshirt. Another family calls these shirts *hoodwinks*.

Yulke. The little grains of dried secretion found in the corner of one's eyes in the morning. The man who gave me "yulke" told me that it had been used in his family for so long he thought it was a real word. It wasn't until he was in the Army and used it that someone told him it wasn't in the dictionary. Other words for yulke: glee, tapioca, and shrum.

One of my favorite verbal heirlooms is this one from Nancy Dougherty of Minneapolis:

Cheesefest. One of those big family get-togethers when grandmother (or somebody) insists on taking "a million pictures" and people must smile a lot.

Snap Judgments

The concept of a family gathering as a "cheesefest" suggests the part that photography plays in the folkways of a family. The key is the humble and ubiquitous snapshot, both an element in the "archive" of family life and a vehicle for the preservation of family history. Or, as social critic Susan Sontag put it in her book *On Photography*, "Through photography each family constructs a portrait of itself, a kit of images that bears witness to its connectedness."

Besides recording family history, photographs also depict family tradition. This was one aspect of family life studied by the Smithsonian's Office of Folklife between 1974 and 1978. The Family Folklore Project was set up to study and collect the stories and customs that constituted American family life. At the beginning there was no plan to include family photography, but that changed the first time the project went public. A Folklore Tent was set up at the Smithsonian's Annual Folklore Festival on the Mall in Washington to foster interest in the project. To decorate the tent and give it a "homey" look, some family photos belonging to the people working on the project were hung up.

The Smithsonian's Amy Kotkin, who worked on the project, explains what happened next, "Right from the outset we started hearing people talk about the photos, both ours and theirs. Those pictures were a powerful impetus in getting people to talk about themselves and their families. We also saw commonality at work. One woman saw a picture of a baby posed on a fuzzy rug and pulled a dog-eared picture out of her wallet and said she had the same photo, but with a different kid."

The following year the team put an ad in the *Washington Post* asking for people who might be interested in showing and talking about their family photo collections. "The responses were overwhelming," says Kotkin. "About 100 were contacted and from them a group of collections were picked for detailed study. It was quickly determined that snapshots and family albums were important expressions of our values, aspirations, and ideals."

The full results of the Smithsonian project appear in the book *A Celebration of American Family Folklore* (Pantheon, 1982), co-authored by Kotkin, Zeitlin, and Holly Cutting Baker. The book, which is based on more than 2,000 interviews, is essential reading for anyone wishing to become a family folklorist. It concentrates on several basic forms of family folklore: family stories, stories for children, family expressions, family customs, and family photography.

The section on photography brings up a number of fascinating points including that the very act of taking pictures has become part of the ritual of certain holidays and special events. At times the camera actually directs events, for instance, the couple who holds its embrace on the wedding altar to accommodate the photo opportunity of "the moment."

Another conclusion was that many shots are so common—the infant in the bath, the family car, a litter of kittens in a basket—that they have become ritual scenes of domestic life. This suggests the conclusion made in the book that "picture-taking creates as much as it records."

It also became apparent that a photograph and the story that goes with it can reveal completely different versions of "the truth." A picture of a family having a good time may elicit a story or recollection that is unhappy. One woman who was interviewed told of her mother who could not look at a fine collection of photographs taken in the 1920s because of the pain of recalling the fact that the family's cherished camera had to be sold during the Depression.

In addition, it was found that legends cropped up around the photos themselves. In one engaging case, the only photo that remained of a woman's great uncle was of him posed on a horse during a short stint with Buffalo Bill's Wild West Show. The man spent most of his life as a tailor in Newark, New Jersey, but the picture of him as a cowboy got him dubbed "One-Gun Blum— the Jewish Cowboy." The photo became a symbol for the man's life for the next generation and yarns were spun about his Western adventures for the children.

Kotkin adds that the snapshot holds a special position in the American family because it is so accessible: "You can touch them, pass them around and leave them on the coffee table without having to haul out a projector or screen." She adds that part of the natural appeal of snapshots is that they provide a shorthanded way for outsiders to get to know the family. "We found that couples recalled that the family snapshot album was often pulled out on a second or third date. It was a person's way of showing another what they were a part of . . . where they came from."

A final observation that came out of the project was the realization that in most families one member takes on the job as "curator" or archivist of the family photos. Sometimes it is the person who takes most of the pictures and sometimes it is another person in the family. Without such a curator or guardian, the pictures are likely to lose their context, and they just become objects and end up being sold off at a yard sale. Kotkin says that the verbal link is extremely important. "If there is nobody to tell you what is going on or who the people are, the pictures lose their meaning."

Steven Zeitlin looks back on the project today and points out that their study of the snapshot predated the home video. "Suddenly people are recording everything. These videos are not just of weddings and graduations but the casual aspects of everyday life." Zeitlin believes that, like the box camera before it, this bit of new technology will have a major impact on the preservation of family culture.

New Rituals

Finally, it must be said that there is a certain importance to all of this that transcends the collecting and appreciation for family folklore. Brett Williams, Associate Professor of Anthropology and American Studies at the American University in Washington, D.C., has studied families who have disturbed children. One of her most powerful findings has been that many of these families did not seem to set aside anything that was special. Tradition and ritual were absent and nothing out of the ordinary ever happened at meals or bedtime. Williams believes that the children got the message that they were not important.

Williams believes that there should be a blend of traditional customs and fresh ones that are indigenous to the household in question. She understands that families today are often "stretched and tired" by the time the evening comes around, but this is just the time that something special should happen. "Whether it's the evening meal, bathtime or bedtime, it is important to create something special."

An example? Williams and her husband realized that giving the children their baths was something of an ordeal. One night neither of them seemed to have the energy for the task at hand and decided the only democratic thing to do was to flip a coin. As she puts it, the kids fell in love with the idea and there is now a coin-tossing ceremony each night at bathtime.

17

Fighting Words

A Muster of Military Terminology

Air support. Bombing. In 1974 an Air Force colonel won a Doublespeak Award from the National Council of Teachers of English for his complaint about reporters writing about a U.S. bombing mission: "You always write it's bombing, bombing, bombing. It's not bombing! It's air support."

Balbo. A massive flight formation involving hundreds of aircraft. It is named after the Italian general Italo Balbo, who led a mass exhibition flight from Italy to the United States and returned in 1933. Balbos are often seen at the ends of movies about World War II, and from the start were used to demonstrate air power.

Balloon goes up, the. Term dating back to the 1950s for a big war, as in "What happens if the balloon goes up?"

Bident. An ancient two-pronged weapon less commonly referred to than the three-pronged *trident*.

Bricole. A harness worn by humans for pulling guns or other heavy loads.

Caltrop. Military device used for stopping cavalry and horse-drawn vehicles. It is a small, four-pointed piece of iron that always presents at least one sharp spike when thrown on the ground.

City-bargaining. A concept in nuclear war strategy by which a war is controlled after it has begun. Specifically, you "bargain" by knocking out one of your enemy's cities in response to his attack on your country.

107

Cocarde. The emblem on the wing of a warplane that indicates which country it is from.

Conservatory. Glass-enclosed machine-gun turret common to large World War II-era aircraft.

Derosing. Word formed from acronym for Date of Estimated Return from OverSEas. To derose is to go home.

DOE reaction. The end; DOE stands for Death Of Earth.

Escalation agility. Ease with which one side or the other can escalate in a weapons exchange.

Foo. A mysterious military onlooker. He was described in a British naval magazine in 1946: "Mr. Foo is a mysterious Second World War product, gifted with bitter omniscience and sarcasm."

Fougasse. A land mine that explodes and blows metal and other debris in a predetermined direction.

Fratricide. When one element of a weapon with more than one warhead knocks out one of its brother warheads. It is used in conjunction with MIRV (Multiple Independently targeted Reentry Vehicle).

Fugleman. Model soldier; one who stands in front of other soldiers to demonstrate, drill, or whatever.

Furphy. A latrine rumor. It is a reference to the Furphy Brothers who furnished field latrines to the Australian Army (1890–1916).

Gaffle. The lever used in cocking a crossbow.

Generalissima. A word that apparently exists only in the abstract. The journal *Word Ways* was able to find four generalissimos (Chiang Kai-shek, Franco, Trujillo, and Stalin), but no woman with the corresponding title, although Sra. Franco may have used it.

Gigaton. A measure of energy released that is equivalent to a billion tons of TNT.

Ground zero. The point over which an air burst explodes and the point at which a nuclear weapon explodes; also the nickname of the small open area at the center of the Pentagon.

Horned scully. An underwater obstacle designed to rip the bottom out of a boat or ship. It consists of long, pointed rails embedded in concrete.

Kopfring. Metal ring welded to the tip of a bomb to reduce its penetration into the ground or water.

Lapidate. To stone.

Machicolation. A floor opening, parapet, or other place from which boiling water, hot lead, rocks, or other objects can be dropped on an enemy. Machicolations are common to castles and fortresses.

Megacorpse. A nuclear-age word for a million dead people.

Meteorskrieg. A super blitzkrieg. The term was coined by American General Stephen O. Fuqua to describe the speed and power of the German drive in France and Belgium in the spring of 1940.

Nth Country Problem. The future proliferation of nuclear weapons. Until France joined the club some years ago, this was known as the *4th Country Problem.*

Permissive-link. An element in the workings of a nuclear weapon that must be completed or supplied before the weapon can be armed or fired. The link itself can be anything from a key to a coded radio signal.

Post-attack economy. Fancy Pentagonese for the America that will exist after a nuclear interchange (if there are enough people left to maintain an economy).

Quakers. Quakers or *Quaker guns* are dummy cannon used to deceive the enemy. They were traditionally placed in the portholes of ships or in the gun holes of forts. Philip Chaplin reports, "In 1941, at least two Canadian corvettes went overseas with quakers mounted on their bandstands because the production of 4" guns had not gotten underway in Canada."

Rug rank. A higher ranking officer; those who rate a rug on the floor of their offices.

Sciamachy. Fighting an imaginary enemy; combat with a shadow. Pronounced *sigh-a-maky.*

Suitcase warfare. A term that drives home the size and portability of new types of weaponry. To quote from the definition of this term that appears in the report of an insurance industry think tank, "It is conceivable that an object the size of a suitcase, and carried as inconspicuously, could contain any of several substances which could destroy whole structures and even whole cities."

Surviving spouse. Department of Defense term to replace the words *widow* and *widower.* The official term for what a surviving spouse is given is a *death gratuity,* which sounds like a tip you give an undertaker.

Tacnuk. Tactical nuclear weapon.

Thalassocracy. Rule of the sea; sea power.

"Total Nuclear War." It says under this entry in the Defense Department's *Dictionary of Military and Associated Terms,* "not to be used. See general war." This squeamishness about total war reaches a peak in the official *Dictionary of United States Army Terms,* which shies away from defining not only *a total nuclear war* but also *general war, nuclear war,* and *war.*

Unk-unks. Short for technological unknown unknowns. Used by military planners whose unk-unks usually pertain to what the Soviet military planners are planning.

Uti possidetis. The principle that states that a nation owns the territory it holds at the end of a war. It is pronounced *you-tea-possa-detis*.

Wargasm. The condition that occurs when all the nuclear and thermonuclear buttons get pushed.

Wild card. The term used to describe a major unforeseen development that could wipe out less dramatic scenarios and projections. A nuclear holocaust, the total downfall of civilization in its present form, a worldwide totalitarian state, and extraterrestrial invasion are all wild cards.

Woompher bomb. Term that emerged in the late 1950s for a technological breakthrough of such magnitude that the country that made it would have a decisive strategic advantage.

Zumbooruk. A small swivel-cannon fired from the back of a camel.

Fillers

*Regional Americanisms
and Foreign Words That Fill
Major Gaps in Mainstream English*

Absquatulate. To leave hurriedly and stealthily. This is an old Americanism in need of revival.

Ambeer. Tobacco spittle in the Ozarks.

Anti-goddlin'. Uneven, out of whack; southern United States.

Baffona. A woman with a not too unpleasant mustache. Italian.

Brindle. Any dark color that cannot be classified. It is often used in New England to describe the color of a cow or horse.

Catawampously. This word was defined in the "Que Paso?" column of the *Arizona Republic* as "Chest-out, big doggin' bravado as in 'Ol' Red, he stomped catawampously into that there saloon and offered to fight ever'body all at once.'"

Cejijunto. Spanish for a person with one long continuous eyebrow. It is both an adjective and a noun and is pronounced *ceh-he-hunto*.

Crème faussèe. French for fake cream. It has so much more style than, say, artificial cream or nondairy creamer.

Culacino. Italian for the mark left on a tablecloth by a wet glass.

Doppelganger. The apparition of a living person, as opposed to a ghost that is the apparition of a dead one. German.

Dozy. In Maine, wood that hasn't been properly seasoned according to E. B. White in his essay "Maine Speech."

Ehestandswinkel. German for incipient balding at the temples.

Espantoon. A police officer's nightstick in Baltimore, which is evidently a varient of *spontoon*, which was a short spear carried by company officers in the British Army in the eighteenth century.

Fantods. The fidgets; the willies. It is a venerable piece of American slang used, among other places, in *Huckleberry Finn:* "They was all nice pictures, I reckon, but I didn't somehow seem to take to them, because if ever I was down a little, they always gave me the fantods."

Het. Past participle of *heat* in northern New England.

Hip-skeltered. Askew, crooked, or irregular in the Ozarks. This is one of a number of fine regional *catawampus* words including *slaunch-wise, skewgee, sky-gogglin', sky-wampus,* and *slantindicular.*

Homme moyen sensuel. Literally, a man of average desires; ordinary man. A wonderful name for an average guy who would like to be called something with a little more zip than average guy. French.

Huskanawed. An expression used to describe a person who appears as if he had been submitted to the action of an emetic or enema. It derives from the word *huskanawing* used by Virginia Indians to describe an ordeal of initiation to which young males were subjected. Part of the ordeal involved heavy doses of emetics.

Jizzicked. Something so far gone that no repair can fix it. New England.

Jorum. A big drink, especially in New England.

Kippage. State of great excitement, anguish, or passion. It is a Scottish word.

Lagniappe. In Cajun country, this is a small present given when a purchase is made, or, more to the point, when a bill is paid. Washington journalist William D. Hickman, originally from East Texas, recalls, "At my grandmother's grocery it was usually bubble gum or a penny Tootsie Roll."

Lagom. Swedish for *just enough.* An American friend who has spent many years in Sweden maintains that *lagom* fills a vacuum in English. It is pronounced *lag-ome.*

Mulligrubs. A state of temporary depression, an archaic but apt term.

Peeze. To leak in small bubbles; a small leak. New England.

Peelie-wally. Scottish term for not feeling all that well. In his Los Angeles *Times* column, Jack Smith quotes Miles Kington on the term, which he had just discovered: "A hundred times more suggestive than feeling a bit off-color, and I've been longing to use the word ever since. Unfortunately my plans have been thwarted by a run of good health. . . . "

Pindling. Small and ill-nourished, such as a pindling chick. The opposite of *thriving* in New England.

Pizzlesprung. Pooped. Kentucky.

Reef. A strong tug. New England.

Saudade. Columnist Dan Rodricks of the *Baltimore Evening Sun* says, "The Portugese have a word *saudade* that means yearning or longing but, more than that describes the mixture of feelings that swim in the heart. . . . [B]est described through example [it is] what a man feels at his daughter's wedding."

Schadenfreude. Taking malicious delight in the misfortune of others. German.

Scurryfunge. According to John Gould in *Maine Lingo*, a scurryfunge is a ". . . hasty tidying of the house between the time you see a neighbor coming and the time she knocks on the door."

Shacklety. Ozarkian for a building that is about to fall down.

Sigogglin. Tilted to the right, as, for example, a leaning barn. A tilt to the left is *antisigogglin*.

Slimpsy. Sleazy, cheap, of poor quality. Yankee talk and a probable blend of slippery + flimsy.

Sloomy. Sluggish, spiritless, and dull.

Sugging. British term for "selling under the guise of doing market research." A *Times* of London headline of June 8, 1991, alluding to Sir Gordon Borrie, the director general of Fair Trading, proclaimed "Borrie lauds a 'sugger' punch."

Tunk. A light blow. "That jar lid won't come off unless you tunk it." New England.

Weltschmerz. Sadness over the evils of the world. Pronounced *velt-shmairtz*.

Whale. To strike vigorously, as in "whaling the bejeezus" out of a fence post. Old Yankee word also found in Canada.

Yuns. Word used in and around Pittsburgh for "you ones"; the long missing plural of *you* that has always been lacking in the English language.

Zàzzera. Italian for the hair that grows on the back of the neck.

Fizzlers

*Terms Whose Time
Has Not Yet Come*

There is something fascinating about new words and phrases that are introduced or suggested and then flop. What follows is a modest collection of such
flops, including a sampling of proposed nonsexist pronouns that were doomed
from the start because they looked and sounded more like Estonian than
English.

Americaid. One of a group of 22 words created by the Nixon administration
in 1972 as possible replacements for the word *welfare*. Among other suggestions were: *Amerishare, Faircare, Sharefare, Americare, Yourfare, Benefaid,*
and *Famfare.*

Autel. An early competitor for the name of a new kind of lodging. The competition was won by *motel. Autotel* also lost.

Banana. When Alfred Kahn, President Carter's resourceful inflation fighter,
was reprimanded by the White House for using the word *recession*, he sub-
stituted the word *banana.*

Cashomat. The first name used for the now ubiquitous electronic tellers attached to American banks.

Chairone. Nonsexist word for chairman/chairwoman that was pushed by a
number of advocates (including members of the National Organization for

Women) in the early 1970s. Rarely does a word have a constituency lobbying for its inclusion in a dictionary, as this one did. It appeared in the 1976 appendix to *Webster's Third International Dictionary*. However, the word was scrubbed from later editions for the simple reason that folks didn't use it, while the alternative—and ever-so neutral—*chairperson* grew in popularity. One reason for its failure may have been that it didn't look like an English word in print. Chairone, however, looks like a great Italian word.

Chirtonsor. In 1924, 3,000 barbers voted to go by this name.

Clothing refresher. A self-descriptive term adopted by the washerwomen of San Francisco in 1849 to upgrade the name of their work. Like so many other attempts to up one's status with a new name, clothing refresher did not take hold. Bartenders are still called that despite an attempt by some to become known as *beverage counselors*. Other failures: *guidance worker* for bill collector and *director of pupil personnel* for truant officer.

Co. Word to replace *he* or *she*, suggested by writer Mary Orovan. The plural is *cos*, and *himself* and *herself* become *coself*.

Cost growth. In 1969 the Pentagon launched an effort, spearheaded by Deputy Secretary of Defense David Packard, to banish the term *cost overrun* and replace it with cost growth.

Cytherean. The adjective for the planet Venus that was informally agreed upon by space scientists who needed a stand-in for the traditional word, *venereal*, which had become too closely associated with earthy behavior. The Greek name for Venus, Aphrodite, had become similarly tied to the flesh. Cytherean comes from the name of the island of Cythera, where Aphrodite first landed after her birth at sea. Similarly, science fiction writers have tended to use *Venusians* for inhabitants of the planet to avoid the association with venereal. Venusian may have a future, but Cytherean has bombed.

District work period. Term created and officially sanctioned by the House of Representatives in late 1976 to replace what then Speaker "Tip" O'Neill called "an ugly term the press likes to use." The ugly term is *recess*, and while representatives may call it a DWP, everybody else still calls it a recess. The Senate, incidentally, has had no better luck with its official replacement, *nonlegislative period*.

E. Neutral stand-in for *he* and *she* created by the Broward County Florida schools in response to the federal call for desexed language in school publications. The same people also came up with *lr*, a neutral personal pronoun for *him* and *her*.

Electrolethe. A less jarring name that has been suggested for the electric chair.

Enco. For years the name for various corporate parts of the giant Standard Oil Company of New Jersey. When the company decided to settle on one international trademark, it considered Enco but decided instead on Exxon when it found that enco sounded like the Japanese term for "stalled car."

Et. Third-person-singular pronoun created from the *e* in *he* and *she* and the *t* in *it*. It was created by Aline Hoffman of Sarnia, Ontario. It appears in Bill Sherk's *Brave New Words*.

Femcee. Female emcee; mistress of ceremonies. The term came into being in the 1950s along with *toastmistress,* which had far greater success than femcee.

Frarority. A collegiate social organization that admits both sexes. Such places are common, but the name is not. Ditto for *freshperson*. The word that seems to be working on some campuses is *frosh*.

Gentlepersons. A saluation that seems to have died at birth.

Girlcott. *Time* magazine's term for a woman's boycott circa 1970.

Hesh. Combined *he* and *she*, one of a number of genderless pronouns proposed by Professor Robert Longwell of the University of Northern Colorado. Also proposed by Longwell:

Hirm: "Him or her" composite.

Hizer: "His or her" word.

-wan: Sexless suffix. The plural is *-wen*—more than one policewan would be policewen.

Huperson. A short-lived suggestion for a neutral replacement for *human*.

Jhe. Coinage to use where *he* is customary but not appropriate. This neutral personal pronoun, pronounced *gee*, was invented by Professor Milton R. Stern of the University of Michigan.

Journey's End. What the *Cincinnati Enquirer* calls its death notices.

Kin-mother. Name adopted in 1942 by the Mother-in-Law Association as a replacement for *mother-in-law*, which the group felt had acquired a bad reputation. Other replacement names that the MILA had considered: *our-ma* and *motherette*.

Klansperson. Nonsexist title advocated by the Grand Dragon of the Ku Klux Klan, according to William Lambdin's *Doublespeak Dictionary*.

MUSIC. (or **MUUSIC**). In 1969 when there was much criticism of the military-industrial complex, some members of Congress tried to get people interested in a new name, MUSIC, for Military University, Union, Science, Industrial Complex. For a while supporters of the new name used lines like "Some critics are out of tune with 'MUSIC' " to get the idea across, but it never caught on.

Newsperson. In his *American Usage and Style: The Consensus,* Roy H. Copperud terms this the "most obnoxious" of the new neuter words as it replaces reporter, which is "as asexual as it can be."

Noctician. A failed attempt to give the night guard higher status.

Norseperson. A Norseman desexed. Former Carter speech-writer Walter Shapiro told of its use in an article in the *Washington Post:* "In 1977, Carter speech-writers, in a puckish gesture, celebrated the anniversary of Leif Ericsson's discovery of America by referring to him as a 'gallant Norseperson' in an official proclamation. Reportedly Carter . . . was not amused."

Nova. Name of a type of Chevrolet that is now marketed in the Spanish-speaking world as the *Caribe*. This change was made after sluggish initial sales were traced to the fact that *no va* means "does not go" in Spanish.

Per. Stand-in for *him* and *her*, derived from *person*. Novelist Marge Piercy used this word in per book *Woman on the Edge of Time*.

Personhole. Term created in 1978 by the Woonsocket, Rhode Island, city council as part of a drive to eliminate supposedly sexist language. It replaced manhole in Woonsocket's official circles.

Pn. Short form of *person* to replace Mr., Mrs., and Ms. It was suggested in the early 1970s by *Everywoman* editor Varda One, who feels we should all be addressed as *Person*. Pn. is pronounced *person* just as Mr. is pronounced *mister*.

Product safety campaign. Term that General Motors attempted to introduce in 1972 as a replacement for *recall*. A GM press release stated that ". . . customers are being notified about three separate product safety campaigns affecting approximately 6,000 vehicles."

Rockoon. A balloon-launched rocket, an idea from the late 1950s whose time has yet to come.

Sanitarians. One of a number of failed attempts to give the busboy (or girl) an upgraded name. Sanitarian was the suggestion of the Wisconsin Restaurant Association in the late 1950s. At about the same time, the Chicago Restaurant Association plumped for *table-service man*. Others that have been suggested: *waiter assistant, restaurant porter,* and *service aide.*

Spose. Term suggested by several readers of *Saturday Review* for two people living together. It comes from the oft-asked question "'Spose they'll ever get married?"

Thon. A suggested third-person genderless pronoun. William Zinsser, in his book *On Writing Well*, wrote, "Maybe I don't speak for the average American, but I very much doubt that thon wants that word in thons language or that thon would use it thonself."

Timmie. Name derived from the French *in time* and suggested by Mrs. Gordon Corbett of Anchorage, Alaska, in the pages of *Saturday Review*. "Now," she wrote, "I can refer to the beloved partners of our children as our own dear Timmies." Along with the aforementioned *spose*, other suggestions sent to *Saturday Review* included: *co-vivante, with-live, shackmate,* and *grynnfink*, which was composed from leftover Scrabble letters.

While others strive to create the right word, it would appear that the term with the best chance of survival is *posslq*, a term invented by the Census Bureau. Posslq (pronounced *poss-ill-que*) is an acronym for Person of Opposite Sex Sharing Living Quarters. The term was made famous by CBS poet-in-residence Charles Osgood, who used it as the subject of a poem that began with the line,

There's nothing that I wouldn't do
If you would be my posslq.

None other than Ann Landers has deemed the word ". . . so simple to pronounce, so non-judgmental and pleasing to the ear." She adds that it is easier on parents than "this person I'm living with."

Waitron. Neutral term suggested for *waiter* and *waitress.*

Womure. Manure. One of a number of new genderless words seriously suggested by Temple University Professor James F. Adams as substitutions for words in which *man* appears. Womure has yet to take off. Neither have *womic* for *manic* nor *womuscript* for *manuscript.*

20

Formations

A Sampling of Shapes and Conditions

One of the most extensive groups of words in the language is that describing the shapes of things. Displayed here are words that capture my fancy and represent less than a tenth of my total "shape" collection.

A logical question that suggests itself is: Who actually uses these words? The answer is that they are used by specialists in certain areas of science and medicine. Dermatologists, for instance, talk of *filiform warts* and *foliaceous growth*.

Acinaciform. Scimitar-shaped.
Acinform. Clustered like grapes.
Actinoid. In the shape of a star.
Aduncous. Bent like a hook.
Aliform. Wing-like.
Ampullaceous. Bottle-shaped; possessing a round body.
Anfractuous. Full of twists and turns.

Anguiform. Snake-shaped; not to be confused with *anguilliform,* which means eel-shaped.

Arcuate. Bow-shaped.

Auriform. Ear-shaped. *Balanoid.* Acorn-shaped.

Belemnoid. Dart-shaped; not to be confused with *beloid* or *belonoid,* which are respectively arrow-shaped and needle-shaped.

Bicaudate. Two-tailed.

Bicipital. Having two heads.

Biomorphic. Free-form; shaped as a living form. It is the opposite of *geometric.*

Boluliform. Sausage-shaped.

Bursiform. Pouch-shaped.

Calathiform. Cup-shaped.

Calceiform. Slipper-shaped—pronounced *cal-see-a-form.* It is not to be confused with *calciform,* which is pebble-shaped.

Campanulate. Bell-shaped.

Carbunculoid. Shaped like a large boil or carbuncle.

Caricous. Fig-like.

Claviform. Club-shaped.

Clithridiate. Keyhole-shaped.

Cordate. Heart-shaped.

Coroniform. In the shape of a crown.

Cristiform. Crest-shaped.

Cucumiform. Cucumber-shaped.

Decussate. X-shaped; intersecting.

Dendriform. Tree-shaped.

Dipterous. Having two wings

Dodecagon. A twelve-sided form.

Dolioform. Barrel-shaped.

Echinoid. Like a sea urchin.

Ensiform. Sword-shaped.

Erose. Uneven and irregular. Rhymes with heroes.

Eruciform. Like a caterpillar.

Esquamate. Without scales.

Evase. Wider at the top; in the shape of a vase.

Falcate. Crescent-shaped.

Favaginous. Like a honeycomb.

Filiform. In the shape of a thread.

Fissilingual. Fork-tongued.

Flabellate. Fan-shaped.

Foliaceous. Leaf-like; leafy.

Forticate. Scissor-like; deeply forked.

Fucoid. Like seaweed.

Fulgurous. Lightning-shaped; charged with lightning.

Furciferous. Fork-shaped.

Fusiform. Spindle-shaped.

Geniculated. Having knee-like joints.

Glabrous. Smooth; bald.

Guttiform. Shaped like a drop.

Hamiform. Hook-shaped.

Harengiform. Herring-shaped.

Hederiform. Shaped like ivy.

Helicoid. Screw-shaped.

Hexagram. In the shape of the Star of David.

Hordeiform. In the shape of a grain of barley. Pronounced *hore-dee-form.*

Hypsiloid. Like the Greek letter *upsilon;* V-shaped.

Incanous. Covered with soft white hair.

Infundibular. Funnel-shaped.

Janiform. Having two faces, like the Roman god Janus.

Lamelliform. Like a thin plate in form.

Lanceolate. Tapered to a point at either end, as with certain leaves.

Lanuginous. Covered with soft downy hair.

Latirostrous. Broad-beaked.

Linguiform. Tongue-shaped.

Lunette. Anything shaped like a half-moon.

Mammose. Breast-shaped.

Margaritaceous. Pearl-like.

Marmoreal. Marble-like; cold and white.

Moniliform. Segmented like a string of beads.

Moriform. Mulberry-shaped.

Muriform. Resembling or suggesting the pattern of a brick wall, such as certain cellular tissue.

Napiform. Turnip-shaped.

Nummular. Like a little coin.

Obconic. Pear-shaped.

Obrotund. Round, but squashed down on the top and bottom.

Oriform. Mouth-shaped.

Ostreophagous. Oyster-shaped.

Palmate. Shaped like a human hand.

Pandurate. Fiddle-shaped.

Papilionaceous. Butterfly-shaped.

Paradigitate. Having an equal number of fingers on each hand. It can also be applied to toes.

Pectinate. Comb-like; having teeth like a comb.

Pedimanous. Having feet in the shape of hands, as is true of monkeys.

Pemphigoid. Bubble-shaped, bubble-like.

Penniform. Having the form of a feather. If this seems to be a word not often used, considered the cases of *bipenniform, demipenniform,* and *semipenniform.* None of these are to be confused with *pinniform,* which means shaped like a pin *or* feather.

Piliform. Thread-shaped.

Pineal. Pineapple-shaped.

Pisiform. Shaped like a pea or peas.

Plataleiform. Spoon-billed.

Plicate. Folded in the manner of a fan.

Pulvinate. Swelling or bulging like a cushion.

Punctiform. Like a point or dot.

Pyriform. Pear-shaped.

Quincunx. An arrangement of five things so that one is in each corner and in the middle of a square. The term is sometimes used to describe the arrangement of plants or shrubs in a garden.

Remiform. Shaped like an oar.

Reniform. Kidney-shaped.

Resofincular. Resembling a wire hanger, a coinage of Lewis Burke Frumkes that first appeared in his 1976 *Harper's* article, "A Volley of Words."

Retiform. Net-shaped.

Rhinocerial. Very heavy, as a rhinoceros.

Samariform. In the shape of a winged seed pod.

Scalpriform. Chisel-shaped.

Scaphoid. Boatshaped.

Sciuroid. Like a squirrel or a squirrel's tail.

Scrotiform. Pouch-shaped.

Scutiform. Shield-shaped.

Selliform. Saddle-shaped.

Sigmoidal. Curved in two directions.

Siliquiform. In the form of a small pod or husk.

Sinorous. Snake-like.

Soleiform. Slipper-shaped.

Sphenoid. Wedge-shaped.

Squaliform. Shark-shaped.

Squamous. Scaly or full of scales.

Stelliform. Star-shaped.

Stirious. Resembling icicles.

Strombuliform. Like a screw or spinning top.

Subulate. Awl-shaped.

Sudiform. Stake-shaped.

Sycosiform. Fig-shaped.

Tauriform. Bull-shaped.

Totipalmate. With fully webbed toes.

Unciform. J-shaped.

Undecagon. An eleven-sided form.

Unifoliate. Having one leaf.

Urceolate. Pitcher-shaped. Pronounced *your-sea-a-lit.*

Utriform. Like a leather bottle.

Velutinous. Having a soft and velvet-like surface.

Vermiform. Having the shape of a worm.

Verruciform. Wart-shaped.

Virgate. Wand-shaped; long and slender.

Vulviform. V-shaped.

Xiphoid. Sword-shaped.

Zosteriform. Girdle-shaped.

Zygal. H-shaped.

Zygomorphous. Yoke-shaped.

21

Game Names

A Leisurely Volley of Terms from Playground and Playing Field

Ape hanger. Extremely tall handlebar on a bicycle or motorcycle.

Aunt Emma. Croquet term for a man or woman who wastes time and talent playing in a dull and conservative manner.

Baby split. In bowling, a split where either the 2 and 7 pins or the 3 and 10 pins are left standing. It is part of a rich collection of terms for bowling splits that includes the *Bedpost* (7 and 10 upright), *Bucket* (leaving 2-4-5-8 or 3-5-6-9), *Cincinnati* (8-10 split), *Four Horsemen* (1-2-4-7 or 1-3-6-10), *Half Worcester* (leaving either the 3 and 9 or the 2 and 8 standing), *Spread Eagle* (2-3-4-6-7-10 split), and *Woolworth* (5 and 10 standing). While it is obvious how the Woolworth got its name (5 and 10), the *Kresge* (one name for the 5 and 7 split) is harder to figure out.

Baff. Billiards. To hit the table before hitting the ball. In golf, *baffing* is striking the ground immediately behind the ball.

Baize. Billiards. The green material that covers the table.

Baltimore chop. Baseball. A ball that is hit just in front of the plate and bounces high enough to allow the runner to make it to first.

Besom. The curler's broom, used to aid the curling stone move down the ice. Pronounced *bee-zum*.

Birling. Log rolling on water. The logger's contest.

Blowout. The proper name for those party table items that unfurl when blown into.

Boondocking. Tiddleywinker's term for sending an opponent's wink or winks far from the cup.

Burger. Skateboarding. A bad bruise or scrape.

Caber. Heavy tree trunk used in the Scottish sport of cabertossing, which is throwing tree trunks for distance.

Canogganing. Winter activity in which one races downhill in a canoe instead of skis. It ranks with *Husskiing* (in which teams of huskies pull individuals on skis) as the most obscure of the winter sports.

Cat. A draw in ticktacktoe.

Cesta. Jai alai. The player's wicker basketglove.

Cleek. The number one iron in golf. Cleek is one of a number of old names for clubs that have been replaced by sternly descriptive standard terms. *Niblick* is the now seldom-heard original name for the sand wedge, and the *brassie* was a wooden club with slightly more loft than a driver. It was commonly shod with a brass plate to protect the wood from abrasions.

Crease. Hockey. The rectangular area in front of the goal that cannot be entered by offensive players without the puck. In cricket, it is the line behind which a batsman must stand when the ball is being bowled at the wicket he is defending.

Crotch. Handball/Racquetball/Squash. The intersection of two court playing surfaces, such as a wall and the floor.

Cuban fork ball. Baseball. A suspected spitball.

Cup of coffee. Baseball. Short time in the major leagues by a minor league player.

Dormie. Golf. A player who leads by as many holes as are left to play, for example, a four-stroke lead after the fourteenth hole.

Double Dutch. Name for the jump rope action that takes place when two turners turn two ropes inward in an eggbeater motion.

Dumpers. Sometimes called *dump words*, they are special words used to clear one's Scrabble rack when it is burdened with too many vowels. *Idiom, melee, bureau,* and *apogee* are well-known and commonly used dumpers. Advanced dumpers, however, use such words as *oribi, aalii, balata,* and *hoopoe.* One would be hard-pressed to come up with a better dumper than *cooee,* which any 17-pound dictionary will tell you is "a prolonged shrill cry used as a signal by Australian aborigines."

Eeph. Lacrosse. Scooping the ball up off the ground and passing it. Rhymes with beef.

Eephus ball. Baseball. An unorthodox pitch popularized by Pittsburgh Pirate Truett "Rip" Sewell in the 1940s. The ball floated high in the air and then fell through the strike zone. Most modern players call it the *blooper.*

The word *eephus* was created by outfielder Maurice Van Robays lest this odd pitch remain nameless. Only one batter, Ted Williams, ever hit one of Sewell's eephus balls for a home run.

Eggies. Borrowed marbles or the act of borrowing same.

Enders. Those who turn the rope in jump rope games.

Endo. Motorcycling. When driver and machine flip end-over-end.

Eskimo roll. A complete rollover in a kayak—that is, into and under the water and up again.

Exotic wagering. Racetrack term for any type of bet other than win, place, or show.

Farthees. Game played with baseball cards in which the object is to see who can flip a card the farthest.

Fizgig. A loud, hissing firework.

Fletch. Archery. To put feathers on an arrow.

Girandole. Cluster of fireworks or water jets.

Glissade. Moving on snow or ice without skis.

Go-devil. A homemade vehicle made by fastening roller skate wheels at either end of a narrow piece of wood with a wooden box on the front end.

Histing. Raising one's hand from the ground when shooting in marbles.

Honda. The eye at the end of the rodeo performer's rope through which the other end of the rope is passed to form a loop.

Hoppo-bumpo. Traditional name for the game played by hopping around on one leg, trying to spill your opponent using folded arms as a bumper bar.

Hot pepper. Fast turning in jump rope. In *Jump Rope!*, Peter L. Skolnik points to a number of synonyms for this term including *bullets, hot peas, hot peas with butter, pepper, vinegar,* and *whipping.* To jump as fast as you can until you miss is the *skin,* and *really* fast turning is *red hot bricks.*

Hunching. Moving one's hand forward when shooting in marbles.

J'adoubovitz. Chess. A player who annoys his opponent by making constant small adjustments to the pieces. It comes from the French *j'adoube,* for "I adjust."

Jaws. In croquet, the entrance to the uprights of a hoop.

Kimmies. One of a number of names for the target marbles in marble games. Besides kimmies, they are also known as *dibs, ducks, hoodles, stickers, immies, peewees, mibs, miggs, commies, crockies,* and *commons.*

Kip. Gymnastics. The move that takes one from a hanging position under the bar to a suppported position on the bar.

Kitchen. Shuffleboard. The minus-10 section of the scoring area.

Lagger. Hopscotch. The pebble or twig tossed in the squares. It is also known as a *peever.*

Lazarus. Pinball term for a ball that drains (seems lost) but then bounces back into play.

Meat hand. Baseball. The hand without a glove. Players rarely used their meat hand on a hard-hit ball.

Mication. "Shooting" or throwing fingers, such as children do when picking odd or even to see who starts a game.

Naismith's formula. Hiking. Common method of estimating the length of a hike. According to the formula, you allow one hour for every three miles to be covered and add an additional hour for every 2,000 feet climbed.

Nerfing bar. Car racing. A bumper that protects the wheels of one car from coming into contact with those of another.

Nock. Archery. The groove at the feather end of an arrow into which the bowstring fits.

Nurdling. Tiddleywinkese for sending an opponent's wink too close to the pot to score easily.

Pantsed. Having your pants taken off against your will. It is a childish prank in the same class with being *teepeed,* which is the business of covering someone's house with toilet paper (t.p., hence teepeed).

Pea. The small wooden ball inside a referee's whistle.

Petticoat. Archery. The white rim of a traditional archer's target. You get no points if you hit the petticoat.

Photon. Racquetball. Powerful shot.

Pips. The spots on dominos and dice. It is also the name for the tiny pimple-like projections on some table tennis paddles and the spots on cards.

Pone. The cardplayer who cuts the cards for the dealer. The pone is usually seated to the right of the dealer.

Razzor. A device, usually made of rubber, that one blows into to create a low, mean noise. Pronounced *razer*.

Schmerltz. A ball housed in a tube sock that is thrown by twirling and releasing the end of the sock. It is caught by the tail. The Schmerltz is one of the many new games advocated by the New Games Foundation, which deemphasizes winning and losing in favor of play for the sake of play. Other New Games include: *Tweezli-Whop,* a form of pillow-fighting; *Fraha,* a cooperative paddle game in which the players try to keep the ball in the air; and *Hagoo,* a game in which a gauntlet of players works to make a person laugh.

Sclaff. Golf. Stroke in which the club hits the ground before hitting the ball.

Scoon. To skip across the water; the act of skipping a flat rock across the water.

Serpentine. Coiled colored strips of paper that are thrown and unfurled at weddings, parties, and other festive occasions. It is sometimes called a *streamer.*

Sights. Billiards. The diamonds on the table rail.

Sitzmark. Skiing. The mark made by a skier who has fallen over backward.

Sling. Badminton. Carrying the shuttle on the face of the racket as opposed to hitting it cleanly. *Slinging* constitutes a foul.

Snooger. In marbles, a close miss.

Snookered. In pocket billiards, to be able to shoot the cue ball directly at an object·ball; stymied.

Sole. In golf, the flat bottom of the club head.

Spillikin. A small wooden peg used to keep score in games.

Squidger. Shooter in tiddledywinks

Squoping. In tiddledywinks, freeing your opponent's winks by putting one of your winks on top of his.

Tappy. In tennis, a light stroke; a poor serve.

Taw. One of several names for the shooter in marbles. Shooters are also known as *bowlers* and *moonies.*

Tennist. One who plays tennis. An old term that is again creeping into coverage of the game.

Thimblerig. To cheat with simple sleight of hand, especially by means of three shells or thimbles and a pea or other small object that is placed under one of the shells and moved around.

Tuck. Diving. The common move in which divers bend their knees and press their thighs against their chest with their hands around their shins.

Void. Along with *nub* and *lock*, one of three major terms associated with jigsaw puzzles. The void is the space into which the rounded projection or *nub* is placed to form a *lock*.

Waffle face. Racquetball. To hit another player in the face with the racquet.

Waggle. The flourish of a golf club prior to the upward swing.

Whelm. Whelm, also known as *release*, or *hatch*, is the first of nine flying disc flight periods, according to Dr. Stancil E. D. Johnson in his classic work, *Frisbee*. The other eight periods in their proper order: *wedge* (insertion), *well* (climb), *wax*, *waft (float)*, wane, waste, warp (turn), and *was* (touch).

Wheel sucker. Bike racing. One rider who uses the slipstream of another rider to conserve energy.

Woodpusher. Chess. Player of moderate (or worse) ability.

Yips. Golf. Pressure affecting players of that game. It is not to be confused with *yip*, another golfing term that means to hit the ball poorly when putting.

Hardware

A Chest of Tools and Such

Aberuncator. A long tool for pruning tall branches. Two blades—one rigid and one movable—are attached to the end of a pole. The movable blade is worked by a rope. As common as these apparatuses are, few people call them by their proper name. Some insist this is an *averuncator*.

Allen wrench. A nonadjustable L-shaped tool for locking screws and set-screws. Either of the hexagonally shaped ends of the Allen wrench can be used.

Bail. The wire handle on a bucket.

Bail rolls. The two small rubber rollers on the bar above the roller of a typewriter.

Becket. A rope grip or handle.

Bibcock. Faucet with a bent-down nozzle, also known as a *bibb* or *bib*. Outside faucets for gardening are practically always bibcocks.

Bilbo. Iron bars with sliding fetters used to shackle the feet of prisoners. From Bilbao, Spain, and its ironworks.

Bubbler. The metal portion of a drinking fountain out of which the water comes.

Cannel. Bevel on the edge of a chisel.

Chatter mark. Mark left by a tool on the surface of an object; drill or saw scars.

Chimb. The rim of a barrel. The final *b* is silent. It is sometimes called a *chime*.

Clevis bolt. A bolt with a hole drilled through the thread end so that a cotter pin can be added for extra holding power.

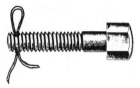

Cramp. Clamp with a movable part that can be screwed in to hold things together.

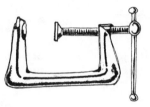

Dibble. Pointed garden tool for boring holes for seeds, seedlings, and bulbs. A *foot dibble* is a dibble that is pushed into the earth with your foot.

Eolith. Tool shaped by natural forces and used by primitive humans.

Escutcheon. Decorative metal plate around a keyhole, drawer pull, or door-knob.

Eye. The hole in the head of an ax or hammer that receives the handle.

Fid. A sharp-pointed tool with a handle for such jobs as making holes in leather; sometimes called a *belt awl.*

Flang. The double-pointed pick of the miner; also known as a *beele.*

Froe. Tool used for splitting or "riving" shingles from wood. It has a heavy blade attached at a right angle to a wooden handle.

Grab. The business end of a crane.

Gusset. Triangular brace plate used to reinforce corners in a structure.

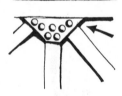

Harp. The frame on a lamp that sticks up around the bulb and holds the lampshade in place.

Helve. The handle of a hammer, ax, or similar tool.

Ironmongery. Hardware store in England.

Kerf. The channel or groove cut by a saw, ax, or knife as a marking or guide. A kerf cut in a tree indicates where it is to be cut down.

Nab. The projecting box into which a door bolt goes to hold the door.

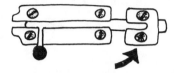

Paper bail. Bar across the top of the typewriter that holds the paper in place.

Peavey. A lumberjack's tool named after its inventor, Joseph Peavey, a Maine blacksmith. It is a strong pole five to six feet in length fitted with a steel pike and adjustable steel hook at the end. It is used for turning and maneuvering logs.

Peen. The rounded end of the head of a hammer. As a verb, to rivet, stretch, or cinch by hitting with the peen of a hammer.

Pintle. The vertical post that runs through the two halves of most door hinges; also, the bolt or hook that attaches a rudder to the stern of a boat.

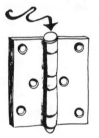

Plunger. The button a phone receiver rests on that connects and disconnects the phone. Some phones, especially older models, have two plungers.

Pulp-hook. Logger's short hook for handling smaller pieces of wood.

Rifflers. Very small wood rasps with rough, pointed, curved ends of various shapes. They are used for finishing details and getting into tight spots.

Scutch. Masonry tool used to cut away and finish rough or broken edges.

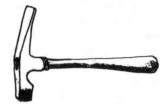

Snath. A scythe handle. A *scythe* is only the blade.

Sprue. The channel through which metal is poured when making a casting.

Stadda. A double-bladed handsaw used in cutting teeth in combs.

Swage. To shape metal by hammering against a form or anvil.

Tang. The thin handle of a file; the thin end of a knife blade that fits into the handle.

Theodolite. Surveyor's telescopic measuring device or *transit*, usually mounted on a tripod.

Toenailing. To drive a nail at such an angle that it penetrates a second piece of wood.

Trammel. Trammel is one of those remarkable words with a number of meanings. It is at once a net, a contrivance used to hold pots and pans over a fire, an instrument for drawing ellipses, a shackle, a device for measuring the necks of animals, and more. For this reason, and because it has such a nice no-nonsense ring to it, trammel is an excellent word to bluff with. If, for instance, someone buys a questionable hunk of metal at an auction, you might wish to comment: "That is one of the finest trammels I have ever seen, and that man got it for only $32."

Traveler. Hand-held tool with a movable disk, used by blacksmiths and wheelwrights to measure with. It is especially handy for measuring the circumference of a circle. It looks like a pizza slicer.

Warren. A heart-shaped hoe.

Water breaker. A hose attachment that creates its own spray pattern. Unlike nozzles, water breakers disperse rather than concentrate the flow water.

Worm. The thread of a screw.

23

Human Conditions

*A Congregation of Beliefs,
Customs, and States*

Adamitism. Nakedness for religious reasons.

Adelphogamy. Marriage in which brothers have a common wife or group of wives.

Agathism. Belief that everything works toward an ultimate good, no matter what the short-term consequences.

Allotheism. The worship of strange gods.

Androlepsy. The government of one nation seizing citizens of another to enforce some right. An obscure term, it came into its own during the Iranian crisis.

Anomie. A situation in which society is not governed by the norms that generally regulate behavior; period of upheaval and disorganization.

Anthropolatry. The worship of a human being as divine.

Anthropophusism. Giving God a human nature.

Autarky. State of national self-sufficiency; importing nothing.

Autolatry. Worship of oneself.

Bardolatry. Excessive worship of Shakespeare.

Bitheism. Belief in two gods, also *ditheism*.

Bourgeoisification. The acquisition of bourgeois characteristics.

135

Contumulation. Lying in the same tomb with another.

Couvade. A husband acting out the motions of childbirth while his wife is in labor. This custom was common in some American Indian tribes. Pronounced *coo-vad.*

Cryptarchy. Secret rule. This word should be in common use, given the number of Americans who believe that the Council on Foreign Relations, the Trilateral Commission, the Rockefellers, or some other force secretly run things.

Decumbency. The act of lying down.

Doulocracy. Government by slaves.

Eidolism. Belief in ghosts.

Eudemonism. The doctrine that makes well-being the ultimate goal of human action.

Eunomia. The state of being well governed.

Floromancy. The belief that flowers have feelings and will respond to kindness as well as cruelty.

Gerontocracy. Government by a council of elders; rule by old men.

Gynarchy. Government by women.

Hecatontarchy. Government by 100 people.

Heliolatry. Worship of the sun.

Henotheism. Belief in one god while not necessarily concluding that that is the only god. Pronounced *henna-theism.*

Hlonipa. A prohibition against saying the name of a dead person.

Hylozoism. The belief that all matter has life.

Hypergamy. The custom that allows a man—but not a woman—to marry one of lower social standing.

In-fare. A wedding reception held by the groom's family.

Inhumist. Referring to a society that buries its dead.

Jumboism. The admiration of things simply because of their largeness.

Kakistocracy. Government by the worst people.

Kleptocracy. Government by thieves.

Maffick. To celebrate with boisterous rejoicing and hilarious behavior. Named after the wild celebration that took place in England after the siege of Mafeking was raised by British troops on May 17, 1900.

Malism. Belief that the world and its inhabitants are essentially evil.

Mariolotry. Excessive worship of the Virgin Mary.

Mechanomorphism. The belief that God is a mechanical force and that the universe is governed by natural law.

Misosophy. Hatred of wisdom.

Monopsony. A situation in which a person or group is the only entity on the demand side of a market. For instance, a collector of used cat-food cans might qualify as a monopsonist in that field.

Moramentia. Absolute amorality.

Noyade. Mass execution by drowning, believed to be an innovation of Revolutionary France. Pronounced *nwayadd*.

Oligopsony. A market in which so few individuals or institutions are involved that the action of one of them can affect price.

Paedarchy. Government by children.

Pancosmism. Belief that nothing exists beyond the material universe.

Pantisocracy. Situation in which all are truly equal and all govern; a Utopian ideal.

Pelagianism. Belief in the basic goodness of nature, including human nature. It is named for Pelagius, a heretic of the fifth century.

Physitheism. Giving God a physical shape.

Pseudogyny. The adoption of the woman's name by a man at the time of marriage.

Ptochocracy. Government by the poor. Pronounced *tock-ock-racy*.

Punaluan. Pertaining to a group marriage in which a number of sisters marry a number of brothers.

Sororate. A custom that obliges or permits a dead woman's sister to marry the widower. The male equivalent is *levirate*.

Squassation. A form of punishment in which the victim had his arms tied, feet heavily weighted, and was jerked up and down on a rope.

Suteeism. The practice of the widow immolating herself on her husband's funeral pyre, a custom once observed by certain Hindu women.

Teknonymy. The practice, noted among certain primitive peoples, of naming a parent after the name of his or her child.

Theanthropism. Giving human characteristics to God or the gods. Giving divine characteristics to humans.

Timocracy. The ideal state in which the love of honor is the ruling principle.

Trigamy. The state of having one more spouse than a bigamist.

Tritheism. Belief in three gods; belief that the Trinity consists of three gods.

Ultimogeniture. A system of inheritance whereby the youngest son or daughter is given property or title. The commoner system whereby the eldest inherits is called *primogeniture*.

Uxorilocal. Living with the wife's family.

Vivisepulture. The practice of burying people alive.

24

Journalese

A Decoder for Deciphering the News

As a fanatical consumer of news, I have been collecting terms that have become indiginous to that business. Here are some of the most important—identified and defined without further ado.

Activist. Not a bureaucrat.

Activity. TV weather word that means nothing, but sounds important. "We can expect some thunderstorm activity in the next 72 hours." Newspapers still refer to them as plain old thunderstorms.

Adult. Dirty, as applied to bookstores, magazines, and movies.

Ailing. When applied to a world leader or important politician, ailing means dying; but when applied to a professional athlete, it usually refers to a torn rotator cuff or pulled Achilles' tendon (two ailments it appears only come to those in professsional sports). It is also what morning newspapers say about afternoon dailies. Banks and S&Ls that are in deep trouble are known as "ailing thrifts."

Alleged. Word used by people in the news business to prevent lawsuits and drive the rest of us crazy. "The alleged murder took place as the victim was shot in the back."

Arguably. Impossible to substantiate, as in "He is arguably the best National League left-handed pitcher ever from Connecticut with three consonants in his middle name."

Array. Used when the reporter hasn't the faintest idea of how many. "Hay fever sufferers can now choose from an array of drugs and treatments."

Backlog. That which happens to the caseload in courts. Any reporter knows that on a slow day a story can be patched together to fit the classic headline: "Judge Complains of Rising Case Backlog." See also, *Logjam.*

Band-aid solution. Used when a solution does not work because not enough money has been spent. If more money is spent, the requisite cliche is to state that the problem will not go away "by throwing money at it."

Beautiful people. Plain folks with lots of money.

Behemoth. Adjective exclusively reserved for describing troubled nuclear power plants. "Seagull droppings cripple behemoth nuclear plant."

Bible-quoting. Prudish activist, as in this Associated Press story lead from July 20, 1985: "Two Bible-quoting mothers who claim that rock n' roll videos promote sex, drugs and suicide have won a battle against MTV, the popular 24-hour music video channel on cable television."

Blue ribbon. Applied to any panel or commission containing a former governor of Pennsylvania.

Brash. Said of those who can only talk about themselves: egocentric.

Buffet. What high winds and hurricanes do to piers and shore communities.

Bureaucrat. Term used to describe a public servant when the story is about red tape, excessive regulation, or anything else negative. The same person becomes a *civil servant* in a positive story.

By all accounts. Term used when details are sketchy and no direct quote can be found.

Cannot be independently confirmed. Said of rumor that is so juicy that it cannot be left out of the story.

Cannot be ruled out. Term used with the highest grade of pure space-filling speculation. Example: "Although a Nixon movement in 1992 cannot be ruled out . . ."

Caring. Not outwardly mean or rotten.

Claimed responsibility. Confessed to a crime, often a heinous one involving more than one death. "A terrorist group today claimed responsibility for taking the lives of 54 innocent people." Terrorists also "execute" their victims, while garden-variety thugs "murder" them.

Clearly troubled. Said of people who are in trouble, but refuse to say so to the press. "The prisoner was noncommital but appeared clearly troubled."

Coming of age. Term used when a newspaper has finally gotten around to writing on a subject, but has no news lead for it save the vague notion that it has come of age. "Woolen Mittens Come of Age," for instance.

Conflict of interest. Nice way of saying, "This really stinks but no indictments have been made."

Conscience. Name for a person who has taken a moral position that agrees with the writer's. If the conscience raises his or her voice a lot, the term becomes *outraged conscience.*

Courage. Universal attribute of people with problems or disabilities who have not attempted suicide. It is also used to describe movie and rock stars who have persisted in the face of minor setbacks: "Despite a failed face lift and the onset of middle age acne, she mustered the courage to continue her career."

Craggy. Said of a face that would stop a clock; ET-like.

Crippled. A ship with a hole in it or a nuclear power plant with serious problems, such as the "crippled Soviet nuclear plant at Chernobyl."

Crusty. Obnoxious

Cure-all. See *Panacea.*

Czar. Bureaucrat who has been given extra authority temporarily. "Pentagon Appoints Mess Hall Czar."

Darker corners of the mind. Obligatory cliche in articles about serious poets. "In her poems about jack-o-lanterns, she explores the darker corners of the mind." It is also used a lot on National Public Radio.

Densely wooded area. Where most "badly decomposed" bodies are found; also target for small planes in trouble.

Diminutive. Short and unassuming; a real mouse (compare with *Peppery*).

Draconian. Term trotted out by the press to describe the Gramm-Rudman deficit-reduction law. The adjective, for that which is cruel or exceedingly harsh, comes from Draco who was a legislator of ancient Athens. "Draco," wrote William Power in the *Wall Street Journal*, "seems to get more press some days than Sen. Ernest Hollings, the law's third sponsor."

Easy answers. See **Panacea.**

Ebullient. Crazy; off the wall.

Eleventh hour. When reprieves arrive on death row and when strikes are averted (after marathon bargaining sessions).

Embattled. Term applied to a subject who tries to get other people to sign petitions.

Emotional. Required adjective for "reunion" and "homecoming."

Ethnically diverse. Obligatory term for all street fairs and urban events where you can buy both egg rolls and tacos.

Execution-style. Shot at close range; hence, a nice way of saying that the reporter on the scene got sick.

Exclusive. We think we were there first and/or nobody else was interested.

Exclusive footage. Anything shown on the 11 o'clock news that the other local channels didn't have on the 6 o'clock news. "Baby turtles hatch in zoo incubator. Exclusive footage on Eyewitness News at 11."

Exclusive interview. Not a press conference.

Explosive situation. TV. Nobody's been shot yet, but we have our cameras there.

Exude. Word paired with *charm* when describing a house in real estate sections. Often used to describe a new tract home with a few extras like a carport or a patio.

Feisty. Belligerent.

Fiercely independent. A descriptive term required by law to appear at least once in any personality profile. The fiercely independent has, invariably, "paid his/her dues."

Fine. Shorthand for "I like this book, play, or whatever."

Flawed. Used by critics in reviews in which they actually enjoyed the film, play, book, or whatever but feel compelled to say something negative lest their boss think that they have gone soft in the head and it is time for them to start covering zoning variance hearings. "Though flawed, it is the best daytime game show to debut in this decade."

Free-wheeling. Chaotic; confused. "In a free-wheeling interview the candidate lashed out against the Kremlin, frequent flier programs, diet colas, supermarket shopping carts with defective wheels, and the arms race."

Fundamental. That which affects the press. A line like "The issue posed is fundamental" is invariably followed by a discussion of freedom of the press, censorship, or copyright.

Gangland-style. Term for murders that involve one or more of the following elements: (1) a late-model car, (2) a victim seated in a barber chair, (3) a victim eating in an Italian restaurant, (4) gunmen wearing suits and shined shoes.

Glass and concrete. Words used to show writer's contempt for a building. "She went to work each morning at 9:00 in a soulless glass and concrete box."

Golfball. Unit of measurement for hailstones.

Goon. Term now tied to labor unions, as in the phrase, "labor goon mentality." There are, according to the papers, no corporate goons.

Grim task. Term used to describe the recovery of human remains.

Guns and butter. Without this metaphor, it would be very difficult for most journalists to write about the federal budget, which in recent years has tended to be typified as "more guns, less butter."

Guru. Any authority who has not made an ass of himself in the last six months, or, in the case of financial gurus, the last two weeks. It is seldom, if ever, applied to Indian wise men any more. Many gurus are in marketing, real estate, and advertising.

Hard charger. Tooth-grinder; person you would not want to sit next to on an airplane.

Hard-working. Plodding and dull.

Head of a pin. Place where thousands of pages of data will be stored in the future.

Heated exchange. Argument; press conference attended by Sam Donaldson.

High tech. Originally applied to that which was new, from California, and contained silicon. It is now applied to everything from kitchen gadgets to electronic wristwatches.

Hot line. Any telephone number with a live person at the other end. "The mayor has set up a hot line for citizens to use to report the locations of uncovered dumpsters."

Human error. Error not made by an animal.

Humanitarian aid. Supplies sent to a warring party who you sympathize with. The other side gets plain old-fashioned aid or worse, "aid and comfort."

Hustings. Word trotted out every time a major electoral campaign gets underway. It is an archaic way of saying that someone is out making speeches.

Hype. Publicity that the reporter does not like. The double-whammy comes when the term "so-called" is used with hype. "The so-called advantage of compact discs is hype," for example, is a line from a recent issue of *Forbes*.

Incarcerated. Jailed.

Ill-fated. Anything that has crashed and whose wreckage is now being "sifted through by federal investigators."

Impromptu. Disorganized, confused, ill-advised. "In an impromptu airport press conference, the congressman defended his two-week, mid-winter, fact-finding trip to Bermuda as essential to national security."

Innocent victim. Not a drug dealer or terrorist.

In depth. Too long; wordy when applied to print. In TV news the term applies to any story lasting more than 90 seconds.

In recent memory. Everyone else has gone home, the library is locked, and this is the only thing I can think of that compares to the situation at hand.

In the shadow of. Where the spouses of the rich and famous stand—Mr. Thatcher, for example.

Indefatigable. A real pest; someone who calls the reporter at home during the World Series to complain about something. "An indefatigable defender of the rights of flatworms, Jones disrupted a council meeting last night to demand the town dump be declared a sanctuary for 'animals without backbones.'"

Inevitable. This is what we have been saying for six months.

Informed sources. Usually, other reporters.

Inside the Beltway. Term used by Washington correspondents to refer to themselves and the people they lunch with. *Outside the Beltway* refers to the rest of the country where people keep abandoned cars and old appliances in their backyards. The Beltway is a circular highway ringing Washington, D.C., where huge trucks regularly overturn.

Interrupted by applause. Scoring system for important speeches. "The State of the Union address was interrupted by applause on six different occasions, comparing unfavorably to last year's near record of eleven."

Irreverent. Swears and shouts a lot.

Job action. Inaction.

Junket. Free trip to which the reporter was not invited. It is often applied to members of Congress who insist that these are "fact-finding missions."

Junta. Example of a word whose pronunciation radio and television broadcasters decided to change. For decades it was *hunta*, but starting in the early 1980s the silent *j* became a hard *j*. This group, known as the "Junta Junta," had been so successful that it launched the Uranus and Halley's Comet conspiracies of late 1985 and early 1986. Now everybody is saying "your-in-us" and "hal-ease" instead of "your-anus" and "hay-lees." These conspiracies are not only meant to make the rest of us look like fools when we say "hunta" at a party, but are motivated by other factors as well. Uranus was changed to keep broadcasters from giggling in front of a live mike, while the Halley's campaign was mounted to distract us from the fact the comet was to be the biggest visual flop since Comet Kohoutek.

Labor of love. The province of eccentrics and borderline crazies. "His campaign to save old outhouses is strictly a labor of love."

Land of contrasts. Said of all foreign countries in travel pieces. Most of these countries also feature a "blend of the old and the new."

Larger truth. The exclusive preserve of journalists who invoke this concept after a few facts have been mangled. Writing on this idea in a 1984 *Time* essay, Roger Rosenblatt said, "When journalists hear journalists claim a 'larger truth' they really ought to go for their pistols. The *New Yorker's* Alastair Reid said the holy words last week: 'A reporter might take liberties with the factual circumstances to make the larger truth clear.' "

Little-known. Used when a reporter is showing off and saying, "Here is something I know, but you don't." Example: "This violates the provisions of a little-known law that prohibits the reuse of cat food cans." See also, and compare with *Obscure*.

Log jam. Term used with litigation (courtroom log jam) and lawmaking (legislative log jam) exclusively. The last time it was used to describe a pile-up of real logs was when Harry Truman was in the White House.

Long-awaited. Recently announced.

Major study. Term used for studies that get reported, even minor ones and just plain old-fashioned studies. Similarly, just about everything that shows up between the pages of the *New England Journal of Medicine* is termed *major*. Such studies are likely to contradict the findings of the last major report on the subject. (Quick! What did the last major study on the health effects of coffee have to say?)

Media baron. Ruppert Murdoch. One of a number of journalistic descriptors attached to well-known individuals. Others include:

Corporate raider (T. Boone Pickens)
Famed baby doctor (Benjamin Spock)
Fugitive financier (Robert Vesco)
Pleasure-loving guru (Bhagwan Shree Rajneesh)
Presidential assailant (John Hinkley, Jr.)
Principal owner (George Steinbrenner)
Soviet dissident (Andre Sakarov)

Media circus. Event that to the consternation of reporters with note pads has drawn more than one television camera. For television people, a media circus is any event that attracts Sam, Barbara, Tom, and Dan and features an open bar and free buffet.

Media representative. Term for reporter that is beginning to creep into print. This is just a guess, but the distinction between reporter and the new term may be that media representatives never spill soup on themselves.

Megaevent. Term for a lot of musicians and singers holding a charity concert. Live Aid and Farm Aid are two recent examples.

Mentioned. Common term used to describe a politician who is running hard for office. If you read that a person has been "mentioned" as a possible Senate candidate, this means that the reporter has already gotten eight phone calls, twelve press releases, and two personal visits from the eager office-seeker.

Mentor. At least one of these must be mentioned in all articles about successful women in business. They must also be able to "network" and "dress for success."

Message. Three or four ads, as in, "We now pause for this message."

Mild-mannered. Deeply introverted; mousey.

Militant. Fanatical.

Mishap. Something terrible with long-lasting consequences. Three-Mile Island and Chernobyl were both widely described as mishaps. Inexplicably, this milder term is displacing *disaster* as the word of choice. Meanwhile, disaster is being applied to plays that flop and baseball teams that lose three games in a row.

Modest. Term applied to most houses and many salaries. It has been observed that journalese has decreed that all houses are either *modest* or *stately*.

Momentum. Term applied to an athlete, team, or political candidate that is making progress, but tends to be mentioned only when it is being lost.

Much-maligned. Seldom-maligned. It is often applied to lesser vegetables in newspaper food sections, as in a *Washington Post* (May 1986) food feature on "The Much-Maligned Artichoke." Such articles always tell you that the artichoke, turnip, brussel sprout, or whatever is actually "far more versatile than you have known until now."

Multidisciplinary. What used to be called a *motley crew*; a mix of specialists.

Myth. A notion we have been pushing for years, but we are now ready to drop.

National disgrace. Subject of news feature; a problem.

Natural causes. What people die of in small towns. Large metropolitan dailies insist on specifying the fatal illness in obituaries.

Neo-. A voguish prefix for younger liberals and conservatives that means "not quite" or, as George Will has written, ". . . I suspect that splicing 'neo' to the sacred word 'conservative' is a form of flinching."

Nestled. Code word for rich. "The Gotrocks home is nestled in among horse farms and rolling estates." Poor folks homes tend to "stand starkly along lonesome dirt roads."

Never suffers fools gladly. Arrogant.

New breed. Said of any group of younger workers, professionals, or athletes. New breeds are usually 10 years younger and 20 pounds lighter than the old breed.

New Hampshire. Place that emerges for a few weeks every four years as a state exclusively populated by political analysts. "The merest bag boy at your typical Nashua supermarket checkout counter," wrote Meg Greenfield in the *Washington Post* at the end of the 1968 campaign, "knows how to toss off a newsy, compact analysis of his feelings about the contest that does credit to both himself and his state on the 6 o'clock news."

No explanation was offered. We forgot to ask; there was nobody there but the cleaning crew.

Not acceptable. Wrong.

Noted authority. Said of anyone whose name appears on the reporter's Roladex.

Obscure. Anything not known to the reporter before working on the story. "She was charged under the provisions of an obscure law making it illegal to bury people alive."

Observers. Cabbies, bartenders, bellhops, and camel-tenders to name a few. They are not to be confused with *thoughtful observers* or *veteran observers* listed below.

Once thought to be. This is what we were saying last Wednesday.

Only time will tell. Sign-off line beloved of television reporters covering summit conferences and unresolved municipal issues. "Will the town dump continue to be open on Sundays? Only time will tell."

Opportunity. A real mess. Bankruptcies, building collapses, and the like are usually seen as opportunities. Worse disasters are known as *challenges*.

Outdoorsman. Man with two or more shotguns and a chainsaw.

Outgoing. A happy drunk.

Outspoken. Very noisy; abusive; a pain in the neck.

Overcrowded. Crowded in articles about schools, mental institutions, and prisons. A group called the Unicorn Hunters, which issues periodic lists of words that should be banished, put it on its 1985 list. It was nominated by James Knight of Nashville, who said, "We have not had a simply crowded prison since 1982." Similarly, *overcommercialized* is becoming popular for things like Christmas, popular tourist areas, and the drive to raise money for large public celebrations.

Overkill. Originally a term applied to nuclear warfare, but now used for any excess no matter how piddling. The word has experienced overkill as it now is as likely to show up in the food pages ("iceburg lettuce overkill at the salad bar," for example) as in an article on the thermonuclear peril. The *Washington Times* recently carried an article on "sewer overkill."

Panacea. Journalistically linked to a negative modifier—"It is not a panacea, he warned." Ditto for *cure-all* and *easy answers* of which there are also none.

Parade. Red-flag word for people who have organized a march. Editors know that if they, say, call an anti-abortion or pro-choice march a *parade*, they will get a bagful of mail for their choice of words guaranteeing them fodder for the letters to the editor page. Other red-flag words that have a proven ability to generate large piles of mail include *apologist* (for spokesperson), and *drivel* (for information).

Paradise. Another word that is almost always used negatively. Articles about problems in places like Sweden, "new towns," Club Med, and Carribean nations are often titled "Paradise Lost" or "Trouble in Paradise." It is only used positively on the religion and travel pages.

Paradox. (1) Obligatory description of two facts that don't match up. "The paradox of a vegetarian big game hunter was not lost on this reporter." (2) Two doctors.

Peasant. People who inhabit the travel pages and who do folkloric things and live on "hearty soups." They do not exist in the United States or Canada, but populate the rest of the world.

Penultimate. This word actually means *next-to-last*, but is beginning to show up as a word for the ultimate in ultimate.

Peppery. Short and overbearing; a real pest (compare with *Diminutive*).

Pop icon. Rock singer who has been around for more than two years, once did something outlandish, and whose name has shown up in the *New York Times*. "Since releasing more than 2,000 lemmings on stage during a 1982 concert, he has become something of a pop icon."

Power broker. Minor politician or union official during an election year.

Precip. Term used by weatherpersons that is short for precipitation as in, "We will be experiencing some precip today." Precip is less awkward than "precipitation-type weather," which is what rain is occasionally called on WTOP, a Washington, D.C., all-news radio station.

Presumably. Code word telling the reader that the writer is about to take a wild-assed guess.

Professional. Virtually anybody who works for a living.

Progress. That which has been reported for years in the fight against the common cold. (This headline usually appears in conjunction with such perennials as "Old-fashioned Treatments for Arthritis Still Popular," "Headaches May Soon be History," and, if it is around New Year's Eve, "Local Experts Offer Hangover Cures.")

Prominent. All doctors, lawyers, bankers, and business executives; never bus drivers, mechanics, teachers, or people from a hundred other occupations.

Quality time. What working mothers spend with their families. Working fathers sit around in T-shirts and drink beer.

Quiet lives. What big city reporters say about the existences of people in small towns. Writers who really want to lay it on put the people in a corner, such as found in this *Washington Post* headline: "Sandy Hook: Residents Lead Quiet Lives in Forgotten Corner."

Quintessential. Word used by writers under 40. Writers over 40 use the word *typical* instead, unless they are describing small villages in New England where the word *quintessential* is obligatory.

Red ink. According to the business press, this is something that always comes in rivers, seas, and pools. It never seeps, but always gushes.

Reportedly. This means that we have no idea if this is so, but it sounds good.

Reputed. Known to all living things, as in the phrases "reputed Mafia kingpin," or "reputed underworld chieftian."

Revolution. Any minor change a reporter has been assigned to write about—"the packaging revolution," "the revolution at the supermarket checkout counter," etc. Not long ago, the Associated Press released a story on the paint roller, which was titled "The Revolutionary Roller: Choosing the Right Type and Size" by the *Washington Post.*

Rhode Island. Unit of measurement for forest fires.

Riveting. Said of potboiler novels involving submarines, nuclear weapons, or terrorists.

Rubenesque. Fat.

Ruddy-faced. Drunk.

Scandal-scarred. Term tied to Teamster's pension fund.

Segue. TV term for a transition. Segues often mean going from the scene of a disasterous flood to a line like "Next, the new faces of Knot's Landing."

Self-evident. I just figured this out myself. "The relationship between excessive dental flossing and antisocial behavior is self-evident."

Self-styled. Adjective used when the reporter is not pleased with the role adopted by a person or institution. It hints that the role is phoney. "Smith, a self-styled consumer advocate, has a lemon tattooed on his forehead." A letter to the editors, which appeared in the *Washington Post*, claimed that the newspaper's word processors are programmed to say "self-styled citizen's lobby" whenever Common Cause is mentioned in an article.

Seminal. Of more than passing interest.

Serial killer. Weak-kneed stand-in for mass murderer; Captain Crunch's assassin.

Sexuality. Sex.

Sexy. Term applied to packaging, stocks, ads, and almost anything else except for sex itself.

Signals. What diplomats send each other.

Simpler times. Fifteen years before writer was born.

Sodium. Term for salt in articles on its bad effects; used in newspaper food sections. Salt, on the other hand, is used when raving about "salt encrusted french fries." Similary "red meat" is bad, while "rare, thinly sliced beef" is fine.

So-called. Bogus and contemptible.

Some observers (SO). Plural noun given to contradictory opinions in news story. On November 6, 1984, Meg Greenfield wrote of SO in the *Washington*

Post, "Some Observers is a fellow who is forever 'thinking,' except when he occasionally 'feels.' But whichever it is that day, there is one thing you can always count on with him. He is fearless. Some Observers *never* thinks or feels what others—in particular those trying to have their way in a news story—think or feel or have the gall to assert as a simple fact. His role is that of unfailing contradictor. Typically, Some Observers will have made himself available for comment—and what a stroke of luck it is!—at precisely that point when the subject of the story, poor thing, has just finished delivering himself of an item of good news concerning his political campaign. 'Some observers think, however, . . .' the next paragraph will begin. And it's all over."

Greenfield refuses to say who SO is, but admits that "I have occasionally cited him myself. . . ."

Spry. Any senior citizen who is not in a wheelchair or coma. (So defined in John Leo's *Time* essay on "Journalese for the Lay Reader.")

Stamp of approval. What is given to anything new at the post office.

Star-crossed. Said of the Kennedys. Other examples of Kennedy journalese include liberal use of the term "dynasty," describing their buildings at Hyannisport as a "compound," and, when one of the "clan" gets in trouble, overblown lines like, "The shimmering legacy of Camelot grew slightly dimmer yesterday when it was disclosed that. . . ."

State of the art. At first this term was used to describe any machine or gadget that did not have a vacuum tube in it or come in a wooden case, but now it has come to mean anything that is not old-fashioned. William Rabe, a professor who has made a specialty out of over-used terms, reports that he has heard it "applied to everything from garbage cans to contraceptives."

Stockpile. What the superpowers do with nuclear weapons.

Strong. Useful headline adjective in describing the local team, which did not fare well in a tournament. "Middletown Hoopsters Finish a Strong Sixth in Holiday Tourney."

Street value. Term used in articles about drug seizures to tip the reader to the fact that a fantastic estimate of the drug's value is about to appear. If all of these estimates were added together for a year, they would probably exceed the amount of the GNP for all of North America and the Common Market combined.

Struggle to come to terms with. What people do after a mishap.

Summit. Any meeting attended by people above the clerical or secretarial level.

Superstar. Person who has been successful at making and selling phonograph records.

Task force. Any group of three or more people in a story with a dateline from Washington or a state capitol.

This. Personal pronoun on radio and television. "This is Peter Poobah reporting from the capitol" instead of "I am Peter Poobah reporting from the capitol." Custom has it that the "This is . . ." announcement is made at the beginning and the end of all television news reports—amounting to a double byline.

Tourist. Person who ends up in the wrong places ("tourist traps", for instance) and who always overtip. Most Sunday travel sections address the reader as a traveler, who is advised to keep away from tourists who are usually boorish jerks always in the market for authentic shrunken heads.

Try. Key word in the section of the paper that discusses "lifestyle." The word is usually tied to goofy suggestions for leading a fuller life ("Try inviting 52 complete strangers over for dinner and watch new friendships bloom"), exercise ("Try pull-ups on the overhead rails on the bus"), or food (Try mesquite-grilled marshmallows").

Twisted wreckage. Place from which survivors emerge miraculously.

Typical household. Any group of 2.69 people living under the same roof.

Ultramodern. Modern.

Uneasy truce. State that exists between the press and most of its subjects (the Pentagon, the Cedar Rapids School Board, the U.S. Senate, etc.).

Unexpected. We told you yesterday that this wouldn't happen.

Unimpeachable source. Anyone other than the President or a federal judge, the only two offices from which the holder may be impeached (per the U.S. Constitution).

Unprecedented. That which has not happened recently; not in our files.

Upscale. Expensive and/or excessive. Used a lot by *USA Today* headline writers and often paired with the term *baby boomer.*

Upwardly mobile. Ambitious, aggressive, and/or obnoxious.

USA. Elusive individual featured in many stories in *USA Today*, for example, "USA Wants Ticket to Miss Liberty Extravaganza," "USA's Health Kick Needs More Oomph," "USA Takes No Fallout Chances."

Venerable. Person over 40 who has not been involved in a major scandal; person with only a few enemies. It has traditionally been applied to the likes of Claude Pepper, Willie Mays, and Kate Smith.

Veteran courthouse observers. The reporter himself, because the city editor will not permit him to state something of common knowledge on his own, unattributed authority. Variations abound including "veteran city hall observers," "veteran Congress watchers," and "long-time White House observers."

Viable. Workable in the abstract. It is applied to options and alternatives.

Visibly moved. Crying or sobbing by a public official or VIP. Regular people are still allowed to cry.

Vital question. That which is important to the reporter.

Voyeurism. What the print media has to say about televised coverage of sensational trials.

Vulnerability. Required male trait of the 1980s. Even Hulk Hogan should show vulnerability when talking to feature writers.

Wag. This term is almost always used when the writer quotes his own cynical or funny line. "As one city hall wag observed, 'It was the first time an alderman had been seen with his hands in his own pockets since last winter's cold snap.'"

In "Sex and Euphemism," an article in the book *Fair of Speech*, Joseph Epstein writes, "A wag—I, actually—once wrote that the novels of the future are likely to be peopled with genitals sitting around discussing fashionable ideas."

Was unavailable for comment. Nobody was home when we called. It is used when somebody is being accused of misconduct.

-watcher. Someone who is at least 2,000 miles from the subject of interest. Moscow-watchers are found in Washington, while Mexico-watchers tend to come from the University of Minnesota.

Watershed. Important, usually applied to whatever political race or piece of legislation a reporter is assigned. "A watershed bill now before the legislature would, for the first time in the history of the state, make it illegal to sell nightcrawlers without a permit."

We. I, as in, "we made our way to the front of the crowd."

Weapons makers. Term used in stories of overcharge and bad performance. If nothing is amiss, they are called *defense contractors*.

Well-groomed. Vain with a touch too much aftershave lotion.

Well-manicured lawns. Used to describe neighborhoods with high-priced houses and small-minded people.

Wetlands. Swamps and marshes: ooze.

What's in a name? Without this headline for stories about corporate names and the changing popularity of first names, newspapers and magazines would be in deep trouble. The March 11, 1985, issue of *Forbes* carried two articles with this title. Other examples of the knee-jerk headline include "Edifice Complex" (for a builder working on a variety of projects) and "Swede Smell of Success" (for the latest generation of Swedish tennis stars).

Whiskey and roast beef. What is served when members of the military-industrial complex get together. These are two items that go fast at such events, while the brie runs and the white wine gets warm.

Without a scratch. Condition of race car drivers who are not hurt in spectacular crashes.

World class. Puffed up term for someone or something that is good. It is one of a list of terms that *Forbes* magazine stated it tended to use and was going to avoid in the future. Quoting a January 27, 1986, editorial on the words to be avoided in the future we have:

"Big Blue (for IBM); Ma Bell (for AT&T); game plan; ongoing; revolution (as in "auditing revolution"); soaring (or plummeting) stock prices on a 1 percent move in the Dow; upscale (for affluent); superstar (what's a mere star?); baby boomers; pricey (for expensive); whopping; bottom line (when numbers are involved); track record (what does "track" add); Young Turks;

Big Apple; downside risk (what's an upside risk?); bells and whistles; free fall; world class; hands-on management; guru, for any vaguely venerated authority . . ."

Within journalese, however, there is a separate set of rules concerning words, phrases, and verbal tricks that get trotted out when a crisis is to be reported. Here is an annotated set of rules and guidelines for crisis journalese. If they are followed carefully, one can take a swarming of termites or a flooded basement and turn it into the breathless stuff of a cover story, front-page special report, or TV news series.

Alliteration adds anxiety. Poets, playwrights, prosecutors, and politicians have long known that a certain drama is imposed when sounds at the beginning of words are repeated. (Recall Spiro Agnew's "nattering nabobs of negativism" and what is worse than "aiding and abetting" an enemy?) So it is not quite by chance that we have crisis headlines about "Crack and Crime," "Faltering Farms," "Troubled Thrifts," and "Coke and Kids." Then there are the D-words, which are a boon at disaster time (death and destruction, doom and despair, diseased and dispirited, dull and dreary, drunk and disorderly).

Hyphenate for the double-whammy effect. For reasons that are unclear, a hyphenated word gives a special pop to the proceedings. "Gangland-Style" murders are more alarming than garden variety killings, but not quite as scary as those deemed to be "Execution-Style." A term like *ill-fated* has a much greater sense of doom to it than *ill* or *fated* have when standing alone. If the reporter wants to cast doubt on something, the hyphen also works in such constructions as *so-called* and *self-styled*. Then there is the drama of *little-known* (used when a reporter is showing off and saying "Here is something I know, but you don't") and *long-awaited* (which often means nothing more than recently announced).

The best verbal inflator is a good prefix. Many are used (mega-, neo-, super-, hyper-, etc.) but the most effective may be over- as "overkill" and "overcrowded."

When in doubt, toss in a military, medical, or religious metaphor. Mix 'n match. For instance, instead of saying that a problem is to be studied by a committee, one should say that the crisis will be attacked by a task force. A proper piece of crisis reporting requires the use of at least two terms from each column.

A	B	C
Frontal attack	Epidemic	Crusade
Defeat/Surrender	Terminal	Evangelical
Task force	Cancer/ous	Missionary
Battle	Festering	Armageddon*
Skirmish	Ailing	Doomsday*
Casualties	Hemorrhaging	Apocalypse*

* These count as two.

Numbers should be expressed early, often, and only in deaths or dollars. (Exception: Shoes can be counted in the case of "deposed despots.") The wildly wrong death count during the initial hours of the Chernobyl incident appears to have done nothing to supress the appetite for big, early numbers.

Don't forget the year 2000. Crisis writing requires a dire prediction of how bad the problem will be in the year 2000 unless something is done now. The beauty of the year 2000 is that it is just far enough away for us to forget the dire predictions by the time it rolls around.

When all is said and done, a good anecdote beats a bunch of stuffy statistics and expert opinion. The press loved to reprimand President Reagan for letting the story of a lone farmer or welfare mother stand in as a token for a much larger issue, but this may be because he was encroaching on one of the tested techniques of crisis journalism. Show me a story on the farm crisis that does not contain a wrenching tale of suicide and I will show you an academic journal.

Turn all positive notions into negative ones. Panaceas are not, nor are "easy answers" and "cure-alls." Paradises are troubled.

Above all, there is no word like a buzzword. A quick primer. Problems are passe; use the word *crisis* at all times. Solutions are for mathematics; *Draconian measures* are called for. When possible mention (a) Watergate, (b) Jonestown, (c) Three Mile Island. Only quote *noted authorities* and *some observers* (who always say that the crisis may be worse than is generally acknowledged). If an institution is involved, say that it is *troubled* and/or *beleagured*. If there is a number to be called, make sure it is called a *hot line*; if a task force is appointed, it must be a *blue ribbon* panel; and anyone given authority to deal with the problem should be called a *Czar* who has *unprecedented powers*.

It never hurts to work in a mention of *Pandora's Box.* This is a nice fatalistic twist if one wants to suggest a host of new ills and evils that are about to be released on a crisis-weary world.

Thanks to Russell Ash, Hal Davis, Sam Freedenberg, Tom Gill, Joseph C. Goulden, Arnold R. Isaacs, Dan Rapoport, Dorothy Repovich, Bob Skole, Anthony A. Spleen, Elaine Viets, and Tony Wynne-Jones for their help with this section.

25

Junk Words

A Catch of Contemporary Clichés

Hopefully, this will have its desired effect, which is to get you to read closely *irregardless* of what you are doing.

There are certain words—*hopefully* and *irregardless* chief among them—that drive 12.7 percent of the population absolutely crazy and simply infuriate another 26.2 percent. So at this point in time, I'd like to speak to the issue of words and phrases that are either incorrect or have become so clichéd that they are irksome.

I'm talking about doing a number on you by listing all those words and phrases I am sick of hearing. . . . Hear me: I am tired of multidisciplinary task forces that examine infrastructure. I have had it with herebys, herins, herinaboves, and with the possible exception ofs. Contexts, syndromes, shortfalls, modules, and root causes are things I can live without. I no longer care to hear that something is just the tip of the iceberg and have decided that the pits are just that. I can think of a whole list of *V* words that are vile including value judgment, verbalize, viability, vibes, visibily moved, and virgin polyester. I find that I can't relate when it is in a sentence like, "Can you relate to peach ice cream?" I am sick of sectors—private and public—and suggest that fines be levied on people who use impact and imput as verbs.

I couldn't care less about couldn't care less, and I worry about not to worry. I would like a piece of the action but don't want to hear about it, and

I think that by now I know that (a) you can't reinvent the wheel, (b) there is no such thing as a free lunch, and (c) that you can't compare apples and oranges.

I walk away from major breakthroughs and meaningful dialogues because neither ever are. I refuse to give feedback, don't like to touch base with, and will only run with the ball when playing touch football. I long ago bit the bullet on bite the bullet.

"We suffer from a shortage of new catch phrases, and what you see—or hear—is what you get." These are the words of Sharon Cohen-Hager in a 1981 article in the *Tampa Tribune* on the nation's ongoing catch-phrase crisis, which has left us stuck with a stale and stuffy collection of popular words and phrases. Her point is underscored by this personal collection of buzzwords that have lost their sizzle.

Absolutely.
Actually.
Accession rate.
Add on.
Against the tide.
Agonizing reappraisal.
All systems go.
All-time record.
Alternative life-style.
Ambience.
An idea whose time has come.
Apples and oranges. A phrase used to indicate that two things cannot be fairly compared, as in "It's not fair comparing their gilhooley to ours . . . why, that's like comparing apples and oranges." Ironically, it is a poor metaphor as there are times when you do compare apples and oranges, such as when picking the best-looking fruit at the market.
At this point in time.
Awesome.
Back burner. "Let's push that one onto the back burner for now" is a response to an idea that is not workable at this time. Though impossible to prove, it has been estimated 99.76625 percent of all back-burner ideas will remain there forever.
Ball of wax.
Ball's in your court, the.
Ballpark figure.
Band-aid approach.
Basically.
Behaviors.
Bells and whistles.
Best shot.
Between a rock and a hard place.

Big picture.
Biggie.
Bite the bullet.
Blah-blah-blah.
Body language.
Boilerplate.
Bottom line. Presumably a bequest from the world of accounting, this term is commonly used when one chooses to avoid detailed explanations, moving directly to something on the order of "So, the bottom line is that we have to raise three quarters of a million dollars by Monday morning at 9:00."
Broad brush.
Business as usual.
Buy into.
Came on board.
Can of worms. How this odd phrase for a group of problems became so popular is beyond fathoming—especially since the going price for a dozen good nightcrawlers last summer was $2.50.
Card-carrying.
Caring. A radio public-service ad proclaims that a group of "warm and caring parents" will meet to discuss summer activities for their children, and a for-profit home for the elderly boasts of its "caring staff." It is an over-used and highly presumptuous word that implies that others are uncaring.
Cast in concrete.
Cautiously optimistic.
Caveat.
Charisma.
Cheap shot.
Chilling effect.
Classy.
Clean up one's act.
Cliché-laden.
Clout.
Cluster.
Cognizant. For *aware.*
Come down on.
Come on strong.
Come to terms with.
Communicate. When he was still part of the Carter administration, Alfred Kahn addressed a conference on communication with this classic opening line: "I will not communicate with you, I will *talk* to you."
Community. When used for a group, such as "the vegetarian community."
Concretize.
Constraint. One of Jimmy Carter's favorites.
Cost effective.

Craft. As both noun and verb.
Crisis-oriented.
Critical mass.
Crunch, the.
Culturally deprived.
Cutting edge.
Deaccession.
Debrief.
Decasualize.
Decisioned.
Deja vu.
Depth.
Deprogram.
Designer. As in Jeans, pizza, etc.
Détente.
Dialogue. As both noun and verb.
Disadvantaged.
Disinterested. For *uninterested*.
Do a number on.
Dog and pony show.
Do-gooder.
Don't have to be a rocket scientist to know . . .
Double digit.
Downsize.
Downside risk.
Effectuate.
Ego trip.
Elitist.
Enclosed herewith. One of a number of words and expressions banned in 1981 from agency correspondence by Secretary of Commerce Malcolm Baldrige. Others on the list were: *maximize, finalize,* and *interface.*
End-run.
Environment. As in one's bathroom environment.
Envisage.
Exacerbate.
Eye contact.
Eyeball to eyeball.
Facilitate.
Facility.
Fascinating.
Fast track.
Faux.
Feasible.
Feedback. This word, along with *input,* has become so overworked that Provost John McCall of the University of Cincinnati received national attention when

he ruled that any administrator who used either of these words in university communications would be fined two bits.

Final destination.

Finalize.

Finite.

First time ever.

For openers.

For sure.

For your convenience. Thomas H. Middleton of the *Saturday Review* identified this as one of his favorite "twaddle terms"—modern balderdash appearing in signs and advertising. "You go into your bank," he wrote, "and there's plaster all over the floor, the ceiling has been ripped out, there are exposed wires to trip over, and you see a sign that tells you, 'for your convenience, we are temporarily destroying the bank. Thank you for your cooperation.' "

Formulate.

Freak. As in *plantfreak*.

Free fall.

Free lunch.

Fully cognizant.

Game plan. The source—NFL, NBA, NHL, or organized horseshoe-pitching—notwithstanding, this sporting term is now applied to virtually every aspect of American life. It is currently used as a synonym for any kind of policy. For example, "Dear, what should our game plan be for dealing with the Nelsons if they insist on three hours of canasta before dinner?"

Gamed.

Get your act together.

Go down the tubes.

Go-fer.

Go for it.

Good news . . . bad news.

Gray area.

Great human being.

Ground zero.

Guesstimate.

Guidelines.

Hands-on.

Hang a left.

Hard ball.

Hard core.

Hard-nosed.

Have sex. The term that Eric Partridge called the "most colourless, ineffectual [and] inadequate" of all English synonyms for sexual intercourse. Partridge was reminded of a character in Nicholas Freeling's novel *What Are the Bugles Blowing For?*, who says to a Frenchman, "In England we have sex. It's exceptionally depressing. In France you say 'Enjoy.' "

Hazy. Hot and humid.

Heartland.

Hereby. One of the most important words in the legalistic-governmental vocabulary. James B. Minor, a lawyer and an expert on legislative drafting, has said of this word, "I think the government would have to cease operation if the word *hereby* were ever deleted from the language."

Herein.

Hereinabove.

High tech.

Hit list.

Holistic.

Hot button.

Hot line.

Human resources.

Humongous. Immense; overpowering; unnaturally big. It began as college slang in the late 1960s—"He gave us this humongous assignment due Monday"—but it has spread so widely since then that it has lost its punch.

I'd like to speak to that.

If we can send a man to the moon.

I haven't the foggiest.

Impact. As a verb.

Implement.

Implementation.

Importantly.

In other words.

In view of.

Infrastructure.

Inoperative.

Input. Also *output* and *thruput*. In 1976 the State Department captured the annual Doublespeak Award of the National Council of Teachers of English for an announcement that said, in part, that a certain person would ". . . review existing mechanisms of consumer input, thruput and output and seek ways of improving these linkages via the consumer consumption channel."

Perhaps the final word on input was uttered in 1980 by cliché-fighter Alfred Kahn when he told a reporter from the *Washington Post*, "When I hear 'input' used as a verb I see a German golfer."

Insufficiency. When used for *shortage*.

Interdependent.

Interact.

Interestingly.

Interface. *Wall Street Journal* found that the Air Force was so in love with this word that it managed to work it twice into one sentence of a press release. The release described engineering services as "studies, [and] analysis to further define interfaces leading to a missile design review-interface with other stages."

The man who has pushed the use of this word to new limits is Alexander Haig, who speaks of "interface areas of complexity and difficulty" and "the great interfaces across the entire spectrum."

In this day and age.
Intimate relationship.
Into. As in "What are you into?"
Irregardless.
Irrespective.
Is of the opinion that.
Level playing field.
Like nailing jelly to the wall.
Lion's share.
Live with.
Locked in concrete.
Low ball.
Low profile.
Mainstream. Noun and verb.
Major breakthrough.
Major thrust.
Make babies.
Management team.
Manualize.
Marvelous.
Matrix.
Meaningful dialogue.
Meaningful relationship.
Media event. For a press conference.
Megabucks.
Methodology.
Mode. Especially "mode of transportation."
Modes.
Modular.
Modules.
Moment. As in, "back in a moment."
Momentum.
Multidisciplinary.
Name of the game.
Negative growth.
New records.
No brainer.
No panacea.
No problem.

Not a happy camper.
Not to worry.
Nurturing. Especially when paired with the word "environment."
Obligational limitation.
Off load.
Off the wall.
On a roll.
Ongoing.
Opt.
Optimize.
Outreach. Alfred Kahn on outreach: "In my office we say 'outreach makes me upchuck.' "
Oversight.
Overview.
Painfully obvious.
Parameters.
Parcelization.
Parenting.
Past history.
Pay one's dues.
Peacekeeping troops.
Peer group.
Phase-in.
Phase-out.
Piece of the action.
Post-modern.
Posture. As in "credibility posture."
Practicable.
Precious few.
Precipitation falling in the form of . . .
Prior to.
Prioritize.
Private sector.
Public sector.
Pursuant to our conversation.
Push comes to shove.
Push the envelope.
Quality time.
Quick and dirty.
Ramifications.
Rattle one's cage.
Really.
Referenced.
Regroup.

Reinvent the wheel.
Relate. As in "Can you relate to barbecued pork?"
Resource. As a word for money.
Revise to reflect.
Rock the boat.
Role model. Along with such terms as *peer group* and *identity crisis*, role model
   has come from the jargon of the behavioral scientist. These terms are fine
   things in doctoral theses, but are being forced into odd places. For instance,
   role model is increasingly being used as a synonym for hero; for example,
   "When I was a kid my role model was Yogi Berra." (This refers to a time
   when Berra's peer group identity was as a New York Yankee.)
Root cause.
Run with the ball.
Scenario.
Sector.
Self-actualizing.
Sell the sizzle not the steak.
Seminal.
Serious crisis.
Sexuality. When one means sex.
Share. As used on talk shows: "Would you share with us your feelings?"
Shoot oneself in the foot.
Shortfall.
Shotgun approach.
Sign off/on.
Significant contribution.
Simplistic. For *simple*.
So-called. As a sign of doubt: "A so-called humanitarian."
Spin off.
Square one.
State of the art.
Stonewalling.
Structured.
Superstar.
Supportive.
Syndrome.
Systematize.
Take a bath.
Task force. William Safire has explained that this is nothing but a committee
   "given a military name to make it sound vigorous."
That's incredible.
The pits.
Third generation. As applied to technology, not people.
Throwing money at the problem.

Throw the baby out with the bath water.
Thrust.
Time frame.
Tip of the iceberg.
Toney.
Too close to call.
Too little, too late.
Top secret.
Touch base with.
Track record.
Transpire. When used as a synonym for happen.
Two-fer.
Two-way street.
Underutilization.
Update. Especially when uttered by newscasters who want to update rather than inform.
Up to speed.
User-friendly.
Using a bomb for a fly swatter.
Utilize.
Value judgment.
Vector.
Verbalize.
Viable.
Viability.
Vibes.
Virgin polyester.
Visibly moved.
Watershed.
Well endowed.
Whatshisface.
When deemed appropriate.
Where the bodies are buried.
Win-win situation.
With the possible exception of.
Within the context of.
Within the framework of.
Working relationship.
Workshop. Kingsley Amis wrote in *Jake's Thing*: "If there is one word that sums up everything that's gone wrong since the war, it's Workshop."
World class.
Would you believe?
Your dime.

Kadigans

*Umpty-Ump Indefinite Nouns
with Xteen Amorphous Adjectives
Thrown in for Good Measure*

There are scrumteen scillion kadigans in English, though the soandsos who produce whatchamacallits seldom pay attention to this sortathing. Moving toward a fuller understanding of the vague precise, here is a basic majaggus.

Booznannie. Sometimes spelled *boozenannie*, not to be confused with a doozandassy.

Chingus. Generally a hoodus that is old, blemished, or obviously defective: a stale jiggus, for instance.

Clanth. An old tool or instrument that once had a specific use now forgotten. Old farm or household clanths are commonly found in the back rooms of antique shops. The word originally showed up in a quiz in the October 1973 issue of *Early American Life* magazine that sought the meanings of such early Americanisms as *holzaxt* ("a special axe with wedge-like head, designed for splitting logs") and *quern* ("simple hand mill, with revolving millstone, for grinding grain into meal"). Clanth was inserted in the quiz as a trick word whose definition was "no such word, no such thing." It seemed a shame to leave a fine construction like clanth without a meaning.

Dingbat. A gadget, but one that is suitable for throwing. According to William and Mary Morris in the third volume of the *Morris Dictionary of Word and Phrase Origins,* a dingbat is also: (1) a printer's term for a typographical ornament not easily described, (2) an Australian name for delirium tremens (the dingbats) or an acute hangover.

Dinglefuzzie. John Gould in *Maine Lingo* says that this is the Down East equivalent of Whoozit or Whatsisname: "Dinglefuzzie stopped in while you were gone, but wouldn't tell me what he wanted."

Dinglet. A small dingus.

Dingus. A thing. The word seems to derive from the South African Dutch *dinges,* for "thing."

Dofunnies. From the old West. Plural of dofunny.

Doings. No-nonsense dodibbles.

Doingses. Plural of doings.

Doodad. Doodah, American style.

Doowhistle. An elaborate gizwatch; a gizwatch embellished.

Eleventeen. Any amount less than a jillion, but not forty-eleven.

Eujifferous. That which is spanglorious; indefinite greatness.

Fidfad. A worthless nubbin; a fiddlestick.

Fizgig. A creation of Lewis Carroll.

Framus. An automotive thingamajig.

Gadget. Although now applied broadly, gadget was originally a Navy term for a tool or mechanical device that one could not recall the name of. One theory of its origin is that it comes from *gachette,* diminutive of the French *gache,* a "catch" or "staple."

Gidget. A gadget; also the heroine of such films as *Gidget Goes Hawaiian.* In their *Dictionary of Word and Phrase Origins,* William and Mary Morris reveal that the name was a Hollywood writer's blending of *girl* and *midget.*

Gilguy. Clamjamtive tosh.

Gilhoolie. Once a thingamabob, now applied to a patented can opener/sealer.

Gimmick. Although the word is now widely applied, it was originally used to describe devices used to deceive, such as those that were used to rig carnival games.

Gismo. Term popularized by GIs during World War II. Also *gizmo.*

Gizwatch. A no-nonsense doowhistle.

Gowser. A recently coined indefinite noun. In an article in the April 1981 issue of the *Maine Antique Digest,* there was a report on a Plainfield, New Hampshire, auction conducted by William A. Smith during which an odd-shaped box came on the block. Smith called it a "gowser" and sold it for $45.

Gubbins. The singular of gubbinses.

Gubbinses. The plural of gubbins.

Hoopendaddy. An outfit; a rathob.

Hootmalalie. Seldom encountered these days, but a useful word to know should one happen to appear.

Ipses. Much the same as gimmick, save for the fact that ipses are generally edible.

Itchicumscratchy. That which irks, infatuates, inspires, irritates, etc.

Jigamaree. A new gadget.

Jiggawatts. Much electrical juice.

Jiggumbob. From Samuel Johnson: "A trinket; a knick-knack; a slight contrivance in machinery."

Kajody. Doowillie for which the correct name is forgotten or unknown.

Kathob. Goofus with ethnic overtones; an imported majaggus.

Majig. Short for thingamajig; also a small thingamajig.

Mathom. A Hobbitish word from J.R.R. Tolkien for something that has no use but is too good to throw away. They were often given to other Hobbits as presents.

Oojah. Can be a majigger, majiggie, majaggus, or a magig.

Optriculum. A shebang with the look of high technology to it.

Polywhatsit. A thingamajig that obviously has more than one use.

Ringamajisser. A ringamajizzer; ringamajiggen.

Snivvie. Ringdingle with an ominous or dangerous look to it. It is not to be tinkered with.

Stromm. Urbane version of a thing-jigger.

Thingummy. No such thing.

Thinkumthankum. A cerebral thingamajig.

Thumadoodle. Generally speaking, a rinktum that can be held and manipulated in one hand. There are, of course, obvious exceptions.

Umpty-umpth. Higher than umpteenth or umptieth.

Wallage. An indefinite quality; an uncertain quality.

Whatsits. Currently common term in the antiques trade for mysterious old tools and objects. The Early American Industries Association, a national group of old tool buffs, has an official Whatsits Committee. Whatsits is used as both a singular and a plural noun.

Whigmaleery. Doflickety with moving parts.

Whimsey. An odd or fanciful object, for instance, an intricate carving made from one piece of wood. The word is currently popular among museum curators and antique dealers to describe objects of uncertain utility.

Whoozit. Prototype widget.

Widget. The commercial version of a whoozit. People in business are always talking about widgets when they begin talking hypothetically: "Suppose you sell 75,000 widgets."

Windge. Jiggus with a nautical aura about it; a whamditty of sorts.

Wingdoodle. A fanciful whatis.

Loutish Words

More Than a Gross of Little-Used but Wonderfully Apt Gibes and Taunts

English is a fine language for insult; yet some of our finest, most precise words of derision have fallen into disuse. Here is an outlandish collection of affronts begging to be revived.

Alcatote. A simpleton; an oaf.

Ballarag. A bully.

Bawdstrot. A procuress or prostitute.

Beau-nasty. Slovenly fop; a man who is dirty but well dressed.

Belswagger. A swaggering bully.

Bezonian. A mean, low person.

Bezzler. A sot who steals for liquor money.

Blatherskite. A boaster and a loud talker.

Borborygmite. A filthy talker.

Botheration. A pest.

Bronstrops. A procuress.

Caitiff. A base, mean wretch.

Chattermucker. A blabberer, gossip.

Chuff. A fat, coarse, blunt person; also, a fat cheek.

Clapperdudgeon. A rapscallion.

Clinchpoop. A lout or jerk.

Clodpate. A stupid fellow; a dolt; a thick skull.

Clodpoll. A stupid person.

Clumperton. A clown; a fool.

Cockabaloo. A bully; a nasty and overbearing boss.

Coistrel. A person of no account.

Cudden. A born fool.

Cullion. A mean wretch; a scoundrel.

Curship. Dogship; meanness; scoundrelship.

Cuttle. A foul-mouthed fellow; a fellow who blackens the character of others.

Dandiprat. A prattling dandy.

Dizzard. A blockhead, dimwit.

Dogberry. An ignorant and officious person who makes a lot of fuss but never takes action. It is named for Dogberry the constable in *Much Ado About Nothing*.

Doolally. Weak in the head.

Dotterel. A sucker; one easily hornswoggled.

Drassock. A slovenly woman.

Drazel. A low, mean, worthless wretch.

Drotchel. An idle wrench; a sluggard.

Drumble. A lazy person or drone.

Dunderwhelp. A detestable numbskull.

Durgen. An awkward, uncouth rustic.

Fadge. A short, obese lump of a person.

Fopdoodle. A fool; an insignificant wretch.

Franion. A man of loose behavior.

Fribble. A foppish lackwit.

Fustilarian. A low fellow; a stinkard; a scoundrel. Shakespeare's word.

Fustilugs. A filthy slob.

Fuzzdutty. A silly person; a simp.

Gangrel. Vagrant rascal; a roguish tramp.

Giddypate. Scatterbrain.

Gigg. A strumpet; a wanton woman.

Gitt. British equivalent of the American jerk.

Glump. A pouting, sulking crank.

Gnoff. A lout or boor.

Gongoozler. An idle person who is always stopping on the street to look at things.

Gormless. Stupid and unattractive.

Gossoon. A big oak. Irish.

Grimalkin. A bossy old woman.

Grobian. A lout. St. Grobianus is the patron saint of coarse people.

Grouthead. Dunce; blockhead.

Growtnoll. A blockhead.

Grumbledory. A clod.

Gulchin. A young or little glutton.

Gundygut. An offensive, mannerless eater.

Haskard. A base and vulgar fellow.

Heanling. A base person; a wretch.

Herkel. A drip.

Hobbil. A dolt; dunce.

Hoddypeke. A cuckold; used as a term of reproach.

Honyoker. A galoot, a rube.

Humgruffin. A creep.

Jack-me-harty. An incipient Jack strop.

Jack strop. An obstropulous member of the British Navy.

Jacksauce. A rude and saucy person.

Jeeter. An ill-mannered slob.

Jobbernowl. A loggerhead; blockhead.

Joskin. A bumpkin.

Kern. A rude peasant; a boor.

Knuff. Lout.

Lickpenny. A greedy, miserly person.

Lickspigot. A sponge; a revolting parasite. Also known as a *lickspittle.*

Lobcock. Sluggish lout.

Lobscouse. A lout.

Lollard. A bum; loafer.

Lollpoop. A particular type of bum who leans out of windows, watches, and occasionally sticks out his tongue at those who pass by.

Looby. A hulking, lazy oaf.

Lorg. A stubborn and stupid person.

Losel. A worthless, sorry person.

Losenger. A flatterer, deceiver, or liar.

Lourd. A stupid, worthless chap (pronounced *lurd*).

Lungis. A ludicrous lout.

Madbrain. An especially temperamental hothead.

Micher. A loiterer who generally skulks about in corners and keeps out of sight.

Milksop. A feeble, docile person; a jellyfish.

Mobard. Boorish fool.

Mollycoddle. A weak and pampered person.

Mollygrubs. A cross and cranky person.

Mome. A blockhead; a stupid person.

Mooncalf. Imbecile, fool, daydreamer.

Moonling. A simpleton.

Muckworm. A miser.

Mudsill. A low-bred person.

Mullipuff. Twerp.

Nigmenog. A nitwit; a fool.

Ninnyhammer. A simpleton.

Nipcheese. A cheapskate.

Nithing. A base coward.

Nobbler. Swindler; sharper.

Noddypole. A simpleton; also known as a *noddypate* or *noddypeake*.

Nup. A silly person.

Nuthook. A sneak thief. It is from a time when thieves used hooked sticks to lift clothes and other goods from open windows.

Omadhaun. Fool or simpleton. Irish.

Pig-sconce. A pigheaded person; a boor.

Pilgarlic. A wretch who feels altogether sorry for himself and wants others to do the same.

Pinchbelly. A miserly person.

Ploot. A slut.

Princock. A pert young rogue, a conceited person.

Puckfist. A braggart.

Puler. A whiner.

Puzzlepate. One who is bewildered by the simplest ideas.

Quakebuttock. Coward.

Quetcher. A constant complainer; a bother.

Quibberdick. A nasty quibbler.

Quoob. A misfit, rhymes with boob.

Ragabash. An idler; a bum. It can be used individually or as a collective noun: "The ragabash that congregates outside the courthouse."

Rakehell. A worthless, debauched, and generally sorry fellow.

Rampallian. A general term of abuse. Used by Shakespeare to nice effect in *Henry IV,* Part II, "Away, you scullion! you rampallian! you fustilarian!"

Ripesuck. Bribable person; easy mark.

Rudesby. An uncivil, turbulent person.

Rumpot. A drunk.

Runnion. A paltry, scurvy wretch.

Scattergood. A spendthrift; a squanderer.

Scelert. A wicked wretch.

Scomm. A buffoon.

Scroyle. A mean or shabby person. Originally, a *scrofulous* swelling.

Skellum. A villain, scoundrel.

Skipkennel. A lackey.

Slubber-degullion. One who slobbers his clothing, a dirty fellow.

Slummock. A cheeky slut.

Smellfeast. Person who will sniff out a major meal and show up uninvited. Sometimes this type is also called a *lickdish*.

Smellfungus. A grumbler who finds fault with everything.

Smellsmock. A lecher.

Smouger. A cheat; chiseler.

Snollygoster. A clever and unscrupulous person.

Snudge. Tightwad; miser.

Spalpeen. A rascal; knave.

Spiv. One who lives flashily with no visible means of support.

Swillbelly. One who eats like a pig; a glutton.

Tatterdemalion. A ragged, dirty fellow.

Tattlebasket. A gossip.

Titivil. A rascal, especially one that tattles.

Toadeater. A sycophant.

Tomnoddy. A simpleton.

Trollybags. A repulsive and dirty person.

Troppop. A slattern.

Troublemirth. A spoilsport.

Tufthunter. A lackey; an apple-polisher, specifically an undergraduate who hung around the sprigs of the nobility at Oxford and Cambridge, so called from the gold tufts (tassels) that the nobs wore on their mortar boards.

Twittletwattle. A tattle, gabble, twit.

VUP. A Very Unimportant Person as distinguished from VIP (Very Important Person) or PUP (Pretty Unimportant Person).

Wallydrag. An unkempt, disreputable woman.

Wheech. Scottish for twerp.

Whiffet. A whiff of air; a nobody.

Whopstraw. A boor.

Xantippe. A shrewish, tart-tongued woman. After Socrates' venomous wife.

Yazzihamper. A lunkhead.

Magic Words

*A Spell of Very Special Words
(Use at Your Own Risk)*

Abracadabra. Originally a magic formula used to rid a person of illness or bad luck. According to Harry E. Wedeck in *Dictionary of Magic:*

Usually the inscription appears on an amulet, in the form of an inverted pyramid; so that the first line reads:

ABRACADABRA

Each succeeding line is diminished by one letter, the last line reading:

A

The disease or ill fortune disappears as the magic formula itself dwindles away.

Abraxas. Word that when carved into a stone or gem is supposed to create a charm of great power. Through a numerological code, the letters add up to 365, the number of days in the year.

Agla. Magic word for the exorcism of demons. It is an acronym formed from the first letters of the four Hebrew words meaning "Thou are forever mighty, O Lord."

Alkahest. The universal solvent that the alchemists tried to find. It would have reduced all substances to their base elements. It was also called *menstruum universale.*

Amaranth. A magic flower that never fades or withers.

Ananisapta. A word that when written on parchment and worn on the body protects one from disease.

Belocolus. A stone that renders the person who holds it invisible on the battlefield.

Bilocation. The ability to be in two different places at the same time.

Coven. A group of people who meet for the purpose of ritual magic and/or pagan worship.

The Craft. Witchcraft to insiders.

Enchiridion. A collection of spells and prescriptions; used to protect against illness and bad luck.

Esbat. A weekly meeting of covens.

Exsufflation. A form of exorcism performed by spitting and blowing on the evil spirit.

Famulus. A sorcerer's assistant.

Grove. A group of covens.

Hocus-pocus. Next to abracadabra, the most famous magic catchall. Most interesting about the word are the two theories of its derivation: (1) from the name of mythical Norse demon/magician, Ochus Bocus; (2) a contraction of the words *Hoc est corpusmeum,* which occur in the Catholic mass when the Communion host is presented. The latter explanation is favored by those who have studied the evidence.

Hola Nola Massa. A magic formula used in the Middle Ages for banishing sickness and other emergencies. Other formulae from the period that were recorded for posterity:

Ofano, Oblamo, Ospergo.
Pax Sax Sarax.
Afa Afca Nostra.
Cerum, Heaium, Lada Frium.

Horse and hattock. The opening words of the spell used by witches when mounting their broomsticks, which was used to get them airborne. The full spell:

Horse and hattock,
Horse and go,
Horse and pelatis, Ho, ho!

Pentagram. A continuous line that crosses itself to form a five-pointed star. Drawn with two points up, it is supposed to show devotion to Satan.

Pentalpha. Design created with five interlaced *A*'s, used in magic rites.

Pyrzqxgl. In L. Frank Baum's *The Magic of Oz* the promise is made that if you can pronounce *pyrzqxgl* properly you can turn yourself or anyone else into whatever you please.

Sabbat Broth. Potion that gave the ability to see the future and fly. It is traditionally made from toads, black millet, the flesh of a hanged man, the flesh of a dead child, and assorted magic powders.

VANARBI. Word used to render another incapable of having sexual intercourse. This and others—including, ironically, RIBALD—were used in the medieval period. For reasons unclear, words of impotence are capitalized.

Y Ran Oui Ran, casram casratem casratrosque. This "charme of wordes" was to be written out, put in an eggshell, and put down the throat of a dog that had been bitten by a "madde dogge," to prevent the bitten dog from becoming mad. From a 1576 *Book of Hunting*.

Markings

*Everything You Ever
Wanted to Know about Specks*

I've always been fascinated by the names for the little marks other than letters and numbers that show up on paper. At first, it is quite easy to collect these names because we all know what a comma or semicolon is. But what of a *paraph*, the *pilcrow*, and the *solidus*?

Aspects. Symbols used to denote positions of planets, such as * and □.

Asterisk (*). It derives from the Greek *asteriskos*, which means little star. It is commonly used in footnotes.* In a 1984 "Words" column, Michael Gartner published an anonymous ditty to help people from mispronouncing the term "asterick":

*Pretty Mary donned her skates
Upon the ice to frisk.
Wasn't she a silly girl
Her little * ?"*

---

* As John Gould observed in one of the footnotes to an essay he wrote on in the *Christian Science Monitor:* "It is doubtful whether some of these things ever get read at all."

Asterism. A triangular cluster of asterisks, used to direct attention to a particular passage:

*   * *
* * or   *

At mark/At sign. One of these: @@@@@@@, but only when it means *at*. When the @@@@@@@ is used for *each*, it is an *each mark*. There is at least one other possibility for this mark: *per*, which shows up in several lists of printer's marks.

Caret. Mark used to show where something should be inserted (∧).

Cartouche. A scroll-inspired ornament, often used as the field for a coat of arms. ⬭

Center point. A period placed higher than the printer's base line. Used, for example, in separating syl·la·bles.

Dieresis. The two dots (¨) placed over the second of two successive vowels to indicate that they are to be pronounced separately: coöperative, for instance. Also, *diaeresis*.

Dingbat. Printer's name for any typographical ornament. Sometimes called a *flubdub*.

Each mark. See *At mark*.

En. Printer's short dash used to represent the word *to*, as the years 1982–83 or pages 50–51. The next longest dash is the *em*, used to mark a faltering or turning of thought ("I—I really don't know"), and the longest, the *2-em dash*, is used for an omission: Ms. ____.

End mark. Mark placed at the end of an article, chapter, or book to indicate that it is done. Common end marks: #, ###, and ㉚.

Engrailment. A ring of dots around the edge of a coin or medal.

Flabbergasterisk. A very strong exclamation point that is represented by the symbol ⅋. It was invented by Fred Flanagan and Stan Merritt in an article in *Printer's Ink*, who suggest it for modern advertising copywriters who have used the standard exclamation point to the point where it has become ineffectual. They also invented the *Stupendapoint* and the *Fluctustress* (see also).

Fleuron. Stylized flower used in printing.

Fluctustress. An underlining created for extra emphasis represented as ﹏﹏ rather than the conventional ────. (I try to use a fluctustress or two from time to time just so I can say, "Now there is a fine fluctustress.")

Flummux mark. Old hobo mark of danger; a house with the mark (⊙) is to be avoided. The bone mark (◇) is, on the other hand, a good mark, and a house marked with it is likely to be the place for a free meal.

Grammalogue. A word that is shown as a sign or letter: & and @ are grammalogues. The & mark is an ampersand, and the @ is the *at mark* or *each mark*.

Harlequins. Heavy decorative type elements.

Interrobang. A mark (?) intended to express a question and an exclamation at the same time; for example, "Who needs it?" It was invented by Martin K. Spector who created the name from *interrogation* and *bang* (printer's slang for an exclamation point). It created a lot of attention when it made its debut in the late 1960s, but has yet to really take off.

Leaders. Lines of dots used to lead the eye to the end of a line. Often used in the contents and indexes of books. Example:

XI. Lola Returns ....178.

Ligature. More than one letter formed as a single character.

Mackle. A printing spot or imperfection, especially one caused by slippage or wrinkles in the paper.

Macron. The horizontal mark used to show a long vowel; for example, mā'krŏn.

Octothorpe. The term created and used by the Bell System in 1967 for the #, which appears on the touch-tone telephone, among other places. Bob Levey of the *Washington Post* used his column to investigate the name for the # and discovered that there was an alternative term, *delimeter* which showed up in the 1973 *Webster's New Collegiate* but which did not show up in seven other dictionaries. It has been variously called a *cross-hatch, gridlet, double-cross, pound sign, tic-tac-toe button, cross of Lorainne*. The # is also a printer's mark meaning *insert extra space here*."

Paraph. A flourish made after a signature.

Patterans. A Romany house-marking system from which tramps and hoboes derived theirs.

Perigraph. An inscription around something, such as the circumscriptions found on coins.

Pilcrow. The proper name for the paragraph symbol: ¶.

Postil. A note or comment made in a margin.

Quadruple quotes. A innovation of Bernard Malamud who used them in his fable "God's Grace" in a dialogue between man and God. Whenever God speaks, his words appear with quadruple rather than the normal double quotes. Malamud told the *New York Times* that the quadruple quotes were simply an example of a writer enjoying his craft.

Quantity mark. One of two marks used to indicate whether a vowel or diphthong is to be pronounced long or short. The macron is the long sound [-], while the breve is the short one [˘].

Schwa. The symbol (ə) in pronunciation used to indicate an indistinct or neutral vowel.

Semiquote. A single quotation mark, as is used in a quote within a quote; an inverted comma (').

Stupendapoint. A super flabbergasterisk represented by the symbol ⚡ . Not to be confused with the six-pointed flabbergasterisk or the overused and now enfeebled exclamation point!

Tailpiece. A small ornament or illustration at the end of a book chapter or magazine article.

Vinculum. A line over a letter or number. In math the vinculum is used to show that a group of elements are to be considered as a whole: $\overline{a+b+2}$.

Virgule. A proper name for the mark (/) that is commonly called a slash, which is used to separate fractions (1/16), to mean *per* (25 miles/hour), and to indicate *either* (has/has not). Other proper names for the same oblique stroke: *diagonal, separatrix, slant,* and *solidus*—all of which sound better than *slash*, which can sound ugly and violent especially when one says "he-slash-her."

Not everybody likes the marking. Charles Aronson wrote in the December, 1980, *Peephole on People*, "Once we get into the habit of slanting things, we come up with salesperson/dealer. And I've seen a whole string of words with slants between. What's wrong with 'and'? Or 'or'? The bad thing about the damn slant is that it pokes itself in your eye as you read."

Volle. The little circle over some Scandinavian vowels. *Volle* is Danish for little round cake (°).

Wing. Slavic mark that commonly appears over *C* to indicate that it is to be pronounced *tch*. Čapek, for instance.

Zollner's lines. Parallel lines crossed with other lines, which give the illusion that they are not parallel.

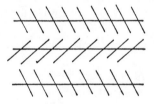

Measured Words

*Four Dozen Ways of Saying
How Much or How Many*

Barleycorn. One-third of an inch.
Barleycorn. One-third of an inch.
Bundle. Two reams of paper; 960 sheets.
Burthen. Seventy pounds, or more specifically, 1 firkin (56 pounds) plus 1 stone (14 pounds).
Chopin. A Scots measure of 20 ounces.
Coffee spoon. Cooking measure equal to ¼ teaspoon.
Coomb. Four bushels.
Cran. Used for fresh herring only; specifically, 45 gallons.
Dash. A scant ⅛ teaspoon.
Demy. Paper size measuring 16×29 inches.
Dessert spoon. Cooking measure equal to ½ tablespoon.
Ell. A measure of length, 1 yard and 9 inches.
Fardel. An old, not-too-accurate measure for 4 cloves. A clove is a fuzzy designation for 7 to 10 pounds of either cheese or wool.
Firkin. Both a British measure of butter—56 pounds—and another name for ¼ of a barrel or 9 gallons.
Frail. Fifty pounds of raisins.

Googol. The number 1 followed by 100 zeros. Coined in fun by the young nephew of mathematician Edward Kasner, the term is now accepted by mathematicians. This makes sense because I'm convinced that numbers over a trillion can only be expressed by kids who say things like "I'll bet you a zillion popplillion grillion dollars that I can spit further than you can," or "I know a kid who has more than a gagillion marbles." My kids happen to like the term *infinity.* They use it when they want to express a number beyond a zillion-zillion as in, "I've got an infinity of baseball cards."

Googolplex. The number 1 followed by a *googol* of zeros or 10 to the googol power. In his 1940 *Mathematics and the Imagination,* Kasner (with J. R. Newman) points out that this number would be impossible to describe in full with all of its zeros ". . . as there would not be enough room to write it, if one went to the farthest stars, touring all the nebulae in the Universe and putting down zeros every inch of the way."

Great gross. Twelve gross; 1,728 articles.

Gross ton. 2,240 pounds.

Hairbreadth. 0.0208 inch.

Hand. A small bunch of bananas, in the banana business. A single banana is, naturally, a *finger,* while the overall bunch from which the hands come is a *stem.*

Heaped measure. A bushel in which the contents are piled high. A *struck measure,* on the other hand, is a bushel in which the contents are level with the top of the basket.

Heer. Six hundred yards of wool or linen yarn.

Hundredweight. A weight equal to 112 pounds in England and 100 pounds in the United States.

Kilderkin. An 18-gallon beer cask.

Kiloparsec. An immense distance equivalent to 3,259 light years. William D. Johnstone says in his definitive guide to measurement, *For Good Measure,* "The length of the kiloparsec is so great that, as an example, it would take an airplane traveling at a constant speed of 600 statute miles per hour more than 3.645 billion years to cover the distance."

Kilopascal. Metric measure of pressure. Atmospheric pressure equals approximately 100 kilopascals. As part of the less than universally loved metric system imposed on Canada, it has become one of those measures more mocked than used by nonscientists. Writing in *MacLean*'s magazine in 1983, Charles Gordon reported on metric: "Around the water cooler, no one was hitting a golf ball 276.92 metres. No one was catching fish measurable in grams. Not a single coffee-break conversation had, as yet, ever contained a reference to a hectare or a kilopascal."

Kip. Half a ton: 1,000 pounds.

Mease. Five hundred herrings.

Megameter. One thousand kilometers or a million meters.

Mho. Reciprocal of the ohm; *ohm* spelled backward.

Oxhoft. Scandinavian measure of approximately 56 to 58 gallons.

Pig. A British measure of ballast equal to 301 pounds.

Pin. A beer cask of 4½ gallons.

Pottle. Four pints.

Puncheon. Enormous cask. Traditionally 120 gallons for brandy and 114 for rum.

Quad. Short for *quadrillion*, or 1×10. It is used when talking of energy to describe one quadrillion BTUs, or British thermal units. The term is used because it is a common unit that expresses the energy content of a fuel regardless of its source (oil, coal, uranium, or whatever).

Quartern. A measure of 5 ounces.

Quinary. In fives; pertaining to the number five.

Quintoquadagintillion. The number 1 followed by 138 zeros—larger than a googol. This is not to be confused with a *nonillion*, which is a 1 followed by 54 zeros or an *undecillion*, which is 1 followed by 36 zeros.

Word researcher Rudolf Ondrejka has compiled a list of names for immense numbers based on the works of the nineteenth-century mathematician Henkle and using Latin cognates. The list includes this sampling: quattuordecillion (45 zeros), novemdecillion (60 zeros), vigintillion (63 zeros), unovigintillion (66 zeros), trigintillion (93 zeros), quadragintillion (123 zeroes), centillion (303 zeros), ducentillion (603 zeros), millillion (3003 zeros), quadcento-millillion (4203 zeros), du-millillion (6003 zeros), dec-millillion (30,003 zeros), duvigint-millillion (66,0003 zeros), sexagint-millillion (180,003 zeros), trecent-millillion (900,003 zeros), billillion (3,000,003 zeros), trigint-billillion (60,000,003 zeros), and sexcent-billillion (1,800,000,003 zeros.)

Quire. Paper measure: 24 sheets, ¹⁄₂₀ of a ream.

Sarpler. A bale of wool that weighs a gross ton (2,240 pounds).

Seam. Eight bushels or 32 pecks.

Septipedalian. Seven feet long. Coined by British wordsman Ivor Brown for its obvious application to athletes. Correspondent C. R. Nowlan of Toronto has suggested, "Might I merely suggest that it describes the mouths of certain sports 'colour commentators', describing as its does the number of feet such mouths often contain."

Sesquipedalian. One-and-one-half feet long, but it is also used as an adjective to describe a lover of long words according to various sources including a *New York Times* editorial of June 26, 1991, entitled "Sesquipedalian." It is also used to mean "having many syllables." The *sesqui-* prefix has other applications including *sesquicentennial* used for 150th anniversaries and *sesquiplane* from a class of World War I planes with a full wing and a half wing (three-quarters of a biplane). Homer K. Shanks, Jr., of San Antonio, who reported this plane, said that the main examples were the French Nieuport 13, Nieuport 17, and Nieuport 21.

Strike. Two bushels.

Tare. The weight of a container that is sometimes deducted from total weight. For instance, the weight of the bag used to weigh a pound of peaches is the tare.

Thou. 0.001 inches.

Tot. One-eighth of a British pint, 2.5 ounces, the daily rum ration in the British Navy, long abolished.

Trillion. A trillion is 1 followed by 12 zeros in the United States and France, but surprisingly is 1 followed by 18 zeros in Great Britain and Germany. What the British and the Germans call a trillion is what we would call a *quintillion*. What we call a billion, the British call a *milliard*.

Tun. When applied to ale or beer, a tun is a cask of 259 gallons (or 216 imperial gallons), but when it is a tun of wine, the amount is 302 gallons (or 252 imperial gallons).

Typp. Yarn measure—the number of yards of yarn in a pound, expressed in thousands. It is an acronym for Thousand Yards Per Pound and is pronounced *tip*.

Wrap. Three thousand yards.

Yaffle. A measure for salt cod in Newfoundland.

Medical Terms

A Plague of Maladies

Accipiter. A bandage worn around the nose.
Accipiter. A bandage worn around the nose.
Acology. The science of remedies.
Acrohypothermy. Cold feet.
Allopathic. Relating to remedies that produce different effects from those of the disease.
Alopecia. Sudden hair loss.
Auriscope. The instrument that doctors use to look inside your ears.
Bariatrics. The branch of medicine that deals with obesity.
Bdellism. Term that covers both infestation with leeches and the practice of using leeches for bloodletting.
Beer drinker's finger. A malady described in the *Journal of the American Medical Association* as the discoloration, swelling, or maceration of one's finger as a result of pulling the rings of pop-top beer cans. This malady and hundreds of others of its type appear in a remarkable dictionary entitled *Folk Names and Trade Diseases.* It was created by Dr. E. R. Plunkett, who not only lists them alphabetically but also categorizes them by the part of the body afflicted. Plunkett, for instance, lists the following thumb maladies: *ampoule snapper's thumb, bowler's thumb, boxer's thumb, drummer's thumb, football keeper's thumb, gamekeeper's thumb, tennis thumb,* and *vaccinator's thumb.*

Blue sweat. A blue-green discoloration sometimes observed in the sweat of copper workers.

Bull men's hand. Pain and numbness of the hand among artificial inseminators.

Circumorbital haematoma. A black eye.

Disco digit. Sore or infected finger that comes from too much finger-snapping while dancing. Disco digit first came to light in the pages of the *New England Journal of Medicine*, which is where many of our less threatening illnesses are first reported.

Dropsy. Swelling of the body tissues with fluid. The term *dropsy* has been replaced with *edema* in modern medical practice.

Dysmenorrhea. Menstrual cramps.

Edentulous. Without teeth.

Emesis basin. The small kidney-shaped basin you are given in a hospital when you feel sick.

Explorer. The pointed instrument that dentists use to check for cavities.

Flip-flop dermatitis. Form of dermatitis identified in the *British Medical Journal* as caused by wearing rubber "flip-flop" shoes.

Floccillation. The deathbed habit of picking at sheets and blankets. Not to be confused with the word *carphology*, which is a neurotic picking at one's bed-clothes.

45,x/46,XXq/46,XXq-dio Karyotype. The technical name for a genetic defect that appeared in the title of an article in a genetic journal. Another title: "A Family Showing Transmission of a Translocation t(3 porq-; CQ+)."

Gomphiasis. Looseness of the teeth.

Graphospasm. Writer's cramp.

Guitar nipple. Term used by the *British Medical Journal* in 1974 to describe the irritation to the breast that can occur from the pressure of the guitar against the body.

Hot pants syndrome. Term used in a 1976 issue of the *Journal of the American Medical Association* to describe a battery burn resulting from carrying a transistor battery in one's pocket.

Humper's lump. An affliction of lumber carriers that results in the swelling of the lower neck.

Iatrogenic. Diseases or symptoms that are caused by doctors. In England the acronym DOMP (for Diseases Of Medical Practice) has come to mean the same thing.

Iatromathematics. The application of astrology to medicine.

Idiopathic disease. An illness of unknown cause.

Irroration. The custom of watering a plant with the discharge of a sick person to rid the person of the disease and give it to the plant.

Mal de raquettte. Pain caused by excessive use of snowshoes. From Quebec, but now used elsewhere.

Mammobile. A mobile unit offering breast screening.

Mithridatism. Immunity from poison that is realized after taking a series of small doses.

Mutagen. An agent that increases the possibility of mutation.

Nosocomial infection. Proper name for illness caused by germs that live in hospitals.

Ochlesis. Sickness induced by too many people crowded under one roof.

Optotype. Chart used to test eyesight on which random letters of diminishing size are printed.

Orchidectomy. Castration. From the Greek word for testicle, *orchid.*

Otorhinolaryngology. The proper name for the branch of medicine that deals with ear, nose, and throat.

Parenteral. Not by mouth; so a medicine that is given parenterally means not by pill, but by injection.

Percussor. Doctor's hammer used in examining patients.

Phlebotomy. Opening a vein for bleeding a patient, as was common in the eighteenth century and before. The instrument used was a *fleam.*

Pruritus scroti. Proper name for jock itch.

Pump bump. A bony bump on the back of the heel that may become irritated by the pressure of shoes.

Purulent. Pus-forming.

Pyrosis. Heartburn.

Radiesthesia. Detecting and diagnosing disease by passing hands over the body.

Rectalgia. Literally, a pain in the ass.

Sequela. A second disease that develops as the result of a first disease.

Singultus. One hiccup in medical parlance; hiccups are singultuses.

Spansule. A capsule containing medicinal particles intended to take effect at different times. A timed-release capsule.

Sphygmomanometer. The common blood-pressure instrument.

Spit sink. The little sink next to the dentist's chair into which one can spit. Increasingly, spit sinks are being replaced by devices that suck the spit right out of your mouth and make horrible gurgling noises.

Strabotomy. Surgical removal of a squint.

Surbated. Bruised, made sore, or beaten—especially used of over-worked feet.

Trepan. A small cylindrical saw used for cutting into the human skull. Also, a powerful tool for cutting into rock, such as is needed to sink shafts. One commentator, Daniel Pettiward, writing in *Punch,* has said, "It always seems to me a most dangerous practice to have two such instruments with a single name. Imagine an inexperienced nurse on being asked by a harassed surgeon to pass the trepan handing him in her ignorance a powerful rock-boring tool. The possible consequences are too appalling even to consider."

Tympany. A swelling, such as that which comes from pride and pregnancy.

Xyster. Surgical bone-scraper.

Zipper trauma. Term used by the *Journal of the American Medical Association* for injury to the penis from catching it in a zipper. The *British Medical Journal,* on the other hand, terms it *zip injury.*

Zomotherapy. Medical treatment using raw meat or meat juices.

Monsters

*A Motley Mob of Demons, Beasts,
Gremlins, and Other Fabulous Critters*

Save for a few superstars (Nessie, Dracula, King Kong, etc.) this is not a particularly good time for monsters. Many are all but forgotten, and those whose names we use are often used without precision. Ogre, for instance, is a term for a very particular fellow: a giant who relishes human flesh. What follows is an attempt to close the modern monster gap.

Androsphinx. Beast with a man's head and a lion's body.

Asmoodeus. The demon of marital unhappiness and vanity. (One can presume that this is the patron demon of daytime television.)

Augerino. Gigantic corkscrew-shaped worm of the Southwest whose main function in life is to let water out of irrigation canals.

Baldersnatch. A fierce imaginary beast, so hideous that nobody has stayed around long enough to get a description.

Belphegor. A vile, slack-jawed demon with a phallic tongue.

Billdad. With the hind legs of a kangaroo, the tail of a beaver, the feet of a duck, and the bill of a hawk, the Billdad is able to leap up to 60 yards. It lives on trout, which it leaps on and stuns with a slap of its tail.

Bingbuffer. An Ozark beast said to be able to kill other animals by throwing rocks with its hinged tail.

Bodach. A small, vile beast of the British Isles who comes down chimneys to carry off naughty children.

Boggart. Yorkshire brownie that indulges in constant household mischief. Save for a tail, its form is human.

Bogle. A Scottish boggart.

Borogove. An extinct shabby bird that looked somewhat like a mop and lived on veal. Borogoves appear in Lewis Carroll's "Jabberwocky" ("All mimsy were the borogoves . . ."). In the original *Words* Borogove was misspelled. Joshua H. Proschau of Lakewood, N.J. wrote to explain, ". . . this was probably due to having left out any mention of the *druckfeblerteufel*, the imp who inserts the errors in printed matter. The *druckfeblerteufel* is nearly extinct, his habitat having been taken over by computers that need no assistance in proliferating errors."

Bucentaur. Monster that is half-man and half-bull.

Bwbachod. A Welsh brownie who will work free for anyone save teetotalers.

Cambions. The offspring of succubi and incubi. Incubi (male) descend on women in their sleep and have sexual intercourse with them, while succubi (female) descend on men. The cambion, incubus, and succubus are all classified as demons.

Champ. Lake Champlain's gigantic serpent.

Chessie. A monster sighted by people in the Chesapeake Bay and Potomac River. It has been named after Nessie, the familiar name for the Loch Ness monster.

Chichevache. A monster from medieval folklore who was always hungry because he lived exclusively on the flesh of virtuous women.

Criosphinx. Sphinx with the head of a ram.

Dat. A crossbred dog and cat with the worst characteristics of each.

Derodidymus. A two-headed monster.

Dipsas. A snake whose bite produces the sensation of unquenchable thirst.

Dungavenhooter. A mouthless alligator-like reptile with abnormally large nostrils. It was once common to the logging regions from Maine to Michigan. Its treacherous behavior was described in Henry H. Tyron's *Fearsome Critters:* "Concealing itself with Satanic cunning behind a whiffle bush, the Dungavenhooter awaits the passing logger. On coming within reach of the dreadful tail, the victim is knocked senseless and then pounded steadily until he becomes entirely gaseous, whereat he is greedily inhaled through the wide nostrils. . . . Rum sodden prey is sought with especial eagerness."

Ectopagus. A double monster united laterally.

Energumen. One possessed by evil spirits.

Fifinelia. Female gremlin.

Flitterbick. A flying squirrel that moves so fast it is never seen. They have been known to kill an ox by hitting it between the eyes.

Galactic ghoul. Force that inhabits a point in space approximately 35 million miles from earth, 130 million miles from the sun, on the route to Mars. The term was created by space scientists after a series of mishaps with unmanned spacecraft in the area. The ghoul has been blamed for no less than three failures and three near or partial disasters.

Gallinipper. A large insect capable of inflicting a sting; a big mosquito.

Gally-wampus. An amphibious monster that lived in Missouri during pioneer times. The Gally-wampus looked like a giant mink.

Galoopus. A tremendous black bird that laid square eggs and was once common in southern Missouri. The richness of the soil in that part of the state came as a result of galoopus dung.

Giasticutus. A monstrous bird of the Ozarks capable of carrying off full-grown cattle.

Gillygaloo. Large bird that lays square eggs.

Gnomide. A female gnome.

Gollywog. A giant salamander-like monster of the Ozarks.

Gowrow. An enormous man-eating lizard said to have terrorized Arkansas in the 1880s. According to Gerald Carson, writing in *Smithsonian* magazine, a salesman named William Miller claimed to have bagged one near Marshall, Arkansas, in 1897. Nobody ever saw it because Miller claims he sent it straight to the Smithsonian (which *claims* no knowledge of it). Carson describes it as

". . . thick-skinned, 20 feet long and enormously tusked, with short legs, webbed feet, a vicious claw on each toe, a body covered by green scales and a back bristling with stubby horns."

Gremlins. Name for the little people who make things go wrong. The term dates back to the 1920s and the Royal Air Force. One theory, expounded in the *Observer* in 1942 by John Moore, is that they were called Gremlins because "they were the goblins which came out of Fremlin beer bottles." This jibes with an account that appeared in *Newsweek*, September 7, 1942, by the magazine's London bureau chief, Merrill Mueller:

The great-grandaddy of all "bloody Gremlins" was born in 1923 in a beer bottle belonging to a Fleet Air Arm pilot whose catapult reconnaissance plane was cursed with perpetual engine trouble. This pilot was overloaded with beer the night before a practice maneuver, and he crashed into the waves when his plane's engine failed the next day. Rescued, and sobered after the cold dip, he said the engine failed because little people from a beer bottle had haunted him all night and had got into the plane's engine and controls during the flight . . . "the bloody Gremlins did it."

Guyascutus. An American animal with two distinct characteristics: telescopic legs that enable it to graze on the steepest slopes, and a tail that can wrap around rocks for added security. In *A Dictionary of Fabulous Beasts*, by Richard Barber and Anne Riches, it is pointed out that the Guyascutus is also known as a *sidewinder, hunjus, ricaboo racker, side-hill ganger, prock gwinter*, and *cutercuss*.

Hieracosphinx. Sphinx with the head of a hawk.

High-behind. A bull-sized lizard with an appetite for humans. Southern United States.

Hippocampus. The great legendary seahorse that pulled the chariots of the ancient sea gods.

Hippogriff. A cross between a horse and a griffin; a winged horse.

Hodag. Given to weeping because of its extreme ugliness, the Hodag has short legs, a spiny back, buck-teeth, and a pointed tail. It is believed to be related to the ever-weeping *Squonk*, which is covered with warts and moles and can be tracked by following its trail of tears.

Hugag. Giant animal of the north woods that is bald, covered elsewhere with pine needles, and cursed with legs without knees. Hugags must sleep standing up and routinely cause trees and buildings to lean over after napping against them.

Jackalope. Jackrabbit and antelope offspring of the Southwest. It has the body of a rabbit and the antlers of the antelope.

Je-Je Bird. Discovered by GIs stationed in Alaska during World War II. It was never seen, but could be heard at night giving out its distinctive call, "Je-Je Jesus it's cold!"

Jersey Devil. Inhabitant of the Pine Barrens of New Jersey and, since 1939, the state's official beast.

Jimp. Cousin of the Gremlin. It haunts automobiles. Jimps were particularly common in England after World War II.

Jimplicute. A nocturnal dragon or dinosaur ghost that walked the roads of Arkansas in the 1870s.

Kigmy. Small animal that enjoys being kicked. Created by Al Capp.

Kingdoodle. A huge collared lizard from the American South, able to upset small buildings and uproot trees.

Kobold. Dwarf goblin or sprite that frequents mines, caves, and homes.

Lamia. A monster that assumes the form of a woman and devours or sucks the blood from human victims; a female vampire.

Luferlang. Described in Walker D. Wyman's *Mythical Creatures of the North Country* as "an animal having a distinctive feature of a tail in the middle of its back; could run in either direction; having a bite that was almost certain death." Another expert, Henry H. Tryon, has further reported: "The biting season usually occurs on July 12. An orange-colored handkerchief conspicuously displayed will invariably afford full protection. Green clothing of any shade should be studiously avoided at this season, as it serves to arouse the animal further."

Manticore. Monster with the head of a man, body of a lion, and tail of a dragon.

Merfolk. Mermaids and mermen as a tribe.

Monoceros. Not quite a unicorn, not quite a rhinoceros; it falls somewhere in between.

Nambroth. A demon that is best conjured on Tuesdays. A *Nabam*, on the other hand, is best called on Saturdays.

Oesophagus. The name of a nonexistent type of bird that appears in Mark Twain's *A Double-Barreled Detective Story* ("...far in the empty sky a solitary oesophagus slept upon motionless wing."). Twain later noted that very few readers caught the bluff.

Ogopogo. Canadian lake monster that has been sighted with some regularity on Okanagan Lake in British Columbia for the last 300 years.

Polyommatous. Having many eyes; a useful word to know when describing monsters.

Rath. An oyster-eating turtle with a shark's mouth, erect head, and curved forelegs (which force it to walk on its knees). Discovered by Lewis Carroll, who said it was often mistaken for a kind of green pig.

Rumtifusel. Vicious, cunning beast that is flat and covered with a luxurious, rich mink-like pelt. It drapes itself over a stump to look like an expensive fur coat to attract its human prey. If a person comes by for a close look, the Rumtifusel covers its victim and cleans him or her to the bone in seconds with its deadly ventral sucking pores.

Senocular. Having six eyes.

Side-hill hoofer. A creature that runs around Ozark mountain tops in one direction because the legs on one side of his body are shorter than the legs on the other side. Also known as a *Side-hill slicker* and a *Side-hill walloper*.

Snawfus. A white deer with great wings and flowering boughs for antlers. An Ozark species exhales blue smoke that becomes the autumn mountain haze.

Sooner-dog. An intensely ferocious American dog that would *sooner* fight than eat.

Spunkie. Goblin that preys on night travelers by tricking them with lights that lead them off cliffs.

Swamp Ape. A 7-foot tall, 700-pound monster that lives in Florida's Big Cypress Swamp. It is known for its offensive smell.

Teratism. Love of monsters.

Thegri. The angel of wild beasts according to Gustov Davidson in his *Dictionary of Angels. Behemiel* is the angel of tame beasts and *Shakziel* is assigned to water insects.

Three-tailed Bavalorus. Now extinct half-animal, half-bird of the northwestern United States. It has a large corkscrew horn on its head, cloven hooves, and three tails, each with a different function. One was a barbed fighting tail, the second was a broad, flat tail that the Bavalorus sat on, and the last was a beautiful fantail used to ward off black flies. Its undoing was the fantail, which it would sit and admire by the hour, allowing its enemies to gain the upper hand.

Tove. Cross between a badger, lizard, and corkscrew, from Lewis Carroll's "Jabberwocky." Toves nest under sundials and mainly subsist on cheese.

Wampus-cat. A bloodthirsty beast of the remotest Ozarks. Mean beyond belief.

Widget. A young gremlin or *Fifinella* (see also).

Willipus-wallipus. A big vague monster of early America.

Wowzer. A super-panther able to kill horses and cows by biting off their heads. Common to the pioneer South.

Yaksha. A Hindu gnome.

Yehudi. During World War II, the American equivalent of the British gremlins were yehudis, because they were always "fiddling about."

Ziphius. A sea monster given to attacking and destroying ships in the northern latitudes. It has an owl's head and a mammoth pit of a mouth.

Neologisms

A Corner for Coined Words

The late Stuart Berg Flexner, senior editor of the *Random House Dictionary of the English Language*, once claimed that if William Shakespeare were to suddenly show up in New York or London today, he would only understand five out of nine words in our vocabulary. The list that follows should help push the ratio to 5:10.

Anglophobia. A dislike for England and things English. It was coined by Thomas Jefferson.

Ansurge. A word that made its debut in the pages of *Word Ways* magazine, for the "irresistible urge to answer a ringing telephone, no matter how inconvenient the hour or the circumstances." It was created by Temple G. Porter, who also suggested *phonercion* and *phoneed* as alternative words for the same condition.

Anthropophaginian. A word formed by Shakespeare from *anthropoghagi* (meat-eaters, cannibals) for the sake of a formidable sound.

Antishoopation. The feeling in the head just prior to sneezing. It was created by Bruce Pelmore of Victoria, B.C., after a radio discussion lamenting the lack of a word for this condition.

Aptronym. Franklin P. Adams's coinage for a name that sounds like its owner's occupation. William Rumhole, for instance, was a London tavern owner. In

Noah Jonathan Jacobs's *Naming-Day in Eden*, we are told of a Russian ballerina named Olga Tumbelova.

Bamama. An overqualified, degree-heavy person. The term was created by columnist Ellen Goodman to describe a friend with one MA and two BAs, who she fondly called Bmama.

Barbecue mode. A term associated with the space-shuttle program. It refers to the period when the Orbiter goes into a series of slow rolls. This NASA creation stands as vivid proof that all government terms are not stuffy and overblown.

Barnacular. The quality of officialese coined by Ivor Brown, who based the term "on the Dickensian family of Tite Barnacles who clung with such tenacity to official posts."

Bladderclock. The use of your bladder as an alarm clock; drinking the right amount of water the night before to get up in time in the morning. It is a coinage of Bill Sherk, author of *Brave New Words,* a brilliant collection of new mintings from Canada.

Blooming verbs. In early 1981 a government official named Paul L. Bloom single-handedly disbursed $4 million in oil company over-charges to various charities. When questioned about this, he said he was "not interested in Robin Hooding." This, in turn, caused the late *Washington Star* to call such constructions Blooming verbs, after Paul Bloom.

Brillig. The time of broiling for dinner; the late afternoon. It was created by Lewis Carroll for "Jabberwocky.'"

Bureausis. An inability to cope with even the most reasonable, simplest rules and regulations. It was attributed to a "political scientist" in *Newsweek,* September 11, 1978.

Calculatoritis. Excessive dependence on electronic calculators. The term was first introduced to the public by Marcia A. Bartusiak in a 1978 article in *Science News* on her own case, which she discovered when, as a physics student, "I was taking a test with my trusty calculator by my side and, without thinking, I actually punched up 200 divided by 2 before putting it on my paper."

Channelfido. A word that first appeared in *Personnel Administration* in 1950, which was defined as "An official, necessarily ineffective, who at all times scrupulously follows proper channels."

Copelessness. Roger Price's word for the inability to cope with life.

Cordodollars. The wood burner's woeful equivalent of the oil burner's inflated petrodollars. It is from Don Mitchell's article on the subject in *Boston Magazine*.

Cotton woolies. Roald Dahl's generic term for what today's children are not interested in reading about. He used it in a quote that appeared in an article about his writing in the *Hartford Courant*: "I write of nasty things and violent happenings because kids are themselves that way. . . . Kids are too tough to read about little cotton woolies."

Cremains. The end product of a cremation. The word was spotted in an ad for a Clearwater, Florida, cemetery. The ad stated, "For a free copy of an 'eye opening' article about handling of the cremains, call..." Presumably the term was created by someone in the funeral business.

Czardine. Assistant czar. The word appears in *Doublespeak Dictionary* by William Lambdin, who says it came from a Los Angeles police lieutenant during the days of the gas lines. In explaining how the police would make sure that service stations were remaining open the proper hours, the lieutenant said, "We have a sergeant in each area who has been appointed energy czar, and he has little czardines out helping him."

Deinstitutionalization. With 9 syllables and 22 letters, this word has been crowned by the *Wall Street Journal* as the king of all recent bureaucratic coinages, beating out such contenders as *Reprioritization* and *unreprocessable*.

Democrapic. Garson Kanin's word for the expression of democratic beliefs by those who cannot tolerate democracy in action.

Dontopedalogy. Natural tendency to put one's foot in one's mouth. It is the creation of Britain's Prince Philip.

Ecdysiast. Stripteaser. This fine word was created in 1940 by H. L. Mencken at the request of a then-famous stripper named Georgia Sothern, who felt that her profession should have a more proper name. It is based on the scientific term *ecdysis*, which refers to the act of shedding skin.

William F. Buckley, Jr., has taken the word one step further by coining *ecdysiasm* to describe what an *ecdysiast* does.

Elechiaondros. An all-purpose but entirely meaningless word created by Phyllis Richman, food editor of the *Washington Post*. It is a marvelous bluff word pronounced *ella-key—andras*.

Eth. A member of an ethnic group, one who displays ethnicity, a subject for study by ethnographers and ethnologists. It was coined by Herbert Kupferberg in his article, "Confessions of an Eth," in *Parade* magazine in reaction to the 1076-page *Harvard Encyclopedia of American Ethnic Groups*.

Extraa. Not actually a new word, but a logical and improved spelling suggested by Canadian columnist Herb Martindale. He also suggests the following spelling reforms in his book *The Caledonian Eye Opener: superfluuouss, maximuum, excesss, swarmmm,* and *glutt*.

Feaseless. The government in general and the military especially have become so infatuated with the word *feasibility* that they have created a number of awkward variations ranging from *defeasible* (no longer feasible) to *prefeasibiity* (a period before something becomes feasible). Of all, however, the oddest is feaseless—presumably, something lacking feasibility.

Globaloney. Cosmic nonsense. The term was invented and introduced by Clare Booth Luce in a speech before the House of Representatives in 1943 while commenting on the views of Vice-President Henry Wallace: "Much of what Mr. Wallace calls his global thinking is, no matter how you slice it, still 'Globaloney.' "

Glot. A person who cannot bear to waste anything. It is from poet Alastair Reid's imaginative *Ounce, Dice, Trice* (see also *Gnurr, Oosse, Poose,* and *Worg*).

Gnurr. The substance that over time collects in the bottoms of pockets and the cuffs of trousers. Gnurr is a small variety of Oosse. Alastair Reid.

Hippism. A philistine's resentment of a curiosity about the meaning of words. This term was coined by William F. Buckley, Jr., after reading an attack on I. Moyer Hunsberger's *Quintessential Dictionary* by a Tampa, Florida, librarian named Joseph Hipp.

Holismo. Exaggerated holism; the belief that holistic medicine is a panacea. The word was created by Fitzhugh Mullan, M.D., in response to the "outpouring of holism" offered by friends and acquaintances when he was sick. The word made its debut in Mullan's article, "The Rising of Holismo," in *Hospital Physician* magazine.

Homerism. Created by William Taaffe, who defined it in the *Washington Star:* (1) The practice of showing partiality to the home team or the side naturally favored in a broadcast area. (2) Excessive partiality, often involving distortion of fact. (3) A provincial form of announcing found in cities with few teams.

Infracaninophile. One who habitually favors the underdog. Christopher Morley.

Infracaninophile. Helper of the underdog. The term was used by Christopher Morley in referring to Sir Arthur Conan Doyle in the introduction to an edition of Sherlock Holmes.

Irage. Rage expressed during the Iranian hostage period, a term coined by an unnamed psychologist and quoted in the *Washington Post* during the crisis.

Irrevelant. Harry S. Truman's way of saying irrelevant. The fact that he was wrong is not terribly relevant.

Kelemenopy. Word created by poet John Ciardi that appears in his *Browser's Dictionary.* It is "a sequential straight line through the middle of everything leading nowhere . . . It is based on the *k-l-m-n-o-p* sequence."

Loyalty laughter. The laughter generated by ambitious underlings when the boss tries to be funny. Fred Allen created the term, which can be applied to other situations: students and professors, sales representatives and big customers.

Mecker. To visit places that have acquired some sort of shrine status, as demonstrated by its inventor, Ivor Brown, "Myriads . . . go meckering at Statford-upon-Avon."

Metropollyanna. The belief that eventually all Americans will move in from the country and live in the cities or suburbs. The term sprang to life at the 1975 National Conference on Rural America after it had been coined by one of the delegates, Clay Cochran of the Rural Housing Authority. Metropollyanna was termed a major problem because it leads to policies that discriminate against rural and small-town America.

Monologophobe. Creation of Theodore M. Bernstein, who defined this creature in *The Careful Writer* as "a writer who would rather walk naked in front of Saks Fifth Avenue than be caught using the same word more than once in three lines." See also *Synonymomania*.

Mux. A mix of many things going through one's head; a blend of mix + flux from *Time*.

Negawatt. Energy not used; the creation of energy expert Amory Lovins.

Nesomaniac. A person who is mad about islands; a creation of James A. Michener, who introduced it in the January 1978 issue of *Travel & Leisure*.

Obeastie. A fat cat according to newspaper columnist Bill Tammeus.

Ochlotheocracy. Mob rule with religious overtones. Created in 1980 by the British magazine the *Economist* to describe the government in power in Iran.

Ocrephobia. Fear of being covered with gold paint, also known as a *Gilt Complex*. One of Roger Price's contributions to the language, it is pronounced exactly like the word for fear of okra.

Ombibulous. H. L. Mencken's word for someone who drinks everything.

Oosse. The airy, furry matter that gathers under beds. Also known as *dust bunnies, trilbies, kittens*. Alastair Reid.

Pedlock. When the number of people exceed the capacity of sidewalks to carry them.

Plentieth. Franklin P. Adam's adjective of indefinite older age, as in "he is about to celebrate his plentieth birthday."

Plimp. To participate, a la George Plimpton, in a professional sport for the sake of participatory journalism. The creation of *Time* magazine.

Plobby. A word created by P. G. Wodehouse to describe a pig eating. He actually used it in conjunction with another word of his own invention to marvelous net effect: It was a "plobby, wofflesome sound."

Poose. A drop that hangs on the end of the nose and glistens. A poose is likely to appear when one has a cold or comes out of the water after swimming. Alastair Reid.

Privish. A portmanteau word combing private + publish, which means to publish with a minimum of fanfare. About the worst thing that can happen to a manuscript is to have it privished. The term has been unofficially bandied about in the book industry since the 1950s.

Proxmites. Those who oppose new technology, especially that which comes from the Pentagon or the Space Agency. The term first appeared in an editorial in the newsletter *Space Daily* in 1971, where it was presented as the modern counterpart to the Luddites, who opposed labor-saving machinery in nineteenth-century England. Although he was not named in the editorial, the term recognized former Senator William Proxmire as the leader of the Proxmites.

Psycherelic. A leftover from the sixties, another coinage from the fertile mind of Bill Tammeus.

Quatressential. Not quite quintessential. One of a number of new words that Lewis Burke Frumkes has offered the English language via his article, "A Volley of Words," in *Harper's* magazine. Two other examples of his fine work:

Copulescence. The healthy afterglow that attends successful sexual intercourse.

Ossis. The contents of a black hole.

Queuetopia. Winston Churchill's blending of queue + Utopia. He created it circa 1950 to describe the Utopia of the Socialist nations where people waited in line for everything.

Quiz. The product of a wager. The manager of a Dublin theater named Jim Daly bet that he could take a word with no meaning and make it the talk of the town in 24 hours. He won the bet with *q-u-i-z* chalked on walls all over the city. At first the word was synonymous with practical joke, but it later came to have its current meaning.

Not all the experts accept the story as authentic, but usually retell it anyhow because it is the only explanation that has ever been given for this word, which is listed in most dictionaries as "origin unknown." In the Morris Dictionary of Word and Phrase Origins, William and Marry Morris say that the story "smacks a bit more of 100-proof Irish whiskey than of 100 percent accuracy."

Ratomorphic. Arthur Koestler's term for a view of human behavior modeled on the behavior of laboratory rats and other experimental animals.

Reaganaut. Government official loyal to Ronald Reagan and his policies. It was created by Richard Allen, once Reagan's national security advisor, to distinguish the loyalists from the rest.

Rectumology. The process of coming up with a price for a custom job when there is no firm criteria on which to base the price. It was first used by Steven K. Roberts in *Industrial Design with Microprocessors.*

Rendezwoo. Columnist Earl Wilson's word for a rendezvous that is clearly romantic.

Renovation. A fresh start beginning with a Reno divorce. Walter Winchell.

Roomscanitis. An affliction of some partygoers that makes their eyes flit about looking for someone more interesting or less dull than you to talk to. It was created by John H. Corcoran, Jr., who introduced it in an article in the *Washingtonian* magazine.

Semantiphony. One who is continually raising alleged semantic questions in an effort to conceal his lack of knowledge and wisdom. Like *channelfido,* this word made its debut in the magazine *Personnel Administration* in 1950. An example was given: "If someone says something no more esoteric than 'How about going to lunch?', the semantiphony is likely to rejoin: 'We have to define terms first. Just what does "going to lunch" mean?' "

Semordnilap. A word that spells another word in reverse. It is the creation of Martin Gardner, who made it by spelling *palindromes* backward. A palindrome is, of course, a word, phrase, or passage that spells the same thing forward as well as backward. Some choice semordnilaps: *straw, reknits, doom,* and *repaid. Serutan* is an intentional semordnilap trade name, whereas *Tums* probably is not.

Serendipity. A word created by Horace Walpole, which made its debut in his *Three Princes of Serendip*. It refers to the ability to make favorable discoveries by accident.

Significa. Term created by Irving Wallace, his daughter Amy, and his son, David Wallechinsky, for "unusual or little-known facts which have too much significance to qualify as mere trivia."

Snoblem. The concern of a small group who see prestige value in the issue; a blend of snob + problem. The word made its debut in the *New York Times* in December 1964.

Spart. "Spart is pretty much the same as fight or pep or gumption. Like the *Spart of St. Louis,* that plane Lindbergh flowed to Europe in." Dizzy Dean.

Strawperson. Columnist Ellen Goodman's stand-in for strawman.

Synonymomania. A word created by Theodore M. Bernstein to describe the "compulsion to call a spade successively a *garden implement* and an *earth-turning tool.*" Both this term and the complementary *monologophobia* appear in Bernstein's *The Careful Writer*.

Tangibilate. Word created by Father Divine when he became disgusted with the theoretical and highly theological musings of others in his field. "The trouble with the world today," he said, "is that there are too many metaphysicians who don't know how to tangibilate."

Ubique. In any place whatsoever, anywhere, and everywhere. This term has served as the motto for the American Geographical Society since 1851.

Universal annoyance. Term coined in the *Smithsonian* magazine by Charles R. Larson for ". . . that indestructable T-shaped piece of plastic that comes attached to almost every object of wearing apparel one buys in department stores, connecting the price tag to the object."

Urbanality. James Thurber's term for self-conscious and plodding urbanity. He used it to describe, among other things, the early issues of the *New Yorker*.

Verbicide. C. S. Lewis's word for the killing of a word.

Videot. The late Red Smith's word for those who watch anything that flickers across the tube. He created it in the days when Liberace and Gorgeous George were major TV figures, but the term is just as useful today. It rhymes with idiot.

Watchpot. Creation of Alexander Haig spotted by William Safire, who wrote, "A watchpot is, presumably, a pot that bears watching to make certain that it does not boil over."

Worg. A plant that never grows. Alastair Reid.

Occupations

A Corps of Job Descriptions

It seems there is no such thing as a job without a name. With the help of various editions of the U.S. Department of Labor's *Dictionary of Occupational Titles* (hereafter referred to as DOT and containing more than 20,000 occupations in its most recent edition) and a number of other sources, here are some unusual examples.

Air Personality. Disc jockey who may work with an *air name*.
Almanagist. Compiler of almanacs.
Astrologaster. A lying or deceitful astrologer.
Ballast scorer. One who inspects and scores the ballast on a railroad line. Ballast is the material—usually crushed stone—in which the railroad ties are imbedded.
Bee hunter. One who follows bees back to their hives for the purpose of taking their honey.
Bersatrix. An old word for baby-sitter, not in general use since the eighteenth century.
Blue-collar worker supervisor. The new official term for *foreman* at the Department of Labor. It may work on paper, but it is hard to imagine a factory worker calling out, "Where's the blue-collar worker supervisor, we've got a problem over here."

Bung puller. A slaughtering/meat-packing job described in the 1949 DOT: "Removes bung from intestines, for use as sausage casing: Grasps bung with one hand and, holding guts down with other, tears bung loose from other guts. Washes bung under water spray and hangs it on rack. Replaces remaining guts on conveyor." It is the kind of job that could lead one to drink, or at least to work as a:

Bung remover. One who removes the plugs, or bungs, from full whiskey barrels in preparation for blending. DOT.

Burger flipper. Person working in a fast food restaurant. It is used in questioning the base of the American labor market in lines like, "Are we becoming a nation of burger flippers?"

Button layer. Lays reflective, ceramic traffic tiles on roads and parking lots.

Camoufleur. Person skilled in use or application of camouflage.

Campanologist. One skilled at bell ringing.

Chicken sexer. One who determines the gender of newborn chicks.

Clicker. An old term for the person who stands at the door of an establishment to invite customers.

Cliometrician. One who uses modern economic techniques to study the past.

Cod tonguer. One of a group of workers likely to be found on a fish-dressing gang, according to the 1949 DOT. A cod tonguer removes the cod's tongue with a sharp knife. Other members of the gang: *blooder, gibber, giller, gutter, header, idler, ripper, scraper, spawner, splitter,* and *throater.*

Dreamer. Officially defined in the DOT: "Sells lucky numbers, which she claims to select by occult means, to policy game bettors. May sell horse-race tips which are derived from similar sources."

Drifter. Runs machines that remove scale from the inside of pipes. DOT.

Drowner. An irrigator of fields in the British Isles.

Faller. In logging, the faller is the logger who puts the initial cut in a standing tree that indicates where it will fall.

Fang manager. According to the British official *Classification of Occupations,* a fang manager is the person responsible for the ventilation of a mine.

Feather renovator. Cleans feathers for reuse in pillows. DOT.

Fellmonger. A dealer in furs and pelts.

Fletcher. One who makes bows and arrows.

Fogger. One who is paid to feed farm animals; sometimes called *fodderer.*

Funambulist. A rope walker.

Handyma'am. Woman working as a handyman and the name of a Detroit-based, female-staffed repair group.

Haruspex. One who practices divination from examining the entrails of animals.

Heresimach. One who combats heresy.

Hwsmon. The headman on a Welsh farm.

Hypertrichologist. The professional name for a person who treats excessive or unsightly facial hair.

Knock-up assembler. Glues and drives wooden parts into such products as door frames and boxes.

Leacher. Tends leach tanks that recover soda ash from black ash. DOT.

Leguillon debeader. One who removes bead wire from scrap automobile tires using a Leguillon wire puller. DOT.

Longshore worker. Neutered form of *longshoreman* adopted by the U.S. Department of Labor. There are many others, including *bat handler* for *bat boy.*

Lump inspector. Inspects lumps of tobacco for defects in wrapper leaf. DOT.

Maturity checker. Tends machine that mashes peas and registers force required to crush them to ascertain hardness. DOT.

Meringue spreader. Fills pies; a pie topper. DOT.

Mesquite grubber. Laborer who clears land of mesquite so that it can be used for cattle. *Cactus grubber* does the same with cactus. DOT.

Moirologist. Mourner for hire.

Mother repairer. One who repairs the metal phonograph matrix, also known as a *mother*. DOT.

Mumbler. Alternate name for a glass blower.

Myropologist. One who sells unguents or perfumes.

Necker. Stitches neckties. DOT.

Peruker. A wig maker.

Protective coating engineer. A housepainter by another name.

Right-fly raiser. A sewing machine operator who turns under the edge of the right-fly lining and sews it to the fly along the seam that joins fly to trousers. The DOT, second edition, lists this but not the *left-fly raiser*.

Santa Claus. The DOT *claims* that this is someone who "impersonates Santa Claus during the Christmas season."

Sequins stringer. Tends machine that automatically interlaces thread around strings of sequins in such a manner as to separate, space, and secure the sequins. DOT.

Siffleur. A professional whistler. A female professional whistler is a *siffleuse*.

Slab smoother. The person who smooths off large ice cream slabs with a large spatula. DOT.

Slime-plant operator. Tends equipment that recovers gold and other minerals at smelting plants.

Slubber doffer. In a textile mill, removes full bobbins from slubber frames and replaces them with empty ones. A slubber is a machine that processes raw cotton and is operated by a *slubber tender*. DOT.

Smasher. Person who operates a power press to crease the folds of the signatures of books before they are bound. Presumably a smasher has helped bring this book to you. Smashers are also known as *book compressors*. DOT.

Squeal, rattle, and leak repairer. Drives automobiles of service customers to determine origin of noises and leaks, and repairs or adjusts components to eliminate cause of complaint. DOT.

Tea-bag tagger. One of three DOT names for the person who ties tags to individual tea bags. The other two: *tea-bag stringer* and *tag threader*.

Thin miner. Miner who works on thin seams of coal as opposed to major veins, according to the official British *Classification of Occupations* which is also responsible for the next two items.

Trolloper. Shrimp fisher on the East English coast.

Visagiste. An expert in cosmetics; a makeup person.

Warping worker. One who clears out ditches.

Webster. Loom operator.

Whizzer. Tends a machine that spins felt hat bodies to remove excess water. DOT.

Oddities

A Sideshow of Very Special Words

Some words are important for reasons that may not be immediately obvious.

Adder. One of a select group of words in English that was created by the misplacement of a letter. Originally an adder was *a nadder,* but somewhere along the way the *n* migrated to the *a.* The same thing happened to *a napron* (but not to *a napkin,* which is closely related), *an ewt,* and *a nauger.*

Aria. Rare four-letter, three-syllable word; *Oreo* is another.

Asphodel. One of a list of words identified some years ago by Dr. Wilfred Funk as the most beautiful in English. The others: *fawn, dawn, chalice, anemone, tranquil, hush, golden, halcyon, camellia, bobolink, thrush, chimes, murmuring, lullaby, luminous, damask, cerulean, melody, marigold, jonquil, oriole, tendril, myrrh, mignonette, gossamer, alysseum, mist, oleander, amaryllis,* and *rosemary.* The asphodel, incidentally, is a flower. Willard R. Espy has added *wisteria, mellifluous, and Shenandoah* to the list.

Balloonnoonnookkeeppoobah. The creation of Joel D. Gaines, an English teacher in Honolulu, who fashioned it to set a record for consecutive pairs of like letters (it has nine). The word that was submitted to and appeared in *Word Ways* magazine describes "an agent who sits on balloons at noon in a corner in order to earn his keep."

Bologna. One of those words that the experts cannot agree how to spell. Various dictionaries yield *balogna, baloney, bolony, bologny,* and *boloney.* Phonetically, *baloney* looks best.

Cleave. A word with opposite meanings: to stick together and to part.

Cuspidor. The word that James Joyce singled out as the most beautiful in the English language.

Designated hitter. The rarest of terms, one that was accepted by the editors at Merriam-Webster on first hearing and without the need for further evidence that it belonged in the dictionary. The term, of course, refers to the 1973 American League ruling that allows for a tenth player, or designated hitter, to be put in the lineup to bat for the pitcher. It was correctly reasoned that the name for a tenth player would come into immediate use.

Dord. This word, which first appeared in the *Merriam-Webster International* edition of 1934 as a synonym for density, was, in fact, an error. It slipped into the dictionary from an abbreviation file that had an entry "D or d"—meaning a capital or small *d*—as an abbreviation for the word *density*. Although it was taken out of the next edition of the *Merriam-Webster,* it has shown up in other dictionaries. *Dord* was brought to public attention by Professor Allen Walker Read of Columbia University at the 1976 meeting of the Modern Language Association in a paper on "ghost words."

Facetiously. One of a handful of words in which the vowels appear in proper order. Other examples include: *bacteriously, abstemiously,* and *arteriously.* They appear in reverse order in even fewer words. One example is *duoliteral.*

Flatulent. One of ten words that were voted the least euphonious in the language by the National Association of Teachers of Speech. The other nine: *phlegmatic, crunch, cacophony, treachery, sap, jazz, plutocrat, gripe,* and *plump.*

Floccinaucinihilipilification. The longest word in the first edition of the *Oxford English Dictionary* (OED). It means "to estimate as worthless." The word is actually used. In January 1979, Senator Daniel P. Moynihan of New York used it in a press conference in response to a question about New York City's fiscal problems when he said, "The floccinaucinihilipilification problem is not behind us." There are many longer words in science and technology, especially science. In his book *Beyond Language,* Dmitri A. Borgman points to a chemical term with 1,185 letters. Incredibly, a year after Borgman's initial discovery, he came up with a 1,913-letter chemical monster, which was announced in the first issue of *Word Ways.*

Fog. The word that the late Professor Raven McDavid, editor of the *Linguistic Atlas of the United States,* said distinguished the different linguistic backgrounds of the candidates in the 1980 presidential campaign. Carter, Reagan, and Kennedy respectively pronounced it "fawg," "fohg," and "fahg."

Ghoti. George Bernard Shaw's spelling of the word "fish" using the *gh* of *laugh,* the *o* of *woman,* and the *sh* of *nation.* The late Russell Dunn of Lakewood, Ohio, came up with this spelling of potato: *gheaughteighptough* using the *p* as in *hiccough*, the *o* of *beau*, the *t* of *naught*, the *a* of *neigh*, the *t* of *pterodactyl*, and the *o* in *though*.

Glottochronology. In the *Morris Dictionary of Word and Phrase Origins* (Volume II), William and Mary Morris cite this word and *lexicostatistics* as the ugliest words from the decade (the 1960s) in which they were coined. What fascinates the Morrises is that both words were coined by *linguists*. Both words are technical names for techniques used to date the age of a word.

Walter de la Mare held that ". . . of all names, perhaps those which grammarians have given to the various species of words themselves are the most unalluring: *adjective, adverb, preposition, conjunction,* for example."

Herein. A word that yields seven other words without transposing any letters: he, her, here, ere, rein, and in.

Hungry. Aside from *angry,* the only other *common* English word that ends in *-gry*.

Each year some 2,500 letters come into Merriam-Webster asking questions about language. These are all answered through its Language Research Service, a fancy name for the fact that the company encourages people who buy its dictionaries to ask questions about words and usage.

One question, however, requires a form response because it is asked so often. For reasons unclear, it is unrivaled as the most commonly asked question about English.

The question always boils down to this: "I have been told that there are three words that end in *-gry. Angry* and *hungry* are easy to find, but what is the third?"

The trick in the question is that the third is hardly a household word. Among the 460,000 entries in *Webster's Third New International Dictionary,* the only other *-gry* word is *anhungry*, an obsolete synonym for hungry, which owes its dictionary survival to the fact that Shakespeare used it. The *Third* also contains *aggry bead*, a form of glass bead, but there is no evidence that *aggry* is ever used without the word *bead*.

Merriam-Webster editors found a few more in the massive 13-volume *Oxford English Dictionary,* but they are so rare that some cannot be found in print outside the dictionary itself. The OED contains *mawgry, magry,* and *maugry*, which are all obsolete variant spellings of *maugre* (an archaic way of saying "in spite of"); *puggry*, which is a variant spelling of the word *puggree* (a light scarf worn around a sun helmet); and *iggry*, which is an English spelling of an Arabic word meaning "to hurry up."

Then there is the question of *pty*. Other than *empty* and excluding proper names like *Humpty* and *Dumpty*, how many . . . .

I. The most commonly spoken word in America. *You, the,* and *a* come in second, third, and fourth.

Indivisibilities. Fine specimen of a word in which one vowel shows up seven times in a row.

Kinnikinnik. A Native American smoking mixture made of bark and leaves but no tobacco. According to John Ciardi, it is the longest palindromic word in *Webster's Third New International Dictionary.*

Kudos. One of those few words that is the same in the singular and the plural. Another is *shambles. Kudos* is an old university colloquialism that was brought back to life by *Time,* which began to use it in 1926 as the title of an annual listing of honorary degrees. David Boardman of West Columbia, South Carolina, collects palindromes and has come up with such treasures as *Kanakanak,* an Alaskan city; *Maylayalam,* a language; and *saippuakivikauppias,* which is Finnish for a dealer in lye. Boardman also raises an important question: "I didn't realize that *radar* was an acronym, but since it is also a palindrome, would that make it an *acrodrome* or a *palidrym* or a *palinym?*"

Latchstring. This may hold the record for a common word with the most consonants (six) in a row.

Milver. Term for a person who speaks out loud during a movie. It was created and defined by Joe Achenbach in the *Washington Post* in 1990 after decades of hunting to find a word that rhymes with *silver.* Achenbach points out that *orange* is still lacking, but that Clement Wood's *Rhyming Dictionary* lists *chirp'll* as a rhyme for *purple.*

Monosyllable. A monosyllable. Ralph Woods, who listed *monosyllable* as a monosyllable in his book *How to Torture Your Mind,* also lists *oxyopia,* which is a seven-letter word with five syllables.

Muzz. British slang for "to study," also "to confuse." The author's research leads him to believe that this would be the last word in the dictionary if all the words in the *Random House Dictionary* were spelled backward. It also would be the first word if the dictionary were completely reversed.

NOON. Noon, when capitalized, comes out the same backward, forward, and upside down.

Oslo. An important city in Czechoslovakia, right in the middle of Czech*oslo*vakia, as a matter of fact. This was once a clue in a crossword puzzle in the London *Observer.*

Ouija. The name of a once-popular board for divination. It is rarest of words because it has roots in two languages: a combination of the word *yes* in French and German.

Pikes Peak. One of the few legislated punctuation bans in history. In 1978 the Colorado legislature outlawed the apostrophe in Pike's Peak.

Pneumonoultramicroscopicsilicovolcanoconiosis. The longest word in *Webster's Third New International Dictionary.* It is a lung disease caused by inhaling fine particles of silicon dust. It can also be spelled with a *k* in place of the last *c* in the word. Since 1982, this word has been the longest word in the *Oxford English Dictionary.*

Queue. A five-letter word that can lose four of its letters—four consecutive vowels—without changing its pronunciation.

Rhythm. One of the longest—if not the longest—words possible without using *a,e,i,o,* or *u.* Other fairly long oddities of this nature: *tryst, Gypsy,* and *lymph.*

Set. According to the *Guinness Book of World Records,* this is the most over-worked word in the English language, with 58 noun uses, 126 uses as a verb, and 10 as a participial adjective. Other words with a multitude of uses: *through, strike, serve, run, draw, cut, cast,* and *point.* Fred Mish, editorial director at Merriam-Webster, has pointed out that the reigning king in his company's *Third International* is *take* with 137 meanings. They list a mere 119 for *set.*

Strengths. The Reverend Solomon Ream claims in his *Curiosities of the English Language* that this is probably the longest word in English with only one vowel—to say nothing of its being one of the longest one-syllable words in the language. *Strength* is the longest eight-letter word with one vowel, but there are a number of seven-letter words including: *flights, frights, groths, lengths, plinths, scrunch, scratch, thrill, thwarts, shrinks,* and *shrills.*

Taxi. Word that is spelled the same in nine languages—English, French, German, Swedish, Spanish, Danish, Norwegian, Dutch, and Portuguese. The *OED* says that it comes from the French word *taxer,* to tax or fix the price of.

Typewriter. One of a small number of longer words that can be typed by using only the top row of letters on a standard typewriter. *Proprietory* is another, and *flagfalls* is one of the few that comes from the middle row only. The vowelless bottom line yields no words.

According to an item in the February 1968 issue of *Word Ways,* the champion "top row" words are two 12-letter medical words: *pituitotrope* (person with a constitution strongly influenced by his pituitary gland) and *uropyoureter* (an infected uroureter).

Underground. Rare English word beginning and ending with *und.*

Unquestionably. Good answer to the question "Are there many English words containing all five vowels?" See also *Facetiously.*

Usher. A word containing four personal pronouns: *us, she, he, her.*

Uu. Tradition says that there are five words with a double *u* in English, but Dr. Timothy Perper of Philadelphia has six of them: *residuum, menstruum, vacuum, continuum, duumvirate,* and *individuum.*

Victuals. "The ugliest word in the language," according to the late Harry Golden, who explained, "You can't say it or write it. The best thing is to forget it." Those who do use it usually pronounce it *vittles.*

Yy. It has been claimed that no English word contains a successive double *y* although one can find *snarleyyow* in *Webster's Second International.*

Zyxomma. An Indian dragon fly. It also stands as the best possible seven-letter word that can be used in a Scrabble game (30 points). Zyxomma emerged as the best Scrabble word after a book published in 1974, *The Best* by Peter Pasell and Leonard Ross, claimed that "the best" Scrabble word was *jonquil* at 23 points and, if one could use a blank tile, that *quiz-er* at 24 points was even better. Immediately, Scrabble buffs began coming up with better offerings such as *squeeze* (25) and *popquiz* (29) until *zyxomma* appeared to best them all.

Zyzzyva. The last of the last words in the major dictionaries. The *zyzzyva* is a South American weevil and is the last word in *The American Heritage Dictionary,* beating such other last words as *zyzzogeton* (a type of South American leaf hopper from *Webster's Third*), and *zyrian* (a Uralic language, from the *Random House Dictionary*).

According to William and Marry Morris (who used the word *zyzzyva* to end their *American Heritage Dictionary*), the *Grolier Universal Encyclopedia,* and the *Dictionary of Word and Phrase Origins,* the word is pronounced *ziz-ih-vuh.*

This is hardly the last word, however, as a letter on the subject from Paul S. Hanson of Stanford, California, attests:

"[Zyzzyva] reminded me of a word that I encountered about ten years ago. It's *Zyzzyx,* a genus of hymenoptera, if I remember correctly. While attempting to verify this word . . . I came across a genus with an even longer name, *Zyzzyxdonta,* which seems to be a kind of terrestrial snail. . . . *Zyzzyxdonta* has the edge over my unverified *Zyzzyx,* but its preeminence is probably temporary anyway. Biologists seem increasingly of late to enjoy devising whimsical or clever names. Whoever first describes a newly discovered species in printed form has the right to christen it, however demonically. There's nothing to prevent a botanist who has just discovered a previously unknown species of stunted buttercup in the Arctic tundra from naming his find *Zyzzyxzyzzyxzyzzyx polycaudata,* for example."

Outdoors Words

Calls of the Wild

Aiguille. A steep, pointed mountain as opposed to one with rounded, soft outlines. The term is used by mountain climbers and rhymes with wheel.

Alpenglow. The reddish glow that appears on mountaintops just before sunrise or just after sunset.

Astrobleme. Scar on the face of the earth made by a meteorite.

Balk. The piece of ground in a field that remains unploughed.

B&B. Balled and burlapped, a nursery term for how large plants are sometimes sold with their root ball wrapped in burlap.

Benthos. The flora and fauna of the sea bottom.

Berm. An earth wall; the shoulder of a road, river, canal, etc.

Birding. What used to be known as "bird watching." People who go birding are known as *birders*.

Cabatoe. A plant that grows potatoes underground and cabbage above. It is one of a number of such creations offered in the catalog of Lakeland Nurseries of Hanover, Pennsylvania. Another is the *topeperatoe*, which grows potatoes for roots and bears peppers and tomatoes above grounds.

Chiminage. A toll paid for going through a forest.

Copse. A thicket of small trees. This word is used a lot in nineteenth-century English novels and is also written as *coppice*.

Culm. An individual shoot or cane of bamboo.

Cultivar. A plant variety that did not occur naturally but was developed by a grower.

Dendrochronological. Tree-dating.

Detritus. Debris, such as the mixture of leaves, twigs, and pebbles found on the forest floor.

Disgorger. Instrument used to remove the hook from the mouth of a fish.

Ejecta. Matter thrown out, such as volcanic ejecta.

Espalier. The lattice or trellis on which a fruit tree is trained to give it an unusual shape. It is also the name of a tree so shaped.

Eyot. A small island in a river or lake. Sometimes called an *ait*. Eyot is pronounced *ite* and ait sounds like *ate*.

Fen. A low-lying land area partly covered by water—also the fen in Fenway Park.

Floc. A clump of solids formed in sewage by biological or chemical action.

Foehn. A warm, dry wind that comes off a mountain. Foehns commonly blow in from the north side of the Alps. It rhymes with main, and it has been described as a European chinnock.

Fumarole. A small hole from which volcanic smoke pours.

Gilpoke. Originally a lumberman's term for a stuck log protruding into a stream that hampered log drives. The term has been adopted by canoeists, who also see gilpokes as hazards.

Gnarr. A knot in wood; an abnormally dense or hard place.

Gnat-ball. A dense swarm of gnats or other small insects. Ozarkian.

Gore. A small, irregular piece of land that can't be fitted into a township. The term is common to Maine, where the map is dotted with such places as Misery Gore and Coburn Gore.

Gowt. A sluice in an embankment for letting water out.

Grike. A narrow opening in a wooden or stone fence that allows people but not farm animals to get through.

Hill-nutty. The outdoor equivalent of cabin fever. According to a column in the *Arizona Republic,* it is a "neurosis brought on by too many months of solitude in the hills."

Hornito. A low, smoke-emitting volcanic mound.

Hortulan. Relating to the garden.

Interamnian. Between two rivers.

Intercolline. Between hills.

Logan. New Englandism for a bog or swamp.

Mephitis. A foul odor from the earth; a great stink. The scientific name for the common skunk is *mephitis mephitis*.

Misly. Raining in minute drops.

Monoecious. A plant, such as corn or squash, with unisex flowers or the ability to otherwise fertilize itself.

Moraine. Piles of debris carried by a glacier.

Onding. Scottish term for a pelting rain. Ivor Brown, among others who have expressed concern over our lack of good terms to describe weather, wrote in his *No Idle Words,* "My degrees and terminologies of rainfall are onding for a pelting storm, snifter for a moderate shower and a smurr for a longish drizzle or incidence of mist."

Orogeny. The process by which mountains are formed.

Parthenocarpic. An all-female plant that requires no outside pollination for fruit or seed production. Some cucumbers are so equipped.

Pergola. An arbor, or a passageway over which plants have been trained to grow.

Piddock. A mollusk that burrows into wood, soft rock, etc.

Pish. Birder term for a noise—pssshhhhh—made to cause birds to sit still. "Yellowthroats like to be pished," said a birder in an article on the subject in the *Portland Press-Herald* for July 10, 1987.

Pudding stick. Canoeist's term for a stiff paddle with little or no give in its shaft.

Pung. A low box sled; also the place in a sled where one sits.

Remontado. One who has fled to the mountains.

Remontant. Said of flowers that bloom twice in a season.

Rime. Frozen fog deposited on objects as a light, feathery coating of ice.

Riparian. Having to do with the bank of a river or stream.

Rock jock. Climbing enthusiast.

Rockmill. A hole in a streambed created by rotating stones.

Rorulent. Dew-covered.

Rough fish. Fish that are (1) of poor fighting quality for sport fishing, (2) of poor eating quality, and (3) more tolerant of environmental pollution. Suckers and gar are rough fish.

Sanibel stoop. Name for the near-permanent stance adopted by people who go to Sanibel Island, Florida, to look for seashells.

Schizocarp. A seed pod that breaks into two or more pieces at maturity. Those winged seeds that fall from maple trees and that kids put on their noses are schizocarps.

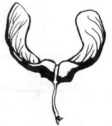

Septage. That which is extracted from home septic tanks.

Slatch. An area of quiet water between areas of disturbed water; the space between breakers.

Slip. An area of uniform width between two townships. Butterfield Slip, for instance.

Snye. A natural channel that leaves the main body of a river or stream and bypasses rapids or a waterfall. Canoeists love that.

Spile. Device for tapping sap from maple trees. It is a hollow spike that drips into a sap pail that is often hung from it.

Subtopia. Area between outer suburbs and open country.

Surplus. A surveyor's mistake, such as Andover North Surplus, which appears on detailed maps of the state of Maine.

Swale. A depression in a stretch of otherwise flat land, which is usually swampy. A comment on this term from Jimmy Jump of Essex, "Interesting that the channel that separates the isle of Sheppy from the rest of Kent is called the Swale. On each side, the land is very flat and low-lying."

Swallet. Place where a stream disappears underground. The term is commonly used by cave explorers.

Tramontane. Located beyond the mountains; also, a cold north wind in northern Italy and the south of France, coming across the Alps. *Transmontane* is an alternative form of the same word.

Twitcher. Name for a birder who travels widely and spends freely to add a species to his or her life list of birds seen.

Virga. Rain that falls but evaporates before it hits the ground.

Watershed. The area drained by a given stream. The term is included here as a reminder that there is something real behind the metaphoric watershed of "watershed study."

Wattle. To bind or intertwine with twigs.

Xenolith. A piece of rock imbedded in another stump.

Zuckle. Old slang word for a withered tree stump.

People

Terms to Fit a Flock of Folks

Acersecomic. One whose hair has never been cut.
Ademonist. Person who denies the existence of the devil or demons.
Agelast. One who never laughs.
Ailurophile. Cat lover.
Ambidexter. A double-dealer.
Ambivert. One who is neither an introvert nor extrovert.
Angelolater. One who worships angels.
Antiscians. People who live in the same longitude but on opposite sides of the equator; northern New Zealanders and New Yorkers, for instance.
Benedick. A newly married man; an eponym from young Benedick in *Much Ado About Nothing.*
Boeotian. A person who opposes works of literature or art because he does not understand them. The term comes from the ancient Greek farming district of Boeotia, which the Athenians thought to be loaded with bumpkins. Pronounced *bee-ocean.*
Burdalone. A solitary person.
Cacographer. One who spells or writes badly.
Centimillionaire. Millionaire with more than $100 million.
Chasmophile. A lover of nooks and crannies.
Cockalorum. A very confident little man.

214

Deipnosophist. One who is good at dinner-table conversation.

Dilling. A child born to parents who are past the age when parents commonly have children.

Dudette. A female dude. According to Ramon F. Adams in *Western Words*, "[a dudette is] described by the cowboy as a young lady who comes west to marry a cowboy." *Dudine* means the same thing.

Dudolo. A Westerner who lives by sponging off dudes and dudettes.

Earthlubber. One who has not been in space.

Ecodoomster. One who forecasts ecological calamity.

Fancymonger. One who deals in tricks of the imagination.

Gemellipara. A woman who has given birth to twins.

Gnof. A curmudgeon.

Gongoozler. One who spends an inordinate amount of time staring at things that are out of the ordinary.

Gradgrind. A person who measures everything, allowing nothing for human nature. From the character Thomas Gradgrind in Dickens's *Hard Times*.

Grammaticaster. A mean verbal pedant; one who views the misuse of the word *hopefully* as a major threat to Western civilization.

Ignicolist. A fire worshiper.

Leptorrhinian. A person with a long, thin nose.

Lychnobite. One who works at night and sleeps in the day.

Marplot. One who frustrates a plan by his officious interference.

Minimifidian. One who puts the least possible faith in something—an afterlife, astrology, UFOs, or whatever.

Misocapnist. A hater of smoking. This old and all but forgotten word has obvious modern possibilities.

Mumpsimus. A person who refuses to correct an error, habit, or practice even though it has been shown to be wrong. It comes from a pigheaded sixteenth-century priest who always said *mumpsimus* when reciting the Mass even though he had been shown many times that *sumpsimus* was correct.

Myrmidon. Someone who carries out commands without hesitation or pity. To speak of a police officer or sheriff as a myrmidon of justice is not a compliment.

Mythoclast. Destroyer of myths.

Nemophilist. One who loves the woods.

Omphalopsychite. One of a sect who practice gazing at the navel as a means of producing hypnotic reverie. *Omphaloskepsis* is the state of contemplation while gazing at the navel.

Oncer. One who does something once and never again; one who has had a number of "once was enough" experiences. A oncer may have had one airplane ride, smoked a single cigarette in 1967, and can still recall that singular occasion when he walked when the signal said, "Don't Walk."

Opsimath. One who has learned late in life.

Paedophage. A child-eater.

Perpilocutionist. One who talks through his hat.

Philodox. One who loves his own opinions.

Pickmote. One who habitually points out and dwells on petty faults.

Plebiocologist. One who flatters the common people.

Pyrrhonist. An absolute skeptic.

Quidnunc. One who seeks all the latest news and gossip; from the Latin *quid nunc,* for "What now?" This rather uncommon word was brought to the limelight in a 1977 ad from Citicorp, which suggested that our own era "is on the way to becoming the Quidnuncs' Golden Age."

Quintroon. A person who is 1/16th black: the offspring of an octoroon and a white.

Salariat. A person with a salary and the security that goes with it. It is in contrast to the word *proletariat.* It is an uncommon word, but Ivor Brown has argued that it is a useful word of distinction at a time when words like *middle class* have become so imprecise.

Spermologer. One who gathers seeds. By extension, a trivia-monger, a gatherer of gossip.

Stegophist. Person whose pastime is climbing the outside of buildings.

Tetrarch. The governor of one part of a country that has been divided into four parts.

Thaumaturgist. One who works wonders.

Ucalegon. A neighbor whose house is on fire.

Utopographer. One who depicts Utopias.

Xanthodont. Person with yellowish teeth.

38

Performing Words

A Cast of Show Business Terms

Academy leader. Standardized film beginning showing a backward countdown from 10 to 3; so called because it was specified by the Academy of Motion Picture Arts and Sciences.

Annie Oakley. Free pass to the theater.

Barney. Sound-deadening housing for a camera, used to prevent camera noises from being picked up by microphones.

Belcher. A person who comes on the air with a frog-like voice or a "frog" in his throat.

Bird feed. Transmission (feed) from an earth-orbiting satellite (bird).

Bloom. A sudden flash on the TV screen caused by a reflection from an object being televised, such as the sun hitting the windshield of a car.

Business, the. The television field, not to be confused with "the industry," which is the motion picture field.

Camerature. A distorted photograph; a photographic caricature.

Capo. A movable bar fitted over the fingerboard of a guitar or banjo to change the pitch of the instrument.

Captation. An attempt to obtain applause or recognition.

Chromakey. Videotape technique in which a person can be inserted over another background.

Clapper. Combination blackboard and noisemaker used to note the scene number and coordinate the sound at the beginning of a "take." The person who holds the board and makes it clap is known as the "clapper boy" or "clapper girl."

Claque. Hired applauders; those who show approval for a fee or self-interest.

Closet drama. A play that is written to be read rather than performed—Shelley's *The Cenci,* for instance.

Comma gig. Musician's term for a performance where one is paid $1,000 or more—all lower sums lacking a comma.

Contour curtain. Curtain that can be opened by loops or scallops.

Cucalorus. Cutout or shade placed over a spotlight to produce a shape on the backdrop of a stage. It is also called a *cookie, cuke,* and *cuckoolorus.*

Dakota. Lines spoken immediately before a song. "Then, in 1927 I wrote," is a Dakota.

Digitorium. A silent piano; for practicing.

Drive time. Radio term for the two periods during a weekday when commuting is at its peak, usually 6 to 9 A.M. and 4 to 7 P.M.

Drooling. Unrehearsed talking to fill in allotted radio or TV program time. Sometimes referred to as *yatata-yatata.*

Early fringe. TV time before prime time.

Eejay. Short for "electronic journalism," the term created some years ago by Eric Sevareid to distinguish television from print journalism.

Flies. The area over the stage, generally out of the audience's sight.

Foreshortening. The compressed distortion caused by telephoto lenses.

George Spelvin. A fictitious name sometimes used in theater programs to indicate that an actor is playing two or more parts. The actor's real name is used for the main role and Spelvin's for the minor role or roles. It is interesting to note that one of the most notorious porno stars of the 1970s was Georgina Spelvin. Raymond Harris of London adds, ". . . the English equivalent is Walter Plinge. He was proprietor of a public house near Drury Lane Theatre, London . . ."

Guard band. Buffer of unused frequency space on either side of a television channel to insure clear transmission.

Halation. The tendency of light to spread in film.

Halflap. Television or movie shot in which two different scenes appear at the same time side-by-side.

Hammocking. Putting a new television show between two established hits.

Hiccup. Opening a movie with a dramatic scene and then bringing on the title and credits.

Iris-in/Iris-out. The classic beginning and ending of a cartoon is to start with the iris-in and end with the iris-out. The iris-in begins with a small dot in the center of the screen, which spreads to reveal the whole scene. The iris-out occurs when the full scene recedes to a dot.

Jerk magnet. Slang for a television camera, also *moron magnet.*

Kilroy. Television camera shot in which the performer's chin is missing. Term comes from the "Kilroy was Here" cartoon in which you cannot see Kilroy's chin.

Kinephantom. The illusion of reverse movement in a fast-moving object, as the spokes of a wheel in a movie.

Lap dissolve. Fading from one scene to another as one is superimposed on the other.

Lavaliere. Small microphone hung around the neck.

Legs. Hollywood talk for a movie with a long box-office life. "*Star Wars* has great legs," said *Newsweek* a few years back. "*Jaws* was said to have 'fins.'"

Limbo. Situation in which a television performer is left standing without a background or with the wrong one.

Lip flap. When a person on television can be seen talking but not heard.

Mike stew. Unwanted background noise picked up by a microphone.

Monomorphic station. Radio station with one thrust—all news, Country and Western, or whatever.

Mooz. A fast zoom-out shot.

MOR. Broadcasting term for a station that plays Middle Of the Road music.

Motor cue. The circular mark that appears in the upper right-hand corner of a film just before the reel is to end (actually, there are 12 feet of film left). The motor cue alerts the projectionist that he should be ready to switch to the second projector and the new reel. A second cue, the *changeover cue,* appears when there is only a foot of film remaining and the time has come to switch to the second projector.

Noodling. Music that is played as titles or credits roll.

Nostril shot. Derogatory term for an extreme close-up.

Octoplex. Movie theater with eight small screens.

Omnies. In broadcasting, background sound of crowd noises.

Peripeteia. A dramatic turnaround in the action of a play, for instance, learning that the hero and heroine are one and the same. Pronounced *pear-a-pa-tee-a.*

Pixillation. Stop-motion photography that gives live actors the appearance of cartoon characters.

Plosives. Explosive sounds that are sometimes produced in broadcasting when a *p* or *b* is overstressed.

Proscenium. The front part of the stage, through which the audience views the play. It is set off at the top by the *proscenium arch.*

Rear mezzanine. The name for balcony in some New York theaters.

Scrim. A curtain that can be opaque or transparent, depending on how it is lit.

Scumble. Making a set look old.

Sustainer. The piano pedal on the right.

Swish pan. Rapid horizontal movement of the camera to get from one subject to another. Also known as a *whip pan*.

Tally light. Red light on a television camera indicating which camera is on.

Thribble. To be vague about your lines while acting.

Upanga. Nose flute.

Verismo. Using everyday material as opposed to the epic or legendary, especially when applied to operatic themes.

Voice wrap. The use of a broadcaster's voice to begin and end a piece of tape or film.

Wipe effect. In film or TV, when one scene appears to be wiped off the screen by a line that reveals a new scene.

"Philophily"

A Collocation of Collections and Collectors

What could be a more natural thing to accumulate than other collectors? The urge is hereby dubbed "philophily."

Aerophilately. Air-mail-stamp collecting.

Arctophilist. A collector of teddy bears. It is believed to have been the coinage of Peter Bull, English actor and bear collector.

Argyrothecology. Collecting money boxes.

Atrocibilia. Term used in the *American Collector* to describe "horrible heir-looms," relics associated with mass murder, execution, Mansonania. It was used in connection with a surge of collector interest in things having to do with Son of Sam.

Baptisaphily. Christian names.

Bibliopegist. A collector of fine book bindings; also, a bookbinder.

Brandophily. Cigar bands. Also, *cigrinophily.*

Cagophily. Keys.

Cartomania. Maps; especially those interested in old maps and map ephemera—or "cartofacts."

Cartophily. Cigarette cards. Collectors in this field are likely to belong to the British-based Cartophilic Society.

Comiconomenclatury. Funny names. This word appears in a recent book published in Australia, Peter Bowler's *Superior Person's Little Book of Words*. Bowler writes, "The serious collector of funny names accepts only those of real people, and abides by certain rules of the game....Chinese names are not fair game, and no self-respecting comiconomenclaturist would include in his collection a Ho Hum, a T. Hee, or a Jim Shoo."

Conchology. Shells.

Copoclephily. Publicity key rings.

Cumyxaphily. Matchbox collecting, not to be confused with *Phillumeny*, which is the collecting of matchbooks.

Deltiology. Picture postcards.

Discophily. Phonograph records.

Entrodentolignumology. Toothpick boxes and other toothpick ephemera. It was coined by the author to describe his collection of antique toothpick boxes and his immodest proclamation that he is among the leading *entredentolignumologists*.

Errinophily. Stamps other than those used for postage (Christmas seals, tax stamps, etc.)

Exonumist. A collector of trade, subway, and other tokens.

Hostelaphily. Inn signs.

Hughesiana. Artifacts that relate to the late Howard Hughes.

Labeorphily. Beer bottle labels.

Laclabphily. Cheese labels.

Lepidopterology. Butterfly collecting.

Moxiana. Memorabilia relating to the soft drink Moxie.

Notaphily. Bank notes.

Onomastics. Name collecting. George Hubbard, a leading onomasticist from New York, has a collection that includes such gems as Aphrodite Chackess, Three Persons Appleyard, and Sistine Madonna McClung.

Oologist. A collector of bird's eggs. By extension, an *ooscope* is an instrument for looking into an egg and an *oograph* is an instrument for drawing the outline of a bird's egg.

Peristerophily. Love of pigeons; pigeon collecting.

Phillumeny. Matchbook collecting. What this hobby may lack in numbers, it makes up for in terminology. Collectors talk of *jewelites* (sparkling covers), *royal flashes* (covers with 40 matches), *odd strikes* (covers with a striking surface in an odd place), and *matchoramas* (covers with full-color photos). Matches are commonly referred to as *strikes*.

Philographer. Term coined by famous autograph dealer Charles Hamilton for serious autograph collectors. Hamilton was quoted in the *American Collector* as saying that such a word "is needed to describe autograph collectors which will instantly establish them as specialists in assembling letters and documents of historic interest, rather than seekers of celebrities signatures."

Philometry. Envelopes with postmarks.

Plangonologist. Doll collector.

Receptary. A recipe collection.

Scripophily. The collecting of antique stock and bond certificates. The term was coined in 1979 as the result of a contest held by a London newspaper to find a name for the stock-collecting craze that was then sweeping England.

Spooner. Spoons.

Sucresacology. The collecting of small paper sugar packets from restaurants.

Syngraphics. Collecting financial documents—cancelled checks, paper money, stocks, and bonds.

Tegestology. Beer coasters and mats.

Timbromania. Along with *timbrophily,* one of the early names proposed for stamp collecting. Philately won out.

Tyrosemiophily. Camembert cheese labels. One would be hardpressed to come up with a more specific collector-term than this one, which was culled from Philippe Julian's book *Collectors.*

Pidgin

Many Half Talks

By all accounts, it came into being some 300 years ago along the China coast as an intensely loose, linguistic shorthand with a severely limited vocabulary. The words were English and the syntax Chinese, which provided enough common ground for Western sailors and Chinese merchants to talk with one another. It was called a business language, but it was hard for the Chinese to pronounce *business,* which came out as something that sounded like *bijin.* It eventually became known as *pidgin.*

Over time other pidgin languages evolved: African pidgins, a Hawaiian version, an Anglo-Indian pidgin (known as Hobson-Jobson), pidgins based in French and Portuguese, and the rich pidgins of the South Seas. The latter are largely compatible languages spoken in Melanesia and Australia. In his *Many Hues of English,* Mario Pei was tempted "to describe as pidgin the Pennsylvania 'Dutch' of York and Lancaster counties, which is not at all Dutch, but a blend of English and High German."

Although there are some who hold pidgin in disregard (it was dismissed in one edition of the *Encyclopaedia Britannica* as a jargon composed of "nursery imbecilities, vulgarisms and corruptions"), it is immensely practical—something that its severest critics will admit. It is especially useful when people from two cultures are trying to communicate. It is also used: pidgin in one form or another is spoken by an estimated 30 to 50 million people worldwide.

Besides being useful, pidgin can also be charming, expressive, and amusing—a magnet for word collectors. Here are some fine examples from the Pacific islands and Australia.

Airmail. Paper-yabber along big fella hawk.

Artery. Rope he-got blut.

Ashes. Shit belong fire. (The phrase for gray is "all-same shit belong fire.")

Automobile. Eat 'im wind cart.

Beard. Grass belong face.

Bicycle. Wilwil (wheel-wheel).

Bishop. Top-side-piecee-Heaven-pidgin-man or No. 1 clistian jossman. (Correspondent Philip Chaplin reports, "There is a story of an Admiral who asked to see the Bishop of Hong Kong using this form, only to be told buy his Chinese butler 'His Lordship will receive you in the garden, sir!' ")

Bottom of . . . Arse belong . . .

Butcher. Man-belong-bullanacow.

Butter. Cow oil.

Contradict. Sack-im talk.

Copulate with. Pushim. (Also *make-im, push-push-im, savvy 'long*, etc.)

Cough. Kuss. A sneeze is "kuss 'long nose," which is not to be confused with the phrase for snot, which is "kuss belong nose."

Edinburgh, Duke of. Fella blong missis Queen.

Elbow. Screw belong arm.

Envelope. Pants b'long chit.

Fifteen. Two-fella hand one-fella foot.

Flashlight. Shoot lamp.

Fattery. Grease.

Foreigner. Man belong far-way place.

Frenchman. Man-a-wee-wee. (The man who says *out-out*.)

God. Big Name; Big Boss. In *Pidgin English* by Edgar Sheappard Sayer, the author translates the Twenty-third Psalm in Australian pidgin. The first few lines:

Big Name watchem sheepysheep:
watchum black fella.
No more belly cry fella hab.
Big Name makum camp alonga grass,
taken black fella walk-about longa,
no fightem no more hurry watta
Big Boss longa sky makum inside glad;
takem walk-about longa too much good fella.

Helicopter. Mixmaster belong Jesus Christ.

Hospital. House sick.

Intellectual. Think fella too much.

Is the water drinkable? Good fella water?

Lantern. Lamp walkabout.

Onion. Apple belong stink.

Only child. One-fish.

Piano. Hit 'im in teeth, out come squeal allasame pig. (Southeast Asian pidgin for piano is "Bokkis [box] you fight him, him call out.")

Pocket. Basket belong trouser.

Poor. Rubbish long money.

Pour the coffee. Capsize him coffee along cup.

Put out the fire. Make-im die fire.

Ruin. Bugger-im-up-im.

Secret. Talk he-hide.

Set the table. Put clothes belong table.

Sun. Lamp belong Jesus. Robert Graves once wrote of an Englishman who told a pidgin speaker to tell others of an impending eclipse of the sun. It came out as: "Him kerosene belong Jesus Christ bimeby all done, bugger up, finish."

Swear (to take an oath). Talk true 'long ontop.

Telescope. Bamboo belong look-look.

Tent. House sail.

Thunder. Fire-up belong cloud.

Tinned peas. Tinpis.

To be or not to be? That is the question. Can do, no can do? How fashion?

Toe. Finger belong leg.

Train. Big fella firesnake.

Twenty. One-fella man. (This refers to the total number of fingers and toes. Ten is "two-fella hand.")

Typewriter. Engine b'long talkee.

Unripe. He-no mow yet.

Violin. Scratch 'im in belly, out come squeak allasame pussycat.

Where. What side?

Whisper. Talk-talk easy.

Word. Half talk.

Worm. Liklik (little) snake.

You need a bath. Skin belong you 'im stink.

Prophetic Words

A Gathering of Omens

Several summers ago I found a copy of the 1859 edition of *Webster's Unabridged,* was browsing through it, and came upon the word *tyromancy.* It means to foretell the future by the examination of cheese. I still have no idea how one performs tyromancy, nor have I found a way to work it into polite conversation (save for contrived comments about words that are almost impossible to work into conversation). However, the very idea that the jargon of divination had become so specific as to include cheese set off a search for other ancient words of prophecy.

Aeromancy. From the state of the air or weather, or by the state of ripples on the surface of water.

Aichomancy. By sharp points.

Alectryomancy. By means of a cock picking up kernels of corn. Commonly, the cock would be encircled by grains placed on the letters of the alphabet, and words would be put together from the order in which the grain was eaten. There is a vivid description of this custom in Thornton Wilder's *Ides of March.*

Aleuromancy. By means of flour. The Chinese, among others, have practiced the custom of baking fortunes in dough. The fortune cookie is a modern example.

227

Alomancy. By means of salt.

Alphitomancy. By barley and barley cakes. This was once used as a means of determining guilt. If the person could not swallow or was made sick by the barley cake, he was deemed guilty. This was also known as *critomancy*.

Amathomancy. By the arrangement of dust.

Ambulomancy. Through taking a walk.

Amniomancy. By observing the caul on a child's head at birth.

Anthomancy. From flowers—presumably the process at work in "She loves me, she loves me not!"

Anthracomancy. By means of burning coals.

Anthropomancy. By examining human entrails. This horrid form of divination was practiced by the Roman emperor Heliogabalus.

Anthroposcopy. The deduction of a person's character, ability, and/or future from his or her face.

Apantomancy. By objects that appear haphazardly.

Arithmancy. By numbers.

Aruspicy. By the entrails of animals.

Aspidomancy. By sitting on a shield within a magic circle and going into a trance.

Astragalomancy. By dice or knucklebones.

Astromancy. By the stars. Astrology.

Augury. By observing birds and serpents.

Auspicy. By the appearance of things being sacrificed.

Austromancy. By observing winds.

Axinomancy. By means of an ax and a stone placed on a bed of hot embers.

Belomancy. By drawing arrows at random from a container.

Bibliomancy. By randomly opening a Bible and using the first passage one sets eyes on to predict the future. The practice had become so common in the fifth century A.D. that several church councils were formed to study and forbid it.

Botanomancy. By means of plants.

Brizomancy. By the inspiration of Brizo, goddess of sleep.

Brontomancy. By thunder.

Capnomancy. By means of smoke wreaths.

Captromancy. By the fumes rising from a poppy thrown on hot coals.

Cartomancy. By the dealing of playing cards.

Cartopedy. By the lines on the soles of the feet.

Catoptromancy. By means of a mirror or lens.

Causimomancy. By fire, specifically flammability. It was often seen as a good omen if something did not burn or took a long time to ignite.

Cephalomancy. By burning the head of an ass on hot coals.

Ceraunoscopy. By the combined phenomena of the air (rain, thunder, etc.).

Ceromancy. From figures produced by dropping melted wax into water. Sometimes spelled *ceramancy*.

Chalcomancy. By brass vessels.

Chaomancy. Through the appearance of clouds; through airborne apparitions.

Chartomancy. By writing.

Cheiromancy. Palmistry.

Chirognomy. A branch of palmistry that deduces a person's intelligence from the shape of his or her hand.

Cledonomancy. By listening to utterances of mantric significance.

Cleidomancy. By a key hanging from a young girl's third-finger nail.

Cleromancy. By throwing dice, bones, or black and white beans; casting lots. It can also be accomplished by studying the shapes formed as pebbles are thrown into still water.

Clidomancy. By means of a Bible and a hanging, moving key.

Conchomancy. By seashells.

Coscinomancy. By means of a sieve (it is usually suspended and the divination comes from observing its motion).

Crithomancy. By grain or particles of flour strewn during sacrificial rites—sometimes over the bodies of sacrificial victims.

Cromniomancy. By means of onions placed on the altar at Christmas.

Cromnyomancy. By means of onions.

Cryptomancy. By mysterious means.

Crystallomancy. By gazing into a crystal ball, precious stone, or bright metal surface.

Cubomancy. With dice.

Dactyliomancy. By means of a finger ring.

Demonomancy. With the aid of demons.

Dophnomancy. By laurel or, more specifically, interpreting the crackle of a laurel branch on a fire. Also spelled *daphnomancy*.

Dririmancy. By dripping blood.

Elaeomancy. By observing a liquid surface.

Empyromancy. By observing objects on a sacrificial fire.

Eromancy. By exposing objects to the air.

Extispice. From entrails plucked from a fowl.

Gastromancy. From (1) the sounds coming from the belly, (2) marks on the stomach, (3) ventriloquism.

Geloscopy. By laughter.

Geomancy. By throwing a handful of dirt on a flat surface to see what figure is suggested. Also, by jotting dots at random on a piece of paper.

Graphomancy. By handwriting.

Gyromancy. By someone walking around in a circle until he falls from dizziness.

Halomancy. By the shape of salt thrown on a flat surface.

Hepatoscopy. By studying the livers of animals.

Hieromancy. By observing things offered as sacrifices.

Hippomancy. By observing a horse's pace.

Horoscopy. By horoscopes; determining one's future by the position of heavenly bodies at the time of one's birth.

Hydromancy. By water (commonly a young boy was used as a medium to report on images he saw in water).

Hyomancy. By the tongue.

Ichthyomancy. By the heads or entrails of fishes.

Iconomancy. Through images.

Idolomancy. By idols.

Keraunoscopy. By thunder and lightning.

Knissomancy. With incense.

Labiomancy. By lip reading.

Lampadomancy. By observing substances burned in a lamp or by a candle.

Lecanomancy. By inspecting water in a basin.

Lithomancy. By stones, by meteorites.

Logomancy. By magic words or formulae.

Lycanthropy. The power of turning a human into a wolf.

Machairomancy. With swords or knives. Sometimes, *macharomancy*.

Macromancy. By the largest thing at hand.

Maculomancy. By spots.

Magastromancy. By magic or astrology.

Manticism. The practice of divination; from *mantic*, for one who has been blessed with prophetic powers.

Margaritomancy. By means of a pearl.

Mazomancy. With the help of a suckling baby.

Meconomancy. By drug-induced sleep.

Meteoromancy. By thunder, lightning, and meteors.

Metoposcopy. From the lines of the forehead.

Micromancy. By the smallest thing at hand.

Mineramancy. By found minerals.

Molybdomancy. By noting images in molten lead.

Moromancy. Through nonsense; foolish divination.

Myomancy. By the movements of mice.

Necromancy. Through communication with the dead; black magic.

Nectromancy. The perception of the inner nature of things.

Necyomancy. From the inspected nerves of the dead.

Nephelomancy. By the clouds.

Nephromancy. By the kidneys.

Normancy. Determining the fate of a person by the letters that form his or her name; also called *onomancy*.

Odontomancy. By examining teeth.

Oenomancy. By the color, sediment, or other wine variations.

Ololygmancy. By the howling of dogs.

Omphalomancy. By the navel; but also predicting the number of children a woman will bear by counting the knots in the umbilical cord of her first born.

Oneiromancy. Through dreams.

Onomancy. By interpreting the person's name.

Onychomancy. By the fingernails. Alternatively spelled *onycomancy, onimancy,* and *onymancy.*

Oomancy. By means of eggs (usually broken); also, *ooscopy.*

Ophiomancy. By watching snakes.

Ornithomancy. By observing the flight of birds; also, *orniscopy, ornithoscopy,* and *ornomancy.*

Osteomancy. From bones.

Pedomancy. By observing the soles of the feet.

Pegomancy. Observing the way that air bubbles rise in fountains or springs.

Pessomancy. From tossed pebbles.

Petchimancy. By examining the skull.

Phyllomancy. By leaves.

Phyllorhodomancy. By rose leaves.

Pneumancy. By blowing. Joseph T. Shipley points out in his incomparable *Dictionary of Early English,* ". . . a vestigium of this is the blowing out of candles on a festival cake."

Psephomancy. By heaped pebbles.

Pseudomancy. False divination.

Psychomancy. By conjuring the dead.

Psychometry. Determining something about a person from an object, such as a piece of clothing, connected with that person; also known as *psychometrics.*

Pyromancy. By interpreting flames.

Retromancy. By looking over one's shoulder.

Rhabdomancy. Through verses. Sometimes this is performed as a needle is stuck through a closed book.

Scapulimancy. Observation of the shoulder blade of an animal; also known as *omoplatoscopy* and *scapulomancy.*

Scatomancy. Through examination of excrement.

Scrying. Crystal-gazing.

Selenomancy. From the moon.

Seyomancy. By means of a cup.

Sideromancy. By burning straws on a red-hot iron.

Sortilge. By casting lots.

Spasmatomancy. By observing spasmodic movements.

Spatalamancy. Through skin, bones, or excrement.

Spatulomancy. With the shoulder blade of a sheep.

Sphondulomancy. By means of spindles.

Spodomancy. By ashes, specifically those of a sacrifice.

Stercomancy. By studying seeds in dung.

Stichomancy. By lines and passages in books.

Stigonomancy. By writing on the bark of a tree.

Stoicheomancy. By opening a poet's book at random and reading from the first verse that presents itself.

Stolisomancy. From the manner of dressing.

Sycomancy. By fig or sycamore leaves.

Tephromancy. By writing in ashes.

Teratoscopy. By monstrosities.

Theriomancy. By observing wild animals.

Theomancy. By the shape of the terrain.

Transataumancy. On the basis of omens seen unexpectedly.

Trochomancy. By wheel tracks.

Turifumy. By incense smoke.

Tyromancy. By examining cheese. Sometimes spelled *tiromancy*.

Uromancy. By urine.

Xenomancy. By the first stranger that appears.

Xylomancy. By interpreting the positions and shapes of twigs and other pieces of wood found on the ground.

Zygomancy. Through weights.

"Psychoneologistics"

A Drove of Manias and Phobias

There is nothing amusing about mental illness; but there is something down-right amusing about the way psychological professionals feel compelled to construct a new word each time they come on a poor soul with a very rare—perhaps unique—fear or fantasy.

Aboulia. Loss of willpower.
Acarophobia. Fear of small insects such as mites and ticks.
Acathisia. The inability to sit down or the dread of sitting down.
Acoria. Unnatural or morbid appetite for food.
Amathophobia. Fear of dust.
Anhedonia. The inability to be happy.
Anthophobia. An abnormal fear of flowers.
Anthrophobia. The fear of people or society.
Anuptaphobia. Fear of remaining single.
Arachibutyrophobia. Fear of peanut butter sticking to the roof of your mouth, according to *The People's Almanac*.
Astraphobia. Fear of being struck by lightning.
Batrachophobia. Fear of frogs and toads.
Blennophobia. Morbid fear of slime.
Boanthropy. The madness in which a man imagines himself to be an ox.

Botanophobia. Fear of plants and flowers.

Bulimy. Insatiable hunger.

Cachinnation. Senseless laughter (or as columnist John Lofton explained on first learning this word, "Any caused by Joan Rivers.")

Castrophrenia. Belief that your thoughts are being stolen by an enemy.

Cathisophobia. Fear of sitting.

Chrematophobia. Fear of money.

Clinophobia. Fear of going to bed.

Counterphobic. Seeking out what is feared; preferring that which one is afraid of.

Cremnophobia. Abnormal fear of cliffs and precipices.

Cynathropy. A form of insanity in which the person imagines himself to be a dog.

Cyberphobia. Fear of computers and high-tech electronics.

Doramania. The compulsion to own furs.

Dromomania. A compulsive longing for travel.

Ecophobia. Fear of home.

Eidetic image. A memory that is as intense and fresh as actual experience.

Eleutheromania. A compelling desire for freedom. Pronounced *i-luth-era-mania*.

Emacity. An itch to be buying.

Eosophobia. Fear of dawn.

Epicaricacy. Taking pleasure in the misfortunes of others.

Ergasiophobia. Fear of work.

Euphobia. Fear of good news.

Factitious disorder. By which a person consciously fakes an illness for psychological gain.

Formication. A feeling that ants are crawling over one's skin.

Friendorphobia. Fear of forgetting a password—one of several new phobias suggested by readers of J. Baxter Newgate's *National Challenge*. Another: *charminphobia*, fear of being squeezed.

Galeanthropy. Belief that one has become a cat.

Gamomania. A form of insanity characterized by odd or extravagant proposals of marriage.

Geniophobia. Fear of chins.

Gephyrophobia. Morbid bridge fear.

Gymnophobia. Fear of nudity.

Hagiophobia. Fear of holy objects, people, and concepts.

Hamartia. A single defect of character in an otherwise decent person; the classic tragic flaw.

Helminthophobia. Morbid fear of becoming infested with worms. It is not to be confused with *scoleciphobia,* which is a simple fear of worms.

Homichlophobia. Fear of fog.

Homilophobia. Fear of sermons.

Hydrophobophobia. According to the *Psychiatric Dictionary,* this is the fear of hydrophobia. Hydrophobia, incidentally, not only means fear of water but is also a medical word for rabies.

Hygrophobia. Fear of liquids.

Hypercatexis. Intense desire or mania for some object.

Iatrophobia. Fear of going to the doctor.

Inficious. Given to denying, not accepting, blame.

Jocasta complex. The desire of the mother for her son.

Kathisophobia. Fear of sitting down.

Levophobia. Fear of things on the left; the opposite of *dextrophobia.* These would seem to have obvious political application.

Linonophobia. Fear of string.

Lycanthropy. The affliction that turns an ordinary human being into a raging beast—usually a wolf. It is a mainstay of horror movies.

Macrophobia. Fear of prolonged waiting.

Misocainea. Abnormal dislike of all things new.

Myophobia. Fear of mice.

Mysophobia. Fear of dirt.

Nebulaphobia. Fear of fog, clouds.

Neurasthenia. Neurosis characterized by boredom, laziness, and fatigue.

Nostopathy. Morbid fear of returning to a familiar place or places.

Nucleomitaphobia. Irrational fear of death by nuclear weapons. Oddly, this is a rare phobia.

Oligoria. Disinterest in former friends.

Ombrophobia. Fear of rain.

Onomatophobia. Fear of hearing a given name, word, or words.

Optophobia. Fear of opening one's eyes.

Orestes complex. The desire of a son to kill his mother.

Paedophobia. Fear of dolls.

Palilia. Repetition of words or phrases with an increasing degree of regularity.

Parthenophobia. Fear of virgins.

Pathophobia. Abnormal fear or dread of disease or germs.

Pediophobia. Dread of dummies, dolls, and mannequins.

Phaneromania. The habit of picking at scabs, biting one's nails, or poking at pimples.

Philoneism. Obsessive interest in fads.

Phobophobia. Dread of fear itself.

Pica. A craving for unnatural food; dust, for instance.

Placophobia. Fear of tombstones.

Pogonophobia. Morbid fear of beards.

Porphyrophobia. Dread of purple.

Sciaphobia. Fear of shadows. (This word tends to get a lot of play around Groundhog Day, when editorialists muse on groundhog psychology.)

Selenophobia. Moon fear.

Stenophobia. Morbid fear of narrow spaces.

Storge. Parental instinct.

Survivor's guilt. Psychological pain felt by one who lives through a disaster.

Symgenesophobia. The fear or dislike of relatives.

Taphephobia. Fear of being buried alive.

Tarantism. The irresistible urge to dance.

Theomania. Belief that one is God.

Topophobia. Intense stage fright; fear of performing.

Trichotillmania. The compulsion to pull out one's hair.

Triskaidekaphobia. Dread of the number 13. It is pronounced *trisk-a-deck-a-phobia*.

Tropophobia. Fear of making changes or moving.

Uranomania. The delusion that one is of celestial origin.

Uranophobia. Fear of heaven.

Zeigarnik effect. The tendency to recall an uncompleted task more vividly than one that has been completed.

Punks

Also, Punkers, Punkesses, Punkaroos, Punkettos, Punkhornes, and Punkabillies

Punk is an unattractive little word. It sounds mean and decadent and for that very reason fits nicely with a fad of music, dress, and behavior that emerged in the mid-1970s. This new use of the word *punk* fascinated me and led to the question, How many other uses and variant forms has the word had?

The question led to a punk hunt that, in turn, led me to a variety of places including the collection of slang dictionaries at the Library of Congress, the citation files at the G. & C. Merriam Company in Springfield, Massachusetts, and the Peter Tamony Collection at the University of Missouri. Humility aside, I believe this to be the definitive work on *punk*.

Punk. (Army) Pre-World War I slang for bread. It was often used specifically for light bread. According to Eric Patridge in his *Dictionary of the Underworld*, it has had the same meaning among prisoners and tramps. Some have said that this use of the word came from the French word *pain*; Patridge contended that it was a new application of punk in the sense of dry, decayed wood—the kind of bread a tramp, prisoner, or soldier might get.

Punk. (Australian) Sea wood; driftwood.

237

Punk. Bad or inferior liquor; also, *punkeroo.*

Punk. (Black jargon) A homosexual.

Punk. (Boxing) A poor or worn-out fighter.

Punk. Bunk; insincerity.

Punk. (Carnival) A toy cat used in a game.

Punk. Chinese insect-repellent.

Punk. Cigarette; cigar. (I have also found an unattributed reference to punk meaning "smoking paper." I am not sure whether this means paper used in smoking, for example, cigarette paper, or paper that is smoldering.)

Punk. (Circus) A young animal, such as a baby lion; any circus youngster, whether it be an elephant or a human.

Punk. (College) Below par; off.

Punk. (College) A box of good things from home, limited use dating from a report on college slang in the 1880s.

Punk. (Construction) A general term for any beginner on a construction job. It is usually designated as carpenter punk, ironworker punk, or even a coffee punk—a novice who goes for coffee.

Punk. (Criminal) Low-level thief; an apprentice hoodlum. An earlier criminal meaning dating back to the turn of the century is that of a boy thief; a very young criminal.

Punk. Decayed and rotten wood.

Punk. (Fire fighting) Charred and partly decayed material, such as old wood, in which fire smolders unless carefully overhauled and extinguished.

Punk. A foolish argument.

Punk. A form of incense.

Punk. A fungus (polyporus fomentarius, etc.) sometimes dried and used as tinder.

Punk. A harlot or prostitute. This use of the word was common from the sixteenth through the eighteenth centuries and was used with this meaning by a number of writers including Shakespeare in *The Merry Wives of Windsor* ("This punk is one of Cupid's carriers . . .") and *Measure for Measure* ("She may be a punk, for many of them are neither maid, widow nor wife").

Punk. Having a dry and flavorless flesh; used of fruits and vegetables.

Punk. (Hobo) A homosexual boy who travels with an older man.

Punk. (Horse racing) An inefficient rider.

Punk. An insignificant person; a nobody.

Punk. Knot cut from crab apple tree, a regional use of the word found in Joseph Wright's *English Dialect Dictionary.*

Punk. A little whore.

Punk. (Logging) The meanings are listed in Dean Walter F. McCulloch's *Woods Words:* "a. The man or boy who passes signals from the choker setters to the donkey puncher. b. A green kid, or any youngster in the woods. c. Rotten wood." Still another meaning appears in *Logger's Words of Yesteryear* by L.G.

Sorden and Isabel J. Ebert: "A bad spot in the wood caused by an injury to the tree when it was young."

Punk. A new nihilism, which began in the mid-1970s; what *Life* termed "hip nihilism."

Punk. A person who has adopted the punk style in music, clothing, and behavior. Some have gone as far as to capitalize the word, as if it were the name of a nationality. "The Punks are also rebelling against a very repressive atmosphere," reads a breathless article on the phenomenon in the *New York Post* for June 9, 1977.

Punk. (Photography) A photographer's assistant.

Punk. (Prison) According to the 1976 *Dictionary of Desperation*, it has the following meanings in prison parlance: "An informer; or an inmate who can't do his own time well; the kept lover of a homosexual." Partridge says in his *Dictionary of the Underworld* that it also means any young prisoner.

Punk. A punctured bicycle tire. (Late-nineteenth-century slang)

Punk. Short for *punk rock* or *punk rocker*.

Punk. Small-time character; chiseler.

Punk. A stick covered with a certain paste that burns very slowly when ignited, commonly used to light fireworks.

Punk. A style of dress and a manner associated with punk rock. From a 1977 *Time* article, "The Punks are Coming!": ". . . punk fans have cultivated an aggressively dumb look: strategically torn T-shirts; safety pins stuck through clothes, cheeks and ear lobes; fishnet hose; cropped and dyed hair." Other elements of the style: skintight pants, stiletto-heeled pumps, black eye-makeup, ugly sneakers.

Punk. (Theater) Child actor; a "juve."

Punk. To be very poor.

Punk. A verb, to procure.

Punk. A verb, to puncture a tire.

Punk. A verb, to urinate.

Punk. Worthlessness; a thing of no value.

Punk. A young elephant.

Punk. A young man; a novice.

PUNC. Acronym for Practical, Unpretentious Nomograph Computer.

Puncke. Old form of punk in the sense of a harlot. "Soe fellowes," runs an old ballad quoted in J. S. Farmer and W. E. Henley's *Slang and Its Analogues*, "if you be drunke, of ffrailtye itt is a sinne, as itt is to keepe a puncke."

Punka. Secondary spelling of *punkah* listed in the *Oxford English Dictionary*.

Punkabilly. Defined in the Arts section of a 1979 issue of *Saturday Review* as a style characterized by "adolescent country pickers with a flair for masochism and audience abuse."

Punkah. A large screen-like fan hung from the ceiling, which is kept in motion by machinery or a servant. The term is from India. It can also describe a portable fan.

Punkah. World War II code name.

Punkah wallah. Servant who operates a punkah. *The Random House Dictionary* lists "punkah coolie" as synonymous.

Punkapog. An Indian village that existed outside Stoughton, Massachusetts.

Punkaroo. (Sports) Second-rate player.

Punkateero. A pimp or panderer. It comes from punk in the sense of a harlot.

Punkie. Tiny sand fly; minute irksome gnat.

Punkola. Lower-class hood, used, for example, by Nathaniel West in *The Day of the Locust*.

Punky. Rotton, gone bad, such as "food gone punky in the heat" from Stephen King's *The Tommyknockers*.

Punquetto. A very old variation of punk in the sense of a harlot. From Ben Johnson's *Cynthia's Revels:* "Marry, to his cockatrice, or punquetto, half a dozen taffeta gowns . . ."

Punk and gut. (Hobo) Bread and sausage.

Punk and plaster. (Hobo) Bread and butter.

Punk and white wine. Prison slang for bread and water; prison food in general. Also *piss and punk*.

Punk culture. Library of Congress subject heading for books on modern punk along with punk rock.

Punk day. Children's day at a circus or carnival.

Punk dunk. (Basketball) "Any sort of dunk that humiliates the defender," according to *The In-Your-Face Basketball Book* by Chuck Wielgus, Jr., and Alexander Wolff.

Punk-folk. Described by Jim Sullivan in the Boston *Globe* (August 23, 1991): "Combining the in-your-face force of punk [rock] with a certain reverence for folk idioms."

Punk for. (Theater) To act as a foil or straight man to a comedian.

Punk hit. (Baseball) Short hit.

Punk kid. A catamite, according to Eric Partridge's *Dictionary of the Underworld*.

Punk oak. A tall water oak of the southeastern United States, sometimes called the *possum oak*.

Punk out. Slang from the early 1950s for quitting.

Punk out. (Street gang slang) To get scared; to refuse to fight.

Punk out. To inform; to rat.

Punk pills. Tranquilizing pills; "red devils."

Punk pusher. (Circus and Carnival) A boss who supervises work done by locals, like the boys hired to set up tents.

Punk rack. (Carnival) Row of funny, fuzzy animals used in games. Normally these are cats that baseballs are thrown at.

Punk ride. (Carnival) Rides that cater to children.

Punk rock. A style of rock music defined by its lack of style. It has been variously described as "minimal art," "two and three chord pedantry," "wind-up monkey musicianship," and "raw, nerve flaying, an aggregate of amplified guitars in a tin garage." The sound was pioneered by such groups as the Buzzcocks, Ramones, Dead Boys, and Sex Pistols. Sometimes it is simply referred to as "punk." The word is sometimes used in tunes like "Nazi Punks Fuck Off" by the Dead Kennedys. Today it is called *Hardcore Punk*.

Punk show. (Carnival) Insiders' name for the shows that display abnormal fetuses in glass jars. See also *Pickle punk*.

Punk stuff. Something useless or contemptible.

Punk tree. Another name for the cajuput, an Australian tree having a pungent smell.

Corn punk. Paste for the treatment of corns and bunions.

Cornpunk. Corn remedy or corn-based patent medicine.

Dental punk. Obsolete term from the time when dentists used dry fungus to dry cavities before they were filled.

Funk-punk. Variation of punk-funk, presumably applied when the influence of funk is stronger than punk. Found in a 1981 article in the *Washington Post* by Mike Joyce on Rick James: "James, the self-annointed high priest of funk-punk, presided over a sold-out celebration of outrageous party music." Also known as, *Funk-punk* or *Funk-rock*.

In the punk. In bad condition; the opposite of "in the pink."

Mess punk. (Nautical) Waiter or steward.

Pickle punk. (Carnival) Name for the abnormal fetuses that are preserved in glass and exhibited. See also *Punk show*.

Post-punk. Quirky rock that emerged after punk rock's mid-70's boom.

Powderpuff Punk. Term used to describe female rock groups such as the Go-Gos.

Pretty punk. From *English as It is Spoken in New Zealand* (1970): "Pretty punk does some of the work performed in America by *lousy*."

Whistle punk. (Logging) A signalman; one employed to signal the operations of machinery.

Sexy Words

A Lusty Lexicon

Aischrolgia. The frank expression of obscenities.

Algolagnia. A term for both masochism and sadism.

Alpha androstenol. The name of a recently isolated substance found in the sweat of human males, which is believed to create sexual excitement in women.

Ambisextrous. Attractive to both sexes; involving both sexes.

Amober. "Maiden fee" paid by a groom to prevent his new bride from having to spend her wedding night with the lord of the manor. The term and the practice comes from Wales.

Ampallang. According to Charles Winick's *Dictionary of Anthropology,* "A metal rod with balls or brushes fixed to the ends. This device is worn transversely through a perforation in the end of the penis by Dyak men and is said to heighten sexual pleasure of their wives."

Anaphroditous. Without sexual desire.

Andromania. Excessive sexual desire in the female.

Antaphrodisiac. Something that reduces sexual desire; the legendary quality of saltpeter.

Antipudic. That which covers the private parts of the body.

Apistia. Faithlessness in marriage.

Arrhenotoky. The bearing of male offspring only.

Bathykolpian. Deep-bosomed.

Blisson. Lusty; with strong sexual desire; in rut.

Brocage. A pimp's wages. It is an old word that appears as far back as Chaucer.

Callipygian. Having beautifully proportioned buttocks. A letter from Joe M. Turner contained this information: "I once intended to write a story featuring Callie Pygian, a lovely Armenian girl and her lard-assed brother, Steato."

Cataglottism. A lascivious kiss; a tongue-kiss.

Catamite. A boy kept by a pederast.

Concupiscence. Ardent sexual desire.

Cornuto. A cuckold; a man horned.

Copesmate. Someone with whom you cope; a lover.

Croodle. A portmanteau word combining crouch and cuddle that sometimes shows up in Victorian novels as a lover's indulgence.

Cullion. A testicle.

Dasyproctic. With hairy buttocks. It is commonly applied to apes.

Dyscalligynia. Dislike of beautiful women.

Ecdemolagnia. The tendency to be more lustful when away from home.

Embonpoint. A plumpness of figure, especially at the bust.

Endogamy. The compulsory custom of marrying within one's own group; inbreeding.

Eonism. A synonym for transvestism. From Chevalier d'Éon, who for years at a time lived alternately as a man and woman.

Ertomania. Abnormally powerful sex drive.

Fanny. An archaic British slang word for vagina, which became popular after John Cleland's *Memoirs of a Woman of Pleasure,* better known as *Fanny Hill.*

Ferk. To jig up and down. In his *Scholar's Glossary of Sex,* Ray Goliad writes, "The word *ferk* is largely forgotten today, but it is the probable source of our most frequently unprinted four-letter word."

Frottage. The practice of rubbing one's genitals against another person, usually of the opposite sex and usually in public. This word is also used to describe the technique of rubbing a raised design with a crayon and a piece of paper to produce an image.

Gere. A sudden fit of passion.

Genetic material. What the American Bar Association called sperm in its "Model Reproductive Services Act."

Iatronudia. The desire of a woman to expose herself to a doctor while feigning illness.

Idiogamist. A man who is only capable of coitus with his wife.

Infibulate. To fit with a chastity belt.

Lectual. Proper for bed.

Lupanarian. Pertaining to a brothel or brothels.

Meable. Easily penetrated.

Melcryptovestimentaphilia. Fondness for women's black underwear. This marvelous word appears in Willard Espy's *Words at Play* and very few other places. The book also contains *cryptoscopophilia,* the desire to look into the windows of homes that one passes, and *genuglyphics,* the practice of decorating the female knee to make her more erotic.

Meretricium. A tax on prostitution.

Merkin. A woman's pubic wig.

Mixoscopy. The secret observation of the sexual act.

Moschate. Musk-like smell, the goal of many perfumes.

Nympholepsy. Trance induced by erotic daydreaming.

Ophelimity. The ability to give sexual pleasure.

Opsigamy. Marriage late in life.

Osphresiology. The study of aromas and olfactory reactions, especially in regard to sexual relationships.

Paizogony. One of a cluster of synonyms for necking and petting. Other high-sounding terms for the same activity: *contrectation, sarmassation,* and *paraphilemia.*

Pansexualism. Total sexual obsession; seeing sex in all activities; belief that sexual instinct is at the basis of all human activity.

Parnel. The mistress of a priest.

Passion purpura. The proper medical name for a hickey, or as it is defined in *A Dictionary of Dermatological Words, Terms and Phrases,* ". . . the erythematous and later ecchymotic mark of a playful bite or pinch, usually on the cheeks (of the face or buttocks), the neck or breasts, inflicted or incurred in hanky-panky."

Penotherapy. Regulating prostitutes as a means of venereal disease control.

Pernocation. The act of spending the night; an overnighter.

Philematology. The art of kissing.

Poke. To brusquely fornicate with. A British term.

Polyandry. A woman who has more than one husband, a form of *polygamy.*

Polygyny. A man with more than one wife, a form of *polygamy.*

Pornerastic. Addicted to harlotry.

Pornocracy. Government by whores. The term is sometimes used to describe Rome during the first half of the tenth century.

Pornogenarian. A dirty old man. This word was created by Norma S. Vance of Florissant, Missouri, for the "National Challenge," a syndicated newspaper game.

Priapus. A penis of enormous size. This is from Priapus of classic times, who was born with a phallus so large that his horror-stricken mother disowned him.

Pronovalence. Only being able to have sexual intercourse in the prone position.

Pyrolagnia. Sexual arousal from watching fires.

Renifleur. One who gets sexual pleasure from body odors.

Roger. To screw. British slang.

Sam. An Egyptian amulet in the shape of a phallus. It was used to foster erotic relationships.

Sarcology. The study of the fleshy parts of the body.

Satyriasis. The condition of intense male lustfulness.

Secundiapara. A woman who has borne two children. A *primipara,* on the other hand, has an only child, and a *nullipara* is a woman with no children.

Shag. British for copulate.

Shunammitism. Contact—visual, tactile, or carnal—with younger girls by old males to encourage or restore their sexual vigor. The practice was common in biblical times.

Starkers. British equivalent of bare-ass. *Starko* is the same thing.

Stasivalence. The inability to have sexual intercourse in any but the standing position.

Strolling hostess. Name used in a New York City courtroom to describe a "streetwaker" when objections were made to the use of that term.

Syndyasmian. Pertaining to temporary sexual union. A *snyndyasmian* relationship would be a one-night stand.

Tentiginous. Lust provoking.

The 3Ps. Current medical slang for "the pill, permissiveness, and promiscuity." It is used when explaining the spread of certain forms of venereal disease.

Thelyphthoric. That which corrupts women.

Theogamy. Marriage of gods.

Urtication. Flagellation with fresh nettles. In ancient Rome urtication was a common means employed to arouse sexual appetites.

Uxoravalent. Pertaining to a man who is only able to have sexual intercourse outside of marriage. *Uxorovalent* men, on the other hand, can only perform with their wives.

Uxorious. Excessively or foolishly fond of one's wife.

Uxorium. A tax imposed on male citizens in ancient Rome for not marrying.

Vanilla sex. Sex without variation.

Viripotent. Fit for a husband; marriageable.

Wittol. A man who encourages infidelity in his wife, the *wittee.*

Xeronisus. The inability to reach orgasm.

Slogans

A Little Prosaic License

Slogans for places have been in the news recently as official boards and bodies try to create new verbal image-builders such as *Dayton—The Innovative Location, Better Yet Connecticut,* and *Salem—Stop by for a Spell.*

Most of these slogans go no further than pamphlets, ads, and bumper stickers, but the most visible and important are written across license plates as official road slogans that now appear on the tags of states from Maine (*Vacationland*) to California (*The Golden State*).

But there is surpirsing flux and controversy in this realm. While it is true that states like New Mexico (*Land of Enchantment*) and New Jersey (*Garden State*) have had the same motto for at least a decade, others have changed with the times. In the 1980s, vehicles from Indiana featured more new slogans than most heavily advertised commercial products—*Wander Indiana, The Hoosier State, Back Home Again,* and *Hoosier Hospitality.* Not that long ago, Arkansas was *Land of Opportunity;* now the message reads *Arkansas is a Natural,* and one imagines that it is just a matter of time until we see *Arkansas—Cholesterol Free.*

As for the controversy, it began in the 1970s when a religious pacifist from New Hampshire went all the way to the Supreme Court to assert his right to tape over the *Live Free or Die* motto on his license plate. A recent lower-court decision has said that the state of Idaho has the constitutional right to say *Famous Potatoes* on its tags, but that it could not prevent the nonfamous from covering the words with tape or displaying alternative slogans along the lines of *Famous Potholes.* People in other states have begun resorting

246

to paste-overs. A wee red lobster on the Maine plate has inspired people to place apt little stickers across *Vacationland* that read *The Crawfish State*.

Americans don't seem to be totally at ease with slogans and symbols imposed from above. Iowa's proposed *A State of Minds* (a reference to the Hawkeye education system) was killed for tag year 1985 by a mix of local outrage and ridicule. Factions emerged pushing for something more agricultural (*Take a Fork to More Pork*) or whimsical (*Iowa: Gateway to Nebraska*), and the Associated Press reported that politicians there said they had never encountered such an outcry.

Like Iowa, the Texas plate has been forced to remain sloganless. In 1989 the Highway Commission proclaimed that future licenses would say *The Friendship State* causing the same anguished outcry and rejection as that which met a 1987 proposal to put *Wildflower State* and a bouquet on everybody's plate.

In 1985, the governor of Wisconsin held a public referendum to determine a replacement for *America's Dairyland*. Not only did the people flatly reject the new ideas (including *We Like It Here* and *America's Northern Escape*) in favor of the old, but they came up with some wild ideas of their own including a dairy country variation on the New Hampshire slogan: *Eat Cheese or Die*.

This brings me to a democratic proposal that I have had in mind for a while. Why don't we allow individuals to put their own custom slogans on their plates? It would greatly expand the limited creative possibilities provided by vanity plates and allow people to escape, for a small fee, the state's promises of Friendship, Enchantment, and *10,000 Lakes*. Those who are content with *Oklahoma Is OK* would accept state issue, but to get the folks at the motor vehicles bureau to sell you a tag saying *The Gibbses Are OK, as Well* would cost extra.

There would have to be a limit on the number of letters and for this purpose the states could rely on the Pennsylvania/Utah Formula, which allows 30 letters. This is based on averaging the 26-letter, 2-part Utah slogan (*Ski Utah/Greatest Snow on Earth*) and the 30-letter (plus apostrophe) minor essay on the Keystone tag (*You've Got a Friend in Pennsylvania*).

In keeping with one's right of free expression one would be allowed to poke fun at official slogans present and past (*You've Got a Friend in Transylvania*) and have one's say about the state (*Land of Hidden Taxes*). Others would ape traditional Chamber of Commerce slogans and brag about their home and family. Some possibilities here would include: *Fastest Growing Family on the Block, Host Family to In-Laws (on Both Sides), Gateway to the Finleys, One of Waco's Interesting Families, Diversity Under One Roof, Athens of the 1200 Block, 15 Elm— All-Season Home of the Halls*, and *Lost Sock Capital of Wayne County*.

Having now proposed this idea and being convinced that 50 state legislatures will tumble to the notion like so many dominoes, I am now at work on my own slogan. Some early candidates included *Never Saw Elvis, Late, Late Bloomer, I'd Rather Be Napping*, and the purposely cryptic *Still Waiting*. The one I'm leaning toward, however, is *Like It or Not, This One Was My Idea*.

Small Talk

A Toddick of Tiny Terms

Perhaps it is because of the excess of Madison Avenue, the NFL, the Pentagon, and other modern institutions; but we have become overburdened by the big, the stupendous, and, recently, the humongous. The result is that we are losing our ability to think and speak small. A diminutive, antidotal offering:

Animalcule. An animal that is either invisible or nearly so.

Bavin. A piece of waste wood.

Beadlets. The small-time release capsules found inside larger capsules in medications like Contac.

Bindle. A small or trifling amount.

Bort. Ground fragments of diamond; diamond dust used in polishing.

Doit. A trifle. The word occasionally shows up in crossword puzzles. Originally, it was a small Dutch coin.

Dole. A scanty share; a lesser allowance. In Britain, unemployment insurance benefits are referred to as "the dole."

Femto. A quadrillionth of a second or a meter. Much smaller than the other hyper-diminutives *nano* (billionth) and *pico* (trillionth).

Flinders. Small things the size of splinters; splinters.

Fribble. Something of little or paltry value.

Funicle. A small cord or fiber.

Glim. A bit; small amount.

Gry. An old, little-used word for anything of little value; for instance, nail parings.

Jerp. A small quantity usually used in reference to sweets. The term comes from the Ozarks.

Jot. A tiny particle.

Micraner. Male ant of unusually small size.

Minikin. Of small and delicate form.

Monad. Something ultimately small and indivisible.

Noil. Piece or knot of short hair or fiber.

Opuscule. A small or minor work.

Piff. Something insignificant; a trifle.

Pigwidgeon. Anything especially small.

Pismire. The hoarding of small things.

Pledget. A small mass of lint, such as that which accumulates at the human navel. In British medical terminology, it is a cotton swab.

Quiddit. A trifling nicety.

Scantling. A little piece.

Scrid. Tiny portion, as in accepting a "scrid of pie" as a second helping. Scrid is a term from New England.

Scuddick. Anything small or paltry.

Sermuncle. A short sermon.

Skimption. Southern talk for a small amount; not enough to bother with.

Snick. A small cut or mark.

Snip. A small person.

Snippety. Ridiculously small.

Sop. A thing of little or no value.

Sup. A small bite or mouthful.

Tittle. A particle; an iota.

Toddick. A very small quantity.

Trig. A stone, brick, or anything placed under a wheel or barrel to keep it from rolling.

Vug. A small cavity in a rock; also, *vugg* and *vugh*.

Waf. Worthless.

Wem. Blemish or spot.

Whit. The smallest imaginable particle.

Sounds

A Cacophony of Words that Make Noise

Armisonant. Resounding with the noise of clashing weapons.
Armisonant. Resounding with the noise of clashing weapons.
Blatter. To make a rattling or senseless noise.
Borborygm. Bowel noise; the noise of a fart.
Bourdon. A bass drone, as can be made by a bagpipe.
Brontide. Seismic noise; the earth making a sound like distant thunder.
Cachinnation. Excessive laughter.
Canorous. Sweet-sounding.
Chirr. Insect sound made by rubbing rough surfaces together. Grasshoppers chirr.
Churr. The sound made by a partridge.
Conflation. Blowing together, as many wind instruments in a concert.
Crepitation. A small crackling; a slight, rapidly repeated sound. Rice Krispies, for instance, are *crepitant*.
Feep. Computerese for the soft bell associated with a display terminal; a melodious bleep or beep.
Frantling. The mating call of a peacock.
Fritiniency. The noise of insects.

Gothele. The noise that water makes when a hot iron is dropped in it.

Glossolalia. Speaking in tongues.

Hirrient. Heavily trilled—as in *Hirrrrrrr*.

Horrisonant. Making a horrible noise.

Kinclunk. The sound of a car going over a manhole cover. Word created by poet Alastair Reid (see *Ploo*, which is also his creation).

Kyoodle. To make loud, meaningless noise.

Lallation. Pronouncing *r* as *l*.

Lumbrage. A term from the Ozarks for a loud rumbling or crashing noise.

Mugient. A lowing or bellowing. This word, which has been out of use for centuries, was recently reintroduced by the Unicorn Hunters, the organizaiton that annually attacks overused words. It felt that the word had modern application, especially in election years. Anyone enjoying mugient should also like *remugient*, to bellow or low again.

Parasigmatism. The inability to pronounce the sound of the letter *s*.

Plangent. Making a sound like the breaking of waves on the shore.

Ploo. The sound of a breaking shoelace.

Poppling. A bubbling sound such as is made when rain falls on water.

Psithurism. Whispering sound of wind through leaves.

Pule. To cry like a chicken.

Raucity. A loud, rough noise.

Reboation. The echo of a bellow.

Rhinophonia. Strong nasality in one's voice.

Rote. Noise made by the surf.

Skirl. The distinctive sound of a bagpipe.

Skirr. Whirr of birds in flight.

Soughing. A soft rustling or murmuring sound. It is pronounced *suhf-ing* and is both a noun and an adjective. In their book *A Play on Words*, a group of word lovers called VERBIA say of this word, "A soughing sound is soft or gentle or muted: It is soft like the deep sigh of a sleeping baby; it is gentle like the rustle of a taffeta gown; it is muted like the shuffle of an old man's carpet slippers."

Stomatolalia. Speech produced when one's nostrils are clogged.

Thrum. To play an instrument coarsely or artlessly.

Tinnitus. A ringing sound in the head.

Tintinnabulation. The sound of bells; bell ringing.

Tonant. Making loud, deep noise.

Tucket. A trumpet flourish.

Ululate. To howl or hoot.

Vagitus. The cry of the newly born.

Wamble. To rumble from the stomach.

Whurr. To pronounce the letter *r* too forcefully.

Soused Synonyms II

Exactly 2,660 (not 2,231) Words and Phrases for Drunk

The Arabs have some 6,000 words for the camel. The Hanunoo, a people of the Philippines, have 92 words for rice. Your average Eskimo can identify snow with five words of his own, depending on whether it's hard and icy or the wet, slushy stuff.

—*Ken Baron writing in the* Washington Post

Ever since I can remember, I have dreamed about setting a record of some sort. I knew that it had nothing to do with the day-to-day realities of making a living or putting bread on the table, but it was still a cherished goal. When I was a kid, the idea of setting an athletic record was appealing, but it was soon clear that I didn't have the necessary talent to set a county record let alone something bigger.

When I got into my early 40s, I decided I had better get on with the business of setting my record if I had any hopes of getting in the record book. But what record book? I had long ago given up the idea of getting in the *Guinness Book of World Records* for the simple reason that I was not up to eating a bicycle or crawling more than 26.5 miles, which is the current record.

Then one day I realized that there was a section in the Guinness book for records having to do with words and that it was missing one important category:

synonyms. I collect synonyms like other people collect matchbook covers or baseball cards, and I quickly concluded that the thing in English that has the most synonyms is the condition of drunkenness. With the help of more than a hundred people—from professional linguists to bartenders—and borrowing from other lists of synonyms for drunk going back to one compiled by Benjamin Franklin, I finally came up with 2,231 words and phrases for drunkenness (which was published in full in the earlier book *Words*) and then fired off a letter to the Guinness people claiming a new category and a record within that category.

I proved my case, and the category "Most Synonyms" is listed in most recent editions and I now have my record. I have been on a lexicographical Cloud Nine ever since, and I feel that I have done something for my odd hobby of word collecting.

But somewhere along the line I forgot something: Records are made to be broken. There is a negative side to all of this. I am starting to worry about other synonym savers who may try to take a shot at my record. It's tough being top synonym slinger because every time you go to the library and see a kid with his nose in a dictionary you wonder if he's working to gun down your record. Now I know what it must have been like to be the fastest gun in the West. So, without further ado, here is an introduction to Soused Synonyms II—a list for the nineties.

As far as can be determined, the first person ever to publish a list of slang terms for drunkenness in the English language was a Benjamin Franklin, who came out with his *Drinker's Dictionary* in 1733. It contained 228 terms for intoxicated including these remarkably quaint expressions:

Has stole a Manchet out of the brewer's basket
Has drank more than he has bled
He's kissed black Betty
He's had a thump over the head with Samson's jawbone
He's heat his copper
He cuts his capers
Sir Richard has taken off his considering cap
It is a dark day with him
He's a dead man
He's Prince Eugene
He's eat[en] a load and a half for breakfast
He owes no man a farthing
His flag is out
He's a king
The king is his cousin
He makes indentures with his legs
He's well to live
He's eat[en] the cocoa nut

He's eat[en] opium
He smelt of an onion
He drank till he gave up his halfpenny
He's as good conditioned as a puppy
He's contending with Pharaoh
He's wasted his paunch
He's eat[en] a pudding bag
His shoe pinches him
It is starlight with him
He carried too much sail
He's right before the wind with all his studding sails out
He makes Virginia fence
The malt is above the water

Others followed Franklin's lead in this admirable pursuit. Edmund Wilson came out with a long list of them in 1927, H. L. Mencley added some in *The American Language* and its supplements, and nearly 1,000 appeared in Lester V. Berrey and Melvin Van Den Bark's monumental *American Thesaurus of Slang*. Over the years, *American Speech* has carried several extensive lists contributed by various authors, and a number of books have recorded other terms. Some of the most important have been Eric Partridge's *A Dictionary of Slang and Unconventional English*, Harold Wentworth and Stuart Berg Flexner's *Dictionary of American Slang*, and Richard A. Spears's recent *Slang and Euphemism*.

All this inspired this word collector to begin work on a master drunk list, a list that not only incorporates all the previous lists but draws from a wide variety of additional sources ranging from "research" conducted by friends and scribbled on the back of cocktail napkins to material from the editorial offices of the *Dictionary of American Regional English* (DARE).

The list that resulted contained 2,231 entries (including the 31 already listed from Franklin's collection) without resorting to slight variations in syntax and resisting the temptation to include one-liners that start with "He's so drunk that—" (such as the nineteenth-century expression, "He's so drunk that he opens his collar to piss," or "He's so drunk the dogs wouldn't piss on him"). Since the first list appeared, a number of people have come forward with documented additions—usually one at a time as they get harder to find after you pass 2,000—and those contributions serve as the basis for S.S.II.

In addition, a number of other extremely valuable sources have been brought to the compiler's attention—some very old, some created since Soused Synonyms I—including J. S. Farmer and W. E. Henley's *Historical Dictionary of Slang* (originally published in 1890 as *Slang and Its Analogues*), the 1984 revised edition of Eric Partridge's *Dictionary of Slang and Unconventional English* (edited by Paul Beale), Robert L. Chapman's 1989 *Thesaurus of American Slang*, Johnathan Green's 1986 *Slang Thesaurus*, and Esther and Albert E. Lewin's 1988 *Thesaurus of Slang*.

Two final points before starting:

(1) All the words and phrases are in "as found" condition, which means that most of the terms that include a personal pronoun refer to men (e.g., Dipped his bill, Has his pots on, etc.). No slight to besotted women is intended.

(2) A number of fine people have helped with the original list and additions to that list. I would like to thank: Jim Agenbrod, Reinhold Aman, Ryan Anthony, Russell Ash, Alan Austin, John Ballou, O. V. Barlow, John Becker, Terence Blacker, F. G. Cassidy, Terry Catchpole, Philip Chaplin, Mary H. Claycomb, Martha Cornog, Don Crinklaw, Alan Currey, William V. del Solar, Frederick C. Dyer, Connie Eble, A. Ross Eckler, Darryl Francis, Jummy Jump, Monika Fuchs, Dan Gardner, Joseph C. Goulden, Dave Hackett, Nancy Hackett, Raymond Harris, Joyce Jackson, Pierre Jelenc, W. L. Klawe, Ray Lovett, John McGuire, Peter T. Maiken, Meghan Mead, Robert M. Monsen, Russell Mott, Fitzhugh Mullan, Dennis Panke, Denys Parsons, Charles D. Poe, Dan Rapoport, Richard E. Ray, Ross Reader, Barbara Rifkind, Somers Ritchie, Randy Roberts, Steve Ross, William Safire, C. W. Sande, Russell Schwalbe, Robert Skole, Marshall L. Smith, Robert C. Snider, Robert Specht, Jim Steigman, William C. Stoke, Bill Tammeus, Wayne Terry, John Thornton, James Thorpe III, Elaine Viets, Stewart Wardell, Stephen Wells, Robert T. West, Robb Westaley, the late Hal John Wimberley and Philip Young: and his rare collection of nineteenth-century British slang books.

The New and Improved List

A

A bit lit
A bit on
A date with John Barleycorn
A guest in the attic
A little gone
A real bender
Aboard
About blowed his top
About drunk
About full
About gone
About had it
About half drunk
About right
About shot
About to cave in
About to go under
About to pass out

Absent
Absolutely done
Abuzz
Aced
Acting silly
Activated
Acts like a fool
Adam's apple up
Addled
Adrip
Afflicted
Afloat
Aglow
Alcoholic
Alcoholized
Alecie (pronounced *ale-see*)
Alcied
Aled up
Alight

Don't Lose Your Grip

Alkied
Alkied up
Alky soaked
All at sea
All fucked up
All geezed up
All gone
All he can hold
All in
All keyhole
All liquored up
All lit up
All mops and brooms
All organized
All out
All pink elephants
All schnozzled up
All shucked up
All there
All wet
Almost froze
Almost intoxicated
Altogetherly
Amiably incandescent
Amuck
Anchored in sot's bay
Anesthetized

Annihilated
Antifreezed
Antiseptic
Ape
Aped
Apple palsy
Arf an' arf
Arfarfanark
Arseholed
A-showin' it
As tight as Andronicus
Ass backwards
Ass on backwards
A-tappin' the bottle
At one's ease
At rest
At rights
Ate the dog
Awash
Awry
Awry-eyed

B

Bacchi plenus
Bacchus-bulged
Bacchus-butted
Back-assward

Back home
Back teeth afloat
Bagged
Baked
Ball-dozed
Balmy
Bamboozled
Banjaxed
Baptized
Bar kissing
Barleysick
Barmy
Barreled-up
Barrelhouse
Barrelhouse drunk
Bashed
Basted
Bats
Batted
Battered
Batty
Beargered
Bearing the ensign
Beastly drunk
Been among the Philippines
Been among the Philistines
Been at a ploughing match
Been at an Indian feast
Been at Geneva
Been barring to much
Been before George
Been elephants
Been flying rather high
Been hit by a barn mouse
Been in the bibbing plot
Been in the sauce
Been in the sun
Been to a funeral
Been to France
Been to Barbados
Been to Jericho
Been to Mexico
Been to Olympus
Been to the saltwater

Been too free with Sir John
    Strawberry
Been too free with Sir Richard
Been too free with the creature
Been with Sir John Goa
Beerified
Beer-soaked
Beery
Beginning to fly
Beginning to get a glow on
Beginning to stagger
Behind the cork
Belly up
Below the mahogany
Belted
Bemused
Bending over
Bent
Bent and broken
Bent his elbow
Bent out of shape
Benused
Besoppen
Besot
Besotted
Better if he's gone twice after
    the same load
Bevvied
Bewildered
Bewitched
Bewottled
Beyond salvage
Beyond the fringe
Bezzled
Bibacious
Bibulous
Biffy
Biggy
Binged
Bingoed
Bit by a fox
Bit one's name in
Bit teed up
Bit tiddley

Bit tipsy
Bit wobbly
Biting the brute
Biting them off
Bitten by a barn-mouse
Black jacked
Blacked out
Blanked
Blasé
Blasted
Blazing drunk
Blazing fou'
Bleary
Bleary-eyed
Blewed
Blighted
Blimped
Blind

Blind drunk
Blind, staggering drunk
Blind staggers
Blinded
Blinders
Blindo
Blinking drunk
Blinky
Blissed out
Blistered
Blithered
Blitzed
Blitzed out
Bloated
Block and block
Bloody drunk
Blotto
Blowed

Blowed-away
Blown
Blown away
Blown out
Blown over
Blown up
Blowzy
Blue
Blue around the gills
Blued
Blue-eyed
Boggled
Boggy
Boiled
Boiled as an owl
Boiled to the gills
Boiling drunk
Bollixed
Bombed
Bombed out of his mind
Bombed out of their kugs
Boned
Bongo
Bongoed
Bonkers
Boosed
Boosy
Booze blind
Boozed
Boozed as the gage
Boozed up
Boozie
Boozified
Boozing
Boozington
Boozy
Boozy-woozy
Borahco
Borracho
Bosco absoluto
Boshy
Bosky
Both sheets in the wind
Bottle-ached

Bottled
Bought the black sun
'Bout had it
Bowzed
Bowzered
Boxed
Boxed out
Boxed up
Brahms and Lizst (Cockney
    rhyming slang for "pissed")
Brained
Brandy-faced
Brannigan
Breath strong enough to carry
    coal with
Breezy
Brick in the hat
Bridgey
Bright-eyed
Bright in the eye
Bruised
Bubbled
Bubby
Bucket is crackers
Buckled
Budgey
Buffy
Bug-eyed
Bugged
Bull-dozed
Bullet proofed
Bummed
Bummed out
Bumpsy
Bung
Bungay Fair
Bunged
Bung-eyed
Bungey
Bungfu
Bung-full
Bungie
Bungy
Bunned

Bunnied
Buoyant
Buoyed
Burdock'd
Buried
Burned to the ground
Burns with a low blue flame
Burnt
Burst
Busky
Busted
Butt Ugly
Buzz
Buzzed
Buzzey
Buzzy

C

Cached
Caged
Cagrin'd
Called Earl on the big white
  phone
Called Ralph on the big white
  phone
Called the wharf cat
Candy
Canned
Canned up
Canon
Can't bite his thumb
Can't find his ass with both
  hands
Can't hit the ground with his
  hat
Can't say National Intelligencer
Can't see a hole in a ladder
Can't see through a ladder
Capable
Capernoited
Capped off
Cap-sick
Cargoed

Carrying a heavy load
Carrying a load
Carrying the dark dog on his
  back
Carrying two red lights
Cast
Casting up his accounts
Cat
Catch'd
Catsood
Caught
Caught off his hobbyhorse
Certified drunk
Chagrin'd
Chap-fallen
Charged
Chateaued
Cherry-merry
Cherubimical
Chickery
Chipper
Chirping-merry
Chloroformed
Chock-a-block
Choked
Chucked
Clear
Clear out
Clipped the King's English
Clobbered
Clinched
Coagulated
Coarse
Cocked
Cocked as a log
Cocked to the gills
Cockeyed
Cockeyed drunk
Cogey
Cognacked
Coguey
Coguy
Cogy
Cold

Comboozelated
Comfortable
Comin'
Comin' on
Commencin'
Commencin' to feel it
Commode-hugging drunk
Completely out of it
Completely squashed
Concerned
Conflummoxed
Conked out
Consumed a rancid oyster
Cooked
Copasetic
Copey
Copped a crane
Corked
Corked-up
Cork high and bottle deep
Corkscrewed
Corky
Corned
Cornered
Cracked
Cramped
Cranked
Cranky
Crapped out
Crapulous
Crashed
Crashed and burned
Crazed
Crazy drunk
Creamed
Croaked
Crocked
Crocko
Crocus
Cronk
Crooked
Crooking the elbow
Cropsick
Cross-eyed

Crump
Crump footed
Crumped
Crumped out
Crushed
Crying drunk
Crying jag
Cruckooed
Cup-shot
Cupped
Cupshotten
Curious
Curved
Cushed
Cut

D
Daffy
Dagged
Damaged
Damp
Daquifried
D and D
Dead drunk
Dead-oh!
Dead to the world
Decanted
Decayed
Decks awash
Deep drunk
Defaced
Deformed
Deleerit
Demented
Derailed
Destroyed
Detained on business
Dew drunk
Dewed
Did the job up right
(Has) Diluted the blood in his
    alcohol system
Ding-swizzled

Dinged-out
Dingy
Dinky
Dipped
Dipped his beak
Dipped his bill
Dipped in the wassail bowl
Dipped rather deep
Dipped too deep
Dipsy
Dirtfaced
Dirty drunk
Discombobulated
Discomboobulated
Discouraged
Discumfuddled
Disguised
Disgusting
Disorderly
Distinguished
Dithered
Dizzy
Dizzy as a coot
Dizzy as a goose
Dog drunk
Doing the emperor
Doing the lord
Done a Falstaff

Done a vanishing act
Done an Archie
Done got out
Done over
Done up
Doped
Doped over
Dotted
Dotty
Double-headed
Double-tongued
Double up
Down
Down and out
Down for the count
Down in drink
Down with barrel fever
Down with the fish
Down with the blue devils
Dragging his bottom
Dragging the load
Dramling
Draped
Draw a blank
Drenched
Drinkative
Drinky
Dripping tight

Drove the big white bus
Drove the brewer's horse
Drove the porcelain bus
Drowned
Drowning brain cells
Drowning the shamrock
Drunk
Drunk and disorderly
Drunk and down
Drunk as a badger
Drunk as a bastard
Drunk as a bat
Drunk as a beggar
Drunk as a besom
Drunk as a big owl
Drunk as a boiled owl
Drunk as a brewer's fart
Drunk as a broken cart-wheel
Drunk as a cook
Drunk as a coon
Drunk as a coot
Drunk as a cooter
Drunk as a cootie
Drunk as Davy's sow
Drunk as a dog
Drunk as a drowned mouse
Drunk as a fiddler
Drunk as a fiddler's bitch
Drunk as a fish
Drunk as a fly
Drunk as forty billygoats
Drunk as a fowl
Drunk as a Gosport fiddler
Drunk as a handcart
Drunk as a hog
Drunk as a kettlefish
Drunk as a king
Drunk as a little red wagon
Drunk as a log
Drunk as a loon
Drunk as a lord
Drunk as a monkey
Drunk as a mouse
Drunk as a newt

Drunk as a Perraner
Drunk as a pig
Drunk as a piper
Drunk as a piper fou'
Drunk as a piss ant
Drunk as a poet
Drunk as a polony
Drunk as a rat
Drunk as a rolling fart
Drunk as a sailor
Drunk as a skunk
Drunk as a skunk in a trunk
Drunk as a soot
Drunk as a sow
Drunk as a swine
Drunk as a tapster
Drunk as a tick
Drunk as a top
Drunk as a wheelbarrow
Drunk as an ass
Drunk as an emperor
Drunk as an owl
Drunk as Bacchus
Drunk as Ballylana
Drunk as blazes
Drunk as buggery
Drunk as Chloe
Drunk as Coote Brown
Drunk as David's sow
Drunk as hell
Drunk as hoot
Drunk as mice
Drunk as muck
Drunk as the devil
Drunk as Zeus
Drunk for sure
Drunk to the pulp
Drunk up
Drunken
Drunkey
Drunker than a boiled owl
Drunker than a cannon
Drunker than a hoot owl
Drunker than a monkey

Drunker than hell
Drunker than Scootum Brown
Drunker than 300 dollars
Drunker than whiskey
Drunkulent
Drunkok
Drunky
Dry
D.T.'s (Delirium Tremens)
Due for drydock
Dull-eyed
Dull in the eye
Dumped
DWIed (Driving While
  Intoxicated)

E

Ears are ringing
Ears ringing
Eating his oats
Ebrios
Ebriose
Ebrious
Edged
Electrified
Elephant's trunk
Elevated
Eliminated
Embalmed
End of the line

Enter'd
Exalted
Exhilarated
Extinguished

F

Faced
Faint
Fairly ripped
Fallen off the wagon
Falling down drunk
Fap
Far ahead (Farahead)
Far gone
Fearless
Fears no man
Featured
Fed his kitty
Feeling
Feeling aces
Feeling dizzy
Feeling drunk
Feeling excellent
Feeling frisky
Feeling funny
Feeling glorious
Feeling good
Feeling groovy
Feeling happy
Feeling high

Here's an Eye-Opener for You !

Feeling his alcohol
Feeling his booze
Feeling his cheerios
Feeling his drink
Feeling his liquor
Feeling his oats
Feeling his onions
Feeling it
Feeling it a little
Feeling juiced up
Feeling no pain
Feeling pretty good
Feeling real well
Feeling right royal
Feeling the effect
Fell off the wagon
Fettered
Fettled
Feverish
Fiddled
Fighting drunk
Fighting tight
Filled
Fired
Fired up
Fish-eyed
Fishy
Fishy about the gills
Fixed up
Fizzed up
Fizzled
Flabbergasted
Flag is out
Flaked
Flakers
Flako
Flared
Flat-ass drunk
Flatch kennurd
Flat-out drunk
Flawed
Flickered
Floating
Floating high

Flooded
Flooey
Floored
Floothered
Floppy
Florid
Flown
Flown with the wild turkey
Fluffed
Fluffy
Flummoxed
Flummuxed
Flush
Flushed
Flusterated
Flustered
Flusticated
Flustrated
Flyblown
Fly-by-night
Flying blind
Flying high
Flying light
Flying one wing low
Flying the Ensign
Fogged
Foggy
Fogmatic
Folded
Fool if you don't quit
Foolish
Footless
Foozlified
45 degrees listed
Fossilized
Fou'
Fou' as a piper
Four sheets to the wind
Foxed (Foxt)
Foxy
Fozzed
Fractured
Frazzled
Freaked

Freefall
Fresh
Freshish
Fried
Fried on both sides
Fried to the gills
Fried to the hat
Fried up
Frozen
Froze his mouth
FUBARed (Fouled Up Beyond
    All Recognition)
Fucked out
Fucked over
Fucked up
Fuddled
Full
Full as a boot
Full as a bull
Full as a fiddler
Full as a goat
Full as a goog egg
Full as a goose
Full as a lord
Full as a pig's ear
Full as a piper
Full as a seaside shithouse on
    Boxing Day
Full as a state school hatrack
Full as a tick
Full as an egg
Full as the family po
Full as two race trains
Full cocked
Full drunk
Full flavored
Full of courage
Full of Dutch courage
Full to the bung
Full to the gills
Full up
Full up to the brain
Fully soused
Fully tanked

Funny
Fur brained
Fur on his tongue
Furry
Fuzzled
Fuzzy
Fuzzy headed

G

Gaffed
Gaga
Gaged
Gaily
Gallows drunk
Galvanized
Gambrinous
Gargled
Gaseous
Gassed
Gassed up
Gassy
Gay
Gayed
Geared up
Geed up
Geezed
Geezed up
Generous
Gestunketed
Get Chinese
Getting a glow
Getting a jag on
Getting a little boozy
Getting a little high
Getting a little inebriated
Getting a little whizzy
Getting a load on
Getting a snootful
Getting a thrill
Getting about all he needs
Getting an answer
Getting barreled up
Getting bleary-eyed
Getting boozed up

Getting boozy
Getting charged up
Getting crocked
Getting dopy
Getting full
Getting goofy
Getting him
Getting his ears back
Getting his load on
Getting in
Getting inebriated
Getting intoxicated
Getting kind of high
Getting kind of woozy
Getting light-headed
Getting likkered up
Getting lit
Getting lit up
Getting loaded
Getting looped
Getting loose
Getting on one
Getting on the band wagon
Getting polluted
Getting pretty full
Getting pretty high
Getting pretty well lit
Getting ready
Getting right

Getting shaky
Getting shot
Getting soft
Getting soused
Getting started
Getting tanked up
Getting teed up
Getting the habit
Getting there
Getting to be a drunkard
Getting to feel his liquor
Getting too full
Getting topsy
Getting under the influence
Getting under way
Getting up high
Getting warmed
Getting warmed up
Getting wasted
Getting woozy
Giddy
Giffed
Giggled
Gilded
Gin crazed
Gin soaked
Gingered up
Ginned
Ginned up
Ginny
Glad
Glassy
Glassy-eyed
Glazed
Globular
Glorious
Glowed
Glowing
Glued
Goat drunk
God-awful drunk
Goes out
Goggle-eyed
Going

Going overboard
Going to Jerusalem
Going under
Gold-headed
Golfed
Gone
Gone Borneo
Gone down in flames
Gone maximum Southern
  Comfort
Gone out
Gone over the hill
Gone to Mexico
Gone to Olympus
Gone to the devil
Gonged
Good and drunk
Good humored
Goofy
Googly-eyed
Gory-eyed
Got a blow on
Got a brass eye
Got a bun on
Got a buzz on
Got a dish
Got a drop in the eye
Got a jag on
Got a little polly on
Got a load on
Got a rum nose
Got a snootful
Got a turkey on one's back
Got about enough
Got barley fever
Got by the head
Got corns in his head
Got his shoes full
Got his snowsuit on and
  heading north
Got kibbled heels
Got on his little hat
Got one going
Got some in him

Got the back teeth well afloat
Got the blind staggers
Got the glanders
Got the good feeling
Got the gout
Got the gravel rash
Got the horns on
Got the Indian vapors
Got the nightmare
Got the pole evil
Got the sun in the eyes
Got the treatment
Got too much
Got up to the third story
Gowed
Gowed to the gills
Grade-A certified drunk
Grapeshot
Graveled
Greased
Greetin' fu'
Groatable
Grogged
Grogged up
Groggy
Guarding the gates of hell
Gutted
Gutter drunk
Guttered
Guyed out
Guzzled

H

Had a bun on
Had a couple of drinks
Had a couple of shooters
Had a dram
Had a few drinks
Had a glow on
Had a few too many
Had a kick in the guts
Had a little too much
Had a number of beers
Had a shot or two

Had a skinful and a half
Had a snort
Had a toothful
Had enough
Had enough to make him noisy
Had it
Had one or two
Had one too many
Hair on his tongue
Half-a-brewer
Half and half
Half-assed
Half-bagged
Half bent out of shape
Half-blind
Half-bulled
Half-canned
Half-cocked
Half-cockeyed
Half-corned
Half-crocked
Half-cut
Half-doped
Half-drunk
Half geared-up
Half-gone
Half-high
Half-iced
Half in the bag
Half in the boot
Half in the tank
Half in the wrapper
Half-lit
Half-looped
Half nelson
Half-on
Half-out
Half-pickled
Half-pissed
Half rats
Half-rinsed
Half-screwed
Half-seas over
Half-seas under

Half-shaved
Half-shot
Half-slammed
Half-slewed
Half-slopped
Half-snapped
Half-sober
Half-soused
Half-sprung
Half-stewed
Half-stiff
Half-stoused
Half-tanked
Half the bay over
Half the bay under
Half-tipsy
Half-under
Half-wrapped
Halfway over
Halfway to Concord
Hammered
Hammerish
Hanced

THE ABSINTHE DRINKER

Hang one on
Happy
Happy drunk
Hard
Hard up
Hardy
Harry flakers
Has a bag on
Has a big head
Has a brass eye
Has a brick in his hat
Has a bun on
Has a buzz
Has a can on
Has a cup too much
Has a drop in his eye
Has a drop too much taken
Has a full cargo
Has a full jag on
Has a full load on
Has a guest in the attic
Has a glow on
Has a jag on
Has a load on
Has a load under the skin
Has a package on
Has a apiece of bread and teeth
   in the head
Has a pretty good glow on
Has a shine on
Has a skate on
Has a skinful
Has a slant on
Has a snootful
Has a turkey on one's back
Has an edge on
Has been kicked in the guts
Has been paid
Has bet his kettle (also Has
   het . . .)
Has burnt his shoulder
Has dampened his mug
Has froze his mouth
Has gallon distemper

Has got the flavor
Has his flag out
Has his gage up
Has his head full of bees
Has his head on backwards
Has his malt above his wheat
Has his pots on
Has hung one on
Has lost a shoe
Has made an example
Has made too free with John
   Barleycorn
Has one's nuff
Has one's soul in soak
Has scalt his head pad
Has sold his senses
Has spoke with his friend
Has swallowed a tavern token
Has taken a chiruping glass
Has taken Hippocrates' Grand
   Elixir
Has the blue johnnies
Has the Indian vapors
Has the jim jams
Has the Mexican vapors
Has the rats
Has the screaming meemies
Has the shakes
Has the uglies
Has the whoops and jingles
Has the yorks
Has the zings
Has yellow fever
Hasn't got no pain
Haunted with evil spirits
Have a tumble down the sink
Having a cooler
Having a warmer
Having the eyes opened
Hazy
He couldn't find his ass with
   two hands
Heading into the wind
Heady

Hear the owl hoot
Hearty
Hebriated
Hee-hawing around
Heeled
Heeled over
Heinous
Helpless
Hepped
Hepped up
Het-up
Hiccius-doccius
Hickey
Hicksius-doxius
Hiddey
High
High as a cat's back
High as a fiddler's fist
High as a Georgia pine
High as a kite
High as Lindbergh
High as the sky
High in the saddle
High lonesome
Higher than a kite
Hipped
His elevator's stalled
His hair hurts
His head is smoking
His lee scuppers are under
His nose is getting red
His nose is red
His teeth are floating
Hit and missed (Cockney
   rhyming slang for "pissed")
Hit on the head by a tavern
   bitch
Hitting 'em up
Hitting it a little
Hitting the jug
Hitting the sauce
Hoary-eyed
Hockey
Hocus

Hocus-pocus
Hog drunk
Holding up the wall
Honked
Hooched
Hooched-up
Hoodman
Hooted
Hopped
Hopped up
Horizontal
Horseback
Hosed
Hot
Hot as a red wagon
Hotsy-totsy
Hotter than a skunk
How-come-ye-so?

I

Iced
Iced to the eyebrows
Illuminated
Imbibed giggle water
Imbibed too freely
Impaired
Impixocated
In a bad way
In a difficulty
In a drunken stupor
In a fix
In a fog
In a fuddle
In a glow
In a head
In a muddle
In a rosy glow
In a stew
In a trance
In a vise
In armor
In color
In drink
In good fettle

In his airs
In his altitudes
In his cups
In his elements
In his glory
In his habits
In his pots
In his prosperity
In it now
In liquor
In Liquor-pond
In Mexico
In one's armour
In one's cups
In orbit
In soak
In the altitudes
In the bag
In the blues
In the cellar
In the clouds
In the gun
In the gutter
In the horrors
In the ozone
In the pen
In the pink
In the pulpit
In the rats
In the sack
In the satchel
In the shakes
In the suds
In the sun
In the tank
In the wind
In the wrapper
In tipium grove
In uncharted waters
Incog
Incognitibus
Incognito
Indentured
Indisposed

Inebriated
Infirm
Influenced
Injun drunk
Inked
Inkypoo
Insobriety
Inspired
Inter pocula
Into it
Into the sauce
Into the suds
Intoxed
Intoxicate
Intoxicated
Inundated
Invigorated
Invisible
Iron-plated

Irrigated
Irrigated the ulcers
Ishkimmisk
It's beginning to kick
It's getting to him
It's got ahold of him and he
    can't let go
It's showing on him
It's working on him

J

Jag on
Jagged
Jagged up
Jambled
Jammed
Jarred
Jazzed
Jazzed up
Jickey
Jiggered
Jim-Jams
Jingled
Jocular
John Bull
Jolly
Jolly fu'
Joplined
Joyous
Jug-bitten
Jug-steamed
Jugged
Jugged up
Juiced
Juiced up
Juicy
Jungled
Just about drunk
Just about half-drunk
Just plain drunk
Just showing signs

K

Ka-floot
Keg-legged

Keel-hauled
Kennurd
Kentucky-fried
Keyed
Keyed up
Keyed to the roof
Killed
Killed his dog
Kind of high
Kind of woozy
Kisk
Kisky
Kited
Knapt
Knee-crawling, commode-
    hugging, gutter-wallowing
    drunk
Knee-walking drunk
Kneed
Knocked for a loop
Knocked off his pins
Knocked out
Knocked over
Knocked to a loop
Knocked-up
Knockered
Knows not the way home
Knus-drunk
Kraeusened
Kursasted
Ky-eyed

L

Laced
Laid
Laid out
Laid right out
Laid to the bone
Lame
Lapped
Lapped the gutter
Lappy
Larruping drunk
Lathered

Laughing at the carpet
Laying out dead drunk
Leaning
Leaping
Leary
Leathered
Leery
Legless
Letting the finger ride the
  thumb
Leveled
Lifted
Lifting the little finger
Light
Light-headed
Light on top
Lighting up
Lights out
Lightsome
Like a rat in trouble
Likker-soaked
Likkered
Likkered up
Likkerous
Limber
Limp
Lined
Lion drunk
Liquefied
Liquor plug
Liquor struck
Liquored
Liquored up
Liquorish
Liquor's talking
Listened to the owl hoot
Listing to starboard
Lit
Lit a bit
Lit to the gills
Lit to the guards
Lit to the gunnels
Lit up
Lit up a little bit

Lit up like a cathedral
Lit up like a Chaunaka bush
Lit up like a Christmas tree
Lit up like a church
Lit up like a kite
Lit up like a skyscraper
Lit up like a store window
Lit up like Broadway
Lit up like London
Lit up like Main Street
Lit up like the Commonwealth
Lit up like Times Square
Lit up like the sky
Lit up to show he's human
Little bit on the go
Little off the beam
Little round the corner
Little tight
Little woozy
Living up a bit
Loaded
Loaded for bear
Loaded his cart
Loaded to the barrel
Loaded to the earlobes
Loaded to the eyebrows
Loaded to the gills
Loaded to the guards
Loaded to the gunnels
Loaded to the gunwales
Loaded to the hat
Loaded to the muzzle
Loaded to the Plimsoll mark
Loaded to the tailgate
Loading up
Lock-legged
Locoed out
Locoed out on an 8-ball
Logged
Longlong (pidgin English)
Longwhiskey (pidgin English)
Looking lively
Looking through a glass
Looks boozy

Loony
Looped
Looping
Looped-legged
Loop-legged
Loopy
Loopy-legged
Loose
Loose in the hilt(s)
Loosening up
Loppy
Lordy
Lost his rudder
Loud and proud
Lousy drunk
Low in the saddle
Lubed
Lubricated
Lumped
Lumpy
Lush
Lushed
Lushed up
Lushington
Lushy

M

Maggoty
Main-brace well spliced

Making a trip to Baltimore
Making fun
Making indentures with one's
 legs
Making M's and T's
Malted
Marinated
Martin drunk
Mashed
Mastok
Maudlin
Mauled
Mawbrish
Maxed
Maxed out
Mean
Meely mouthed
Mega-drunk
Mellow
Mellowing
Mellowish
Melted
Merry
Merry as a Greek
Mesmerized
Messed
Messed up
Methodistconated
Mexican-fried
Mickey-finished
Middlin'
Middling
Miffy
Milled
Miraculous
Mitered
Mixed
Mixed-up
Mizzled
Moist around the edges
Moistened
Mokus
Moon-eyed
Moonlit

Moony
Moored in sot's bay
Mopped
Moppy
Mops and brooms
More or less in liquor
Mortal
Mortallious
Mortally drunk
Motherless
Mountous
Mouthy
Muckibus
Muddled
Muddled up
Muddy
Muffed
Mug blotto
Mug blots
Mugged
Mugged up
Muggy
Mulled
Mulled up
Mullet-eyed
Mushy
Muzzed
Muzzy

N

Nailed to the floor
Nappy
Nase
Nasty drunk
Native (as in "He went native")
Nazy
Nearly off his rocker
Needing a reef taken in
Newted
Nice
Nimptopsical
Nipped
Nodded
Noddy-headed

Noggy
Nolo
Non compos
Non compos poopoo
Not able to see through a
    ladder
Not all there
Not feeling any pain
Not in any pain
Not suffering any
Numb
Nuts
Nutty
N.Y.D.

O

Obfuscated
Obfusticated
Oddish
Oenophlygia (pronounced *ee-no-fly-gia*)
Off
Off at the nail
Off his bean
Off his feet
Off his nut
Off nice
Off nicely
Off one's nut
Off the deep end
Off the nail
Off the wagon
Off to Mexico
Off to the races
Oiled
Oiled up
Oinophluxed
On
On a bat
On a bender
On a binge
On a bout
On a brannigan
On a bus

On a bust
On a drunk
On a fool's errand
On a jag
On a merry-go-round
On a skate
On a spree
On a tear
On a tipple
On a toot
Ona
On fourth
On his ass
On his ear
On his fourth
On his last legs
On his oats
On his way down
On his way out
On his way to a good drunk
On instruments
On sentry
On the batter
On the beer
On the bend
On the booze
On the drink
On the drunk
On the edge
On the floor
On the fritz
On the fuddle
On the go
On the grog
On the juice
On the lee lurch
On the loose
On the muddle
On the ooze
On the piss
On the ramble
On the randan
On the ran-tan
On the razzle dazzle

On the ree-raw
On the rampage
On the sauce
On the sentry
On the shikker
On the skyte
On the spree
On the sway
One over the eight
One too many
Oozy
Organized
Orie-eyed
Oscillated
Ossified
Out
Out cold
Out for the count
Out getting a head of bottles
Out in left field with a catcher's
    mitt on
Out like a lamp
Out like a light
Out like Lottie's eye
Out nibbling the grape
Out of altitudes
Out of commission
Out of control
Out of funds
Out of his mind
Out of his mind drunk
Out of his skull
Out of his tree
Out of it
Out of key
Out of kilter
Out of one's element
Out of one's head
Out of register
Out of the picture
Out of the way
Out on the roof
Out owl hooting
Out to it

Out to lunch
Over the bay
Over the limit
Over the line
Over the mark
Over the top
Overboard
Overcome
Overdone
Overloaded
Overseas
Overseen
Overserved
Overset
Overshot
Oversparred
Overtaken
Over the edge
Over-wined
Owled
Owl-eyed
Owly-eyed
Oxycrocium (pronounced *oxy-crock-eum*)

P
Pabbed
Packaged
Padded
Pafisticated
Paid
Paint the town red
Painted
Paintin' his nose
Palatic
Palatio
Palled
Paralytic
Paralysed
Parboiled
Pass out cold
Passed
Past going
Pasted

Peckish
Pee-eyed
Pegged too low
Peonied
Pepped
Pepped up
Peppy
Pepst
Perked
Perpetual drunk
Pertish
Petrificated
Petrified
Phfft
Pickled
Pickled his debts
Pickled the mustard
Pie-eyed
Pied
Piffed
Pifficated
Piffle
Piffled
Pifflicated
Pigeon-eyed
Pilfered
Pinked

Pinko
Pious
Piped
Piper-drunk
Piper-full
Piper-merry
Pipped
Pipped up
Pissant drunk
Piss-completed
Pissed
Pissed as a fart
Pissed as a newt
Pissed as a pig
Pissed as a rat
Pissed in the brook
Pissed out of one's mind
Pissed to the earlobes
Pissed up
Pissed up to the eyebrows
Pissing drunk
Pissy-arsed
Pissy-drunk
Pistol-shot
Pitted
Pixillated
Pixy-laden
Pixy-led
Pizzacato
Placated
Plain drunk
Plain old drunk
Planted
Plastered
Plated
Played out
Pleasantly intoxicated
Pleasantly plastered
Plenty drunk
Plonk
Plonked
Plootered
Plotzed
Ploughed

Ploughed under
Plowed
Plucked
Plumb drunk
Pocito
Poddy
Podgy
Poffered
Poggled
Pogy
Polished
Polished up
Polite
Polled-off
Polluted
Poopied
Popeyed
Potated
Potched
Pot-eyed
Pots on
Potsed
Pot-shot
Pot-sick
Potted
Potted off
Potty
Potulent
Potvaliant
Pot-walloped
Powdered
Powdered up
Practically down
Praying to the porcelain god
Preaching drunk
Preserved
Prestoned
Pretty drunk
Pretty far gone
Pretty happy
Pretty high
Pretty silly
Pretty well intoxicated
Pretty well organized

Pretty well over
Pretty well plowed
Pretty well primed
Pretty well slacked
Pretty well started
Priddy
Primed
Primed to the barrel
Primed to the muzzle
Primed to the trigger
Primed up
Pruned
Psatzed
Puggled
Puggy drunk
Pulled a Daniel Boone
Pungey
Pushed
Put in the pin
Put to bed with a shovel
Putrid
Putting one on
Pye-eyed

Q

Quadded
Quaffed
Quarrelsome
Quartzed
Queer
Queered
Quenched
Quick-tempered
Quisby
Quilted
Quite gone

R

Racked
Racked-up
Raddled
Ragged
Raised

Raised his monuments
Rammaged
Ramping mad
Rat-assed
Rather high
Rather touched
Ratted
Rattled
Ratty
Ratty as a jaybird
Raunchy
Razzle-dazzle
Reached a hundred proof
Ready
Ready to pass out
Real drunk
Real mellow
Real tipsy
Really
Really feeling his drinks
Really clobbered
Really gassed
Really got a load
Really had a load
Really high
Really lit
Really lit up
Really saturated
Really soused
Really tied one on
Red-eyed
Reeking
Reeling
Reeling and kneeling
Reeling ripe
Reely
Relaxing
Religious
Re-raw
Rich
Right
Right down and out
Right royal
Rigid

Rileyed
Ripe
Ripped
Ripped and wrecked
Ripped to the tits
Rip-roaring drunk
Ripskated
Road hugging
Roaring
Roaring drunk
Roaring fou'
Roasted
Rockaputzered
Rocked
Rocky
Rolled off the sofa
Rolling
Rolling drunk
Roostered
Rorty
Rosined
Rosy
Rosy about the gills
Rotten
Round as a glass
Royal
Royally plastered
Rum-dum
Rum-dumb
Rummed
Rummed up
Rummied
Rummy
Rung one up
Running drunk
Rye-soaked

S

Salt junk
Salted
Salted down
Salubrious
Sank like a brick
Sank like a rock

Sank like a stone
Sap-happy
Sapped
Saturated
Sauced
Saw Montezuma
Sawed
Scammered
Schicker
Schizzed
Schizzed-out
Schlitzed
Schlockkered
Schnapped
Schnockered
Schnockkered
Schnoggered
Schwacked
Scooped
Scorched
Scotch mist
Scrambled
Scratched
Scraunched
Screaming drunk
Screeching
Screeching drunk
Screwed
Screwy
Scronched
Scrooched
Scrooched up
Scrooped
Scudded
Seafaring
Seasick
Seeing a flock of moons
Seeing bats
Seeing by twos
Seeing double
Seeing pink elephants
Seeing the bears
Seeing the devil
Seeing the elephants

Seeing the French king
Seeing the snakes
Seeing the yellow star
Seeing two moons
Seguéd
Semibousy
Sent
Served-up
Set-up
Several slugs behind the midriff
Sewed
Sewed up
Sewn up
S.F. (Shit-faced)
S.F.'ed
Shagged
Shaggy
Shaking a cloth in the wind
Shaky
Shaved
Sheet and a half to the wind
Sheet in the wind
Shellacked
Shellacked the goldfish bowl
Sherbetty
Shicer
Shicker
Shickered

Shifassed
Shikker
Shikkered
Shined
Shined up
Shiny
Shiny drunk
Shipwrecked
Shit-faced
Shitty
Shoe the goose
Shot
Shot away
Shot down
Shot full of holes
Shot in the arm
Shot in the mouth
Shot in the neck
Shot in the wrist
Shot the cat
Shot-up
Showing his booze
Showing his tipsiness
Showing it
Silly
Silly drunk
Singed
Sinking like a rock
Six sails to the wind
Six sheets to the wind
Sizzled
Skew-whiff
Skulled
Skunk drunk
Skunked
Skunky
Slammed
Slap drunk
Slathered
Slewed
Slewy
Slick
Slightly buzzed
Slightly clobbered

Slightly draped
Slightly drunk
Slightly high
Slightly looped
Slightly tightly
Slightly under
Slightly woozy
Slippery
Slipping
Slobbered
Slopped
Slopped over
Slopped to the ears
Slopped to the gills
Slopped up
Sloppy
Sloppy drunk
Sloshed
Sloshed to the ears
Sloughed

Slued
Slugged
Slurks
Slushed
Slushed-up
Slushy
Smashed
Smashed out of his mind
Smashed to the gills
Smeared
Smeekit
Smelled the big cork
Smelling of the cork
Smitten by the grape
Smoked
Snackered
Snapped
Snerred
Sniffed the barmaid's apron
Sniffy

Snockered
Snockkered
Snockkered up
Snonkered
Snoot full
Snooted
Snootered
Snoozamorooed
Snotted
Snozzled
Snubbed
Snuffy
Snug
So
Soaked
Soaked to the gills
Soaked-up
Soaken
Soako
Soapy-eyed
Sobbed
Socked
Sodden
Sodden-drunk
Soft
Soggy
Somebody stole his rudder
Some-drunk
Sopped
Sopping
Sopping wet
Soppy
Sore footed
Soshed
So-so
Sot drunk
Sotted
Sottish
Sotto
Soul in soak
Soupy
Soused
Soused to the ears
Soused to the gills

Southern-fried
Sow-drunk
Sozzled
Sozzly
Spak (pidgin English)
Speared
Speechless
Spiffed
Spifficated
Spiffilo
Spiffled
Spiflicated
Spirited
Spliced
Sploshed
Sponge-eyed
Sponge-headed
Spoony drunk
Spotty
Spreed
Spreed up
Spreeish
Sprung
Squamed
Squared
Squashed
Squiffed
Squiffed out
Squiffy
Squiffy-eyed
Squirrelly
Squished
Staggering
Staggering around
Staggering drunk
Staggerish
Staggers
Staggery
Stale
Stale drunk
Standing too long in the sun
Starched
Starchery
Starchy

Stark drunk
Starting to feel pretty good
Starting to feel rosy
Starting to get lit up
Starting to glow
Starting to show his drink
State of elevation
State of temulency
Staying late at the office
Steady
Steamed
Steamed-up
Steeped
Stewed
Stewed as a fresh boiled owl
Stewed like a prune
Stewed to the ears
Stewed to the eyebrows
Stewed to the gills
Stewed-up
Sticked
Stiff
Stiff as a carp
Stiff as a goat
Stiff as a plank
Stiff as a ramrod
Stiff as a ringbolt
Stiffed
Stiffo
Still on his feet
Stimulated
Stinkarooed
Stinking
Stinking drunk
Stinko
Stitched
Stocked-up
Stoked
Stolled
Stolling
Stone blind
Stone cold drunk
Stoned
Stoned out of his mind

Stoned to the gills
Stoney blind
Stonkered
Stove in
Stozzled
Street-loaded
Stretched
Striped
Strong
Stubbed
Stuccoed
Stuffed
Stumble-drunk
Stung
Stunko
Stunned
Stupefied
Stupid
Stupidlegged
Sucked
Sucky
Suffering from the flu
Suffering no pain
Sun in the eyes
Sunk like a brick
Super-charged
Sure feeling good
Sure 'nuff drunk
Sure petrified
Sure tied one on
Suttle
Swacked
Swacko
Swallowed a hare
Swallowed a tavern token
Swamped
Swatched
Swatted
Swattled
Swazzled
Sweet
Swigged
Swiggled
Swilled

Swilled up
Swillo
Swine-drunk
Swiney
Swinnied
Swiped
Swipey
Switchy
Swivelly
Swizzled
Swozzled

T

Tacky
Taken a segué
Taken a shard
Taken in some O-be-joyful
Taking a trip
Taking it easy
Talking loud
Talking to Earl on the big white
  phone
Talking to Jamie Moore
Talking to Jim Beam
Talking to Ralph on the big
  white phone
Tangled
Tanglefooted
Tanglelegged
Tanked
Tanked out
Tanked up
Tanky
Tanned
Tapped
Tapped out
Tapped the admiral
Tap-shackled
Tattooed
Tavered
Taverned
Tead up
Ted
Teed

Teed up
Teeth under
Temulent
Temulentious
Temulentive
That way
Thawed
There
There with both feet
There with the goods
There with what it takes
Thick-headed
Thick-legged
Thick-lipped
Thick-tongued
Thirsty
Thoroughly drunk
Thoroughly intoxicated
Three bricks short of a load
Three sheets in the shade
Three sheets in the wind
Three sheets in the wind and
  the other one flapping
Three sheets to the wind
Three sheets to the wind's eye
Throw down
Tickeyboo
Tiddled
Tiddley

Tied one on
Tiffled
Tight
Tight as a brassiere
Tight as a drum
Tight as a fart
Tight as a goat
Tight as a mink
Tight as a tick
Tight as Andronicus
Tight as the bark on a tree
Tight-wadded
Titled
Tin hats
Tinned
Tip merry
Tipium grove
Tipped
Tipping
Tippling
Tipply
Tippsified
Tippy
Tipsy
Tip-top
Tired
Tired and emotional
Tishy
Toasted
Toasty
Tol-lol
Tongue-tied
Took a dive
Too many clothes on the wind
Too numerous to mention
Toped
Toper
Top-heavy
Top-loaded
Topped
Topped off his antifreeze
Topped up
Topper
Toppy

Topsy-boozy
Topsy-turvy
Tore-up
Torn
Torn up
Torrid
Tossed
Tosticated
Tostified
Totalled
Totally drunk
Touched
Touched as a boiled owl
Touched off
Touched with drink
Tow up
Towered
Toxed
Toxicated
Toxified
Toxy
Trammeled
Translated
Trashed
Trashed out of one's gourd
Trifle maudlin'
Trimmed down
Tripped up
Tripping
Trying Taylor's best
T.U.B.B. (for tits up-but
    breathing)
Tubed
Tumbling
Tumbling drunk
Tuned
Tuned up
Tuned up a little
Turned on
Turugiddy
Tweeked
Twisted
Two sheets to the wind
Two-thirds kicked in the ass

U
U.I. (Under the influence)
Ugly
Ugly drunk
Umbriago
Unbalanced
Unco' happy
Uncorked
Under
Under full sail
Under full steam
Under the affluence of incohol
Under the influence
Under the table
Under the wagon
Under the weather
Underway
Unglued
Unkdray
Unsensed
Unsober
Unsteady
Up a stump
Up a tree
Up in one's hat
Up large
Up on blocks
Up on Olympus
Up the pole
Up to the ears
Up to the eyeballs
Up to the gills
Upholstered
Uppish
Uppity
Upsey
Upside down

V
Valiant
Vapor-locked
Varnished
Vegetable
Very

Very drunk
Very high
Very relaxed
Very weary
Vulcanized

W
Walking on his cap badge
Wall-eyed
Wallpapered
Wam-bazzled
Wamble crop'd
Wapsed down
Warming up
Wassailed out
Wassailed up
Wasted
Watching the ant races
Watered
Waterlogged
Water-soaked (also water-
  soaken)
Waving a flag of defiance
Waxed
Wazzocked
Weak jointed
Wearing a barley cap
Weary
Weaving
Well away
Well bottled
Well-corned
Well fixed
Well greased
Well heeled
Well in for it
Well into it
Well jointed
Well lathered
Well lit
Well loaded
Well lubricated
Well oiled
Well on

Well on his way
Well primed
Well soaked
Well sprung
Well under
Well wrapped
Wellied
Wet
Wet both eyes
Wet-handed
Wettish
Wet within

Whacked out
Whacky
What-nosed
Whazood
Whiffled
Whipcat
Whipped
Whipsey
Whiskeyfied
Whiskey-frisky
Whiskey-raddled
Whiskey-shot

Whiskied
Whistle drunk
Whittin stewed
Whittled
Wholly-wassailed
Whooshed
Whoozy
Whopped up
Wide-eyed and legless
Wild
Willy-wacht
Wilted
Wine-potted
Winey
Wing-heavy
Winterized
Wiped
Wiped out
Wiped over
Wired
Wired up
Wise
With a binge on
With a bun on
With a jag on
With a load on
With a skate on
With a slant on
With an edge on
With the main brace well
  spliced
With the sun in one's eyes
With the topgallant sails out
With too many cloths in the
  wind

With too much sail
Wobbly
Woggled
Woggly
Wollied
Womble-ty-cropt
Wooshed
Woosy
Woozy
Wounded
Wrapped up in warm flannel
Wrecked

Y

Yappy
Yaupish
Yaupy
Ydrunken

Z

Zagged
Zapped
Zigzag
Zigzagged
Zipped
Zippered
Zissified
Zoned
Zonked
Zonked out
Zonkers
Zooted
Zorked
Zozzled

49

Studious Words

An Academic Assortment

ABD. Abbreviation for "all but dissertation." It is applied to doctoral candidates who have completed all the required courses, but who have yet to write their dissertations. It is used facetiously in some circles, as M.A. and Ph.D. are.

Algriology. Study of savage customs.

Aliterates. Those who know how to read, but won't.

Autology. The scientific study of oneself.

Axiology. In philosophy, the science of values in general. It is a relatively recent coinage.

Balneology. The study of the therapeutic effects of bathing in mineral waters.

Biometeorology. The effect of weather on people.

Cart. Campus-course slang for cartography. There are many of these—*trig, calc, Brit lit, poli sci,* etc.—but they reach their highest form as rhyming pairs such as *rocks for jocks* for introductory geology. A fine collection of these appears in an article, "Course Names" by Paul A. Eschholz and Alfred F. Rosa, in the Spring 1970 issue of *American Speech.* Among them:

Slums and Bums: Urban local government.

Nuts and Sluts: Abnormal psychology.

Stones and Bones: World prehistory.

Chokes and Croak: First aid and safety education.

More recent additions to the collection include:

Rocks for Jocks: Introductory geology.
Nudes for Dudes: Art 1–2.
Gods for Clods: Comparative religion.
Monday Night at the Movies: Introduction to film.
Baby Shakes: Introduction to Shakespeare.
Monkies to Junkies: Anthropology.
Clapping for Credit: Music appreciation.
Cut 'em and Gut 'em: Anatomy.
Bag 'em and Tag 'em: Field zoology.
Chem for Cromagnons: General chemistry, also known as a *Kinder Chemistry*.
Art in the Dark: Introduction to Art.

Even the places with the toughest academic reputations have their *Heroes for Zeroes* (Harvard's concept of the Greek hero), *Breathing for Credit* (Dartmouth's breathing voice for the stage), and *Moons for Goons* (Oberlin's planets, moons, and meteorites).

Donnism. Academic self-importance.
Enigmatology. The study of enigmas and puzzles. According to an Associated Press story of March 1981, there is only one academically confirmed specialist of this sort in the United States. He is Will Shortz, who designed his own course in enigmatology at Indiana University.
Ichnology. The study of footprints, commonly applied to those who study fossilized prints.
Kalology. The study of beauty.
Ktenology. The science of putting people to death.
Lirripoop. A learned person who lacks common sense; an academic dolt. It is also applied to the hood and long tail of an academic gown.
Melittology. The study of bees.
Momilogy. The study of mummies.
Nassology. The science of taxidermy.
Nidology. The study of birds' nests.
Oikology. The science of housekeeping.
Orology. The study of mountains.
Osmology. The study of odors.
Parietal. Of or relating to life within a college or university.
Phobiology. The study of phobias.
Photics. The scientific study of light.
Polemology. The study of war.
Polymath. One who has mastered many fields of knowledge.
Pomatology. The science of sealing containers.

Pomology. The science of fruit growing.

Pteridology. The study of ferns. The *p* is silent, as it is on the next word.

Pterylology. The study of the distribution of feathers on a bird's body.

Pud. An easy college course; a university blow-off. There are dozens of well-established terms covering snap courses starting with the traditional *snaps, guts,* and *cakes.* They are also widely known as *mick* courses (from Mickey Mouse) and *slides* (by extension, a professor known for easy classes is likely to be known as *Dr. Slide*). Depending on the campus you are on they are also variously known as *crip courses,* or *crips, loan-savers, blow-offs, easy A's, sleep courses, cruise courses, fluffs, bluffs, punts,* and *skates.* Rare, but in use, are the terms *sop* and *bunny.*

According to *Lisa Birnbach's New and Improved College Book,* schools tend to opt for their own common name, so what is a *cake walk* at Pepperdine is a *cake* at George Washington University. Some places have constructed their own easy course vocabulary. The journal *American Speech* carried an article in 1980 on the *boat* courses at landlocked Gettysburg College, which were the ones you could "sail through." A *yacht* was a super-*boat,* and a professor who taught *boat* was known as an *admiral.* One professor, aware of his status as an *admiral,* greeted his class with a hearty "Welcome aboard" and word that the course was about to set sail.

Pyrgology. The study of towers.

Sphragistics. Study of engraved seals.

Teacherage. Housing provided for a teacher; the academic equivalent of a parsonage or vicarage.

Telmatology. The study of swamps.

Theogony. The study of the genealogy of the gods.

Toponomy. The study of place names.

Trichology. Study of the hair, especially as it relates to baldness.

Vexillology. The study of flags.

Wonk. Current slang for one who studies excessively. A student who wrote to William Safire on the occasion of a column on student slang suggested that *wonk* is *know* spelled backward.

50

Temporal Terms

Words of Diverse Duration

Baton. The stroke that is sometimes used on a clock or watch instead of a number.

Bezel. The rim, usually metal, that holds the glass of a watch or clock in position.

Biduous. Lasting two days.

Bimester. Two months.

Bissextile. The correct term for leap year. The day itself, February 29, is called the *bissextus*.

Centenarian. Person 100 years or older.

Chiliad. A period of 1,000 years; a millennium.

Chronon. One billionth of a trillionth of a second.

Decennium. A period of ten years.

Enneaeteric. Occurring every nine years. Pronounced *any-ate-eric*.

Gnomon. The pin or plate of a sundial that throws its shadow on the dial.

Grandfather Paradox. Science-fiction dilemma that classically occurs when a time-traveler goes back and murders his grandfather before his father is born. The paradox: If this happened, the murderer not only would have never been born, but also would be incapable of going back in time to perform the deed.

Hebdomadal. Happening every seven days. Pronounced *heb-do-maddle*.

Hesternal. Pertaining to yesterday.

Kalpa. About 4,320 million years in the Hindu calendar.

Light-foot. One billionth of a second.

Lug. The shaped portion of a watch to which the wristband, or in the case of a pocket watch, the strap, is attached.

Lustrum. A period of five years.

Matutine. Relating to the early morning.

Noctivagant. Wandering by night.

Nonagenarian. Persons in their nineties.

Nudiustertian. Relating to the day before yesterday.

Nycthemeron. The space of 24 hours; day plus night.

Octogenarian. Persons in their eighties.

Octongentenary. The 800th anniversary. In his book *British Self-Taught: With Comments in American*, Norman W. Schur points out that this is essentially a British word, because Americans are still piddling around with things like bicentennials.

Penteteric. Recurring every five years.

Picosecond. One trillionth of a second. Pronounced *peak-o-second*.

Piscean Epoch. The 2,000-year era that preceded the present Aquarian Age. The Piscean Epoch ended in March 1948.

Pissing-while. An instant; a short period of time. It was used, according to J. E. Barlough in his book *The Archaicon*, from the sixteenth through the nineteenth centuries. He adds, "The allusion is blatantly obvious."

Premundane. Before the creation of the world. *Postmundane* refers to the period after the end of the world.

Quadragenarian. Between 40 and 49 years of age; a person of that age.

Quinquagenarian. Persons in their fifties.

Quadrennium. A period of four years.

Quinquennial. An event that occurs every five years, see also *Penteteric*.

Quotidian. Recurring each day, especially what is ordinary.

Raith. A Scottish word for three months; a quarter of a year.

Sennight. The space of seven days and nights; half a fortnight.

Septuagenarian. Person between the ages of 70 and 79.

Sexagenarian. Persons in their sixties.

Shake. One-hundred-millionth of a second.

Sublapsary. Occurring after the fall of man.

Tertian. Occurring or recurring every third day.

Trinoctial. Lasting three nights.

Vicennial. Every 20 years.

Widdershins. Counterclockwise; to go against the natural direction. It is the opposite of *sunwise* in magic terminology.

Yestreen. Yesterday evening.

Yonk. An indefinately long time.

Tongues

A Babble of English Languages

Some of the many we speak and write:

Agglomerese. A shortening of language common to people in the military and the civilian bureaucracy. It is typified by the use of initials, acronyms, and portmanteau words. If someone in the U.S. Navy says "CINCLANT is dismayed that BUPERS has not gotten JCS the information it needs to get to SHAPE for the upcoming NATO meeting," you are listening to pure Agglomerese. The term was coined by writer Robert C. Doty in a 1959 article in the *New York Times Magazine* entitled "Parlez-Vous NATO?"

Bafflegab. Alternative term for gobbleygook. It can be used to greater effect with the words *sheer* and *utter*. It was coined by former counsel for the U.S. Chamber of Commerce, Milton Smith, who is quoted in William Lambdin's *Doublespeak Dictionary:* "I decided we needed a new . . . word to describe the utter incomprehensibility, ambiguity, verbosity and complexity of government regulations."

Baltimore-ese. Howard K. Smith once had this to say of Baltimore: "They can't speak English there. They call their city this: Balamer, Murlin. They call garbage: gobbidge. Legal is pronounced liggle. Paramour is their word for power mower. And if you ever ask directions there, remember that Droodle Avenue means Druid Hill Avenue." Some other examples:

Umpahr. Person who calls balls and strikes at *Awrioles* games.

Pahret. Name of the Pittsburgh baseball team.

Council. Cancel.

Idn't. Is not.

Downey Beach. Down at the beach.

A recent master's thesis written by Ann Marie Hisley of the University of Maryland claims that the key influence in all of this came from the northern England settlers who colonized Maryland.

Basic English. The invention of Professor C. K. Ogden of England's Orthological Institute, it stands for "British, American, Scientific, International Commercial" English. It was introduced in 1933 as a quick and easy way of teaching someone to write and speak English. The Basic vocabulary is limited to 850 words that its inventor felt could express all fundamental thoughts in English. It features only 400 nouns ranging from *account* to *year*. One gets a flavor of Basic from an article in the *Baltimore Sun* that used Basic to tell how the words were selected:

The selection of the 850 words came about after deep thought about this complex business and the words given were taken because they were the most simple and most necessary. They go around the dangers of connection with tricky groups of letters in words and strange ways of sounding them."

The language was used during World War II to teach Chinese and other Orientals enough English to function with American and English units. "It takes only 400 words of Basic to run a battleship," one advocate told *Time* in 1945; "With 850 words you can run the planet."

Basic has had many staunch supporters—Winston Churchill and Franklin D. Roosevelt to name two—and only a few critics. One critic was Alden H. Smith, who waggishly suggested it would not work as it left out such basics as *ouch* and *plop*.

Cablese. A particular form of expression based on compressing as much meaning into as few words as possible. It is predicated on the fact that telegram charges have been based on so much per word no matter how long or short the word. Many years ago this took the first prize in an English contest for the longest 12-word cable.

ADMINISTRATOR-GENERAL'S COUNTER-REVOLUTIONARY
INTER-COMMUNICATIONS UNCIRCUMSTANTIATED STOP
QUARTERMASTER-GENERAL'S DISPROPORTIONABLENESS
CHARACTERISTICALLY CONTRA-DISTINGUISHED
UNCONSTITUTIONALIST'S INCOMPREHENSIBILITIES STOP

Cincinnada Dutch. Term used by author and novelist Dorothy Weil in an article in the *Cincinnati Enquirer* magazine to describe the manner of speaking in that city. Some of Weil's prime examples are:

Wer's ziz office? Where's his office?

Denist. Dentist.

Quarder. Quarter (not to be confused with *quata,* which is New Yorkese).

Er. Or.

Wat's zat fer? What's that for?

Constabulese. The talk of on-duty police that dictates that they say "in the vicinity of" instead of *near,* "ascertain as to whether" when they want to *find out,* and "as to why" when *why* would do. This manner of speaking is not limited to the United States. British writer Spike Hughes points out in *The Art of Coarse Language* that in his country the same high-sounding language is used—that is, "utilized and employed." Hughes has collected a number of favorites including that from a mobile unit running about "taking informationary numbers."

This is different from the station house slang that police use among themselves: *hole* for subway, *poke* for pickpocket, *KG* for known gambler, and so forth.

Crosswordese. A vocabulary that is little used outside the confines of crossword puzzle boxes. They are usually short, vowely, and obscure. In a statement that clears the air of any pretense about crosswords, Eugene T. Maleska, crossword puzzle editor of the *New York Times,* wrote in his *A Pleasure in Words,* "Who cares that an *anoa* is a Celebes ox, a *moa* is an extinct bird, or an *Abo* is a member of an Australian tribe?" Not to be too harsh, some of these words have a certain presence about them, although their use in daily conversation is severely limited. *Oese,* for instance, is the name for the small looped wire used by bacteriologists in making cultures and is pronounced *U-say;* a *nene* is a Hawaiian goose and a *stoa* is a Greek porch. The first cousin of Crosswordese is *Scrabble-babble,* which deals in terms like *xu, taroc, ranid,* and *pyruvates* (all of which appear in the *Official Scrabble Players Dictionary*).

DCD. DCD, or the D.C. Dialect, is an argot that was revealed to the nation during the Watergate era. In their book *The D.C. Dialect,* authors Paul Morgan and Sue Scott explore the new language in terms of ten easy lessons (be impersonal, be obscure, be pompous, be evasive, be repetitious, be awkward, be incorrect, be faddish, be serious, be unintelligible) and end with a glossary of DCD words and phrases. A few examples are in order:

English	*DCD*
begin	implement
break-in	entry operation
cover-up	contain the situation
criminal conspiracy	game plan
fired	selected out
kidnap	segregate out
won't work	counterproductive
workable	viable

Educanto. High educational jargon. For instance, proper *Educanto* for text-book is an "empirically validated learning package" and a library is a "media access center." A teacher who is able to operate a movie projector is an "Audio-visually qualified person," and if older kids are allowed to help younger ones, it is known as "cross-age tutoring." A few years ago, a group of Texas parents were sent a note from a school principal that baffled the parents but showed the principal's mastery of the jargon. It read in part:

Our school's cross-graded, multi-ethnic individualized learning program is designed to enhance the concept of an open-ended learning program with emphasis on a continuum of multi-ethnic, academically enriched learning.

In some circles it is known as *Pedageese.*

Gobbledygook. Term for bureaucratic language coined by Representative Maury Maverick when he was the wartime chairman for FDR's Smaller War Plans Corporation. Maverick was so infuriated with the bloated language in the memos that were landing on his desk that he wrote a scathing memo of his own on the subject, containing such direct lines as, "Anyone using the words 'activation' or 'implementation' will be shot." In 1977 his son, Maury Maverick, Jr., wrote to the *Christian Science Monitor* to reveal how his father came up with the name: "He stated at the time that most bureaucratic language reminded him of his days as a boy back in Texas when he could hear a foolish old turkey gobble endlessly, saying 'gobble, gobble, gobble' and then ending it with a 'gook.'"

Everybody has their pet examples; here are mine:

Anticipatory retaliation. Attacking your enemy on the assumption that he would do the same if given the chance.

Health alteration committee. The name the CIA once gave to one of its own assassination teams.

Individualized learning station. A desk renamed by the U.S. Office of Education.

Information processing center. A typing pool.

Intermodal interface. A term that was translated by former Transportation Secretary William Coleman as, "When you get off the train, a bus is waiting."

Personalized, recreational eco-unit. A garden.

Medicant. The jargon of people in medicine who say "deglutition" when they mean swallowing, or call a headache "cephalalgia."

Mellowspeak. Term popularized by Doonesbury cartoonist Garry Trudeau for the "laid back" hip and slangy new language of ego and emotion—a whole new "language trip" that includes such "upfront" expressions as "to go with the flow," "I hear you," "I know where he/she is coming from," "to die for," "to make some space," "to get one's head together," "can/can't relate to it," "high energy," "swing with," "mellow out," and more.

It is called *psychobabble* in a book of the same title by R. D. Rosen, who writes of it as "a set of repetitive verbal formalities that kills off the very spontaneity, candor and understanding it pretends to promote."

Meta-Talk. It has been given various names—"meta-talk" in a book of the same title by Gerard I. Nierenberg and Henry Calero, "meta-communication" in Julius and Barbara Fast's *Talking Between Lines,* and "super language" by others—but it amounts to the silent messages that are generated when we talk. Examples abound. One that is used by the Fasts is the line that bosses use on employees: "Are you sure you're feeling all right this week?" In reality the boss is not asking about the person's health, but saying that the person's work is unsatisfactory. The authors of *Meta-Talk* cut through such classic lines as "Oh, don't worry about me" and "I'll do my best," to reveal that the first is often an appeal for help and the second is an admission of failure before the fact.

Noo Yawkese. Sometimes called Brooklynese (though not limited to that borough), this is one of the few distinct manners of speaking that people actively try to shed. One linguist, William Labov, told the *New York Times* in 1971, "A great many New Yorkers feel that it's a compliment to be told 'You don't talk like a New Yorker,' " adding, "The average working-class Philadelphian doesn't see anything wrong with Philadelphia speech but in New York City the average working-class person feels there is something wrong with the way he talks." Some classic examples:

Toidy toid and toid. 33rd and Third.
Waddaya dune? What are you doing?
Alodda dem. A lot of them.
Jalettum? Did you let him?

Padress. Awkward manner of speaking that afflicts those who speak into public address systems, especially at airports. Some of the commonest words in Padress include *de-plane, pre-board,* and *equipment* for airplane. For example, "Due to the late arrival of equipment in the area, the pre-boarding period has been extended." The rules of Padress require that all announcements of great inconvenience ("All planes have been delayed 48 hours") end with the line "Thank you for your cooperation."

Pittsburghese. One of the more pronounced and easy-to-recognize urban dialects, which, according to University of Pittsburgh linguist Dr. Robert Parslow, has unique speech patterns heard no place else in the world. Some of the words with which to recognize a Pittsburgher:

Still. Steel.
Dauntaun. Downtown, where the streets get *slippy* when it snows.
Yuns. You ones, used the way "You all" is further south.

Gumband. Rubber band.

Worsh. As in Worshington, D.C.

Igle. The national bird, which it is *illigle* to shoot.

Plannish. Plannish is the term that Lloyd A. Kaplan, an analyst for the New York City Planning Commission, created in the late 1960s to cover the "epidemic technicalese used by urban planners to confuse the public." Kaplan told a reporter for the *New York Times* that the single most useful word in plannish is *facility,* meaning "things." "For example, there are waterfront facilities, health facilities, recreation facilities, and," Kaplan added, "even facility facilities." Another example: "Money is never mentioned, as such. Resources is the prime substitute, although expenditures (allocations, appropriations and funds) are also popular." Additionally, planners call those who move from the city "gross out-migrants," and if a planner drives through a neighborhood to look around he is making "a field windshield survey."

Platform Talk. Every four years, after the primary elections are over, the political world turns to the special metaphor of platform carpentry. To be sure, these are terms that fit together nicely, and the metaphor of a wooden platform is an almost pure one. The elements of a platform are *planks*, and *splinter groups* are forever trying to get their issues into the platform lest they *fall between the cracks.* Some planks, of course, are hard to *nail down*, and platform builders have to *hammer away* at them. Once finished, the platform should be solid and sturdy enough so that the party that created it can *stand on it*, and the other party can jump on it without it *collapsing*. The one place the metaphor is less than perfect is in calling those who build the platform "platform architects" rather than "carpenters," which would be more appropriate.

As we listen to the sounds of the platforms being erected every four years, we can admire that the metaphor is never mixed—we will hear nothing of accounting, baseball, or stonecutting. Nobody will try to make a *ballpark* estimate of when they will be finished . . . there will be no *bottom line* statements and—knock on wood—nobody will claim that the planks are *etched in stone.* Carved in wood, maybe but not etched in stone.

The hard-wood images of the political platform bring up the natural question of why certain metaphors attach themselves to certain activities. The platform imagery for a place on which to stand is a logical one, but others are much less so. When I was in the Navy, I kept finding highway images even at sea. People talked about *getting the green light* to go ahead with things; we had message *traffic*; and even the rules of the sea were called *The Rules of the Road.* Imagine my surprise when I came out of the Navy and found nautical images in a brokerage house where I went to work for a year. There people routinely *jumped ship,* produced *boilerplate,* and went *full speed ahead* . . . trying, of course, not to go *overboard* in the process.

R.A.F. slang. One by-product of modern warfare is slang, but for reasons that are not clear, those serving in the R.A.F. during World War II produced a remarkably broad and rich slang vocabulary. In 1942 an example of R.A.F. talk along with its translation appeared in the *New York Times*:

Three ropey types, all sprogs, pranged a cheeseye on bumps and circuits. One bought it; the other two went for a Burton. The station-master took a dim view and tore them off a strip. They'd taken along a shagbag wofficer, who was browned off. The queen bee was hopping mad.

Translation: Three unpopular individuals, all brand new pilots, crashed a wornout airplane while practicing circuits and landings. One was killed; the other two were reprimanded severely. The station commander disapproved strongly and roundly berated them. They had taken along with them a somewhat plain WAAF officer, who was bored. The station's WAAF commander was very angry.

While the only place this slang can still be heard in full bloom is in the old World War II movies, some of its words and phrases have become part of the language—"good show," "in the drink," "get cracking," "to tick off."

Reverse gobbledygook. A banquet-table form of English that revels in its terse directness. It is the exact opposite of written gobbledygook. It was first discussed in an unsigned article in *Fortune* in 1950, which further explained:

Thanks to reverse gobbledygook, the less you have to say, the more emphatically you can say it. All one has to do is use certain hard-hitting expressions, and refer as frequently as possible to the fact that these expressions are being used. A sure forewarning of its on-rush, accordingly, is a prefatory announcement by the speaker that he is not going to beat around the bush, pull any punches, pussyfoot, use two-dollar words, or the like. The rest is inevitable; so standardized are the expressions of reverse gobbledygook that an audience would be stunned to attention were a single one of them altered by so much as a word. (One of these days a clever speaker is going to capitalize on this. "Gentlemen," he will say, "I offer a panacea.")

Slurvian. An American dialect without geographic limitations, which was discovered, named, and reported on by John Davenport in an article in the *New Yorker* in 1949. A few examples of phonetically spelled Slurvian:

Bean. n. A living creature, as in *human bean.*
Cactus. n. The people in a play or story.
Murca. n. Nation to which Slurvians return after *Yerpeen* trips.
Plight. adj. Courteous.

Sociologese. The bloated, awkward language of sociologists. Russell Baker may have had the last word on it when he wrote, "There are many dead languages, but the sociologists' is the only language that was dead at birth."

Strine. Australian way of running words together, often practiced by those who can speak distinct proper English:

Emenyjiwant? How many do you want?
Hammachizit? How much is it?

Texlexical. Manner of speaking in Texas, whether it be in a big city like *Yewst'un* or in the *rule* areas of the state. Chase Untermeyer, state legislator, has been involved in the *whored bidness* of collecting fine examples for his Tex-lexicon, which is now in preparation. Several of his best finds, revealed in a recent column by George Will, include:

Lowered Barn. An English poet (1788–1824).
Forced. A large group of trees, as "Lemme showya mah pine forced."
Hard. Employed, as "I hard him to do the job." Also a man's name, as "Mah wife's a cousin of Hard Hughes."

Texlish. Another name for Texlexical. This is the term used by Jim Everhart in his *Illustrated Texas Dictionary of the English Language.* Some examples from Everhart's collection:

All crisis. That embargo which began with the oil embargo.
Bob wahr. Fencing material.
Mihyon. $1,000,000.
Tarred. Exhausted.

Vietlish. Term created by Richard Lingeman for the jargon created by official Washington to explain the war in Southeast Asia. It was well described by the late Peter Lisagore: "A whole language was created to minimize that we were in war, and didn't know how to fight it." Although this archly euphemistic language has fallen into disuse since the end of the war, it stands as an example of how lies, ruses, dodges, and distortions can be wrapped in words and simple phrases. Among many, were:

Strategic hamlet. Refugee camp, or as a *New York Times* reporter explained, "A few people are driven together, a roll of barbed wire was thrown over their heads and the strategic hamlet was finished."
Search and destroy. Destroy and then search.
Positive response. One of Lyndon Johnson's terms for bombing.
Incursion. Invasion.
Returnee. Defector.
Structure. A hut, once destroyed. One of a number of "before and after" terms. A bomber pilot explained these in a 1966 letter to the editors of *Aviation Week & Space Technology,* pointing out that once destroyed, a "straw-thatched hut" officially became a "structure"; a dead pig or

goat became a "pack animal"; a splintered set of logs felled across a stream became a "bridge"; and a sunken one-man dugout became a "boat." This process was called "target verification."

Windyfoggery. The linguistic condition that embraces the gobbledygook of government and business with such afflictions from other fields as pseudoscientific jargon and unintelligible art criticism. This broad term is the creation of Theodore M. Bernstein, who explained that wind and fog do not normally exist in nature, but do in language, where "the greater the wind the more impenetrable the fog."

Travel Words

Terms in Transit

Aclinic-line. The imaginary location near the equator where the magnetic needle has no dip.

Afterbody. Something (debris, another craft) that follows a spacecraft in orbit.

Apolune. The point in lunar orbit that is farthest from the moon. *Perilune,* on the other hand, is the point in the orbit closest to the center of the moon.

Bollard. The traditional name for the large posts to which ships are tied, bollard is being used increasingly to describe those inverted rubber cones used to mark traffic lanes and detours. The word is also used to describe the posts that are strategically placed near supermarkets to keep you from walking off with a shopping cart.

Break-off phenomenon. The feeling that occasionally occurs during high-altitude flight when one feels totally separated from the earth and human society.

Bumping post. The upright device at the end of a railroad track to keep the train from rolling too far.

Calash. The upper, collapsible portion of a baby carriage.

Cat's paw. A slight breeze that shows itself on the surface of the sea as a slight ripple.

Cisatlantic. On this side of the Atlantic. The opposite of *transatlantic.*

Davit. Crane used to hold a lifeboat and swing it out over the water and lower it.

Deadlight. Metal covering clamped over portholes in storms.

Diaphragm. The flexible corridors between railroad passenger cars.

Eyre. The circuit taken by itinerant judges.

Fiddles. Rails or battens placed across shelves on boats and ships to keep objects in place when the vessel rolls and pitches at sea.

Fishybacking. Transporting loaded trailers by ship. It is akin to *piggybacking*, which is moving trailers by railroad flatcars.

Fluke. One of the points of an anchor; designed to catch on the bottom. It consists of the *palm*, which is the flat part, and the *pea* or *bill*, which is the point.

Frog. The central part of a turnout switch on a railroad. It is a Y-shaped switch from which one route can diverge into two, or two converge to one. A *diamond* is a crossing of two tracks at any angle.

FTL. Faster-Than-Light travel. Modern physics shows that it is impossible, but science fiction writers have found a number of imaginative ways around the objection of impossibility.

Gnotobiotics. The use of germ-free animals in space probes.

Gobbles. To say that a car gobbles is to say that it runs fast, presumably gobbling up gasoline.

Gurry. An old New England sailor's term for a combination of sewage, decayed fish or whale meat, rancid oil, and brackish seawater. Gurry gave off a powerful smell that tended to stay with a ship even after it was washed down.

Guzzle. Cape Cod talk for a channel between two sandbars.

Howdah. The seat on the back of an elephant. (Howdah is also New Yorkese for "how to," as in "Jatellum howdah get dere?")

Impact attenuation devices. Back in the 1960s, Representative H. R. Gross of Iowa issued periodic Gobbledygook Awards for overblown terms for simple objects. One award went to the Bureau of Public Roads for calling the old oil drums used to block off construction areas "impact attenuation devices." Gross also honored the Air Force for calling a parachute an "aerodynamic personnel decelerator" and the Army for calling a shovel a "combat emplacement evacuator."

Intermodal transportation facility. The name given to a bike rack in a train station by the Department of Health, Education and Welfare in the 1970s.

Jiggle-bar. Noisy rough-spot intentionally put on a road or highway to keep drivers awake or alert them to a toll area or something equally important. They are also known as *rumble strips*.

Lagan. Goods that have been sunk, but that are marked with an attached buoy. Not to be confused with *flotsam* (floating debris) and *jetsam* (cargo thrown from a ship to lighten it).

Lanai. Hotel term for a private terrace or balcony that comes with a room. Pronounced *lan-eye*.

Lightening holes. Holes found in bridge elements to make them lighter. Lightening holes are also found on ships.

Lingtow. A rope for pulling contraband ashore.

Mobility aid. What the Space Agency calls a handrail or footrail in a spacecraft. It is used in NASA descriptions of Skylab and the Shuttle.

Ocnophile. Person who dreads travel; a homebody.

Oilberg. Alternate name for the new Very Large Crude Carriers (VLCC). These gargantuan ships are the largest moving things ever built by man, with decks as long as a quarter of a mile. These ships employ the iceberg principle, in that 80 percent of their great size is underwater.

Ornithopter. A flying machine with wings that flap.

Pantograph. The upward-pushing apparatus that extends between a streetcar or electric train and the overhead electric wires from which it gets its power.

Philobat. Person who loves to travel.

Pirogue. A canoe fashioned from the hollowed trunk of a single tree. Pronounced pierogg.

Pillowed. Flight attendant term, as in "Would you like to be pillowed?"

Plimsoll mark. A circular mark prominently displayed on a ship's hull. It is used as a safe-load line to indicate how heavily the ship can be loaded. It is named for Samuel Plimsoll (1824–1898), British statesman and maritime reformer.

Rack rate. Hotel equivalent of "list price"—the officially stated price of a room from which discounts are sometimes made.

Scud. Aviator's term for small masses of cloud moving below a solid deck of higher clouds.

Sinistrodextral. Moving from left to right.

Snubbing post. The post around which a ship's line is thrown.

Taffrail. The rail around the stern of a ship.

Thwart. A structural member of a boat reaching from side to side. In small pulling boats, they also serve as seats, but in canoes they do not.

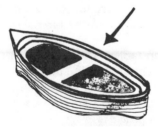

Viaggiatory. Traveling frequently.

Waveson. Goods floating on the water after a shipwreck.

Waywise. Skilled or talented at not getting lost.

Wheel guards. The small cement or asphalt bars that you park your car wheels against in parking lots.

Xenodocheionology. A love of hotels and inns. Pronounced *zeno-deckion-ology*.

Wordland

Coming to Terms in Springfield

In 1985 I spent a few days in Springfield, Massachusetts, preparing an article on a dictionary company for the *Newsday* magazine. Here is that report updated by a brief return visit in August 1991.

Few Americans have heard of James Lowe, but since 1973 he has had more influence over what "becomes a word" and what gets into the dictionary than any other person in the country. He is a one-man linguistic Supreme Court who decides what new words are granted admission to future editions of our most influential line of dictionaries. His title is senior editor in charge of new words at Merriam-Webster Inc. in Springfield, Massachusetts.

Lowe is a slim, friendly man with an easy laugh whose unassuming manner does not even hint at the linguistic power he possesses. Sitting at a desk piled high with paper and surrounded by stacks of books, he looks more like a professor deep in his research than like a book editor. He speaks softly and listens attentively giving the impression that he's always ready to pick up a new word or verbal nuance.

He readily admits that he *loves* his work and relishes each day's odd surprise or two, such as finding that *chimichanga* is a product of the American Southwest and neither the dish nor the word came from Mexico. He discovered this as he started looking at the word to see if it had wide enough distribution to be admitted.

A self-confessed trivia buff with a master's degree in English from the University of Florida, he delights in the fact that he may work on Tex-Mex cuisine in the morning and then spend part of the afternoon assessing the influence of "Hill Street Blues" on the same language used by Chaucer (who probably would have loved *hairball, dogbreath,* and *sleazeball*).

There are few routinely typical days in Lowe's working life, but he tries to devote at least one hour a day to reading magazines and newspapers with an eye to new words and new uses of older words. On most days, he spends a good part of his time looking at words on a case-by-case basis. On the day of my visit he was taking a hard look at *sequelization* (not in any dictionary), *cross-dress* (as a verb), *open-captioned* (where you see the subtitles, as opposed to *closed-captioned* where you don't), *weaponization, slicks* (for a racing tire), *Baby Doe, slidewalk* (for a moving sidewalk), *erotiphobe* (for the fear of pornography), and *mocktail* (a drink for kids who would prefer not to ask for a Shirley Temple).

Part of each day also is spent working with other editors pinning down the exact pronunciation, etymology, and definition of a new word. This is not as passive and scholarly as it might sound. Lowe says that he has been working on the definition of *break-dance* and has had to spend a good deal of time watching break-dancing in order to describe the motions involved. He adds, "It hasn't been an easy word to define."

Lowe says that before a word is actually added to one of the company's dictionaries a case must be made for its inclusion. Other editors note the use of new words on small slips of paper called *citations*, and it is from these written references that Lowe decides on the case. Usually, a word must have appeared in a variety of sources over time and must be used over a wide geographical area before admission is granted. "If it has only been used by a small number of people or never gets outside a small area we don't even consider it," says Lowe.

A very few words gain instant access because of their immediate importance. *Ayatollah*, for instance, became an English word in 1979, and *designated hitter* wasted no time in getting to first base in 1973, the year the American League approved it.

Generally speaking, Lowe tends to look for ten or more citations from different sources. He is also quick to point out that he does *not* buy words—despite occasional letters and calls from people who believe that the company does. (These words for sale are generally so bad that Lowe can't even recall one: "I try to forget them as quickly as I can.")

Lowe is very careful when it comes to tradenames and trademarks: "We only include the most common ones." *Velcro* was one of the elite that made it into the most recent *Collegiate* dictionary, and *Nutra Sweet* seems a sure bet for the future.

I met Jim Lowe because I am a self-confessed dictionary lover. I maintain that a dictionary is more than just another book. I think that picking one out is, as a critic of word books once put it ". . . the closest most Americans ever come to choosing a household god." It is the oracle in the living room used as a Scrabble judge, a spelling checker, a crossword puzzle co-conspirator, and an argument settler.

It is consulted in times of gleeful discovery, as kids try to pin down the exact meaning of a naughty word heard on the playground, and in times of sadness, as we pull it out to make sure we don't misspell condolence (is it -*ence* or -*ance*?) when struggling with a letter of sympathy. There are times when we are simply looking for a correct spelling and get joyfully lost finding all sorts of oddities. Other times we use dictionaries to keep egg off our collective faces as we check to see if we have used a word like *fulsome* correctly in a letter. We give them for graduations, confirmations, and bar mitzvahs in the genuine hope that they will be a key to a young person's success.

If one makes a living with words, as I do, a dictionary is picked with practically the same care used to choose a constant companion. Then one day we can't find *Heimlich maneuver* or we discover that half of the pages containing the t-words have fallen out. The dictionary is dog eared and obsolete; it is time to shop for a new one.

These are the best of times for dictionary buyers, a point that can be underscored by a trip to any large library or bookstore. There are numerous good ones on the market ranging from the old standbys to newer additions like *The American Heritage Dictionary*, which made its debut in 1969 and is now in a second edition, and the monster *Random House Dictionary*, which first came out in 1966.

As one who is infatuated with American dictionaries to the point of owning almost all of the major editions now on the market as well as older collector's items dating back to the early nineteenth century, I have been less than monogamous in my dictionary love life. A happily married man, who wouldn't know a singles bar if one opened next door, I have become a reckless, dictionary lover who callously throws over one faithful word mistress for another without a pang of remorse—an admitted bounder and cad.

Lest there be any question, these are close, passionate relationships while they last. Writing a few hundred magazine articles and more than a score of books has required daily dalliance with these good books. When I am writing about language, an orgy sometimes takes place as I get my hands on a half-dozen of them in the space of an hour.

I am writing this article during a torrid affair with *Webster's Ninth New Collegiate Dictionary*, but by the time you read it my wandering lust may be refocussed on the sexy new *American Heritage* or may have returned to an old flame like *Webster's New World Dictionary of the American Language*.

Given my present assignment, however, it was logical to latch onto *Webster's Ninth*, hereafter known by her nickname, "W-9," as a case study—the case being that dictionary making is a dynamic and fascinating art. The case could have been made elsewhere, but I chose to hop a plane to Springfield, Massachusetts, the location of the Merriam-Webster company. For this word lover, it amounted to a pilgrimage.

The company is housed in an attractive brick box-like building on tree-lined Federal Street on a hill overlooking the small recently renovated, but still quintessentially New Englandish, downtown. The present building was built in 1939, but contains ready proof that this is a bastion of tradition. In the lobby is a beautiful display case that was used in a world's fair exhibit—the World's Columbian Exposition of 1893 to be exact. The working atmosphere inside is decidedly more academic than corporate, and the lack of things electronic—a few copy machines and word processors notwithstanding—remind one of a bygone pre-digital age. There are no eyeshades or sleeve garters in evidence, but it seems there should be.

The main attraction is on the second floor, which holds what is believed to be the most complete collection of citations on English language words and their usage in the late nineteenth and twentieth centuries. It is the key to W-9 and other Merriam-Webster dictionaries and reference books of which there are now 26 ranging from *Webster's Sports Dictionary* to *A Pronouncing Dictionary of American English.*

These more than 13-million citations are packed in row upon row of metal file cabinets. A citation is a slip of paper on which the word and its usage is noted, dated, and filed. Not only Jim Lowe, but every editor is expected to spend a portion of each workday reading from a diverse menu of magazines, newspapers, and other printed sources to spot new words or new uses of existing ones. To the extent possible, an editor is given things to read that are of personal interest, which makes working here something of a utopia for people who love to read. All this reading results in some 10,000 to 12,000 new citation slips a month.

These new slips arrive on Jim Lowe's desk in piles as he looks for legitimate new word candidates. Lowe must be especially alert to the subtle changes in meaning that will account for a second or third definition. For instance, he is aware that the recent coinage *gridlock* is being applied to nonvehicular situations. The word is now being used for congressional deadlocks as well as other standoffs where things have come to a halt. Even with this system, Lowe admits that occasionally a term takes a tad too much time to spot, define, and get into the dictionary. The term *strip search*, which began showing up in print in 1975, is only now going in. Other words are on hold as Lowe waits to see if they stick or are just a fad. On hold is a new definition of *streak* in which one runs naked in public.

The citations are also used to determine which words come out of the book. If the citations show that the word has not been used for a long time, any editor can suggest that it be deleted; however, the editor in chief has the final say in making cuts. Words used by Shakespeare and other famous writers are exceptions. They are not pulled even if they have not been in common use for centuries.

Over time, the collective case study of a word becomes most impressive. A relatively minor word like *beachcomber*, for example, yields a pile of citations more than a half-inch thick, noting its use all over the English-speaking world dating back to 1840. For years it was clearly just a pejorative term for an out-of-work sailor or a maritime hobo looking for flotsam. Then in 1952 an editor noted that it was used in a travel ad in which it was synonymous for a tourist wandering at the beach. A lone citation notes that the word is sometimes applied to a powerful wave.

Set, the word that nets a spot in the *Guinness Book of World Records* as the English word with the most meanings (58 noun uses, 126 verbal uses, and 10 as a participle adjective), fills hundreds and hundreds of citation slips. As you wander through the files, you are likely to stumble on all sorts of oddments: a letter from a pharmacist on the origin of the term *sundae*, a postcard from the Panama-Pacific Exposition of 1914 noting the use of the term *red herring* in a column by a young writer named Walter Lippman, and a captioned picture from a 1938 issue of *Life* containing the lone citation on the word *stroom* (a verb meaning to run one's tongue along the inside of one's cheek so as to produce a moving lump, presumably coined by a *Life* editor). Perhaps the most famous citation in the files is a 1917 entry on *atomic bomb*, which was termed "fanciful" by the editor who reviewed it.

Looking at this forest of file drawers, one is reminded of an earlier time, specifically that time before computers. Word processors are used here, but primarily to generate more paper citations. The company has no plans to fully automate for several simple reasons. First, it would be prohibitively expensive to transfer and store 13 million citations. Second, the editors feel that they would be limited by what could be put on a screen and that, when dealing with a word like *take* with its hundreds of meanings and submeanings, there is an advantage to physically dealing with slips of paper.

Today's Merriam-Webster company is the literary successor to the great Noah Webster who died in 1843. In 1844 the Merriam brothers of Springfield purchased from Webster's estate the right to use the Webster name and to publish and revise the monumental *American Dictionary of the English Language*. The Merriams apparently did not buy all the published works held by the estate, which, it is believed, is why the the name Webster began its slide into the public domain. Now anyone can produce a dictionary with the name Webster on it. In fact, dozens of companies have done so, ranging from the producers of cheap discount store dictionaries last updated when Ike was in the White House, to the absolutely first rate *Webster's New World Dictionary of the American Language*, which is published by Simon and Schuster and competes directly with W-9. To make it all the more confusing, Houghton Mifflin, which publishes *The American Heritage Dictionary*, has come out with a dictionary it calls *Webster's II*. In other words, three of the four major publishers in the field have at least one book with the Webster name on it (Random House being the lone holdout).

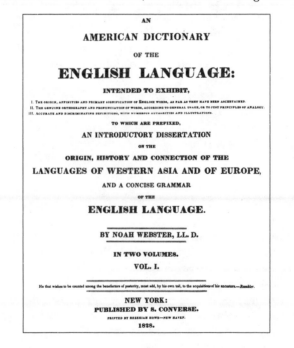

W-9 is the ninth generation of a new breed of desk or college dictionaries, which Merriam-Webster started in 1898 with new editions about a decade apart. Most of the competition occurs with college dictionaries—about two million of these are sold each year. "Of these," former Merriam-Webster President and Publisher William A. Llewellyn estimated, "we sell about half."

This brings us to W-9 itself, which was born here in 1983 under the chief editorship of Frederick C. Mish. It took three years to prepare and employed 28 editors. Although conservative in business terms, the company is linguistically liberal and open-minded when it comes to admitting new words. Unlike some critics who see the language as dead or dying, Mish says that his editors see English as flourishing, vital, and ever-changing.

W-9 was fed no less than 11,000 new words and new meanings including *vanpooling, veggie, food processor, cellulite, ecofreak, salad bar, theme park, dirt bike, glitter rock, shuttle diplomacy, acid rain, sunshine laws, workfare, stagflation, antinuke, amaretto, bong, hit list, zit, sitcom, Jacuzzi, missionary position, high tech, blow-dry, workaholic, up-front,* and *bottom line.* Old words with new meanings included *live-in,* which had become a word for a lover as well as a maid, *disco,* which is now a form of music not just a place to dance to records, and the listing for *smart* had to be appended to include the sense of smart as used in "smart bomb." A few words that were left out of the first edition of W-9 have been added to the latest printing. AIDS, the disease, has just been added in grim deference to current events.

The leading sources of new words, says Mish, are science and technology, which account for almost half of them. The news media and cuisine, especially that of foreign origin, tie for second place. Ethnic food presents a special case, as there comes a moment when a word like *sushi* ceases to be just a Japanese word and becomes an English word of Japanese origin. That moment occurs when the word no longer appears in italics, has a commonly accepted spelling, and is no longer explained in the text of a magazine or newspaper article. Although sushi dated back to the 1890s in text, it was not until a few years ago that it "became" an English word making its first appearance in W-9. One food word has not made it simply because it has more than a dozen variant spellings and therefore cannot yet be considered English. It is sometimes written as *babaganooj* and is an eggplant dish of Arabic origin.

One of W-9's most seductive new features is that words are dated, noted by the year in which they were first found in print or writing. The dates were established by a special staff using the citation files and other sources to determine that first appearence on paper. The purpose of the dating was to give more of the word's actual history and put it in perspective. To say that this feature invites browsing is like saying that a bowl of peanuts invites nibbling. If you try to look up the spelling of *brassiere,* as I did one day, your eye is likely to jump to brass knuckles, which came along in 1855, brassiere, which was unheard before 1911, and brat, which—I was astonished to find—dates back to 1505.

As these dates of origin were added to W-9, the editors were often surprised to find how early or late a word came into the language. Here are some that came in earlier than one might expect and were, in fact, eye-openers for editor Mish: *astronaut* (1926), *contact lens* (1888), *electoral college* (1691), *politicize* (1758), *verbalize* (1609), *euthenasia* (1742), *warmonger* (1590), *yogurt* (1625), *energize* (1752), and *health food* (1882, but *junk food* didn't come in until 1971). *Chairwoman* was dated back to 1685, when it was used by John Locke in a letter, and *marshmallow* was found to go back before the twelfth century. On the other side, two words associated with the old west—*bounty hunter* and *gunslinger*—could not be traced to a date earlier than the l950s.

Another feature that sets W-9 apart from her predecessors and a number of other dictionaries is a collection of small usage essays attached to words that tend to be disputed, misused, or confused. The usage essays are, as a group, liberal in the sense that people who equate the use of the words *hopefully*, and *ain't* with the decline of Western Civilization are not going to be pleased. *Ain't* is seen as a reasonable term for emphasis and attention gathering at all levels of society, as in "I'm figuring a million dollars and that ain't hay." It treats *hopefully* as standard and compares it to other adverbs—interestingly, presumably, and fortunately—which have not drawn the same "critical fire."

All of this was greatly consoling to this writer who could never figure out why critics made such a big deal out of using the word *hopefully* and who grew up with a generation of school teachers who equated ain't with the vilest of four-letter words. I was doubly consoled when in my 1985 interview, then-President Llewellyn himself used *ain't* in my conversation with him. Llewellyn pointed out that the usage paragraphs have not been written to satisfy pedants and purists but are there, "to answer the question, will it stigmatize my arguments if I say it this way." He added, "We tend to warn people about what is incorrect, but we also tell them not to get too uptight about it."

These usage paragraphs were written by senior editor E. Ward Gillman, who reports that he came upon some surprises when looking into word histories for a key to their proper usage. The biggest of these was with the distinction between *infer* and *imply*. For years we have been told that one means to state indirectly (*imply*), while the other means to draw a conclusion based on the facts (*infer*). We have been told that they are not interchangeable, but Gillman discovered that the first person to use the words, Sir Thomas More in the sixteenth century, was the first to confuse them. Gillman says that this blurring continued until after World War I when a professor of logic wrote to Merriam-Webster and convinced the editors to make the distinction. That distinction was made until W-9, which says, in as many words, not to fret about *infer* and *imply* since the meaning of the word will be clear from its context.

If this approach to usage has raised a few eyebrows, it is nothing compared to the storm that was whipped up when the company brought out the most recent edition of its great mothership dictionary *Webster's Third New Interna-*

tional Dictionary in 1961. This is the giant unabridged work with 458,000 entries which W-7, W-8, and W-9 have all been based on. It took 757 editor-years and more than $3 million, under the leadership of Philip B. Gove, to prepare the *Third.*

Gove and his editors were not prepared for the reception it was given. It was broadly perceived as a bad influence, a debaser of English. The *New York Times* declared in an editorial that the editors had "surrendered to the permissive school"; *Life* termed it "abominable"; and the *Washington Post* told people to hang onto their *Second Internationals.* An article in *The Atlantic*, titled "Sabotage in Springfield," said that it had thrust upon the public "a dismaying assortment of the questionable, the perverse, the unworthy, and the downright outrageous."

Mish says that the editors were "flabbergasted" at being branded as radicals for simply accepting and recording the vast changes that had occurred between 1934 and 1961. What had so upset the critics was opening the book to find words and phrases like *corny, someplace, anyplace, one for the book, upsurge, finalize, to level with, shindig, passel, wise up,* and *fetch.* Not only were these words listed, but they were not tabbed as substandard, another way of saying they were not used by cultured and educated people. Even when a term like *irregardless* was listed as substandard, some critics blew their tops just because such an abomination of a word had been given a slot at all.

Since all of this took place almost a quarter of a century ago, it is safe to say that the controversy that surrounded the *Third International* is gone. Those who comment on it today seem to be more tolerant of twentieth-century words and to see it for the great work that it is. It is a comment on the monumentality of this big book that it is a sure bet we won't see a *Fourth International* until early in the twenty-first century, if then.

Because of bad weather, the plane that I took home from the Hartford-Springfield airport after my 1985 visit was two hours late. It was a rough flight and to calm my nerves I bought a martini. More effective, however, in making the trip less stressful was the time I spent alone with W-9. Want to know what I found out? *Airsick* dates back to 1785, *martini* was coined in 1894, and *deplane* was first spotted in 1923. *Stewardess*, I am amazed to find, dates back to 1631 but *flight attendant* came along in 1956 making it one of the first genderless nouns. I wondered what new word from the world of aviation was now bidding to become part of the language. Jim Lowe would know.

Word Words

*A Glossary of Terms for
Things We Say and Write*

Abecedarius. An acrostic in which the initial letters appear in alphabetical
order. This is one of several acrostic words. Another is *mesostich,* which refers
to an acrostic composition in which the middle letters form a word or phrase.
The garden-variety acrostic is a composition in which the first letter of each
line forms a word or message. An acrostic in which the final letters form a
word or phrase is called a *telestich.*

Ablaut. The changing of a vowel in the root of a word to modify use or
meaning, as the change from get to got.

Acromonogrammatic. Applied to a passage or verse in which each line begins
with the letter with which the preceding line ended.

Addisonian termination. The scholarly name for the habitual practice of using
prepositions to end sentences with. Named for Joseph Addison, who was
addicted to the terminal preposition. Among others, Winston Churchill sided
with Addison when he termed the rule against sentences ending in prepositions "nonsense up with which I will not put."

ADEHINORST. Not a word but the ten letters that make up 70 percent of all
English words. It is believed to be an abomination of modern design that
only three of these letters are where the fingers normally rest on the standard

QWERTY keyboard, which is so-called because those letters appear on the top letter row.

Adoxography. Writing cleverly on a trivial subject.

After-wit. The wisdom or cleverness that comes too late. Clifton Fadiman's term was *staircase wit,* or "what you would have said if you had happened to think of it at the time."

Amphigory. Writing that sounds good but lacks sense.

Anacolouthon. A sudden switch from one grammatical construction to another in the same sentence: a sudden shift of direction in the middle of an utterance. "I can't believe that you—Oh! forget it!" Pronounced *anna-co-luthon.*

Anagrammatist. One who composes anagrams and when asked for the four points of the compass is likely to reply *thorn, shout, seat,* and *stew.* This is also a good place to point out that *stifle* is an anagram of itself.

Ananym. A name written backward.

Aphaeresis. Omitting the initial letter or letters of a word—*'neath* for *beneath* or *'gainst* for *against.* Pronounced *afar-ee-sis.*

Aphthong. A letter or letters not sounded in a word.

Apocope. Omitting some of the final letters of a word—for instance, *tho'* for *though.*

Aposiopesis. Breaking off in the middle of a statement, as if suddenly realizing that someone's feelings are being hurt or about to be hurt: "The reason that people find you so hard to get along with, Fred, is that...well, I'd better not say it."

Battology. Excessive repetition in speech or writing.

Boustrophedon. A system of writing in which the words proceed from right to left for a line and then head back in the other direction as in:

The quick brown fox jumped
.daeh s'god yzal eht revo

The early Greeks experimented with this system and gave it a name that means, literally, "as the ox turns." It refers to the way in which an ox moves when ploughing a field. The adjective form of the word is displayed in this fine verse by David P. Stern of Greenbelt, Maryland, which appeared in the *Science* magazine of March 5, 1982:

Strange new words I relish
Like nectar or tonic.
I now know my line printer
Is boustrophedonic.

Cacography. Bad spelling; cramped or indistinct writing.

Catagraph. First draft.

Chiasmus. A change in word order in two parallel phrases or lines: Chess is the game of kings and the king of games.

Clerihew. A short biographical quatrain verse-form created by E. Clerihew Bentley (1875–1956), who is also known as the mystery writer whose most famous work was *Trent's Last Case.* What is required of the proper clerihew is that a proper name occur in the first line and that the quatrain contain two rhyming couplets (aabb).

Typical examples:

Sir Humphry Davy.
Abominated gravy.
He lived in the odium
Of having discovered Sodium—

And:

The people of Spain think Cervantes
Equal to a half dozen Dantes:
An opinion resented most bitterly
By the people of Italy.

Cheville. An unnecessary word; in poetry, a word used to extend the length of a line.

Chiastic. Inverting words in otherwise similar phrases or sentences: "He went to the door, to the door went he."

Cledonism. Using circumlocution to avoid using words believed to be unlucky; for example, counting "twelve, twelve plus one, fourteen . . ."

Counterword. A word that has been used so much it has lost its original meaning: *darling, great,* and *cool,* for example.

Dialect geography. The proper name for the branch of linguistics concerned with the regional differences in vocabulary, accent, and usage. Dialect geographers are, for example, fascinated by the fact that a *hero* in New York City is a *grinder* or *torpedo* elsewhere in New York State, an *Italian* in northern New England, a *hoagy* in Philadelphia, a *sub* in Washington, D.C., and so forth.

Diasyrm. Damning with faint praise.

Digraph. A single sound expressed by writing two letters—*th, ph,* etc.

Dilogy. Rhetorical trick in which a word or phrase is intentionally used ambiguously. Columnist Michael Gartner cites this example, which appears in the Second Edition of *Webster's New International Dictionary*: "I have said that the gentleman is a liar—it is true—and I am sorry for it."

Dithyramb. A wild, emotional outpouring whether it take the form of a poem, speech, hymn, song, or writing.

Doublet. (1) An unwanted repetition of letters, words, or passages. The newsletter *Editorial Eye* has commented on them:

Doublets most often occur within wordds and figures
(1,50000), between tween words . . .
            . . . and at the end of a line and the beginning
beginning of the next.
(2) Also the same word borrowed twice from another language: the Latin *paralysis* becoming both paralysis and palsy in English.

Elide. To slur or cut off, as a final vowel.

Emblem poetry. A poem arranged typographically into a recognizable shape that suggests the subject of the poem. Pyramids, butterflies, crosses, wineglasses, and columns are among the most common forms. Sometimes called *shaped verse.* An example is this old prohibitionists' poem:

TURNING THE WINE-CUP.
by John P. Trowbridge.

Hail! all ye children of this land!
A cheerful, mirthful, numerous band,
With your eager faces
And your graces,
Come,
Come,
Come,
Every one,
And let us
Take
Hold
Upon
This
WINE CUP,
Yes,
This
Great
WINE CUP,
This red wine cup,
This CRUEL wine cup,
This accursed wine cup,
This all-intoxicating cup,
That from the ancient times
Has been filling up with crimes,
And with anguish and with tears,
And with sin, and hate, and fears,
And with bitter pains and dread,
And with cursings strongly said;
While it slowly swelleth higher,
Higher, with an all-consuming fire
That from out the lustrous wine
Darts its forked flame, to twine
Round its victims, like a breath
Mixed with want, or woe, or death.
Ah! dear children, come and stand,
One great Home Guard in the land;
Take this treacherous, gilded cup,
Take and place it right side up;
Right side up, in glebe and town,
Which always should be upside down.
And let
The fears,
And wine,
And tears
Escape
Forevermore.
From the Home Guard.

Embolalia. Hesitation forms in speech—*you know's, um's, uh's,* extra *okay's,* and, *like,* other things said when we aren't sure what to say. Right? Okay?

Enjambment. Carrying the thought or phrase of a poem from one strophe to the next.

Epibole. Beginning consecutive clauses or statements with the same word, for rhetorical effect.

Epizeuxis. The repetition of a word for emphasis.

Eponym. A real or mythical person whose name is given to an invention, attribute, institution, nation, etc. The earl of Sandwich, Lord Cardigan, and the earl of Davenport are among the most famous examples in English.

Escape words. Words used in place of those that might be considered sacrilegious or obscene. *Golly, gosh,* and *gad* are all escape words for God. It has also been referred to as "Deconic swearing."

Grammatolatry. The worship of words.

Grues. Term coined by Robert Louis Stevenson to describe the morbid rhymes popular in Victorian times. Many featured "Little Willie" and a few are still recalled from time to time, such as this high school mnemonic for chemical formulae:

Little Willie is no more,
For what Little Willie thought was H_2O
Was H_2SO_4.

Hendiadys. The figure of speech in which one idea is stated by the use of two words joined by *and*—for example, "Look and see if anyone is coming."

Holophrase. A single word that expresses a complex idea.

Homophone slip. The use of one homophone for its counterpart—*too* instead of *two, there* instead of *their,* and so forth.

Hyperbaton. The transposition of words, usually to create a different effect. Example, "He wandered earth around." It is, however, hard to find better examples than *cow girl* and *girl cow* and *good looking* and *looking good*—the later pair showing the difference in what is said of a person over the course of 20 years.

Hyperurbanism. A usage that comes from the overcorrection of "bad" English; giving an overly elegant pronunciation to a word. Examples: using "she and I" excessively; pronouncing the *t* in *often.*

Idioglossia. The invented speech of children who are closely related, used for private communication.

Klang association. Hearing one word in the sound of another and being influenced in our use or understanding of it. *Fakir* suggests *fake,* but has nothing to do with that word. *Dastardly* has the klang of *bastard* in it, and *noisome* is offensive but generally quiet. It can be assumed that certain words and meanings die out because the klang is too great, such as may have been the case with the old plural form of penny, *penis,* and the all-but-forgotten word of "thrush-like, looking like a thrush," which was *turdiform.*

Lethologica. The temporary inability to recall a word or a name: that which is on the tip of your tongue.

Lipogram. A piece of writing that lacks a certain letter or letters. E. V. Wright's novel *Gadsby* is a 50,000-word lipogram without any *e*'s. Wright, whose book was published in 1939, wrote the whole thing with the *e*-typebar of his typewriter tied down. Columnist Cedric Adams once pointed out that a natural lipogram takes place in counting. One can count to a thousand before using an *a* in spelling a number.

Logodaedaly. The capricious coining of words.

Logogogue. Person who lays down the law concerning words and their use.

Logomachy. A dispute about words and their meanings.

Meiosis. The opposite of *hyperbole*—making less of something rather than more of it. For instance, saying that winning the Nobel prize was "not bad." Columnist Sydney J. Harris has pointed out that the British have a passion for meiosis. "They say 'not half bad' about something we would call terrific, call a World War 'the late unpleasantness,' and the Atlantic Ocean a 'pond.' "

Merism. A figure of speech in which a whole is expressed by two contrasting parts: young and old, head to foot, and ins and outs are all merisms.

Meronym. A term that falls in the middle of a verbal polarity. Gray is the meronym that falls between white and black.

Metanalysis. Word misdivision that sometimes leads to amusing results; for example, Londonderry Aire becoming London derriere.

Metathesis. The transposing of consonants that turns "sons of toil" into "tons of soil." Metathesis can sometimes become newsworthy as attested to by this item in the London *Telegraph* of April 27, 1991: "The news about Turks and Kurds was bound to cause an accident sooner or later and it duly happened to a presenter on Radio Four's *Today* programme, when he transposed the consonants. No, he did not say "Kurks.' "

Metotymy. Replacing the name of one thing for the name of another, such as saying "today the White House announced . . ." when it is understood that you mean the President or his administration.

Misguggle. A sentence or passage that is worked over by so many hands that it is no longer intelligible; any form of mishandling. This old Scottish term for bad handling has found new users in recent years, including some in computers who talk of misguggled data and misguggled programs.

Mnemonic device. Something, often a sentence or series of words, that helps one to remember something else; an aid to memory. "Did Mary Ever Visit Bill?" can be used to recall the order of English peerage (duke, marquess, earl, viscount, baron).

Orthoepy. The study of pronunciation. The fascinating thing is that some orthoepists pronounce it with an emphasis on the *or* while others stress the *tho*.

Palindrome. Word or passage that reads the same forward and backward. "Sex at noon taxes," "Too hot to hoot," "A slut nixes sex in Tulsa," "Dennis and Edna sinned" are one sentence-palindromes.

Palinode. A poem that retracts something the poet said earlier. One of the most famous palinodes was written by Gelett Burgess, who wrote "The Purple Cow":

I never saw a Purple Cow,
I never hope to see one;
But I can tell you anyhow,
I'd rather see than be one.

It became so popular that five years later, in 1900, he wrote:

Ah, yes, I wrote "The Purple Cow"—
I'm sorry now I wrote it!
But I can tell you anyhow,
I'll kill you if you quote it.

Pangram. A sentence or verse containing all of the letters of the alphabet. It is often used to test typewriters, as in, "The quick brown fox . . ." Here are several fine examples for people tired of the quick brown fox:

Pack my box with five dozen liquor jugs.
Waltz, nymph, for quick jigs vex Bud.
Jackdaws love my big sphinx of quartz.
The five boxing wizards jump quickly.

A. Ross Eckler, editor of *Word Ways, the Journal of Recreational Linguistics*, reported in the May 1986 *GAMES* that more than a dozen 26-letter pangrams have been created. He added that the most sensible was this Clement Wood creation: "Mr. Jock, TV quiz Ph.D., bags few Lynx."

Paragoge. The addition of a meaningless sound to the end of a word, such as the New England *r* sound heard at the end of law*r* and umbrella*r*.

Paralipsis. A statement that pretends to conceal what is really said. For example, "I will not call him a mean-spirited lout, because this is neither the time nor the place for character assessment."

Paronomasia. Punning, a playing on words.

Pasimology. The art of speaking through gestures.

Pathetic fallacy. Ascribing human passions to nature: cruel snows, caressing clouds, and the like.

Periphrasis. Roundabout speech or writing—what Charles Morton of the *Atlantic* magazine dubbed "the elongated yellow fruit" school of describing a banana.

Phatic. Pertaining to speech that is meant to express friendship or sociability rather than convey information. The conversation in a receiving line is invariably phatic.

Pleonasm. The introduction of superfluous words: the use of more words than are required for the expression of an idea; excessive verbiage; over-explanation in which too many words are used.

Portmanteau word. A word formed by the blending of two or more other words. *Smog*, for instance, is a portmanteau of the words *smoke* and *fog*. The term comes from *Alice in Wonderland* and appears as Alice asks Humpty-Dumpty to explain the word *slithy* from the opening line of "Jabberwocky": "Twas brillig and the slithy toves . . ." He tells Alice, "Well 'slithy' means lithe and slimy . . . You see there are two meanings packed into one word." A small collection of examples:

Bash. Bat + Mash.

Bit. Binary + Digit. (Computerese)

Blot. Black + Spot.

Bonk. Bank + Conk.

Brunch. Breakfast + Lunch.

Chortle. Chuckle + Snort. Lewis Carroll's most famous portmanteau word.

Clump. Chunk + Lump.

Clash. Clap + Crash.

Contrails. Conversation + Trails.

Convair. Conveyed by Air.

Doff. As "to doff one's clothes," from *do off.*

Don. As "to don a garment," from *do on.*

Flare. Flame + Glare.

Flurry. Flutter + Hurry.

Flush. Flash + Blush.

Frumious. Fuming + Furious, from Lewis Carroll's "Jabberwocky."

Gidget. Girl + Midget. (1959)

Knoll. Knell + Toll.

Liger. Lion + Tiger. The offspring of a male lion and a female tiger. The opposite mating produces a *tigon.*

Mimsy. Miserable + Flimsy. A Lewis Carroll creation from the "Jabberwocky."

Mingy. Mean + Stingy.

Mixaphor. Mixed + Metaphor, a short form created by Theodore M. Bernstein.

Motel. Motor + Hotel.

Napalm. Naphthene + Palmitate.

Noxema. Nox (for knocks) + Eczema, commercial skin preparation.

Pixel. Picture + Element.

Porridge. Pottage + Porrets.

Quasar. *Quas*i-*Stellar* radio source.

Slang. It has been guessed that this originally came from Slovenly + Language.

Slithy. Slimy + Lithe. From Lewis Carroll's "Jabberwocky."

Slosh. Slop + Slush.

Smaze. Smoke + Haze.

Smice. Smoke + Ice. A fog containing ice crystals.

Smist. Smoke + Mist.

Smog. Smoke + Fog. The *Oxford English Dictionary* says that this word was created in 1905 by a Dr. Des Voeux.

Smust. Smoke + Dust.

Socialite. Social + Light. This blend, which first appeared in *Time*, January 7, 1929, may be that magazine's most successful coinage.

Sparcity. Sparseness + Scarcity.

Splatter. Splash + Spatter.

Splutter. Splash + Sputter.

Telethon. Television + Marathon.

Transistor. Transmitter + Resistor.

Twirl. Twist + Whirl.

Prolepsis. In a narrative or drama, a hint of coming events.

Psellism. Defective pronunciation.

Retronym. A noun that has been forced to take on an adjective to stay up-to-date. For instance, *real cream* and *live performance* are retronyms for cream and performance that have been brought about with the advent of nondairy creamers and prerecorded performance. The term was created by Frank Mankiewicz, president of National Public Radio.

Rhopalic. A line or passage in which each word has one more letter or syllable than the one before it. Writing on this arcane topic in the May 1986 *GAMES*, A. Ross Eckler writes: "The longest rhopalic that reads naturally and makes logical sense appeared in a science article in *Time* magazine on January 10, 1977: 'O to see Man's stern poetic thought publicly expanding recklessly imaginative mathematical inventiveness, openmindedness unconditionally superfecundating nonantagonistical, hypersophisticated, interdenominational interpenetrabilities.' "

Rumbelow. A combination of meaningless syllables, such as the "yo-ho-ho's" of rowing sailors.

Sandwich words. Words of two or more syllables that have been split open and spread with spicy filling. *indegoddampendent, obligoddamgation,* and *irrefuckingsponsible* are classic examples. In *Anatomy of Dirty Words,* author Edward Sagarin tells of several British soldiers who were playing cards with the radio on during World War II. One of the cardplayers realized that he was hearing the infamous Axis Sally and yelled to one of his buddies sitting nearer the radio, "Turn off the propafuckinganda!"

The term *sandwich word* was coined by linguist Harold Wentworth. The number of sandwich words that have been created over the years is tredamnendous and they exist in fandamntastic variety.

Schizoverbia. The phenomenon that occurs when one takes a compound word, splits it, and turns it into a descriptive phrase. Examples are calling income tax forms the most "rigged up marole" imaginable or calling children "ragged little muffins." The term was coined by Frederick Packard in a 1946 *New Yorker* article entitled "Schizoverbia."

Semantic infiltration. Term created by Fred C. Ikle to describe the process by which we come to use the language of our adversaries in describing political or military situations. Examples are calling invading forces "peace-keeping forces," or "liberation forces."

Syncope. Omitting some of the middle letters of a word, usually for the sake of brevity—*med'cine* for *medicine* or *o'er for over.*

Tacenda. Those things that should not be mentioned.

Tapinosis. Use of degrading diction when talking of someone.

Thunk. A light verse that plays with syntax. An example that appeared in an article on thunking in the magazine *Country Journal* goes like this:

> *The peeping Tom designed to peep*
> *At Miss Godiva when she's sleep,*
> *Wherefore on hands and knees he crept*
> *And underneath her curtain pept.*
> *Behind him, though, a watchman crope,*
> *Pursuing peepers while she slope,*
> *and pounced on Tom because he pope.*

Tmesis. The separation of a compound word by an intervening word or words.

Univocalic. A piece of writing containing only one vowel. "Eve's Legend," a short story written by Lord Holland in 1824, omits all the vowels except *e*. The first paragraphs of "Eve's Legend":

Men were never perfect; yet the three brethren, Verses, were ever esteemed, respected, revered, even when the rest, whether the select few, whether the mere here, were left neglected.

Peter wedded Hester Green—the slender, stern, severe, erect Hester Green. The next, clever Ned, wedded sweet Ellen Herber.

Steven, ere he met the gentle Eve, never felt tenderness; he kept kennels, bred steeds, rested where the deer fed, went where green trees, where fresh breezes, greeted sleep.

Xenoglossia. Understanding a language one has never learned.

Words at Work

*A Mix of Terms from the Salesroom,
Law Office, and Other Places
Where People Make a Living*

Additur. The power of a judge to increase the amount of money awarded to a plaintiff by a jury.

Asporation. The act of illegally taking things and carrying them away.

Barratry. The stirring up of lawsuits or quarrels. It is often applied to lawyers who inspire suits they benefit from.

Beback. Perjorative name used by salespeople to describe prospective customers who leave saying they will be back but are never seen again. The word sounds especially good in context: "If you are going to stereotype all salesmen as dishonest, then all customers might be stereotyped as chiselers, squirrels, flakes, pipe smokers, bebacks." (From an article in the *Washington Post* by salesman Bill Adams.)

Bezel. An upper facet of a cut gem. It is above the *girdle* but beneath the *table*.

Bulletproof. Said of a contract or other document that has no loopholes.

Byte. Computerese for a group of bits, often eight, that are convenient to work with. A bit is an abbreviation for *bi*nary digi*t* and is the standard unit of computer information.

Cartnapping. Retail food industry term for the theft of shopping carts.

Chad. The droppings of a computer card when it has been punched up with information.

Champerty. Taking over a lawsuit being brought by another, either by buying the other person's claim or sharing the winnings. Champerty is illegal.

Congeneration. Generation of electricity from a source that would normally be wasted—wood chips, steam that escapes into the air, trash, etc.

Escheat. The state acquiring money or property because the proper owner cannot be found.

Estoppel. In court, being stopped from proving something because something said before shows the opposite. For instance, if one signs a deed, he can be *estopped* later from going to court to prove that it is wrong.

Extended review cycle. Nineties term for the postponement of salary increases.

Firmware. Data-storage devices and other elements of a computer system that are neither hardware nor software.

Fungible. Things that are easily replaced with other things. A pound of coffee, for instance, is fungible, while a Monet is not.

Gazump. In real estate, raising the price of a property after a deal has been struck.

Gentrification. The process by which the well-off swarm into an old neighborhood, rehabilitate the houses, escalate property values, and attract new businesses. It forces out the poor, who cannot afford to live in the area anymore.

Issue. Lawyer's word for children. When the will of John B. Kelly, millionaire contractor and the father of Princess Grace of Monaco, was read, it contained this small lecture on legalese: "Kids will be called 'kids' and not 'issue,' and it will not be cluttered up with 'parties of the first part,' 'per stirpes,' 'perpetuities' . . . and a lot of other terms that I am sure are only used to confuse those for whose benefit it was written."

Liveware. Computer scientists, technicians, and other humans found around computers; what is left in the room when you eliminate hardware and software.

Mingling. Current real estate term for one or more unrelated single people, couples, or families sharing a house or apartment for the purpose of saving money and coping with inflation.

Modesty panel. The name of an optional panel on the front of a woman's desk that makes it difficult to look at her legs.

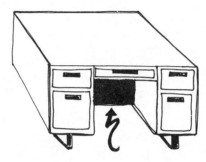

Mooch. Term used in the automobile trade for customers who think they can outsmart the salesperson. Mooches often carry calculators into the showroom.

Multure. The miller's fee for grinding grain.

Novation. The substitution, by agreement, of an old contract for a new one with all of the rights under the old now ended.

Outsourcing. Using goods or services from outside the company; sometimes used euphemistically for layoffs.

Ranchplex. Two-story houses with no basement, current realtor's term.

Remittitur. The power of a judge to decrease the amount of money awarded to a plaintiff by a jury.

Replevin. A lawsuit to get back personal property in the hands of another.

Seisin. Full and complete ownership and possession of land.

Sharpshooter. Current legal slang for the lawyer who aims at loopholes.

Trover. An old type of lawsuit involving property in which you claimed a piece was lost and showed that it was now in the hands of another. It got around the difficult business of actually showing that the property was taken.

Twitching. Northwoods term for dragging a log along the ground with the help of a *scoot,* a short, stubby sled.

Usufruct. Old legal term for the right to use something as long as it is not broken, used up, or changed.

Waldo. Mechanical hands used to extend human hands, such as are used in handling nuclear material. The name comes from a science fiction story, "Waldo," by Robert A. Heinlein, in which such hands were envisioned.

Wall-breaking. Variation on the theme of a ceremonial groundbreaking; for instance, a bank that is about to install an electronic teller or a drive-up window may choose to hold such an event, replete with a ceremonial sledgehammer.

Personal Postscript

I am one of millions of Americans who work from home. I've been doing it for 15 years now and I love it. But one thing that has always bothered me about working at home is that home workers don't have our own jargon. People who commute to offices and factories have rich, complicated jargons. Depending on who you are talking to, you hear of marvelous sounding things like perks and rifs; bottom lines and suboptimizations; kilobucks and petty cash vouchers; and so much more.

In the morning when I walk a few feet to my office, I think of all the people fighting traffic so that they can congregate in front of the watercooler and use their work jargon.

Now I've given this some thought and have come up with a few words that might help other homeworkers. It's just a beginning, mind you, but it shows that a cottage jargon is possible.

Keep-home pay. Our equivalent of take-home pay.

Outlier. This is an old, seldom-used word that means a person who does *not* work at home. I presume it dates back to a time when most everyone worked at home and there were a few outliers commuting on horseback or mules. Now that I know the term, I use it around other work-at-homes, as in the sentence, "I had to go downtown yesterday and I grabbed a ride with an outlier."

Manual cottage. So much has been made of the electronic cottage, Alvin Toffler's term for the computer-based home business, that I thought it might be a good idea to have a name for a plain old-fasioned home-based business.

Associate. Term for everyone else in the house. It is used in communicating with the outside world. A case in point would be when the kids are having a big fight in the next room and you're on the phone with someone important to your business. You don't want to make a big deal about the fight, so you say, "Could I call you back in a few minutes as two of my associates are having a problem." I've used the term for a long time starting when my associates needed diapering.

I hope these few words are enough to get us started. Who knows, before long the outliers won't even know what we're talking about.

Written Words

A Font of Printer's, Writer's, and Editor's Terms

Ascender. The part of a letter that rises above the main body, as in *b*.

Bastard title. The title of a book printed by itself on the odd page preceding the full title page. Also called *half-title* and *bas-title*.

Below the fold. A reference to a page-one newspaper story that is important, but not important enough to appear above the fold.

Best food day. The day of the week on which a newspaper places heavy emphasis on food or carries a special food section. The "best food day" is therefore the best day to advertise food.

Biblioclast. A destroyer of books.

Bildungsroman. A novel that specifically deals with a young man's road to maturity. Created from the German word *bildung*, for growth, and the French *roman*, for novel.

Blow-in card. The name of the piece of paper that falls out of a magazine and falls into the lap. These cards, usually appeals to subscribers, are also known as *lap cards* and *insert cards*.

BOM. Business Office Must. A news story generated by the business department of a newspaper, often to please an advertiser.

Breaker. A biblioclast who rips illustrated books apart to sell the plates individually.

Card plate. Book page that contains a list of books by the same author. The card plate traditionally backs the bastard title page.

Catchword. Word at the head of a page, such as those found at the tops of pages in dictionaries.

Ceremonial opening. Beginning a chapter of a book with a large ornamental letter.

Circus makeup. The use of many different typefaces on one page to create attention.

Clip Job. Newspaper article created from clippings in the paper's files or *morgue*.

Descender. The part of a letter that falls below the main text body, as in *p* and *q*.

Doublet Doublet. Matter that is set by mistake a second time.

Ear. A small box of information to the right or left of the title line of the front page of a newspaper. Ears commonly contain weather synopses, the edition (Late City Edition), or the paper's slogan. The Boston *Globe* features daily "weather ears" with punning heads along the lines of "Rise in Fall," "Curses, Foul Again," "Moist we go on," and "A braisin' in the sun." During times of national stress, such as the San Francisco Earthquake, the Challenger explosion, and the Gulf War, the punning heads are dropped.

Elhi. Publishing jargon for the elementary through high school book market. It is known more widely as *K-12* (that is, kindergarten through twelfth grade).

Etaoin shrdlu. Two words produced when one runs one's fingers down the two vertical left-hand rows of a linotype machine. Traditionally, if a mistake was made, the operator would run his finger down one or both of these lines to fill in the line, which would be discarded later. Since they were sometimes left in by accident, newspapers have been known to inform us that, "The Revolutionaries were running short of ammunition, medical supplies, fund and etaoin shrdlu."

Evening lid. At the White House, the moment at which no news is expected and the press can go home. On May 2, 1989, George Bush personally announced the evening lid.

Filler. Small factual sentence used to fill out a column of newsprint.

A personal digression is called for here:

When I was 13 years old, I started delivering newspapers, and the one that I carried used fillers—there were yards of them. I say "were" because fillers are rare today, mostly showing up in small papers with a circulation of 25,000 or less. Apparently, there isn't that much call for them in this age of news glut and electronic typesetting.

But they were common when I was a kid, and I took great delight in them. As I walked along my paper route, I made a point of reading and memorizing as many as I could. "In 1888 Jack the Ripper murdered six women in London," I would repeat to myself several times and then move onto "The common flea can jump over 200 times its own length" or "The average human liver weighs 3 pounds."

Some were so dramatic that I can recall them verbatim 30 years later. I can vividly remember the day I came upon "A popular method of committing suicide in ancient China was to eat a pound of salt," one of those rare fillers so stunning that it caused me to stop in my tracks. It also caused me to momentarily consider giving up pretzels.

Many of these are still buried in the folds of my brain and pop up, but only with the proper stumulus. Not long ago, I heard the name Euripides and within a split second I heard myself say: "Euripides was killed when attacked by a pack of hunting dogs."

While fillers are still useful to me, it is little compared to their importance at age 12 or 13 when, among other things, I knew another guy who admired and collected them. In the playground at school we would occasionally stage quick fact fights with the idea being that one of us would lead with an item that the second had to equal or better. "Turtles have no teeth," I would blurt out and he would counter with, "Cows have four stomachs."

We had rules; for instance, no "Franklins." To us it seemed that a full fifth of all fillers had to do with Benjamin Franklin. If it wasn't something he had said, it was something he had done—as in, "Ben Franklin was one of the first people to manufacture playing cards in America." It just seemed too easy to bluff with phoney Franklins, so they were all banned.

There was bluffing of another sort, however. Over time, we came up with the devilish concept of "cheaters," which were totally false fillers made up to sound like real ones. If others were listening and the mood hit, one of us would secretly signal for cheaters and we would start with something fairly believable—"Hyenas often laugh themselves to death"—building up to a level of absurdity on the order of "The ancient Sumerians learned to teach oysters to do simple household tasks" that would finally get an onlooker to accuse us of faking. The idea was to see how absurd we could get before being caught. We could not do this too often.

We also had to be careful not to memorize cheaters lest one come out at the wrong time. Other kids, who didn't know when we started using the bogus items, may have taken them as fact. I'd like to think that they were absorbed, lay dormant, and emerged many years later to cause embarrassment in a game of *Trivial Pursuit*.

Over time I noted the decline in the filler, and it was not long before one could go into any major city, pick up the morning paper, and *not* find one word about Benjamin Franklin.

A few years back a friend gave me a subscription to the weekly *Inquirer and Mirror* of Nantucket, Massachusetts. It uses a lot of them. Each week I bypass the front page for the inside. On page 1-C of the issue at my elbow I learn "People have believed dill would scare away witches" and "Ketchup was once sold as a medicine." On 7-C, however, I was stunned when I saw "Back in 400 B.C., a flying wooden pigeon made by Archytas of Tarebtum became the talk of the Old World." I have learned that there are 60,000 miles of blood vessels in the human body, that the common garden snail travels at .03 miles per hour and, to quote one of my favorites, a rare fungus filler, in its entirety, "In one case on record, strong winds behind a cold front carried spores of a fungus from Minnesota to Georgia in two days."

Curiosity compelled me to check with an editor of that newspaper to find out where its fillers come from. Assistant Editor Steve Sheppard says most of them come out of books offered by a filler service in New York, but that he writes a number of them himself. He adds, "Most big papers have problems with too much copy, we're always trying to fill holes." He seems pleased that I enjoy the fillers in the paper and I passed along some of my favorites including the one about doing oneself in by eating a pound of salt.

The special service Sheppard uses is the Barbara Thompson Free Filler Service, which is a product of the North American Precis Syndicate, a New York publicity distribution agency. Ronald Levy, who is the president of the company, says that he sends fillers to more than 3,000 smaller newspapers. He adds that they are free because many of the items are paid for by clients who wish to pass along a message about themselves or their products. The rest are nonsponsored fillers that are passed along as a service to editors and are created by Levy's staff, which checks them for accuracy. There are other filler services, but none the size of Levy's operation (Barbara Thompson was Levy's wife's maiden name), which has 75 people working for it.

Fortunately, I have run out of things to say about fillers, which means the editors of this book will have to find a way to fill up the rest of this page:

"Silver Threads Among the Gold" was Billy the Kid's favorite song.

Baboons, according to legend, were trained to wait on tables in ancient Egypt.

Cows sweat through their noses.

Jimmy Carter was the first American president to have been born in a hospital.

Nickels are the coins least likely to show up in pocket change.

The name Mississippi is spelled with 11 letters, but only four different letters.

English is the second most widely spoken language on earth.

Evidence suggests that popcorn was enjoyed as early as 3500 b.c.

Fly/Fly boy. As explained in the newsletter *Typography Today*, ". . . a printshop worker who removed printed sheets from the press as soon as they were finished, for the sake of speed, most often with newspapers. The term survives in modern usage as a single, quickly printed sheet: *Flier.*"

French fold. Arrangement by which all the printing is done on one side of a page and then the page is folded so that the blank side does not show, such as is done with most greeting cards.

Furniture. Pieces of wood or metal that are used to create margins of white spaces in printing.

Grangerize. To illustrate a book by adding your own prints, photographs, and clippings. The term comes from James Granger, who published his *Biographical History of England* with pages left blank for just this purpose.

Gutter. The space created by the inner margins at the fold of a book.

Incavo. The hollowed-out portion of an intaglio or engraved work.

Index. In addition to the one appearing in the back of a book, an index is a stylized hand with a pointing index finger pointing to something the reader should take special notice of.

Lacunae. The space allowed in a medieval manuscript or an incunable for the placement of an initial letter by a rubricator.

Lobster trick. The newspaper shift that comes on after the last edition has gone to press. It is usually a reduced shift that comes on in the early morning.

Newshole. That portion of a newspaper reserved for news.

Off its feet. Term for type that is not standing straight and is making an incomplete impression.

Opisthosgraphy. Writing on the back of a piece of paper.

Palimpsest. Parchment that has been written on, erased, and then written on again.

Paste-down. The half of the endpaper that lines the inside front cover of a hardback book. The other half is called the *free endpaper.*

Peculiars. Infrequently used characters in a type font.

Pell. Parchment in a roll.

Pi. Printer's term for mixed type; jumbled, unusable type.

Piling. Typing term for those times when letters pile on top of one another.

Recto. The front side of a book leaf; the right-hand page of a book, which always bears an odd page number.

River. Undesired band of white space   that runs through a number of lines of type because one word in   each line ends at a given point.

Second Coming type. The largest, boldest headline type available to a newspaper.

Sinkage. The lowered position of type matter on a page that starts a chapter or special section.

Slug. Very brief identifying headline used at the top of the continued portion of a newspaper or magazine article. The slug for an article headlined "Administration Plans Massive Budget Cuts" might simply say "Budget."

Tail. The margin at the bottom of a book page. The upper margin is called the *head*.

Topstain. Color applied to the top edge of a book page. It is usually a darker color, as the purpose of topstain is to prevent fingerprints from soiling the top of the book.

Verso. The left-hand page of a book, bearing an even page number; the reverse side on the leaf.

Where list. A list accompanying a graph or diagram that gives the values of symbols and letters.

Widow. A line containing an awkwardly small amount of type, such as part of a word.

Wrongfont. In printing, a piece of type of a face different from the other letters around it.

The Last Word

A passion for words is not something that can be turned on and off like a faucet. So it follows that just because this collection has been exhibited, there is no reason to stop collecting. In fact, the urge becomes stronger.

At present I am beginning a new set of things to collect, including these:

Gudgeons. This is one of those remarkable words with dozens of meanings. In this case gudgeons tend to be obscure and diverse pieces of hardware. A few of the gudgeons I have already collected: (1) A pin holding two pieces of stone together; (2) a ring that fits over a gate hook to keep it in place; (3) the socket for the rudder of a boat; (4) either of the two supporting knobs that keep a cannon in its carriage; (5) the round pins on a window shade roller; (6) a sheath knife; (7) a small sluggish fish; (8) a dupe.

Klangers. Words that give the wrong impression—*aprosexia, gnomic, inspissed, ideotropic,* and so forth. They are also words that do not mean what people think they mean: *literally* (which some think means figuratively), *chauvinism* (which does not mean male bigotry), *relevant* (which does not mean related to contemporary problems), etc.

Mibstionary. The definitive collection of marble terms. One could create a fairly sizable dictionary of marbles terms if one wanted to. While researching an article for the *Smithsonian* magazine on the game of marbles, the author noted 459 of them—from *abacus* (a marbles game) to *zebras*—and there are doubtlessly many more. Many were archaic when Coolidge was in office and others are regional, but some are as essential to the game as a good shooter. Should you wish to partake for the first time or after many springs away from the game, you will want to know such terms as:

Histing, for instance, refers to the act of raising one's hand from the ground when shooting, while *hunching* is moving one's hand forward while shooting. This is—or, at least was—an important distinction. Marbles also has a synonym-rich vocabulary in which one's shooter can be a *taw, bowler, reeler,* or *moonie,* which one uses to shoot at target marbles that are variously known as *ducks, stickers, dibs, hoodles, kimmies, immies, commies,* and *miggs.* The material of the marble invokes a list of terms including *steelies, aggies, crockies,* and *glassies. Glassies,* in turn, can be *solids, rainbows, bumble-bees, milkies, cat's eyes, pureys,* and *clearys.* (For readers born after 1960, a *purey* is a pure *cleary*—that is, one without a single air bubble.)

Some of the terms have a distinct childish charm:

Deegle. A marble that leaves the game area and ends up in the weeds or involved in a nearby game.

Fourbles. Four target or prize marbles. The term is used as the ante is increased from one marble to two (*dubs*), to three (*thribs*), and then four.

Snooger. A near miss.

20-er. A marble that is so desirable that it is worth 20 run-of-the-mill glass marbles.

Others sound "official":

Pot. The hole in hole games.

Slip/Slips. Call made when your shooter slips out of your hand and rolls a short distance. It allows you to shoot again, but only if agreed to before play starts.

When such terms are used in a sentence, they sound like a separate dialect. A few lines from Henry A. Shute's 1906 *The Real Diary of a Real Boy* attests to this, "Pewt dreened 18 marbles, and two chinees out of me. We was playing first in a hole."

Food Slang. A rich American tradition including *Cincinnati oysters* (pork products, to short-order cooks), *pep tires* (GI term for doughnuts during World War II), *burnt offerings* (roast beef in the Navy), and the *5B*'s (a meal of Boston baked beans and brown bread).

Chronisms. Not long ago, I went into a store and told the man behind the counter that I needed a needle for my record player.

"Oh," he replied, "what kind of stylus do you want for your turntable"

This took place in a shopping center, which people keep reminding me is now called a *mall.* One difference between the two may be that the former sold sneakers and the latter athletic shoes.

It made me think about the way words date what we say. For instance, I count myself among those who are more terrified by the image of an *atomic bomb* than a *nuclear device* (which sounds like it should be used to describe a smoke detector). If you listen to me talk long enough, you'll know that I come from the group just before the baby boom: the one that listened to *rock 'n roll*, not the one that listened to *rock* music.

I was therefore thrilled when I came upon an article by William Safire in which he announced the coining of *chronism* for "words quivering in the aspic of time, perfect for use by dramatists who want to give historical scenes the flavor of authenticity, starring Vera Similitude, my 1940s *heartthrob*."

Now that I knew what to call them, I decided to begin a chronism collection.

Some chronisms are simply words that apply to things that were once common, but are now rare: milk bottles, slide rules, dime stores, adding machines, linoleum, and soda jerks.

Others have changed with a turn in technology, sensibility, or fashion. Ice boxes first became *refrigerators* and now, according to an ad in a recent *Better Homes and Gardens* from one of the leading manufacturers, should be called *food storage systems*. The Victrola, of course, became the *phonograph*, a *hi fi*, then a *stereo*, and now a *stereo system* (or *system*, for short). Meanwhile, the jump from record to disc is being speeded up with the advent of the *CD*. On the food front, spaghetti, noodles, and macaroni are now terms used by middle-aged people who can't hear the word *pasta* without thinking of *pasta fazool*.

Pals have turned into *peers* and heroes into *role models*. Pep is now *energy*, the blues now have a number of clinical, latinate names, and to admit that you feel like a *sap* (or a *chump*) is to admit your age rather than your foolishness. If you say *teenager* more often than *adolescent*, it proves you were one a long time ago. Sometime back, brothers and sisters gave way to *siblings*, pinups to *playmates*, boundaries to *parameters*, and simple to *simplistic*. Sex is fast becoming a real verbal antiquity as it is now widely referred to in terms of *sexuality*. Job applications now ask for *gender* rather than sex.

No realm is safe. I recently read in a newspaper stamp and coin column that the term *magnifying glass* was passe and today's magnifier is a "lupe, glass or scope." In photography, the totally appropriate term *snapshot* has been driven out by the word *print*.

I find that I am often being amended, corrected, or confused. At a meeting not long ago, I suggested appointing a committee; it was rephrased by someone else so the final motion had me creating a task force. To these ears, a *task force* requires at least a few destroyers, an aircraft carrier, and an admiral. A college administrator corrected me recently when I said "higher education." He said, "The proper term is now post-secondary education, many people felt that higher education was elitist." Near where I live there is a "career center," which I suddenly discovered was a vocational high school when I read an article about it in the paper. Time was when these places were called *trade schools*, but that was when dinosaurs roamed the earth. Jails are now *detention centers*, and junior colleges are likely to be called *community colleges*. There is a swamp not too far from my home, which they now call a *wetland*.

Then there are the special chronisms:

The *boomerang chronism* occurs when an old term is replaced by a new one only to have the old one fight its way back. A case in point is *media center*, which was a term brought in to replace *library*. It stuck for a while and then headed off into the sunset with the open classroom and areas they called *pods*. Speaking of schools, about a year ago I allowed myself to be on a parent-student committee to review sex education material that was going to be used in my son's school. At one point in our initial meeting, the teacher of the course pointed out that much attention would be paid to STD's. An eighth-grader with no idea that the initials stood for *sexually transmitted diseases* said that she hoped they would talk about VD as well because this was something the kids were talking about.

The *bouncing* chronism is a term that is likely to change so quickly that one is hard-pressed to have the latest one on the tip of one's tongue before the next comes along. Such is the case with junior high schools which were soon just plain *junior highs*, until they became *intermediate schools* and *middle schools*, which, if nothing else, has been a boon to the sign painters. In some places there were distinctions between the three, but they got lost in the confusion. The other night I was at a meeting at a local school where the principal referred to "jim schools." The term produced a murmur of confusion in the roomful of parents, so he stopped and explained, "That's a general reference to junior, intermediate, and middle schools—JIM for short." If he had not stopped to explain, I would have been forced to conclude that he was talking about schools with gymnasiums.

Then there is the *slang* chronism. "The modern ballplayer," said Vin Scully during a 1986 World Series telecast, "calls them flares, not Texas Leaguers." Scully was referring to that particular hit that looses oomph in mid course and drops in for a hit. No matter what they say, they will always be Texas Leaguers to me, and the new term will always sound like something from the realm of dressmaking.

Perhaps, this is as it should be: a way of marking time and generations with words. I think of my childhood and the people who said *divan* when I said *sofa* and who could never break themselves of the habit of saying they were going to *listen* to the television.

I would love to hear from readers with chronisms and other collectibles to pass along, as well as ideas for new collections and additions to the collections in this book. With any luck, there will be a *Second Word Treasury* that will contain, among other things, the world's finest collection of chronisms. This collector can be reached at Box 80, Garrett Park, MD 20896—0080.

ACKNOWLEDGMENTS

A number of people have helped me find words for this book. In addition to those I have already acknowledged for their efforts in helping me compile the list of synonyms for *drunk,* I would like to thank the following people for their particular help in creating the original *Words*: Ernest Hildner, Fitzhugh Mullan, Tracy Connors, Bob Skole, Norman Mark, Joseph C. Goulden, Bill O'Neill, Ellen T. Crowley, Elaine Viets, Don Crinklaw, Bill and Virginia Cressey, and, as always, Nancy Dickson. I would also like to thank Andrew Dickson for his help with the illustrations.

Those who helped in the creation of the tome in your hands are:

Don Addis, J. A. Allen, Reinhold A. Aman, Jay Ames, W. R. Anderson, Russell Ash, Jack Van Auken, Joseph Badger, Don G. Baker, O. V. Barlow, Paula Berg, Terence Blacker, David Boardman, Bruce Boston, Gene Botkin, Lynne Bronstein, David S. Brown, M. M. Bruce, Caroline Bryan, Larry Bryant, Wendell E. Bulger, Judy Burr, Samuel Cabot, Duane Campbell, T. D. Campbell, Martha Cornog, Frank Celentano, Howard Channing, Philip Chaplin, Pete Christianson, William Rossa Cole, John Clark, Kate Contos, Bertram C. Cooper, John Corcoran, Norman Corwin, Raymond G/A Cote, Jean Scott Creighton, Don Crinklaw, Neil Croll, Charles W. Davis, L. Sprague de Cam, Al deQuoy, Gordon B. Dean, S. Percy Dean, Gene Deitch, Louis Delpino, Charles F. Dery, Lisa Dickson, J. Edward Dirr, Stephen B. Dudley, the late Russ Dunn, Sr., John Duffie, Frederick C. Dyer, M. Mack Earle, Charley Eckhardt, Gerald M. Eisenhower, Owen Elliott, Bryan Embray, Thomas D. Engel, George Englebretsen, Willard R. Espy, Nona West Eudy, Jim Evans, James E. Farmer, Felix Fellhaur, Wayne H. Finke, Henry Fischbach, Barbara Rainbow Fletcher, Charles B. Forster, Alex Fraser, Lewis Burke Frumkes, Monika Fuchs, Martin Gardner, Bill Gerk, Walt Giachini, Joan Gilbert, Dorethea Gildar, Robert B. Giles, Thomas E. Gill, Kay Gleason, Patricia Goff, E. S. Goldman, Joseph C. Goulden, Shane Graham, Gayle Grove, Stephen Haase, the late Irving Hale, Joan Hale, Paul S. Hanson, Kelsie Harder, Raymond Harris, Edwin A. Haselbauer, John Hazlitt, George A. Heinemann, Anne Higgins, Archie Edward Hinson, Donald B. Hofler, Janet W. Hook, Colin Howard, Madeline Hutchinson, Geof Huth, Arnold Isaacs, Lane E. Jennings, Warren R. Johnston, Jon B. Jolly, Jimmy Jump, John Kessel, Maseo Kinoshita, George Kirby, W. L. Klawe, Glenn Knickerbocker, Tim Knight, David C. Kopaska-Merkel, Martin S. Kottmeyer, Bobby Kraft, Chris Kucharski, Edwin D. Lawson, John L. Leckel, Richard Lederer, Joann Lee, Ray Leedy, Joel Levis, Alan G. Lewis, Lewis P. Lipsitt, E. A. Livingston, Mel Loftus, Ed Lucaire, Ruth E. Lunas, Joe McCabe, Blaine C. McKusick, Cynthia MacGregor, Irving MacGregor, Pete Maiken, the

347

late John Main, Ivan Martin, Stephen V. Masse, Steve Masse, Edward Mayo, Bill Mead, Louis Milliner, Charles Mintzlaff, Charles D. Moss, Suzie Mundell, G. D. Myers, Raymond J. Nelson, J. Baxter Newgate II, D. K. Noller, C. R. Nowlan, Michael J. Olin, William O'Neill, Rudolf Ondrejka, Mike Page, Margaret Moreau Palmer, Herbert Paper, Denys Parsons, Myra Patner, Bernadine Z. Paulshock, Timothy Perper, William Petkanas, Cate Pfeifer, Gerald M. Phillips, Louis Phillips, Phillip B. Phillips, M.D., Fred Powell, Kay Powell, Joshua H. Proschan, Suzie Radus, Mary Ann Raimond, Rainbow, Dan Rapoport, Allen Walker Read, Ross Reader, Susan Fenwick Reed, Joe Reilly, Joe and Joyce Rizzo, Mary M. Roberts, Randy Roberts, Ursula Roberts, Dan Rodricks, Jack P. Roe, William A. Rooney, the late Cornelius Van S. Roosevelt, Jane Ross, Lee Saegesser, W. H. Sage, M.D., Carl H. Scheele, Patricia L. Schley, W. N. Scott, Homer Shanks, Jr., Robert S. Shaver, Louise Sherman, Rob Simbeck, Bob Skole, Don Sloan, Jean E. Smythe, Bob Snider, Patricia Spaeth, Michael A. Stackpole, Ron Stall, Ashley H. Steele, Warren E. Steffen, Norman D. Stevens, J. O. Stevenson, Dick Stewart, Carol N. Stix, Warren Sturgis, William Sunner, Bill Tammeus, Robert J. Throckmorton, William S. Tilton, Joe M. Turner, R. E. Tuttle, Jr., Laurence Urdang, Elaine Viets, David Walsh, Stuart Wardell, Elizabeth Watts, Roger D. Way, Martin Weiss, Bob and Mary West, Roy West, J. van de Weyer, Robert D. Wheeler, Margaret Whitesides, Neal Wilgus, Bruce S. Williams, Ben Willis, Rick Winston, Anita Marion Niederer Wirta, E. R. Wirta, Mrs. Kenneth Worthing.

In preparing this book, I have used hundreds of books, pamphlets, magazine, and newspaper articles. The bibliography includes a listing of the most important sources I used. To conserve space, I have not listed the major general-purpose dictionaries, which, of course, were invaluable.

BIBLIOGRAPHY

Adams, Charles C. *Boontling: An American Lingo.* Austin: University of Texas, 1971.

Adams, J. Donald. *The Magic and Mystery of Words.* New York: Holt, Rinehart and Winston, 1963.

Adams, Ramon F. *Western Words.* Norman, Okla.: University of Oklahoma Press, 1948.

Allison, Norman and Sonia. *Drink's Dictionary.* Glasgow: Collins, 1978.

Bacon, Kenneth H. "When the Navy Says ABRACADABRA It Isn't Really Magic." *The Wall Street Journal* (August 31, 1977), pp. 1, 33.

Barber, Richard, and Anne Riches. *A Dictionary of Fabulous Beasts.* Ipswich, England: Boydell Press, 1971.

Barlough, J. E. *The Archaicon.* Metuchen, N.J.: Scarecrow Press, 1974.

Barnhart, Clarence L., Sol Steinmetz, and Robert K. Barnhart. *The Barnhart Dictionary of New English since 1963.* New York: Harper & Row, 1973.

————. *The Second Barnhart Dictionary of New English.* New York: Harper & Row, 1980.

Barron, John N. *The Language of Painting.* Cleveland: World Publishing, 1967.

Bender, James F. "Ourway Ecretsay Anguageslay." *The New York Times Magazine* (December 31, 1944), pp. 14–15.

Bendick, Jeanne. *How Much and How Many.* New York: Whittlesey House, 1947.

Berg, Paul C. *A Dictionary of New Words in English.* New York: Crowell, 1953.

Bernstein, Theodore M. *Dos, Don'ts & Maybes of English Usage.* New York: Quadrangle, 1977.

————. *More Language That Needs Watching.* New York: Atheneum, 1962.

————. *The Careful Writer.* New York: Atheneum, 1978.

Berrey, Lester V., and Melvin Van Den Bark. *The American Thesaurus of Slang.* New York: Crowell, 1952.

Blumberg, Dorothy Rose. *Whose What?* New York: Holt, Rinehart and Winston, 1969.

Bombaugh, C. C. *Oddities and Curiosities of Words and Literature.* Edited and annotated by Martin Gardner. New York: Dover, 1961.

Borgman, Dmitri A. *Beyond Language: Adventures in Word and Thought.* New York: Scribner's, 1967.

Bowler, Peter. *The Superior Person's Little Book of Words.* Melbourne: The Hawthorne Press, 1979.

Boycott, Rosie. *Batty, Bloomers and Boycott.* New York: Peter Bedrick, 1982.

Brandreth, Gyles. *More Joy of Lex.* New York: Morrow, 1982.

————. *Pears Book of Words.* London: Pelham Books, 1979.

British Broadcasting Corp. *More Words*. London: BBC Publishing, 1977.

Brown, Ivor. *A Rhapsody of Words*. London: Bodley Head, 1969.

————. *A Ring of Words*. London: Bodley Head, 1967.

————. *A Word in Your Ear*. London: J. Cape, 1942.

————. *Having the Last Word*. New York: Dutton, 1951.

————. *I Break My Word*. London: J. Cape, 1951.

————. *I Give You My Word*. New York: Dutton, 1948.

————. *Just Another Word*. London: J. Cape, 1943.

————. *Mind Your Language*. New York: Capricorn, 1962.

————. *No Idle Words*. New York: Dutton, 1951.

————. *Say the Word*. New York: Dutton, 1948.

————. *Words in Our Time*. London: J. Cape, 1958.

Bruton, Eric. *Dictionary of Clocks and Watches*. New York: Bonanza, 1963.

Burgess, Gelett. *Burgess Unabridged*. New York: F. A. Stokes, 1914. (Also reprinted in 1986 by Archon Books, Hamden, Connecticut, with a new foreword by Paul Dickson.)

Byrne, Josefa Heifetz. *Mrs. Byrne's Dictionary*. Secaucus, N.J.: Citadel, 1974.

Carling, T. E. *The Complete Book of Drink*. New York: Philosophical Library, 1952.

Carter, John. *ABC for Book Collectors*. New York: Knopf, 1966.

Ciardi, John. *A Browser's Dictionary*. New York: Harper & Row, 1980.

Colby, Elbridge. *Army Talk*. Princeton, N.J.: Princeton University Press, 1943.

Copperud, Roy H. *American Usage and Style: The Consensus*. New York: Van Nostrand Reinhold, 1980.

Crowley, Ellen, ed. *Acronyms, Initialisms and Abbreviations Dictionary*. Detroit: Gale Research, various dates and editions.

Dalrymple, Denis. *Pub Talk*. Henley-on-Thames, England: Gothard House, 1975.

Darling, Charles H. *The Jargon Book*. Aurora, Ill.: Aurora, 1919.

Day, Harvey. *Occult Illustrated Dictionary*. New York: Oxford, 1976.

De Funiak, William Q. *The American-British, British-American Dictionary*. Cranbury, N.J.: A. S. Barnes, 1978.

Dennett, Daniel, and Karel Lambert. *The Philosophical Lexicon*. Privately published and available from Prof. Daniel Dennett, Tufts University, Medford, Mass. 02155.

De Sola, Ralph and Dorothy. *A Dictionary of Cooking*. New York: Meredith Press, 1969.

Dickson, Paul. *Family Words*. Reading, Mass: Addison-Wesley, 1988.

————. *Words*. New York: Delacorte Press, 1982.

Dickson, Roy Ward. *The Greatest Quiz Book Ever*. London: Wolfe Publishing, 1974.

Doty, Robert C. "Parlez-Vous NATO?" *The New York Times* (October 18, 1959).

Doxat, John. *International Distillation of Drinks and Drinking*. London: Ward Lock, 1971.

Drepperd, Carl W. *Primer of American Antiques*. Garden City, N.Y.: Doubleday, 1944.

Durant, Mary. *The American Heritage Guide to Antiques*. New York: American Heritage Press, 1970.

Eckler, A. Ross. *Word Recreations*. New York: Dover, 1979.

Ellyson, Louise. *A Dictionary of Homonyms*. Mattituck, N.Y.: Banner Books, 1977.

Epsy, Willard R. *An Almanac of Words at Play*. New York: Potter, 1975.

_____. *Say It My Way*. Garden City, N.Y.: Doubleday, 1980.

_____. *Thou Improper, Thou Uncommon Noun*. New York: Clarkson N. Potter, 1978.

Evans, Bergen. *Comfortable Words*. New York: Random House, 1962.

Ferm, Vergilius. *A Brief Dictionary of American Superstitions*. New York: Philosophical Library, 1965.

Flexner, Stuart Berg. *I Hear America Talking*. New York: Van Nostrand, Reinhold, 1976.

_____. *Listening to America*. New York: Simon and Schuster, 1982.

Frazier, George. "Doubletalk." *Life* (July 5, 1943).

Frommer, Harvey. *Sports Lingo*. New York: Atheneum, 1979.

Garber, Aubrey. *Mountainese*. Radford, Va.: Commonwealth Press, 1976.

Gaynor, Frank. *Dictionary of Mysticism*. New York: Philosophical Library, 1953.

Goliad, Ray. *Scholar's Glossary of Sex*. New York: Heinemann, 1968.

Gould, John. *Maine Lingo: Boiled Owls, Billdads, and Wazzats*. Camden, Maine: Down East Magazine Press, 1975.

Green, Jonathan. *The Slang Thesaurus*, London: Elm Tree Books, 1986.

Hall, Robert A., Jr. *Melanesian Pidgin Phrase-Book and Vocabulary*. Baltimore, Md.: Linguistic Society of America, 1943.

Hayakawa, S. I. *Language in Thought and Action*. New York: Harcourt Brace, 1941.

Haywood, Charles F. *Yankee Dictionary*. Lynn, Mass.: Jackson and Phillips, 1963.

Henke, James T. *Courtesans and Cuckolds: A Glossary of Renaissance Dramatic Bawdy*. New York: Garland, 1979.

Hinch, Derryn. *The Scrabble Book*. New York: Mason Charter, 1976.

Hinsie, Leland E., and Robert Jean Campbell. *Psychiatric Dictionary*. New York: Oxford University Press, 1960.

Hofford, Tony, and Martha Wright. *What's That Word*. Wakefield, R.I.: Times Press, 1954.

Hollander, Zander, ed. *The Encyclopedia of Sports Talk*. New York: Corwin Books, 1976.

Homer, Joel. *Jargon*. New York: Times Books, 1979.

Hook, J. N. *The Grand Panjandrum*. New York: Macmillan, 1980.

Hughes, Spike. *The Art of Coarse Language*. London: Hutchinson, 1974.

Hunsberger, I. Moyer. *The Quintessential Dictionary*. New York: Hart Publishing, 1978.

Hunt, Bernice Kohn. *The Whatchamacallit Book*. New York: Putnam's, 1976.

Jacobs, Jonathan Noah. *Naming-Day in Eden*. New York: Macmillan, 1969.

Jennings, Charles B. *Weigh the Word*. New York: Harper & Brothers, 1957.

Johnson, Burges. *The Lost Art of Profanity*. New York: Bobs-Merrill, 1948.

Johnstone, William D. *For Good Measure*. New York: Avon, 1977.

Jordanoff, Assen. *Jordanoff's Illustrated Aviation Dictionary*. New York: Harper & Brothers, 1942.

Kimball, Warren Y. *A Selection of Fire Terminology*. Boston: National Fire Protection Association, 1961.

King, Aileen. *Dictionary of Cooking Terms*. London: Forbes Publishing, 1976.

Kurzban, Stan, and Mel Rosen. *The Compleat Cruciverbalist*. New York: Van Nostrand, Reinhold, 1980.

Lambdin, William. *Doublespeak Dictionary*. New York: Pinnacle Books, 1979.

Leider, Morris, and Morris Rosenblum. *A Dictionary of Dermatological Words, Terms and Phrases*. New York: McGraw-Hill, 1968.

Levinson, Leonard Louis. *Webster's Unafraid Dictionary*. New York: Macmillan, 1967.

Loane, George G. *1,001 Notes on "A New English Dictionary."* Privately published, 1920.

Lucas, Alan. *The Illustrated Encyclopedia of Boating*. New York: Scribner's, 1977.

Maleska, Eugene T. *A Pleasure in Words*. New York: Simon and Schuster, 1981.

Markus, John. *Electronics Dictionary*. New York: McGraw-Hill, 1978.

Mathews, Mitford M. *Americanisms*. Chicago: University of Chicago Press, 1966.

Matthews, C. M. *Words, Words, Words*. New York: Scribner's, 1979.

Mawson, C. O. Sylvester. *The Dictionary Companion*. Garden City, N.Y.: Halcyon House, 1932.

McAdam, E. L., and George Milne. *Johnson's Dictionary: A Modern Selection*. New York: Pantheon, 1963.

McCulloch, Dean Walter F. *Words Words*. Portland: Oregon Historical Society, 1958.

Mencken, H. L. *The American Language*. New York: Knopf, 1937.

————. *Supplement One: The American Language*. New York: Knopf, 1945.

Mendelsohn, Oscar A. *The Earnest Drinker*. New York: Macmillan, 1950.

Merriam-Webster. *6,000 Words: A Supplement to Webster's Third New International Dictionary*. Springfield, Mass.: G. & C. Merriam Co., 1976.

Michaels, Leonard, and Christopher Ricks. *The State of the Language*. Berkeley: University of California Press, 1980.

Milberg, Alan. *Street Games*. New York: McGraw-Hill, 1976.

Mitchell, Edwin Valentine. *It's an Old New England Custom*. New York: Vanguard, 1946.

Mitchell, G. Duncan. *A Dictionary of Sociology*. Chicago: Aldine, 1968.

Moore, W. G., *A Dictionary of Geography*. New York: Praeger, 1969.

Morgan, Paul, and Sue Scott. *The D.C. Dialect.* New York: The Washington Mews Press, 1975.

Morris, William and Mary. *Morris Dictionary of Word and Phrase Origins,* Vols. I-III. New York: Harper & Row, various dates.

_____. *The Word Game Book.* New York: Harper and Bros., 1959.

Moss, Norman. *What's the Difference?* New York: Harper & Row, 1973.

Mouat, Lucia. "What's in a name? Kirstin's in, Henry's out." *The Christian Science Monitor* (August 22, 1983).

Muir, Frank, and Patrick Campbell. *Call My Bluff.* London: Methuen, 1972.

Murphy, John J. *The Book of Pidgin English.* Brisbane: W. R. Smith and Paterson, 1962.

Opie, Iona and Peter. *The Lore and Language of Schoolchildren.* London: Oxford University Press, 1959.

Oran, Daniel. *Law Dictionary.* St. Paul, Minn.: West, 1975.

Partridge, Eric. *A Dictionary of Slang and Unconventional English.: Two Volumes in One.* New York: Macmillan, 1961.

_____. *A Dictionary of the Underworld.* New York: Bonanza, 1961.

_____. *The Gentle Art of Lexicography.* New York: Macmillan, 1963.

Pei, Mario, and Frank Gaynor. *Dictionary of Linguistics.* New York: Philosophical Library, 1954.

Pei, Mario. *Language of the Specialists.* New York: Funk & Wagnalls, 1966.

_____. *The Many Hues of English.* New York: Knopf, 1967.

_____. *Words in Sheep's Clothing.* New York: Hawthorne, 1969.

Pflug, Raymond J. *The Ways of Language: A Reader.* New York: Odyssey Press, 1967.

Picken, Mary Brooks. *The Fashion Dictionary.* New York: Funk & Wagnalls, 1973.

Plunkett, E. R. *Folk Names and Trade Diseases.* Stamford, Conn.: Barrett, 1978.

Pollock, Alben J. *The Underworld Speaks.* San Francisco: The Prevent Crime Bureau, 1935.

Quinn, Jim. "A Nose by any Other Name—Would It Still Smell?" *The Washington Post* (October 14, 1977).

Randolph, Vance, and George P. Wilson. *Down in the Holler: A Gallery of Ozark Folk Speech.* Norman, Okla.: University of Oklahoma Press, 1953.

Ream, Rev. S. *Curiosities of the English Language.* Cleveland, Ohio: Central Publishing House, 1925.

Reid, Alastair. *Ounce, Dice Trice.* Boston: Little, Brown & Co., 1958.

_____. *Passwords.* Boston: Atlantic Monthly Press, 1963.

Reifer, Mary. *Dictionary of New Words.* New York: Philosophical Library, 1955.

Rocke, Russsell. *The Grandiloquent Dictionary.* Englewood Cliffs, N.J.: Prentice-Hall, 1972.

Safire, William. *On Language.* New York: Times Books, 1980.

Sagarin, Edward. *Anatomy of Dirty Words.* New York: Lyle Stuart, 1962.

Salak, John S. *Dictionary of American Sports.* New York: Philosophical Library, 1961.

———. *Dictionary of Gambling.* New York: Philosophical Library, 1963.

Sayer, Edgar Sheappard. *Pidgin English.* Toronto: Privately published, 1943.

Schaun, George and Virginia. *Words and Phrases of Early America.* Annapolis, Md.: Greenbury Publishing, 1963.

Schur, Norman W. *British Self-Taught: With Comments in American.* New York: Macmillan, 1973.

Schwartz, Alvin. *Chin Music: Tall Talk and Other Talk.* New York: Lippincott, 1979.

Severn, Bill. *Place Names.* New York: Ives Washburn, 1969.

Sherk, Bill. *Brave New Words.* Garden City, N.Y.: Doubleday, 1979.

Shipley, Joseph T. *Dictionary of Early English.* New York: Philosophical Library, 1955.

———. *Playing With Words.* Englewood Cliffs, N.J.: Prentice-Hall, 1960.

———. *Word Play.* New York: Hawthorne, 1972.

Simon, André L. and Robin Howe. *Dictionary of Gastronomy.* New York: McGraw-Hill, 1970.

Spears, Richard A. *Slang and Euphemism.* Middle Village, N.Y.: Jonathan David, 1981.

Sperling, Susan Kelz. *Poplollies and Bellibones.* New York: Potter, 1977.

Steible, Daniel J. *Concise Handbook of Linguistics.* New York: Philosophical Library, 1967.

Stonebone, Brig. Gen. Cyclops. *A Pamphlet on the Four Basic Dialects of Pig Latin.* Los Angeles: William Murray Cheny, 1953.

Stoutenburgh, John, Jr. *Dictionary of the American Indian.* New York: Philosophical Library, 1955.

Syatt, Dick. *Country Talk.* Secaucus, N.J.: Citadel Press, 1980.

Taylor, A. Marjorie. *The Language of World War II.* New York: Wilson, 1944.

Tyron, Henry H. *Fearsome Critters.* Cornwall, N.Y.: Idlewild Press, 1939.

U.S. Army. *Dictionary of United States Army Terms.* Washington, D.C.: Department of the Army, 1975.

U.S. Department of Labor. *Dictionary of Occupational Titles.* Washington, D.C.: Department of Labor, various dates and editions.

U.S. Nuclear Regulatory Commission. *A Handbook of Acronyms and Initialisms.* Washington, D.C.: NRC, 1979.

VERBIA with Miriam Berg. *A Play on Words.* New York: Macmillan, 1969.

Versand, Kenneth. *Polyglot's Lexicon: 1943–1966.* New York: Links Books, 1973.

Vogt, Arno R. *Can You Classify Sciences?* New York, Conn.: Privately printed, 1958.

Wedeck, Harry E. *Classical Word Origins.* New York: Philosophical Library, 1957.

———. *Dictionary of Aphrodisiacs.* New York: Philosophical Library, 1961.

———. *Dictionary of Magic.* New York: Philosophical Library, 1956.

Weekley, Ernest. *The Romance of Words.* London: John Murray, 1913.

Wentworth, Harold. *American Dialect Dictionary.* New York: Crowell, 1944.

Wentworth, Harold, Flexner Wentworth, and Stuart Berg. *Dictionary of American Slang.* New York: Crowell, 1960.

Weseen, Maurice H. *Dictionary of American Slang.* New York: Crowell, 1938.

Whitbread and Co. *Word for Word: An Encyclopedia of Beer.* London: Whitbread and Co., Ltd., no date.

Whittaker, Otto. *Such Language.* New York: Grosset & Dunlap, 1969.

Wilson, Everett B. *Early America at Work.* New York: A.S. Barnes, 1963.

Winick, Charles. *Dictionary of Anthropology.* New York: Philosophical Library, 1956.

Woods, Ralph L. *How to Torture Your Mind.* New York: Funk & Wagnalls, 1969.

Worth, Fred L. *Incredible Super Trivia.* New York: Greenwich House, 1984.

———. *More Super Trivia.* New York: Greenwich House, 1981.

———. *Super Trivia Encyclopedia.* New York: Brooke House, 1977.

Wright, Joseph. *English Dialect Dictionary.* Oxford, England: Oxford University Press, 1923.

Wyman, Walker D. *Mythical Creatures of the North Country.* River Falls, Wisc.: River Falls State University Press, 1969.

SUBJECT INDEX

This rather bodacious index was prepared with the help of Jeremy Bender, Alex Dickson, Curtis Jepsen, and Jonathan Redburn who were fueled by several large pepperoni pizzas.

INDEX OF TERMS